MAKING A DIFFERENCE

MAKING A DIFFERENCE

ADVOCACY COMPETENCIES FOR SPECIAL EDUCATION PROFESSIONALS

CRAIG R. FIEDLER

University of Wisconsin–Oshkosh

Allyn and Bacon

Boston   London   Toronto   Sydney   Tokyo   Singapore

Senior Editor: Virginia Lanigan
Series Editorial Assistant: Karin Huang
Marketing Manager: Stephen Smith
Manufacturing Buyer: Suzanne Lareau

Library of Congress Cataloging-in-Publication Data

Fiedler, Craig R.
    Making a difference : advocacy competencies for special education professionals /
Craig R. Fiedler.
        p.   cm.
    Includes bibliographical references and index.
    ISBN 0-205-30629-2
        1. Handicapped children--Education--United States.   2. Handicapped children--Services
for--United States. 3. Special education--Law and legislation--United States. I. Title.

LC4031 .F52   2000
371.91--dc21
                                                                                    99-049036

CEC citations in Chapters 3 and 12 are from *Code of Ethics and Standards for Professional Practice* by The Council for Exceptional Children, *Exceptional Children, 50,* November 1983, pages 205–209. Copyright 1983 by The Council for Exceptional Children. Reprinted with permission.

Printed in the United States of America

10   9   8   7   6   5   4   3   2   03   02   01

To my parents, Russell and Betty Fiedler,
who provided me with the support and
encouragement to pursue my goals;

and

To my family—my wife, Sharon, and my daughters,
Jennifer and Lindsay—who have patiently
tolerated my absences and sustained my energy
and commitment during the writing of this book.
I owe a special debt of gratitude to my daughter
Jennifer, who has taught me firsthand about the
importance of special education advocacy.

Contents

I was motivated to write this book because the topic—the role and responsibility of special education professionals to serve as advocates for students with disabilities and their families—is critically important as the field of special education enters the twenty-first century. Special education advocacy by both parents and professionals was responsible for securing basic rights and services for children with disabilities during the 1970s. We are now entering a new era that will require sustained and committed advocacy to maintain the rights and services won during the first wave of special education advocacy. This second wave of special education advocacy must respond to the increasing needs of children with disabilities and their families and to the significant challenges facing schools and educators working with limited resources.

Effective advocacy seeks to inform and challenge institutions and individuals to respond to the individual needs of children with disabilities, not to alienate or antagonize institutions and individuals who may come under an advocate's scrutiny. In *Making a Difference,* I do not try to offer simplistic panaceas for the challenges facing families, special education professionals, and schools in responding to the increasingly complex needs of children with disabilities. Instead, I will raise difficult issues and suggest possible responses in an effort to fulfill a professional's responsibility to act in the best interests of children with disabilities.

When I started to formulate the outline for this book, I quickly discovered there were many excellent books and articles on the subjects of special education law, educational ethics, collaboration, and conflict resolution strategies. However, there were no professional publications that comprehensively addressed the topic of advocacy by special education professionals. Specifically, I wanted to integrate information from a number of related fields of study by identifying and discussing *essential advocacy competencies for special education professionals*. This book is the result of that integration process.

Multiple Perspectives

In writing *Making a Difference,* I approached the topic from three diverse perspectives. First, I am a parent of a child with a disability who has been receiving educational services since nine months of age. My daughter is now 21 years old. My parental perspective is interwoven throughout the book. In most cases, my family and I have been effectively supported and empowered by wonderfully dedicated special education professionals. In some cases, however, we have experienced negative professional attitudes and actions. My point in sharing this parental perspective is to illuminate experiences (positive and negative) that I believe are typical for many families of children with disabilities.

Second, I write from the perspective of a professional who worked as a lawyer for a few years and served as a special education due process hearing officer for nine years. The topic of advocacy must inevitably address legal rights and procedures, and my background and experiences related to special education law surface in several chapters.

Finally, I have addressed the topic of special education advocacy from the point of view of an educator. The demands and diverse responsibilities facing educators today are immense. Although this book argues for another job responsibility—advocacy—I believe an advocate's role is complementary to the basic duties of any effective, caring educator. That is, an educator cannot be a caring, dedicated, and effective professional without serving as a child advocate. The vast majority of special education professionals, I believe, are caring, dedicated individuals. In this book, I highlight professionals' advocacy responsibilities and provide some useful tools in functioning as an advocate for children with disabilities and their families.

Book Features

There are three unique features of this book. The first of these is my introduction of four brief advocacy vignettes in Chapter 1. Each vignette involves a special education professional who has encountered an advocacy dilemma. I intersperse these four advocacy vignettes throughout the book to illustrate issues, concepts, and strategies that are discussed in subsequent chapters. The advocacy vignettes seek to provide a more realistic and practical application of the advocacy skills addressed in this book. Another feature included in most of the chapters is Advocacy Anecdotes. These brief stories are boxed in the chapters and offer the reader some real-life examples of advocacy issues and concerns. Many of these Advocacy Anecdotes discuss my personal experiences as a parent of a child with a disability, as a lawyer or due process hearing officer, or as an educator. The third feature incorporated into most of the chapters is Advocacy Actions. Like the Advocacy Anecdotes, this material is boxed in the chapters and provides the reader with quick reference advocacy pointers, checklists, or other advocacy-related information (e.g., a sample IDEA complaint letter, law and advocacy related Internet websites, etc.).

Book Organization

Making a Difference is organized into five parts. Part I (containing Chapter 1) discusses the need for professional advocacy in special education. Specifically, five arguments are posed to establish a need for special education professionals to function as child advocates: the historical discrimination experienced by individuals with disabilities, the frequent denial of educational rights and needs of children with disabilities, the political and bureaucratic structure of schools, the lack of parental advocacy, and the findings from special education outcomes research.

Parts II, III, and IV categorize the essential professional advocacy competencies into *dispositions, knowledge,* and *skills.* Part II (containing Chapters 2 through 4) describes three essential

advocacy dispositions: an advocacy disposition (Chapter 2), an ethical disposition (Chapter 3), and a family support and empowerment disposition (Chapter 4). Part III (containing Chapters 5 through 7) examines three essential knowledge bases for effective special education advocacy: knowledge of special education law (Chapter 5), knowledge of dispute resolution mechanisms (Chapter 6), and knowledge of systems change (Chapter 7).

Part IV (containing Chapters 8 through 12) reviews five essential advocacy skills: interpersonal communication skills (Chapter 8), collaboration skills (Chapter 9), conflict resolution skills (Chapter 10), advocacy skills and strategies (Chapter 11), and ethical analysis skills (Chapter 12). Part V (containing Chapter 13) discusses the desired outcomes of special education advocacy, including an enhanced sense of professional development and growth, family empowerment, improved educational services for children with disabilities, and a more responsive and collaborative educational system.

Acknowledgments

I am indebted to the contributions and insight provided by the following educators who shared their special education advocacy experiences with me: Barbara Bauer, Beth Binz, Jan Blume, Gail Bowers, Terri McCall Burkham, Mary Dees, Dick Dorn, Pat Dugan, Phyllis Gillespie, Pam Griesbach, Joan Helbing, Kathy Jacobson, Amy Jordan, Jeanne Kapszukiewicz, Sandy Kletti, Cheri Kuehn, Deb Larson, Theresa Liebham, Jon McCluskey, Laurie McCulloch, Colleen Perrine, Tom Phillips, Kris Sauter, Nancy Schererman, Al Schroeder, Suzette Stewart, and Sheila Stojak. I owe a special thank you to Joan Helbing, who helped identify these educators as effective advocates for students with disabilities. In addition, I thank Kim Ellenbecker, a graduate student who provided library research assistance to me.

My thanks also to the following reviewers for their comments on the manuscript: Beverly H. Johns, Four Rivers Special Education District's

Garrison School; Allan Osborne, Snug Harbor School, Quincy, MA; and Richard L. Simpson, University of Kansas.

The administrative assistant in the Department of Special Education at the University of Wisconsin–Oshkosh, Becky Thorson-Randall, provided invaluable computer and word-processing assistance in the preparation of this book. Jane Jacobson did an independent study project that identified several of the Internet sites that are listed in Chapter 5.

Finally, I am grateful to Ray Short, now retired, who, as senior education editor at Allyn and Bacon, provided me with support and encouragement to write this book. I have also received support and assistance from Karin Huang, editorial assistant at Allyn and Bacon.

CHAPTER 1

THE NEED FOR PROFESSIONAL ADVOCACY IN SPECIAL EDUCATION

We are not advocating futile heroics, only personal courage.
Such courage requires calculated risk in conditions that
offer some opportunity for change. Individuals often
underestimate their power to change things.
—*Michael Fullan and Andy Hargreaves (1991)*

Mary Kinney is the only speech and language clinician employed by a small, rural school district. In the past five years, the school district has grown dramatically, primarily because of two large industries moving into the area, creating jobs and bringing new families into the community. Unfortunately, the school budget has not kept pace with the influx of new students. At the beginning of the school year, the director of pupil services informed Mary and other professional staff serving students with disabilities that no additional staff would be employed to address increasing caseloads. So, in effect, everyone was told to do the best job they could with limited resources. Mary is presently serving a full caseload of children eligible for speech and language services. After two months of the new school year, she received 12 new referrals of children in potential need of her educational services. Mary suspected that the majority of those newly referred children would, in fact, qualify for speech and language services. However, she was unable to meet their needs adequately, given her full caseload. She decided to meet with all the parents of the recently referred children. At this meeting, Mary explained the situation and informed the parents of their educational rights. She encouraged the parents to contact the school administration to demand appropriate services.

The students in Steve Kern's special education program at Central High School are difficult to teach. The school has labeled these students as emotionally/behaviorally disordered and almost all of them have poor school attendance and are involved with the juvenile justice system. For two years, Steve has complained to his school administration about inadequate vocational/career education services, nonexistent participation of community agencies and personnel in transition planning, and the use of excessively punitive disciplinary interventions, such as repeated school suspensions. Steve maintained that the school district lacked sufficient commitment to his students' educational needs and has taken an "out of sight, out of mind" approach. The state protection and advocacy agency recently convened a task force to address the transitional needs of secondary students with emotional/behavioral disorders. Through Steve's membership in the state Council for Exceptional Children, he was appointed to serve on this task force. Over the course of the next six months, Steve's participation as a task force member was critical in formulating policy recommendations submitted by the task force to the state Department of Education. The task force recommendations served as an impetus for the promulgation of new administrative regulations. The new administrative regulations expanded vocational training for special needs students, provided closer monitoring of transitional programming, and developed statewide inservice training on positive behavior management techniques and procedures.

As principal of Wilson Elementary School, Karen Snyder was concerned about the appropriate inclusion of students with disabilities into general education classrooms. Karen was convinced that most of the school's students who are learning disabled and mildly mentally retarded could be successful, with support, in general education. The problem was that many teachers were not implementing the accommodations listed on the individualized education plans (IEPs) of students included in general education classes. At the monthly staff meeting, Karen reviewed IEP legal requirements and emphasized the obligations of teachers to adhere to all the accommodations listed in a student's IEP. In addition, Karen personally reviewed all IEPs for classroom accommodations and she made regular classroom visits to ensure compliance with IEP provisions.

Miguel Hernandez works as a school counselor in a culturally diverse urban school district. At Martin Luther King Jr. Middle School, where Miguel serves as a counselor, the school population is 40 percent Hispanic, 40 percent African American, and 20 percent Caucasian. Many of the students at King Middle School live in poverty. Miguel meets twice a week with seventh-grader Susie Ortiz. Susie is in the learning disabilities program. Susie's mother is dissatisfied with the school program because she feels Susie has not made any academic progress in two years. The mother is also frustrated because whenever she raises a concern, school personnel dismiss her or, alternatively,

state they will make changes but they never do. Although Susie's mother is angry at the school, she feels incapable of changing the situation. Further, Susie's mother is overwhelmed as a single parent of five children, as she works three jobs to pay the bills. Miguel has established a trusting relationship with Susie and her mother. Aware of Susie's home situation, Miguel put Mrs. Ortiz in touch with the local respite care program, a free financial budgeting service, and a food pantry. Miguel also informed Mrs. Ortiz of her options for changing Susie's IEP, and introduced Mrs. Ortiz to a representative of a parent advocacy center. The advocacy center provided an advocate who assisted Mrs. Ortiz in preparing for an upcoming IEP meeting.

What do these four scenarios have in common? In each, a special education professional (e.g., special education teacher, school administrator, school psychologist, related services personnel, school social worker) is engaged in some form of educational advocacy work on behalf of students with disabilities and their families. These scenarios also illustrate that special educational advocacy work is not "one size fits all"; it is as multifaceted and diverse as the needs and circumstances of children with disabilities and their families. The potential impact of professional advocacy in special education is best captured by one teacher's comment, "We have the power to make a difference" (Taylor, Coughlin, & Marasco, 1997, p. 178).

ADVOCACY DEFINED

Advocacy has been variously defined in the professional literature. Consider the following definitions:

- "Advocacy . . . means seeing that one's own organization plans with people rather than just for them, and is sufficiently representative of groups to be served that planning with them is possible. It means changing by-laws, scrapping policies, changing procedures that are part of the problem rather than a part of the solution. It means orienting the service delivery to the consumers in terms of time, place, type of service, type of staff and attitude. It means using the power we have. It may mean altering or holding in abeyance the agenda of the agency in order to begin with the agenda of the client group" (Riley, 1971, p. 14).

- "Advocacy is intervention when needed services are not accessible; are not available; are not appropriate; are not effectively provided; or when the voice of a child is not being heard" (Herbert & Mould, 1992, p. 118).
- Advocacy is a problem-solving strategy to correct problems in service delivery (Hines, 1987).
- An advocate is someone who acts on behalf of or for another person's cause (Alper, Schloss, & Schloss, 1994). Similarly, Stoecklin (1994) described an advocate as a person who speaks on behalf of or in partnership with someone else, such as a child or a parent, in order to procure needed services.
- "Advocacy is defined as information, advice and representation provided to individuals and their families to assist them to acquire appropriate services for a person with a disability" (Bonney & Moore, 1992, p. 7).
- "Child advocacy is intervention on behalf of children in relation to those services and systems that are injurious to children, that are inadequate to prevent harm, or that provide inappropriate help to children" (Cahill, 1986, p. 547).
- An advocate is one who speaks on behalf of another person or group of persons in order to bring about change (Anderson, Chitwood, & Hayden, 1997).

Upon consideration of these definitions, the following essential characteristics of professional advocacy emerge: (1) where advocacy is concerned, allegiance must first be to those we serve and not to the employing agency; (2) advocacy actions typically seek a change in the status quo; (3) advocates speak up for individuals or in concert with another person; and (4) the intent of advocacy is to correct an identified problem or to improve services for children with disabilities.

An advocate's primary allegiance or loyalty must be to children with disabilities and their families. In this allegiance, special education professionals face potential conflicts of interest in their advocacy in that they are employees of a school district that they may be challenging. Their primary commitment, however, ethically rests with children and families. Because professionals who challenge their school district may face disciplinary sanctions for their perceived "insubordination," special education professionals must carefully consider possible consequences of their advocacy actions. This issue will be discussed more completely later in this chapter and in Chapter 2.

The second characteristic, that advocacy seeks a change in the status quo, duly notes that such work is action and change oriented. Advocacy for change requires professional dedication, time, energy, and a clear vision of desired outcomes. The third essential characteristic of advocacy is that professional advocates work to empower parents as the natural advocates of their children with disabilities. For reasons discussed later in this chapter, not all parents are able to function as effective advocates. When this is the case, professionals have the opportunity to fill the advocacy void by speaking up for children with disabilities. The fourth characteristic of advocacy emphasizes the problem-solving nature of this endeavor—that is, the need to identify advocacy issues and the manner in which to address them. Advocates seek positive change through improved educational systems and services for children with disabilities and their families.

THE HISTORICAL LEGACY OF ADVOCACY ON BEHALF OF INDIVIDUALS WITH DISABILITIES

Both parents and professionals have historically engaged in advocacy on behalf of children with disabilities. Turnbull and Turnbull (1997) have chronicled the historical roles parents have assumed throughout the twentieth century. One of those roles involved parents acting as political advocates. In an effort to initiate appropriate educational services for their children with disabilities in the late 1960s, parents turned first to the courts and then to Congress. In a landmark case, *Pennsylvania Association for Retarded Citizens (PARC)* v. *Commonwealth of Pennsylvania* (1972), a group of parents prevailed in a lawsuit to obtain free appropriate education for children with mental retardation. After several similar parent-initiated court victories across the country in the early 1970s, parents turned their attention from the courts to Congress. The political advocacy of parents was instrumental in convincing Congress to pass the Education for All Handicapped Children Act (now known as the Individuals with Disabilities Education Act or IDEA) in 1975. Turnbull and Turnbull noted that the legal and political successes of parents were accomplished in collaboration with professionals serving as advocates.

The roots of professional advocacy can be traced to the "child-saving" era of the late nineteenth and early twentieth centuries. During this era, professional child advocacy efforts led to the creation of many agencies to address the increasing needs of children and families. With this evolution of child welfare agencies, Herbert and Mould (1992) identified a new advocacy function for professionals: "Supporters of children's rights, whose efforts had resulted in the evolution of child-serving agencies, now found a new role, that of ensuring that these agencies remained truly responsive to the needs of the children they had been founded to serve" (p. 114). Professionals have functioned both as **external advocates,** working for change from outside an organization, and **internal advocates,** committed to changing organizations from within.

Kagan (1989) correctly depicted the dichotomy experienced by professionals in terms of advocacy when she stated, "There can be no doubt that the early childhood profession is divided in its attitude toward the role, function, and desirability of advocacy. While some, including many practitioners,

feel threatened and overwhelmed by the work of advocacy, others are invigorated by and actively engaged in advocacy activities" (p. 465). Kagan attempted to understand this professional ambivalence toward advocacy by tracing the history of child advocacy. Prior to the 1960s, professional training programs for special education personnel stressed curricular and instructional strategies to the almost total exclusion of advocacy. Child advocacy was not considered to be within the scope of special education professionals' responsibility. A perspective shift, however, occurred in the 1960s, coinciding with the increasingly militant advocacy of parents. During the 1960s, professionals teamed with parents to employ advocacy strategies that successfully procured new rights and services for individuals with disabilities.

Many professionals paid a price for their unending advocacy efforts of the 1960s: professional burnout due to increased stress and role responsibilities. During the 1970s and early 1980s, a professional pessimism toward advocacy pervaded the field of special education. As Kagan (1989) noted, "There was a pervasive sense that advocacy did not matter. Advocacy became the David pitted against a governmental Goliath" (p. 466). In the 1990s, however, new educational reform efforts emphasizing professional collaboration and empowerment have rekindled interest in and commitment to educational advocacy. The significance of this rekindled interest should not be minimized, as, historically, securing new rights, improving educational services, and positively impacting societal attitudes toward individuals with disabilities can be attributed primarily to one phenomenon: advocacy (Fiedler & Antonak, 1991).

THE RELUCTANCE OF PROFESSIONALS TO SERVE AS ADVOCATES

Notwithstanding the rich tradition of professional advocacy on behalf of children with disabilities and their families, as well as the success of these advocacy efforts, many special education professionals are reluctant to assume an advocacy role and its corresponding responsibilities. It is crucial that professionals overcome this reluctance, as there are many reasons why professional advocacy continues to be necessary in special education, including: (1) to preserve programs for children with disabilities; (2) to increase service capacity and enhance program quality; (3) to change educational systems, thereby making special education services more accessible and equitable; and (4) to generate public awareness of educational issues affecting children with disabilities and their families (Kagan, 1989). Given the compelling need for professional advocacy, why are many special education personnel unwilling to function in this capacity?

There are several reasons for the reluctance of professionals to be advocates. Fiedler (1986) noted, "Special education professionals have historically avoided advocacy responsibility because of insufficient training, legal ramifications, pressure from superiors, and competing time and energy demands" (p. 7). Because advocacy is still perceived as tangential to special education professionals' immediate work, most preservice educational programs do not address the topic of advocacy in any comprehensive fashion. Therefore, most professionals enter the field of special education with a perceived lack of knowledge and skills necessary for advocacy (Herbert & Mould, 1992).

Many special education professionals are intimidated when contemplating potential legal implications of their advocacy work. As stated earlier, it is important that special education professionals systematically evaluate the risks and potential of legal liability emanating from their advocacy. As part of this evaluation process, typical questions should include: What are the child's educational rights in this situation? Do I have a legal right to disagree with the parents? Can the school district fire me for challenging school policies and practices? The safe action is not to make waves by serving as an advocate. Professional advocacy, by its very nature, requires some risk taking but the benefits outweigh the risks. As one teacher put it, "Advocating for a child against the school system is not a smart choice, but it is my only choice" (Taylor, Coughlin, & Marasco, 1997, p. 27).

Professional advocacy is constrained by school bureaucratic barriers (Herbert & Mould, 1992; Kagan, 1989; Taylor et al., 1997). To some school administrators, professional advocacy is viewed as aberrant radical behavior instead of behavior that fulfills a professional ethical obligation. Professionals who do not fit the expected norms within the school culture of being a "good employee" face the anxiety of doing something wrong or not being liked (Taylor et al., 1997). In this context, a good employee does not challenge the school bureaucracy. Harste (1990) pinpointed this form of school bureaucratic control of special education professionals when he stated, "In the past, schools seem to have been better at silencing children and teachers than at hearing them. Silent classrooms have been more than unfortunate; they have been wrong. In a democracy, the role of the school is to hear people, not to silence them" (p. 31).

Finally, many special education professionals avoid or ignore advocacy responsibilities because of competing time and energy demands. To function as an advocate requires additional time and energy commitments from professionals that go beyond typical job descriptions and expectations. Many professionals feel overwhelmed by basic job and family demands that preclude advocacy work (Kagan, 1989). In fact, in a structured interview I conducted in the fall of 1997 with 27 professional educators on the topic of advocacy, the most frequently mentioned reason why many educators do not serve as advocates was excessive time and energy demands required in being an advocate. Other reasons for professional reluctance to serve as advocates are as follows (Fiedler, 1997):

- Excessive time and energy demands in being an advocate
- Fear of reprisals from school administration
- Different perceptions on what being a child advocate is all about

- Belief that being an advocate is not part of their job responsibilities
- The fact that advocacy can be exhausting, frustrating, and emotionally draining work
- Professional burnout
- Lack of necessary advocacy skills
- Intimidated by potential legal implications
- Possibility that advocacy may lead to "inconvenient outcomes" for individual educators
- Assumption that advocacy is solely a parental responsibility
- Personality traits—being an advocate is easier for individuals who are outspoken and assertive
- Feeling overwhelmed with regular job duties —tendency to focus only on personal needs, not the needs of others
- Uncomfortable with taking risks
- Uncomfortable with change
- Lack of administrative support to serve as an advocate
- Insufficient patience
- Lack of professional passion in one's work

THE NEED FOR PROFESSIONAL ADVOCACY IN SPECIAL EDUCATION

The need for professional advocacy in special education has been increasingly recognized (Alper et al., 1994; Balcazar, Keys, Bertram, & Rizzo, 1996; Fiedler, 1986; Fiedler & Antonak, 1991; Kagan, 1989; Simpson, 1996; Turnbull & Turnbull, 1997). Some have argued that advocacy should be part of every special education professionals' job description (Kagan, 1989). In the aforementioned interviews I conducted, a number of reasons were cited why professional educators need to serve as advocates (Fiedler, 1997):

- Educators have important insight about what a child needs.
- Every child needs a "voice."
- Advocacy is part of one's professional responsibility.
- Advocates can serve as positive role models for colleagues.

- Professionals are usually not hindered in their advocacy by emotionality, like some parents may be.
- Advocacy is necessary to cut through bureaucratic red tape.
- The educator might be the one to make a difference.
- Advocacy is necessary in working with the "whole child."
- Advocacy is part of being a child's mentor.
- Advocacy may be legally necessary (e.g., to avoid discrimination).
- Advocacy is necessary to enhance others' understanding of children with disabilities.
- Advocacy is part of one's responsibility in establishing a partnership with families.

This section will present five arguments supporting the need for professional advocacy in special education: (1) the historical discrimination experienced by individuals with disabilities, (2) the frequent denial of educational rights of children with disabilities, (3) schools as political and bureaucratic entities, (4) lack of parental advocacy, and (5) the findings from special education outcomes research (in terms of successful community adjustment after leaving school).

Historical Discrimination Experienced by Individuals with Disabilities

Individuals with disabilities have minority status in this country; thus, they share the conditions of discrimination, segregation, and subordination with certain ethnic, racial, social class, and gender groups (Brantlinger, 1991). From this perspective, advocacy is needed to foster basic civil rights. Individuals with disabilities are at risk in this society (Fiedler & Antonak, 1991). Herr (1984) stated that "as a banished and insular minority, such persons were isolated and stigmatized in ways that matched and sometimes exceeded the most vicious regimes of racial segregation" (p. 3). The segregation, isolation, and discrimination experienced by individuals with disabilities takes many forms, including separate housing, separate schooling, separate medical care, and separate employment.

The at-risk status of many individuals with disabilities was noted by Fiedler and Antonak (1991):

> The ebb and flow of society's attitudes and treatment of persons with mental retardation resulted in bleak periods where they were thought of as a menace, a threat to society, and where Social Darwinism was the driving force behind perceptions of society's responsibilities. During these bleak times, the societal response to people with mental retardation emphasized solutions such as institutional incarceration, immigration restriction, eugenic control, and sterilization. (p. 23)

These kinds of discriminatory and pernicious practices were justified because individuals with disabilities were considered deviant. That is, they were perceived as being significantly different from others in aspects that were negatively value.

In terms of public schooling, children with disabilities were not deemed worthy of any education until the late nineteenth century (Stainback, Stainback, & Forest, 1989). This period of total educational neglect was followed by a period of institutionalized, segregated education. Public school programs for children with disabilities were sporadic until the 1960s. When educational services were provided, children with disabilities were placed in segregated, self-contained special education classrooms. This placement model was indicative of a philosophy that believed children with disabilities must be separated from nondisabled students in the interest of school efficiency and efficacy (Skrtic, 1987).

Clearly, U.S. society and the public educational system have made great strides in the way individuals with disabilities are viewed and treated. New rights and entitlements have evolved over the past 50 years. Most of these societal and educational advancements in both thinking and acting toward individuals with disabilities are directly attributable to advocacy efforts. Undoubtedly, it will take continued advocacy by parents and professionals to maintain and expand on these legislative and service gains.

Frequent Denial of Educational Rights/Needs of Children with Disabilities

Even though the federal special education law, the Individuals with Disabilities Education Act (IDEA), has been in existence since 1975, there are still legitimate concerns about compliance with legal mandates and best educational practices. For many children, advocacy is the "squeaky wheel that gets the grease," in the form of appropriate, individualized educational services. Conversely, children without an effective advocate may experience an inappropriate education. Schloss (1994) advanced four typical reasons why the rights of children with disabilities are often denied:

1. The presence of a condition or circumstance for which there are no legal precedents
2. The inability to function as a self-advocate to ensure one's rights and the unavailability of others to serve as advocates
3. The denial of rights due to lack of information by educational service providers and families
4. The denial of rights due to lack of good-faith efforts by educational service providers

It is widely maintained that many children with disabilities are routinely denied their rights and deprived of appropriate special educational services because those services are not truly individualized (Audette & Algozzine, 1997; Hines, 1987; Kauffman, 1993). That is, for many children with disabilities, there is nothing "special" about their special education services. The anecdote presented in Box 1.1 is based on some of my research and is illustrative of this point. This lack of individualized programming is amplified by Audette and Algozzine:

> Individualized education programming is rarely a process of sophisticated tailoring of learning strategies to meet the needs of children and youth.... Too often, Individualized Education Programs mean replicating (with minor variations) existing programs of other children and youth in a class. In too many programs, individualized education has become merely the obedient rewriting of the same goals

Box 1.1_____

Advocacy Anecdote

A few years ago, I conducted a study on secondary programming for students with emotional/behavioral disorders (EBD). As part of the data collection, I reviewed all of the current IEPs for 10 students enrolled in a high school EBD program. I was shocked to discover that every single IEP was identical, word for word. All of the services provided and the goals and objectives were the same. The only difference from one IEP to the next was the demographic information for each student. What is "special" about special education? In this case—nothing.

_____

and objectives for individual students—one student at a time. (p. 382)

Many IEP meetings primarily operate as mechanisms for the identification of problems within students and for procedural compliance with the law (Christensen & Dorn, 1997). That is, many IEP meetings provide limited focus on individualized instruction. Instead, these meetings merely legitimize the teacher's identification of the student as the problem. This practice reflects the internal deficit model of disability, whereby the problem resides solely in the student. The result is to blame the student and his or her family for school failure. Instead of the individual needs of children driving educational programming decisions, as is the legal requirement, too many programming decisions are based primarily on administrative convenience—whether there is an existing program in which to readily place a given child.

When parents or advocates maintain that the special educational rights of a child have been violated, the ultimate conflict resolution mechanism is a due process hearing. Although a school district may also request a due process hearing to challenge parental decisions, the vast majority of these hearings are initiated by parents or advocates on behalf of children with disabilities. A report prepared for the Office of Special Education Pro-

grams, U.S. Department of Education (Ahearn, 1997) analyzed the number of due process hearing requests filed nationally during a five-year period (1991 to 1995). Although data on the number of due process hearing requests are not a totally accurate measure of the frequency of children's educational rights violations (because it is not known in how many cases the school ultimately prevailed and no violations of the law were found), this information is still some measure of parental satisfaction with how schools are meeting the educational needs of children with disabilities. The number of due process hearing requests nationally increased from 4,125 in 1991 to 5,497 in 1995, an average annual increase of 7.5 percent.

There is no doubt that the IDEA has increased access to educational services for many children with disabilities. Yet, inequalities in access and appropriateness of services still exist for many children (Cuban, 1996). Des Jardins (1993) offered several reasons why parents and professionals are often unable to secure appropriate educational services for children with disabilities: (1) trying to fight entrenched bureaucracies and the status quo, (2) lacking sufficient financial resources to meet the increasing demand for services, (3) providing services to those consumers and advocates who are more vocal and assertive (the squeaky wheel phenomenon again), and (4) working with children who are suffering from low expectations by parents and professionals. Effective professional advocacy can address all of these reasons for denying children with disabilities their educational rights.

Schools as Political and Bureaucratic Entities

Advocates for children with disabilities must first recognize that schools are bureaucracies, and thus are conservative by nature. This means that schools tend to be inflexible and resistant to change (Cutler, 1993; Sailor & Skrtic, 1996; Stoecklin, 1994). A common feature of bureaucratic institutions is that they tend to respond more to their own needs rather than to the needs of those they serve (Shields, 1989; Taylor et al., 1997). In other words, schools often base decisions on administrative convenience and not on the individual needs of children with disabilities. An example of this administrative convenience decision making is provided in Box 1.2. This anecdote is based on a due process hearing I presided over as a hearing officer. Sailor and Skrtic (1996) have argued that the organizational structure of schools, as typical bureaucracies, is antiquated. Instead, it is argued, schools need to evolve into "learning organizations" (Senge, 1990). The limitation of bureaucratic schools is noted by Sailor and Skrtic: "Bureaucracies are designed to perfect a given product or service by standardizing work processes and worker behavior, but learning organizations invent new products or services by deploying their workers on collaborative teams" (p. 268).

Another feature of schools as bureaucracies is the pressure toward conformity. Schools as institutional work environments demand compliance and conformity by its employees (Glickman, 1990). Teachers have been conditioned to conform rather than to be autonomous and involved as initiators of change. This teacher conditioning was identified by Glickman: "Administrators prize conformity, privacy, dependency, quietness, and routine in their teachers and consider unconventionality, public attention, creativity, assertiveness, spontaneity, and collective action among teachers to be threatening and 'unschool-like.' As a result, teachers are rewarded for conforming and penalized for being intellectually critical" (p. 38). Given this working environment, the risks of serving as a professional advocate are obvious. A destructive consequence of this pressure to conform is that many teachers and administrators who started their careers with idealism and a strong sense of purpose become disillusioned. This tragedy is depicted in Box 1.3.

Lack of Parental Advocacy

The Individuals with Disabilities Education Act clearly acknowledges that parents are their children's first and best advocates (Anderson et al., 1997). The IDEA empowers parents to be active

Box 1.2 _____

Advocacy Anecdote

I used to serve as a due process hearing officer for the state department of education. My first case as a due process hearing officer involved a small, rural school district. This district had one elementary building and one secondary building. Both schools were antiquated and overcrowded. This school district had historically sent their students with severe disabilities to a regional program 20 miles away in another district. The district decided to bring their six students with severe disabilities back to their home district the next year. This decision was based on the least restrictive environment legal principle of educating children with disabilities as close to their home as possible.

The only problem with the decision to bring the six students back to their home district was where to place them. There was no space for an additional classroom in either of the two existing school buildings. The district's solution was to lease an old muffler shop storefront in the small downtown area and convert that space into a special education classroom. The closest school building was over one mile away. The storefront was converted over the summer and the six students started their new school year in this downtown facility.

One parent objected to this arrangement and filed for a due process hearing. The district's rationale for their placement decision was simply that they had no space in any school building; therefore, this was a suitable arrangement in an effort to have the students back in their home district. In other words, the district's decision was based on administrative convenience. In dealing with the space problem, it was more convenient to renovate a nonschool facility than to disrupt the school environment by rearranging existing classroom space. The school district lost this case.

educational decision makers by bestowing the following rights:

- To be notified whenever the school wants to evaluate a child, wants to change a child's educational program or placement, or refuses a parent's request for an evaluation or a change in program or placement
- To initiate an evaluation if the parent thinks his or her child is in need of special education

Box 1.3 _____

Advocacy Anecdote

Cutler (1993) wrote:

> *These teachers may have asked many times for more services and space, only to be refused, ignored, or intimidated through subtle messages that their contracts might not be renewed if they continued to bother people. When they compared notes with friends, they found other school systems were not really different. They grew tired of asking and getting nothing in return for their efforts. If the disillusioned people are administrators, their experience may have been the same, with too much work, too few resources to build effective programs, too many requests for personnel denied, and too many attempts to create new ways of doing things that were frustrated by a system insisting that we've always done things this way. (pp. 50–51)*

- To request a reevaluation if the parent suspects his or her child's present educational program or placement is no longer appropriate
- To provide informed consent prior to an educational evaluation and placement into a special education program
- To obtain an independent educational evaluation if the parent disagrees with the outcome of the school's evaluation
- To review all of the child's educational records
- To participate in the development of the child's IEP
- To request a due process hearing to resolve differences with the school that could not be resolved informally

It is generally accepted that parents are their child's ideal advocates if they are informed and involved (Fiedler, 1993; Friesen & Huff, 1990; Simpson, 1996; Stoecklin, 1994; Turnbull & Turnbull, 1997). Parents are natural advocates because they know their child better than anyone else. Further, there is more than 20 years of research strongly correlating active parent involvement with increased child development (Stoecklin, 1994). Other reasons why parents should function

as educational advocates include the following: parents have been given this social and legal responsibility; parents have an emotional investment in their child's welfare that goes well beyond the emotional investment of professionals; parents are more constant in their child's life than professionals; parents can be persuasive advocates because they have direct, firsthand experiences with the school system; parents' advocacy motivation is less likely to be viewed with suspicion than possible self-serving motives of some professionals; and, as parents do not have potential conflicts of interest as professionals sometimes do, they are more free to speak out (Friesen & Huff, 1990).

Although professionals should assist parents in acquiring the necessary knowledge and skills to function as effective advocates (discussed further in Chapter 4), some family situations preclude parents from being effective advocates. In such circumstances, professionals must be able to serve as a child's advocate. There are a variety of barriers to family advocacy. Some families are hindered in their advocacy efforts because of certain family characteristics and circumstances (Friesen & Huff, 1990; Schloss & Jayne, 1994; Simpson, 1996). For example, a single mother may be struggling with economic survival to the point that worrying about the quality of her child's educational program is a luxury she cannot presently afford. In some blended family circumstances, issues of merging two families under one roof can sometimes take priority over educational matters. Another family circumstance that interferes with effective parent advocacy is mobility. Family involvement and advocacy often suffers when a family moves from school district to school district because the parents never gain a good understanding of local issues and the school administration. This lack of local district information can hamper advocacy efforts. Families experiencing a crisis situation or chronic stress often have their time and energy consumed and are thus unable to expend any additional time and energy on advocacy.

Additional barriers to family advocacy arise from parental knowledge and skill deficits (McBride, 1992). Without a good understanding of special education legal rights, it is impossible to function as an effective advocate. Some families lack information about what services are available for their child. The communication or conflict resolution skills necessary for effective advocacy may not be possessed by some families. Certainly, families can acquire the requisite knowledge and skills to serve as an advocate. However, a professional commitment of training and support, along with sufficient family time and energy, are required. Some parents lack the self-confidence to advocate, perhaps as a result of how special education procedures operate. As an example, one father commented: "It is an intimidating process. . . . Everyone in the room talks about and makes decisions about my kid like I'm not even in the room, and they put the piece of paper in front of me to sign" (Smith, 1992, p. 10).

Some parents shun advocacy because of fear of reprisals if they challenge the school in any manner. An example of this fear was shared by one parent who said, "Our son is not disabled and we tried to fight the school district. The school district became more and more entrenched in their position and more and more punitive to the point of saying, 'You let us test your kid again or he can't go into third grade'—which is probably illegal. So the regulations get used in ways that aren't appropriate because the officials have taken a stand and they are not willing to back down from that position" (Taylor et al., 1997, p. 67). In addition to threats of school reprisal, some parents are discouraged from advocacy because their interactions with school personnel are characterized by being blamed for their child's problems.

Findings from Special Education Outcomes Research

In recent years, there has been increased emphasis on the postgraduation success of special education students. This demand for educational accountability has spawned numerous studies investigating the impact of special education programming on student performance upon leaving school (Destefano & Wagner, 1993; NASDSE, 1993;

Schalock, Holl, Elliott, & Ross, 1992). This outcomes research focus has been concerned with the educational, occupational, social, and independent living status of students with disabilities after leaving school.

Most special education outcomes research has employed Halpern's (1985) conceptual model that maintains that the desired outcome of special education programming should be successful community adjustment. Community adjustment consists of three components: employment, residential adjustment, and establishment of desirable social and interpersonal networks. The vast majority of outcomes studies paint a pessimistic picture of adult adjustment for students with disabilities exiting from special education programs (Blackorby, Edgar, & Kortering, 1991; Chadsey-Rusch, Rusch, & O'Reilly, 1991; Edgar, 1991; 1995; Edgar & Polloway, 1994; Hasazi, Gordon, & Roe, 1985; Levine & Edgar, 1994; Mithaug, Horiuchi, & Fanning, 1985; Nelson, 1996; Wagner, 1989). Simply stated, many studies reveal that special education graduates are

- not employed
- not living on their own
- not integrated into their communities
- not very satisfied with their lives

Nineteenth Annual Report to Congress on the Implementation of the Individuals with Disabilities Education Act

In its most recent report on the implementation of the IDEA, the U.S. Department of Education (1997) estimated a special education student cohort dropout rate of 28 percent. This is a particularly ominous statistic because special education graduates are significantly more likely to be engaged in productive activities of employment, postsecondary education, and independent living than dropouts. Since, as numerous studies have reported, the postschool outcomes for special education graduates are not very promising, the outlook for dropouts is especially dismal. The U.S. Department of Education report was particularly discouraging for urban students with disabilities, indicating that such students were less likely to graduate, less likely to enroll in postsecondary education, and less likely to be employed after exiting school than other special education students in nonurban settings. Further, African American students with disabilities were at greater risk of poor community adjustment outcomes when compared to Caucasian students with disabilities. The Nineteenth Annual Report to Congress concluded that advocacy is necessary to ensure full participation for students with disabilities in their schools and communities.

ESSENTIAL PROFESSIONAL ADVOCACY COMPETENCIES FOR MAKING A DIFFERENCE

In this chapter, I have cited several reasons why special education professionals should be willing to serve as advocates for children with disabilities and their families. First, individuals with disabilities have historically experienced discrimination as a result of societal attitudes, treatment, and school practices. The primary impetus for the improvement of societal attitudes and practices can be traced to advocacy efforts. Rights and services for children with disabilities have improved tremendously in the past 25 years, but improved services and continued progress are necessary. Advocacy is essential in monitoring current practices and seeking improvements. Second, even with state and federal special education laws and regulations, children with disabilities still experience frequent violations of their educational rights. Parent and professional advocacy provides the enforcement mechanism to assert children's rights. Third, schools function and are structured as political and bureaucratic organizations. Such organizations tend to demand conformity from its employees while attempting to silence dissenting voices. To spark school change, professionals must be willing to empower parents to serve as advocates or be willing to function as advocates in the parents' absence. Fourth, although parents are their children's first and best advocates, many families, for a variety of reasons, are unable to

function as effective advocates. In those situations, professionals must be willing to fulfill this advocacy void. Finally, the overwhelming conclusion of special education outcomes research is that special education graduates are often not successful in their postschool community adjustment efforts. Advocacy is necessary to improve educational services, transition services into the community, and accountability.

Willingness to serve as a professional advocate and the ability to be an *effective* advocate are two different issues. Whether special education professionals become effective advocates and make a difference depends on their *dispositions* (or attitudes), their *knowledge,* and their *skills* (Shields, 1989). Figure 1.1 identifies 11 essential professional advocacy competencies. The competencies are categorized as follows:

- **Dispositions.** Dispositions reflect the values and attitudes of professionals in terms of their commitment, sense of responsibility, and ethical behavior on behalf of children with disabilities and their families. There are three essential dispositions:

   Advocacy disposition. Professionals with an advocacy disposition recognize that advocating for children with disabilities and their families is a legitimate part of their job responsibilities (Chapter 2).

   Ethical disposition. Professionals with an ethical disposition have a strong ethic of caring and a commitment to their professional code of ethics (Chapter 3).

   Family support/empowerment disposition. Professionals with a family support and empowerment disposition seek to understand families from a family systems perspective and to collaborate with and empower families in a supportive partnership (Chapter 4).

- **Knowledge.** Knowledge refers to awareness of the essential information to effectively advocate in an effort to bring about educational change. There are three essential knowledge bases:

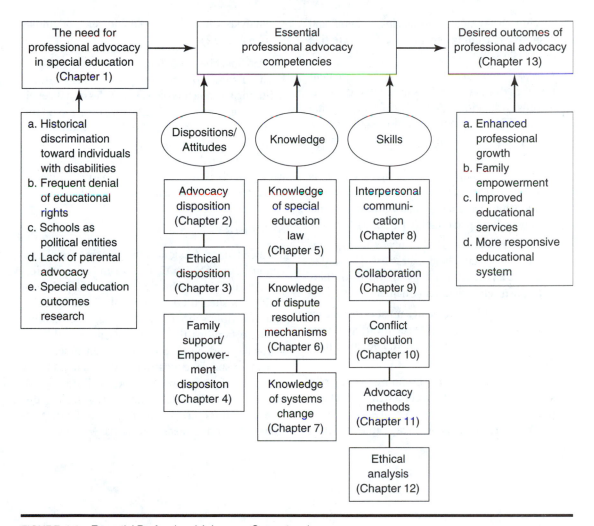

FIGURE 1.1   Essential Professional Advocacy Competencies

Knowledge of special education law.   Effective advocacy is dependent on a solid understanding of special education laws, procedures, and regulations (Chapter 5).

Knowledge of dispute resolution mechanisms.   Advocacy often creates conflict, which requires an understanding of informal and formal dispute resolution mechanisms in special education (Chapter 6).

Knowledge of systems change.   Advocacy seeks change in the status quo, sometimes on an individual level and sometimes at a systems level. Knowledge of systems change issues and effective strategies can ensure the implementation of legal pronouncements or negotiated settlements (Chapter 7).

— **Skills.**   Skills involve performance abilities in interpersonal communicative interactions, resolving differences, influencing others, and cognitive reasoning capabilities. There are five essential skills:

Interpersonal communication skills. The context for advocacy involves interpersonal interactions with families, school professionals, and others. Effective communication skills are essential in fostering understanding and change (Chapter 8).

Collaboration skills. Advocating for change is usually more effective if good collaborative relationships have been established with families and school personnel (Chapter 9).

Conflict resolution skills. In advocacy, conflicts are inevitable and necessary. The key to effective advocacy is resolving those conflicts in a constructive manner (Chapter 10).

Advocacy skills. Advocates must possess specific strategies and awareness of different avenues of advocacy to successfully advance their causes (Chapter 11).

Ethical analysis skills. Deciding whether to serve as an advocate for a child with disabilities presents ethical dilemmas. A professional must be able to recognize and engage in a reasoned analysis when confronted with such dilemmas (Chapter 12).

The final chapter (Chapter 13) discusses the desired outcomes of professional advocacy efforts, including an enhanced sense of professional development and growth, family empowerment, improved educational services for children with disabilities, and a more responsive and collaborative educational system. The outcomes of advocacy provide both intrinsic and extrinsic rewards along with tangible and intangible results.

SUMMARY

The need for professional advocacy in special education is great. Historical discrimination against individuals with disabilities, frequent violations of children's special education rights, unresponsive and inflexible school bureaucracies, the inability of some families to function as their children's advocate, and bleak postschool adjustment outcomes for special education graduates point to the necessity of professional advocacy. Professionals who serve as advocates in an effort to make a difference will require a number of specific dispositions, knowledge bases, and skills.

CHAPTER 2

AN ADVOCACY DISPOSITION

The greatest discovery of my generation is that a human being can alter his life by altering his attitude.
—William James

As stated in Chapter 1, advocacy, ethics, and family support/empowerment dispositions reflect the values and attitudes of special education professionals in terms of their commitment, sense of responsibility, and ethical behavior on behalf of children with disabilities and their families. Special education professionals with an advocacy disposition acknowledge the importance of special education advocacy and accept this responsibility as a legitimate part of their jobs. The requisite professional dispositions (advocacy, ethics, and family support/empowerment) may be more important than knowledge and skill competencies. Without a sufficient disposition toward advocacy, professionals will lack the motivation to acquire the necessary knowledge and skills to function as effective advocates. When the educational system is unresponsive to the needs of children with disabilities and their families, professionals lacking an advocacy disposition will accept this lack of responsiveness as a fact of life (Shields, 1989). Obviously, this disposition prevents professionals from serving as advocates and maintains the status quo. Alternatively, professionals who serve as advocates must, among other beliefs, expect that children who require special services are entitled to receive them; that professionals and schools exist in order to serve; and that the need for special services is a normal, acceptable need and not a sign of inadequacy. For professionals lacking this requisite advocacy disposition, there is hope that one can, as the William James quotation above notes, alter one's attitude.

An advocacy disposition is critical to professional success. To truly make a positive difference in children's lives, advocacy must become a state of mind—an attitude of constant watchfulness to ensure the responsiveness of the educational system (Herbert & Mould, 1992). Professional advocates must possess additional dispositions, such as a willingness to learn, persistence, consistency, and self-confidence (Stoecklin, 1994). Persistence and self-confidence are especially important dispositions because most people are taught that it is inappropriate to disagree or to confront anyone (Hines, 1987). Advocacy, however, often requires disagreement and confrontation. Advocates must be prepared to be labeled as "troublemakers" or "radicals"; they must be willing to withstand criticism.

Professionals often stand alone when they advocate. There are no guidelines for advocacy; however, special education professionals are wise to reflect on the limits to their advocacy as dictated by legal safeguards. Instead of providing prescriptive guidelines, this chapter will discuss some of the factors and issues revolving around acquiring and enhancing this necessary advocacy disposition. Topics in this discussion include (1) the dilemma faced by special education professionals as they try to fulfill a dual role, (2) characteristics of effective advocates, (3) values inherent in an advocacy disposition, (4) developmental phases in becoming an advocate, (5) legal safeguards in professional advocacy work, (6) factors fostering a professional advocacy disposition, and (7) advocacy educational issues.

DUAL ROLE DILEMMA

Professional advocates face an advocacy dilemma that results from their dual roles as advocates for children with disabilities and school employees (Frith, 1981; Rock, Geiger, & Hood, 1992). Frith defined this advocacy dilemma "as a conflict that arises when a professional must decide whether to actively defend a child's rights when doing so would contradict the stated or implied directives of the professional's employing agency" (p. 487). This advocacy dilemma poses a most difficult question of whether a professional's primary loyalty should be to his or her employer or to the children for whom services are provided (Fiedler & Antonak, 1991). Fiedler and Antonak stated, "In attempting to answer such a question, special educators must reflect upon their personal reasons for entering the teaching profession, thus trying to ascertain their role responsibilities" (p. 24). The perspective I present in this book is that a professional's commitment to a child with disabilities must take primacy over a commitment to the employer, provided professionals temper their child commitment according to the realities of legal protections (as discussed later in this chapter). In situations where the child's and employer's interests conflict, if the professional chooses not to promote the best interests of the child, that professional ceases to be an advocate (Schloss & Jayne, 1994).

The potential conflict between the child's rights and the employer's directives are evident when reflecting on some of the typical advocacy activities identified by Rock and colleagues (1992):

- Actively participate in an organization seeking to improve services.
- Educate groups in the rights of individuals with disabilities.
- Collaborate with others to improve services.
- Contact elected or appointed state officials to improve services.
- Contact elected or appointed federal officials to improve services.
- Testify on funding, legislation, or regulations.
- Inform individuals of their rights.
- Encourage initiation of a due process hearing.
- Refer persons to advocacy organizations.
- Obtain or provide resources to improve services.
- Spend extra time to secure rights or services.

Some actual examples of special education advocacy where the commitment to the child is the professional's first priority are contained in Box 2.1. Although these anecdotes do not involve direct conflicts between the students' rights and the employer's directives, this conflict is ever present when professionals place their primary loyalty with their students.

What motivates special education professionals, regardless of external pressures from the school administration, to assume an advocacy role? Some insight into this question was gathered through structured interviews I conducted with special education professionals who are acknowledged to be effective child advocates. The following are responses to the question: What motivates you to serve as an educational advocate for children with disabilities and their families (Fiedler, 1997)?

- Accepts advocacy as part of job responsibility and as an ethical obligation
- Had personal experiences in parenting a child with a disability; empathy toward children with disabilities
- Recognize that parents sometimes need a spokesperson
- Recognize that sometimes advocacy is necessary to do what is in the child's best interests
- Recognize the need to right an injustice
- Have experienced some negative personal situations as students themselves
- Possess a strong sense of personal efficacy; believe that one can make a difference

Box 2.1_____

Advocacy Anecdotes

- A music teacher took a particular interest in one of her students with disabilities. This young man, who was severely learning disabled and had a seizure disorder, had been in an institution for most of his elementary school years. He was rejected by peers and experienced a very lonely adolescence. He did exhibit an interest and some talent in writing poetry. The music teacher wrote a grant to hire a local musician to compose music for the student's poetry. The student's poetry, set to music, was played at a community concert. This young man with disabilities, through his poetry, finally found a way to belong, which greatly enhanced his self-esteem.

- An early childhood exceptional educational needs (EC:EEN) teacher devoted extra time and energy to interact with a mother of one of her students. This mother had been criticized by several school personnel due to her irrational and hostile behavior directed at professionals. Instead of operating from a similar judgmental perspective, the EC:EEN teacher carefully listened to this "hostile mother." After several interactions, the mother finally confided to the teacher that she was anxious about successfully parenting a child with special needs. This anxiety and lack of parental confidence was exacerbated by the fractured relations with her own mother. The fractured relationship was caused by the grandmother's inability to deal with the reality of having a grandchild with disabilities. By looking beyond the overt behavior of the "hostile mother," the EC:EEN teacher was able to support, collaborate with, and empower a very needy family.

- A principal became an advocate for a seventh-grade student with school phobia. In an effort to provide comprehensive buildingwide support for this student, the principal conducted an inservice workshop for all staff. A psychologist discussed school phobia with staff and the staff engaged in roleplay simulations to enhance their understanding and empathy of this condition. With this building-based support system, the student with school phobia was eventually successful and graduated from high school.

- A school psychologist consulted with a general education teacher on classroom accommodations for a fifth-grade student with emotional/behavioral disorders. Initially, the general education teacher was very reluctant to make any modifications in his classroom expectations or operations. The school psychologist was very patient and respectfully listened to all of the teacher's concerns. Over the course of several months, the school psychologist dealt with each teacher concern while providing weekly consultation support to incorporate classroom accommodations. The classroom accommodations were phased in over time to allow the teacher to feel comfortable and confident with each new modification.

- Recognize that children who have an advocate tend to get more from the educational system than children without advocates
- Like a challenge
- Believe that advocacy is necessary due to "system failures"
- View teaching as a "mission"
- View advocacy as an opportunity to work with others; to get to know colleagues on a deeper level

Similarly, the following are responses to the question: What rewards do you receive for serving as an advocate (Fiedler, 1997)?

- See children with disabilities progress and develop as a result of receiving appropriate services
- Experience an intrinsic feeling of personal satisfaction
- Receive positive feedback from parents, children and colleagues

- Enhance sense of self efficacy
- See attitudinal and behavioral changes in others
- Feel as though one did all that was possible to support a child
- See families become empowered

In reviewing these responses, the following advocacy dispositional characteristics are revealed: (1) substantial empathy toward individuals with disabilities, (2) a strong sense of "justice," (3) a strong sense of self-efficacy or ability to make a difference, (4) a need to be stimulated by a challenge, (5) a passion in performing one's professional job responsibilities, (6) an ability to clearly see deficiencies of the educational system, and (7) a strong intrinsic motivation for knowing that you have done a job well. Additional dispositional characteristics of effective advocates will be discussed in the next section.

CHARACTERISTICS OF EFFECTIVE ADVOCATES

A number of characteristics are common to effective advocates, such as:

- A great concern for the child's best interests
- A commitment to the child's welfare and to being the child's advocate
- Knowledge of the present needs of the child
- Assertiveness in persistently pointing out the child's needs to the people responsible for meeting those needs
- The ability to work with others to develop appropriate and beneficial educational goals and objectives for the child
- The ability to find and use information, allies, and resources to put the needed educational plans to work (Cutler, 1993; Stoecklin, 1994)

Most of these characteristics are essential advocacy competencies that will be discussed in subsequent chapters on interpersonal communication (Chapter 8), collaboration (Chapter 9), conflict resolution (Chapter 10), and advocacy skills (Chapter 11). In terms of dispositional characteristics, three essential ones will be addressed: the willingness to be a risk taker, self-confidence, and persistence.

Willingness to Be a Risk Taker

Advocacy inevitably involves some risk taking. Essentially, the risk is in going from the certainty of the status quo to the uncertainty of change. Prior to embarking on a course of advocacy, professionals consider a number of typical questions: What if I am wrong in advocating for this change? How will my colleagues and the school administration view my advocacy efforts? What happens if I fail in my advocacy? What if my advocacy puts me in conflict with the child's family? Will I have enough time, energy, and support to continue advocating when it becomes difficult? Without a sufficiently strong risk-taking disposition, the anxiety created by these typical questions and other issues will probably lead to the "safe course of action," which is not to make any waves. Professionals can gain some insight into their own risk-taking disposition by completing the Risk-Taking Questionnaire (Simpson, 1996) shown in Figure 2.1.

Educational change and improvement are accompanied by anxiety and stress (Fullan, 1991). Taking risks is largely a matter of will (personal disposition). Fullan and Hargreaves (1991) identified three criteria for developing a risk-taking disposition: (1) be selective initially in the risk-taking ventures, (2) take risks on a small scale, and (3) take a positive rather than a negative risk. As an example of being selective, consider a potential advocacy problem where a secondary special education teacher is dissatisfied with the quality and comprehensiveness of his district's transitional services. Instead of trying to revamp the district's entire transitional services philosophy and programming all at once, the teacher chooses to advocate for better services for one of his students who will be leaving the school this year. By instituting positive changes for one student, the teacher's advocacy can stimulate a larger discussion and review of the transitional services for all students

FIGURE 2.1   Risk-Taking Questionnaire

How comfortable are you in . . .	Very Comfortable	Somewhat Comfortable	Neutral	Somewhat Uncomfortable	Very Uncomfortable
1. telling parents that you don't know?	☐	☐	☐	☐	☐
2. telling parents that you made a mistake?	☐	☐	☐	☐	☐
3. suggesting to parents that another professional made an error?	☐	☐	☐	☐	☐
4. suggesting to parents that they should consider therapy for themselves?	☐	☐	☐	☐	☐
5. telling parents that there are behaviors displayed by their children that you dislike?	☐	☐	☐	☐	☐
6. displaying your emotions in a parent-educator conference?	☐	☐	☐	☐	☐
7. confronting parents with their failure to follow through on agreed-upon plans?	☐	☐	☐	☐	☐
8. talking about your own problems in a parent-educator conference?	☐	☐	☐	☐	☐
9. praising parents for things they do well?	☐	☐	☐	☐	☐
10. having parents take notes during conferences?	☐	☐	☐	☐	☐
11. allowing parents to observe in your class while you are teaching?	☐	☐	☐	☐	☐
12. allowing parents to tutor their own child at home?	☐	☐	☐	☐	☐
13. allowing parents to use behavior modification procedures with their own child at home?	☐	☐	☐	☐	☐
14. telling parents their "rights"?	☐	☐	☐	☐	☐
15. having parents assume an active role during IEP conferences?	☐	☐	☐	☐	☐
16. having parents ask you to defend your teaching strategies?	☐	☐	☐	☐	☐
17. having parents bring a friend to IEP conferences?	☐	☐	☐	☐	☐
18. having parents call you at home about a problem their child is having at school?	☐	☐	☐	☐	☐
19. having parents recommend a specific curriculum for use with their child?	☐	☐	☐	☐	☐
20. having parents review school records on their child?	☐	☐	☐	☐	☐
21. having parents collaborate on various problems and issues?	☐	☐	☐	☐	☐
22. maintaining relationship parity with parents?	☐	☐	☐	☐	☐

Source: From Working with Parents and Families of Exceptional Children and Youth: Techniques for Successful Conferencing and Collaboration by R. L. Simpson, 1996, Austin, TX: Pro-Ed. Reprinted by permission.

with disabilities in the district. This advocacy scenario is also an example of the second criteria for developing a risk-taking disposition—take risks on a small scale. Finally, the third criteria—take a positive risk rather than a negative risk—means it is easier to advocate for a particular positive vision than to take up an advocacy situation where the professional must refuse to do something. For example, advocacy is less confrontational and threatening to the school administration if the professional leads an effort to increase school personnel's understanding and implementation of positive behavioral management techniques as opposed to taking an advocacy position refusing to suspend any students (even after the principal orders to do so).

Hargreaves and Fullan (1998) have argued that educational professionals' continued learning and development is largely dependent on their willingness to embrace risk and uncertainty. These authors see a certain level of risk and anxiety in one's work life as stimulating creativity. Risk, however, must be harmonized with security. The relationship between risk, security/insecurity, and certainty/uncertainty is discussed by Hargreaves and Fullan.

A work environment characterized by security and certainty, instead of being an ideal situation, breeds excessive employee caution and complacency. In such an environment, a dull routine sets in where staff lack a sufficient questioning attitude. This kind of work environment will not foster sufficient motivation nor risk taking to improve educational services. The school environment where insecurity and certainty exist describes top-down school change efforts where front line staff have very little input into change initiatives. This type of work environment creates fear and hopelessness as well as demoralizes staff. A third type of school environment characterized by insecurity and uncertainty is chaotic. Chaotic school environments proliferate when schools jump blindly from one educational fad to another. This leads to staff frustration, anxiety, and burnout. The optimal risk-taking school environment is where staff accept some uncertainty but in a secure environment. School officials can establish a culture that fosters more risk taking among professional staff by valuing diverse opinions, by making it safe to disagree and challenge the administration, and by encouraging mentorships and collaborative working relationships. This school climate decreases the fear of failure and thus should foster more risk-taking behavior.

Professional Self-Confidence

In too many schools, there is a pervasive culture that, as noted by Fullan and Hargreaves (1991), stifles risk taking and decreases professional self-confidence: "Uncertainty, isolation and individualism are a potent combination. Almost by definition, they sustain educational conservatism, since the opportunity and pressure arising from new ideas are inaccessible. Such narrowness of orientation and experience lead to 'safe,' and non-risk taking forms of teaching. . . . This sense of powerlessness eats away at the teacher's sense of his or her own capacity to 'make a difference' in children's education" (p. 39). This mindset further narrows a professional's perceived role and responsibilities. Given this disposition, professionals will not likely take up "a cause beyond oneself" (Glickman, Gordon, & Ross-Gordon, 1998). Advocacy involves taking up a cause beyond oneself by putting one's values and convictions on the line and taking a risk to advance the educational rights and services for children with disabilities.

Without sufficient self-confidence, professionals will lack the personal courage to take risks that offer some opportunity for positive change. Conversely, professionals who are self-confident display the following characteristics:

- A strong sense of their own efficacy
- The ability to admit that they made a mistake
- A willingness to tell a parent or colleague that they do not know
- Not being defensive when a parent or colleague questions their decisions or services

- A constant thirst for new knowledge and skills
- Humility in the face of realizing how much there is to learn about appropriate educational services for children with disabilities

Of course, this is not an exhaustive list of all the characteristics of self-confident professionals, but some important attributes are highlighted. There is strong evidence that professionals who possess confidence and a strong sense of their own efficacy, who believe they can make a difference, actually do (Ashton & Webb, 1986). Specifically, research on parent and professional self-efficacy shows that professionals with higher perceived self-efficacy report higher levels of parent participation, suggesting that professionals who perceive themselves as effective may encourage more active parent educational involvement (Hoover-Dempsey, Bassler, & Brissie, 1992). Similarly, professionals with higher perceived self-efficacy characterized parents as likewise having higher efficacy. Finally, higher parent perceptions of self-efficacy are significant because it is correlated with increased parent volunteerism in schools and increased parent participation in educational activities and communication with school professionals.

Professional Persistence

Most advocacy efforts require a long-term commitment. Professional advocates need persistence and tenacity to maintain their vision and energy for the long haul. Consider this sentiment expressed by Rees (1991): "It is not sufficient merely to recognize an injustice. You have to believe that this issue should be fought for, and if necessary over a long period of time" (p. 146). This level of commitment is difficult in today's quick fix, immediate gratification world. I believe that many classroom educational interventions are characterized as failures because the teacher did not persist in implementing the intervention for a sufficiently long period of time. Most people are terribly impatient when it comes to change. As an example, I recently

received a call from a former student of mine who is now in her first year as a special education teacher. This new teacher was distraught that inclusion in her building was not proceeding as quickly as she thought it should. In her despair, she was ready to give up and go back to the old self-contained, isolated special education delivery model. Lack of professional persistence leads to superficial solutions and a defeatist disposition. To maintain an advocacy disposition and the necessary long-term commitment to advocacy work, Box 2.2 describes some advocacy disposition strategies adapted from the best-selling book by Richard Carlson (1997) *Don't Sweat the Small Stuff . . . and It's All Small Stuff.*

VALUES INHERENT IN AN ADVOCACY DISPOSITION

Values drive an individual's beliefs and convictions. It is important that advocates recognize that their personal values are often inherent in advocacy efforts (Peck, 1995). This is because many advocacy efforts are based on a sense of what "ought to be." Advocates must be able to articulate their values clearly and acknowledge when there are value differences with others in an advocacy situation. Professional disposition goes a long way in determining actions. There are many reasons why individuals have the value bases they do. "Many factors are important in the making of a teacher. Among them are the times in which teachers grew up and entered the profession, and the value systems and dominant educational beliefs that went with those times. Also important is the stage in life and career that teachers are at, and the effect this has on their confidence in their own teaching, their sense of realism, and their attitudes to change" (Fullan & Hargreaves, 1991, p. 25).

Hargreaves and Fullan (1998) argued that educational professionals must "go deeper" which "means hard thinking and soul searching about the fundamental value and purpose of what we do as educators" (p. 29). They believe that going deeper involves (1) purpose, (2) passion, and (3) hope.

Box 2.2 _____

Advocacy Actions

1. *Choose your battles wisely.* One of the dangers in becoming a persistent professional advocate is that your vigilance is always on the lookout for the next "educational injustice." If you take up each and every cause, you will become burned out and not act as an effective advocate for anyone. Develop some criteria by which you pick and choose which battles are worth fighting and which ones you will ignore.

2. *Life is a test. It is only a test.* If you see each new advocacy issue you face as a life and death battle, you will be stressed out and ineffective as an advocate. Instead, take the perspective that advocacy problems are like tests, and you can learn something from these tests.

3. *Argue for your limitations, and they're yours.* There are hundreds of reasons not to assume the responsibilities of serving as an advocate—you have some knowledge or skill deficiencies, or you are afraid of possible consequences, or you are afraid of making a mistake. If you fill your head with nothing but limitations, you will become paralyzed to any sort of positive action.

4. *Make service an integral part of your life.* If you constantly ask yourself, How can I be of service to someone? you will stretch yourself and experience personal and professional growth. Advocacy involves a "cause beyond oneself" or service to others. By making service a part of your professional work life, you will diversify your job responsibilities and enhance your learning and skills.

5. *When trying to be helpful, focus on little things.* If you go into your advocacy work with grandiose notions of all of the sweeping educational changes you will spark, you will probably be disappointed most of the time. As an alternative, learn to focus on the small changes brought about by your advocacy—a child is now getting appropriate accommodations in a general education class, nondisabled peers have formed a circle of support for a student with severe disabilities, a family has been empowered to advocate for changes at their child's next IEP meeting. If you fail to focus on the small victories, you will not be sufficiently reinforced for your advocacy efforts.

6. *If someone throws you the ball, you don't have to catch it.* Another occupational hazard of being a professional advocate is that you quickly get a reputation as a caring, dedicated person who takes up any and all injustices. Similar to choosing your battles wisely, it is important sometimes to not catch the ball when it is thrown to you. Recognize what your time and energy resources allow you to tackle and then set those limits.

Source: Adapted from *Don't Sweat the Small Stuff . . . And It's All Small Stuff* by Richard Carlson, 1997, New York: Hyperion.

These three values are crucial in forming and sustaining an advocacy disposition.

Purpose

According to Hargreaves and Fullan (1998), there are four purposes of schooling that have a special moral value. First, **to love and care** is a fundamental purpose in establishing caring and supportive relationships between children with disabilities and professionals. This professional caring means having empathy for students and their families.

Empathy is noted by Goleman (1995) as a fundamental attribute of what he calls "emotional intelligence." Empathy allows professionals to step inside the lives of a child and/or a child's family and see the world from their perspectives. Professional empathy is the emotional bond that is necessary for an advocate to take up another's cause.

The second purpose is **to serve**. Hargreaves and Fullan (1998) stated that "service to others should be one of the most basic purposes of family life and schooling" (p. 42). It is difficult to serve others when one's personal and professional lives are frenetic and exhausting. As noted earlier, advocacy requires a substantial amount of time and energy. Many busy and stressed professionals are more inward oriented and thus dwell on their own personal and/or professional issues. Service to others requires an outward orientation where one recognizes that true personal and professional satisfaction comes from helping others. This realization deepens a professional's commitment and enriches his or her life.

The third purpose is **to empower** (discussed more fully in Chapter 4). Professionals should strive to empower their students and families. When professionals empower people, they give those individuals a voice and more control over their own destinies. Advocacy is a primary vehicle for empowering children with disabilities and their families. "Empowering parents . . . means interacting with all of them more extensively. Listening to them more sincerely, soliciting their opinions and feedback, more determinedly, and involving them in curriculum development and in decisions about their own children's learning more widely—all on a regular basis" (Hargreaves & Fullan, 1998, p. 46). Instead of empowerment, some professionals seek control over families by controlling access to information and decision making (Shields, 1989). This creates unnecessary dependence and is indicative of a failed service system.

A final purpose of schooling is **to learn**. This value involves a lifelong commitment to learning and professional growth. I fear that some preservice education majors, in their eagerness to graduate from college and enter the teaching field, possess the attitude that now, finally, their learning is over, instead of realizing that their learning has just begun. Advocates have this value of lifelong learning. Professional advocates are highly motivated individuals who constantly seek challenges in a desire to grow, learning from their students, colleagues, and families. Unfortunately, many professionals fail to establish close relations with their students, preferring a traditional teacher/student relationship that is totally teacher directed where students are merely passive receptacles of the teacher's knowledge. Unfortunately, many profes-

sionals continue to work in isolation in schools. Also unfortunate is that many professionals are unable or unwilling to learn from parents. Instead, as Vincent (1996) concluded from her research on parent/teacher relationships, most teachers prefer a relationship where parents support or learn about what teachers already do. That is, these relationships are not characterized by teachers learning from parents.

Passion

Professional advocates are passionate in their commitment to children with disabilities and their families and to improving educational services. This passion springs from intense emotions (both negative and positive). Conventional wisdom has asserted that emotions impair rational thinking. Most educators have heard stories of the overly emotional parent at the IEP meeting. Usually, these stories are told in a critical tone, describing the emotional parent as irrational and unrealistic. However, new research maintains that emotions enhance rational decision making (Damasio, 1994). Hargreaves and Fullan (1998) explain: "In today's turbulent and complex environments, we operate with multiple goals and imperfect knowledge. We can't be perfectly rational by pinning down and choosing between all the possible ends and conceivable means for reaching them. Emotions help us narrow and judge among the range of possibilities. In healthy individuals, emotions don't distort rationality, they enhance it!" (p. 52).

Certainly, in many special education situations, one often operates with imperfect knowledge where decisions among legitimate competing goals must be made. If everyone listens in a careful and nonjudgmental fashion, that emotional parent or advocate may offer important insight about long-term values and visions for a child with disabilities. This information needs to be factored into educational decision making. A more helpful and empowering stance, then, is to assist that emotional parent or advocate in clearly articulating his or her vision for the child. Box 2.3 shows an example of how one professional disempowered a family by

Box 2.3 _____

Advocacy Anecdote

I am the parent of a daughter with severe and multiple disabilities. My wife and I have maintained for several years that our daughter, Jennifer, could educationally benefit from some general education classroom experiences. We knew that Jennifer was not capable of performing grade-level work in the general education classes. However, as parents, we were concerned about providing our daughter with sufficient opportunities to be exposed to more appropriate language and social/behavioral peer models than the self-contained special education class could offer. We were also hopeful that general education class participation could foster some much needed peer relationships between Jennifer and nondisabled students.

The most stressful year we had in Jennifer's school career was when she transitioned to the high school. Her new special education teacher did not believe in any general education class participation for students with severe and multiple disabilities. The teacher operated a completely self-contained special education program. At IEP meetings, my wife and I got rather emotional (and frustrated) as we attempted to explain our vision for Jennifer's future and why we felt some general education class participation was an important educational goal. The special education teacher could see us only as "irrational and unrealistic parents" simply because our educational philosophy and goals for our daughter were different from the teacher's theoretical framework. Instead of truly listening to our values and vision for our daughter, the teacher became defensive and intractable. The teacher simply dismissed our "emotions" and our feelings did not enter into her decision making at all. It was only our persistence and willingness to proceed to a due process hearing that brought about any general education class experiences for our daughter.

---

failing to acknowledge the parents' emotions and vision for their child.

One final comment about passion as a component of an advocacy disposition bears mentioning. By speaking up passionately about an educational injustice, one makes oneself vulnerable for frustration, disillusionment, and exhaustion. Therefore, professional advocates must build collaborative relationships with others to combat the emotional vulnerability that comes with advocacy work. Passionate professionals must actively seek interaction with and support from colleagues; professional isolation is destructive: "Studies done over two decades involving more than 37,000 people show that social isolation—the sense that you have nobody with whom you can share your private feelings, have close contact—doubles the chances of sickness or death" (Goleman, 1995, p. 226).

Hope

"The best definition of hope is 'unwarranted optimism.' There is no advantage to being hopeful when the conditions warrant it. Hope's real value is when the conditions are not hopeful. Hope should never disappear" (Hargreaves & Fullan, 1998, p. 57). Professionals and parents engage in advocacy because they are hopeful that educational services for children with disabilities can improve. Having hope is linked with a strong sense of self-efficacy—a belief that one's advocacy can make a difference in people's lives. Hope is not pie-in-the-sky wishful thinking. Instead, hope fuels an advocate's desire to solve difficult problems. Goleman (1995) discussed the emotionally beneficial effects of hope: "From the perspective of emotional intelligence, having hope means that one will not give in to overwhelming anxiety, a defeatist attitude, or depression in the face of difficult challenges or setbacks. Indeed, people who are hopeful evidence less depression than others as they maneuver through life in pursuit of their goals, are less anxious in general, and have fewer emotional distresses" (p. 87).

Turnbull and Turnbull (1997) acknowledged the importance of hope as one of the five elements that foster family motivation, which is essential for family empowerment. The Turnbulls define *hope* as a "belief that you will get what you want and need" (p. 41). Hope is the opposite of learned helplessness, which is a psychological state characterized by perceptions that one's life is controlled by external forces (Seligman, 1990); in other words, a person has no control over his or her own destiny. Therefore, when individuals with learned helplessness experience a challenge, they typically assume they will fail. For special education professionals, hope is important for two reasons. First, professionals need to cultivate a sense of hope in families of children with disabilities. Without hope, families will lack the motivation to advocate for their children. Second, professionals must remain hopeful to sustain their own advocacy efforts.

DEVELOPMENTAL PHASES IN BECOMING AN ADVOCATE

There are numerous reasons why many professionals do not function as advocates (see Chapter 1). This section will review several theories and research findings that examine professional willingness and ability to serve in an advocacy capacity from a developmental perspective.

Fuller (1969) identified three phases of concern in the development of educators: preteaching phase, early teaching phase, and late teaching phase. During the *preteaching phase,* preservice education majors think about teaching primarily based on their own experiences as students. Unless a teacher-to-be was exposed to a strong educational advocate as a student, the issue of professional advocacy is probably not even at a conscious level of thinking for most preservice education majors. The lack of attention to the issue of advocacy by most professional education programs further exacerbates the situation that most educators enter their careers without an advocacy disposition. During the *early teaching phase,* beginning educators are preoccupied with their own performance in the traditional classroom roles of content expert, behavior manager, and instructor. That is, most edu-

cators are not inclined at this phase of development to be focused on a "cause beyond oneself." During the third phase, *late teaching,* experienced educators can shift their focus from their own concerns to the concerns and progress of their students. At this point in their careers, professionals are more likely to be receptive to advocacy responsibilities. Fuller's theory of teacher development bolsters the argument for teacher induction and mentoring programs to foster professional support and collaboration in becoming an advocate.

Moore (1992) discussed teacher development as a process of reconciliation between one's *personal identity,* that aspect of the person most closely related to personality, and one's *social identity,* that aspect of the person related to a role one chooses and for which members of the community have certain expectations. During the first phase, the beginning professional fears failure in reconciling the conflict between the ideal social identity of the good student and a feared social identity as incompetent teacher. Again, similar to Fuller's early teaching phase, the professional preoccupation will be with one's own performance, not with fulfilling an advocacy role. In the second phase, the professional has resolved the earlier conflict by assuming the idealized personal identity as dutiful employee. Obviously, as discussed in Chapter 1, this perspective favors conformity and compliance—the antithesis of an advocacy disposition.

In the third phase, the professional is frustrated by the dual role conflict that emerges in a bureaucratic organization. This conflict is between the ideal social identity of a professional as a child advocate versus the personal identity of the dutiful and compliant employee. In fact, I believe that many individuals who are drawn to educational careers are at a disadvantage in terms of acquiring an advocacy disposition. I base this statement on my belief that most preservice education majors have chosen their prospective career paths because they had quite favorable experiences as students themselves. In schools, given their bureaucratic operations, successful students succeed due to their compliant rule-following behavior. Given their own school experiences, it is contrary to many educators' innate dispositions to make waves as advocates. Finally, in Moore's fourth phase, the professional has matured in both personal and social identities to the point of being able to consider an advocacy role.

Glickman and colleagues (1998) reviewed research on adult development and life span transitions and applied those findings and implications to teacher development. Research on adult development is engaged in the study of adults' capabilities to improve over time. Research on life span transitions focuses on typical events and experiences that individuals encounter as they age.

According to Glickman and colleagues (1998), research findings (Glickman & Tamashiro, 1982; Oja & Pine, 1981) have concluded that most teachers are in the conformist to conscientious stages of ego development. In these stages of ego development, teachers exhibit conventional behaviors, depending on others for solutions to problems (Loevinger, 1976). It is only at the higher stages of ego development that teachers display autonomous thought and behavior. Levine (1989) suggested that ego development in teachers can be enhanced by providing experiences that require teachers to take the perspectives of other persons. This is a prerequisite to developing an advocacy disposition.

In terms of conceptual development, the majority of teachers were categorized in the unilateral-dependence stage (Harvey, 1970). That is, their conceptual thinking was characterized as absolute and concrete with dependence on authority. Low-concept teachers tend to view issues in black and white and respond to the same problems in a habitual manner, even though those responses are not resolving the problem (Glickman et al., 1998). Effective advocates must rely on creative problem-solving skills and an ability to act autonomously, which is indicative of high-concept teachers.

Research on moral reasoning concluded that the majority of teachers were in the conventional-reasoning stage, which is governed by adherence to external rules of a group (Rest, 1986; Wilkins, 1980). It is only at high levels of moral development that individuals seek to uphold the rights of others and moral behavior is equated with helping others (Gilligan, 1982; Kohlberg & Armon, 1984). Glickman and colleagues (1998) noted that research conclusions about the ego, conceptual, and moral development of teachers are probably not any different from the adult population at large.

What are the implications of these adult development findings for professional advocacy pursuits? For professionals to assume an advocacy role or a "cause beyond oneself," highly reflective and autonomous thinking will be necessary. Based on the foregoing summary of adult development research findings, a majority of school professionals think and behave in a highly conforming, authority-dependent, and rule-governed manner. In other words, a majority of school professionals will not automatically nor naturally possess an advocacy disposition. Glickman and colleagues (1998) did offer a general prescription for improving this situation when they stated: "Thinking improves when people interact with each other, when they break routine by experimenting, when they observe others at work, and when they assess and revise their own actions. A cause beyond oneself becomes the norm, and the school becomes successful" (p. 77).

Research on the life transitions of teachers is equally as sobering as the findings from the adult development literature (Adams, Hutchinson, & Martray, 1980; Ayers, 1980; Gehrke, 1979). The all too frequent scenario is that the typical teacher enters the profession with high ideals and expectations. After a few years in the field, the teacher's ideals give way to an attitude that reflects the climate of the school. This phase is followed by a loss of enthusiasm and commitment to the job. Professionals who follow this life transitional path will obviously not be disposed to an advocacy role. An appropriate advocacy disposition is predicated on (1) an overriding concern for the student, (2) autonomous actions, (3) principled moral reasoning, and (4) altruistic motivation. Glickman (1990) concluded with a positive vision: "The autonomous teacher wants to succeed with every student, even at the risk of being different. His or her thinking is altruistic in that actions are motivated by the needs of others and not of self. The autonomous teacher is willing to help other teachers, to work on school-wide change, and to address larger issues of education and the profession" (pp. 64–65).

LEGAL SAFEGUARDS IN PROFESSIONAL ADVOCACY WORK

Professional advocacy will often result in challenging school policies, practices, or individual personnel working in the school district. A professional's appropriate disposition must not only recognize advocacy as a legitimate job responsibility but there must also be some contemplation of possible consequences from one's advocacy efforts. Special education professionals encounter ethical obligations (see Chapter 3) to advocate for the best interests of students with disabilities, but disciplinary sanctions and "legal liability may loom behind and beyond these professional precepts" (Zirkel & Suppa, 1986, p. 10). Professionals may be dissuaded from assuming an advocacy role out of fear of possible legal consequences, such as job termination or other retaliatory actions from the school district employer. This section seeks to minimize the fear of professionals in assuming advocacy responsibilities by articulating limits to advocacy and legal safeguards.

Prior to 1968, the prevailing judicial thinking was that public school personnel had a limited right of freedom of expression to criticize school policies or practices because public employment was considered to be a privilege rather than a right (LaMorte, 1996). In 1968, the U.S. Supreme Court expanded First Amendment freedom of expression protections for public school personnel in *Pickering* v. *Board of Education of Township High School District 205*. This case involved a public high school teacher, Marvin Pickering, who published a critical letter in the local newspaper. In his letter, Pickering criticized his superintendent and school board on their methods of raising and spending school funds. The board of education terminated Pickering's teaching job, claiming his letter damaged professional reputations of the superintendent and board members and was detrimental to the efficient operation of the schools. The U.S. Supreme Court ruled on behalf of

Pickering and ordered that his job be reinstated with back pay. In reaching its decision, the Court employed a balancing test to determine the scope of a public employee's First Amendment freedom of expression safeguards. The judicial inquiry must balance the interests of school personnel as citizens to comment on matters of public concern versus a consideration of the interests of schools in promoting an efficient operation of their services.

Courts employ a two-step inquiry in determining whether a school professional's speech is protected by the First Amendment. First, the critical speech must address a matter of public concern. It is important to distinguish commentary on matters of public concern versus private concerns. In *Connick* v. *Myers,* the U.S. Supreme Court ruled that personal employee complaints are not protected by the First Amendment. This means that school professionals' criticism about employment conditions—such as classroom materials, room conditions, and similar complaints—are not protected speech under the First Amendment. For example, in one court case, a special education teacher was nonrenewed because, in part, she complained to some parents about the principal's action in reducing her paraprofessional's schedule (*Saye* v. *St. Vrain Valley School District,* 1986). The courts view such private concerns as personnel matters and are reluctant to intervene.

Second, if the school professional's speech involved a public concern, the courts apply the *Pickering* test and balance the professional's interests as a citizen discussing public issues versus the school administration's interests as an employer in promoting an efficient operation of services. In this balance test, courts weigh a number of factors:

- The need for harmony in the schools
- Whether the criticism injured close working relationships
- The time, manner, place, and context of the speech
- The degree of public interest involved
- The effect of the speech on the professional's ability to work effectively

There are circumstances when a school professional's critical speech on a matter of public concern would probably not enjoy First Amendment protection. These circumstances involve (1) speech where the school professional knowingly or recklessly makes false statements; (2) speech that breaches an important confidentiality right of another individual; (3) speech that substantially damages close working relationships so that the professional's ability to work effectively has been impaired; and (4) speech that is not informative on a matter of public concern and is, instead, primarily a vile personal attack on a school official. In considering a special education professional's limits to advocacy protection, particular attention must be paid to the issue of advocacy actions that damage close working relationships. In such circumstances, many courts balance the interests in promoting efficient operation of school services in favor of the school district employer. For example, in *Kibodeaux* v. *Jefferson Parish School Board,* a special education teacher, who refused to confer about her students with her administrative supervisors unless the students' parents were present, was not protected in her advocacy by the First Amendment.

What about a circumstance where the school professional is not terminated but is transferred with no loss of pay or rank? An illustrative case on this issue, *Bernasconi* v. *Tempe Elementary School District No. 3,* was decided by a federal appeals court. In *Bernasconi,* a guidance counselor publicly criticized evaluation procedures the school district used in placing Mexican American children in special education classes for students with mental retardation. The Mexican American children were tested in English, not Spanish. The guidance counselor encouraged the Mexican American parents to sue the school district to stop this evaluation-placement process. Subsequently, the school district transferred the guidance counselor to another school with few Mexican American students. The court acknowledged that school professionals have no legal right to be assigned to work in any particular building, but once the counselor was assigned to work with Mexican American students, school officials could not constitutionally transfer her because of her public criticism.

Will a professional who privately criticizes school policies or practices in regard to a public matter (e.g., a violation of the special education legal rights of a child with disabilities) be protected by the First Amendment? This question was addressed by the U.S. Supreme Court in *Givhan* v. *Western Line Consolidated School District.* In *Givhan,* an English teacher was terminated after several private conversations with her principal over concerns of racial discrimination. The Supreme Court extended the *Pickering* ruling of First Amendment protection to apply to private as well as public criticism.

Does the *Pickering* First Amendment protection apply to nontenured school professionals? That is, can school districts refuse to rehire probationary school professionals for any reason whatever? In *Mt. Healthy City School District Board of Education* v. *Doyle,* the U.S. Supreme Court upheld the constitutional rights of probationary school professionals. In analyzing these cases involving probationary public employees, courts apply the two-step *Pickering* test discussed earlier in this section. In addition, the courts must determine if the employee's protected speech was a "substantial or motivating factor" in the school's nonrenewal action. If yes, the school district may still show that the probationary employee would not have been rehired, even in the absence of the protected speech or conduct.

Are private school employees protected by the First Amendment? Even if the private school receives state public funds, most court cases have decided against the private school employees. The rationale is that the First Amendment does not apply to private school actions since they are not state actions.

A majority of states now have whistleblowing statutes that protect public employees who, in good faith, report a violation of law. Most of these state statutes protect public employees against termination, coercion, discrimination or any form of employer retaliation for employee reporting of legal violations, gross waste of public funds, or dangers to the public health, safety, or welfare (Fischer, Schimmel, & Kelly, 1999).

Professional advocates can take some comfort

in the knowledge that there are constitutional (First Amendment) legal safeguards for protecting public employees who criticize school policies and practices that are illegal. These legal protections are intended to right injustices. Professionals need not be paralyzed in their advocacy out of fear of employment retaliation. However, special education professionals must remember Zirkel and Suppa's (1986) admonition: "One cannot automatically assume in such 'whistle blowing' cases that ethical guidance means legal protection" (p. 13).

FACTORS FOSTERING A PROFESSIONAL ADVOCACY DISPOSITION

The necessary disposition for professionals to serve as advocates would be greatly fostered by developing what Fullan and Hargreaves (1991) have referred to as "interactive professionalism." In a school culture with interactive professionalism: (1) school personnel are allowed more decision-making discretion on behalf of children with disabilities, (2) professionals' decisions are made in a collaborative environment of support, (3) decisions are based on critical reflection of professional values and purposes, (4) professionals are committed to continuous improvement and life long learning, and (5) professionals experience more accountability for student performance. These are the critical institutional supports to foster greater professional acceptance of an advocacy role.

On an individual level, Fullan and Hargreaves (1991) offered a number of guidelines for increasing a sense of professionalism or, as I argue, instilling an advocacy disposition in professionals. The guidelines are as follows:

- *Listen to and articulate your inner voice.* This involves personal reflection on your values and goals as a professional. What do you stand for? What makes you passionate about your job? Do you really want to make a difference?
- *Develop a risk-taking mentality.* As discussed earlier in this chapter, an advocate must be willing to take risks. Risk must be viewed as a vehicle to foster your professional growth and improvement.
- *Trust processes as well as people.* Professionalism requires interpersonal collaboration, and you cannot effectively collaborate if you lack trust in your colleagues. Another kind of trust is also essential for advocacy work—trust in processes and procedures. For example, to disagree at an IEP meeting, you must be able to trust in the integrity of that process. Or, before you criticize a school policy or practice on behalf of a child with a disability, you must be able to trust in the legal process to protect your rights.
- *Appreciate the total person in working with others.* You will be more trusting and successful in your collaborative relationships if you make the effort to know your colleagues or parents of your students on a more personal level. When this level of interaction is not possible due to privacy concerns, at least look for ways to show personal interest in the other person.
- *Seek variety.* Professionals who lose their enthusiasm and commitment in their job often do so as a result of excessive routine or "falling into a rut." You need challenges to stimulate professional learning and growth. Advocacy provides an avenue to diversify your job and to acquire new competencies.
- *Redefine your role to include responsibilities outside the classroom.* Advocacy work typically extends your responsibilities beyond the classroom and into other arenas. For example, your advocacy may have you working with a professional organization to improve educational services for children with disabilities, or you may be engaged in political advocacy work trying to change public policies, or you may be educating a parent group on their special education legal rights.
- *Balance work and life.* Quite simply, an advocate must be selfish to safeguard his or her personal life by developing the capability to "walk away from it" when leaving school. If you cannot successfully separate your work and personal worlds, you will likely burn out.

— *Commit to continuous improvement and perpetual learning.* "The single distinguishing characteristic of the best professionals in any field is that they consistently strive for better results, and are always learning to become more effective, from whatever source they can find" (Fullan & Hargreaves, 1991, p. 82).

ADVOCACY EDUCATIONAL ISSUES

Special education professionals who perceive themselves as lifelong learners are more likely to engage in advocacy. Therefore, an advocacy disposition and skills can be fostered in school settings. Kieffer (1983) proposed four development phases for individuals engaged in advocacy activities: entry (the initial step of getting involved), advancement (belonging to an advocacy oriented organization and receiving advocacy mentoring), incorporation (developing an initial sense of mastery and competence), and commitment (developing a strong sense of mastery and participatory competence).

At the *entry phase,* school officials should set expectations that new professionals will engage in child advocacy activities. In addition, schools must establish a culture that permits professional disagreement with existing school policies or practices. In the *advancement phase,* school officials should strongly encourage special education professionals to get involved in advocacy organizations such as the Council for Exceptional Children. This kind of professional involvement is best not viewed as a threat to schools but as a mechanism to foster lifelong professional growth and commitment. School officials should also establish a mentoring program whereby new professionals are matched with experienced professionals who have previously functioned in an advocacy capacity. During the *incorporation phase,* inexperienced professionals should be allowed to shadow experienced professionals engaged in advocacy actions. Gradually, over time, as inexperienced professionals gain more confidence and skills, the mentors should phase themselves out of this support role. Ideally, during the *commitment phase,* a new generation of experienced and committed professional advocates will have been nurtured by this support process.

SUMMARY

An advocacy disposition fuels the motivation for professionals to serve as advocates. An initial dilemma confronting all special education professionals evolves from their dual role as child advocate and school district employee. When the interests of child and employer conflict, a true professional advocate must place primary loyalty with the child.

Professional advocates possess a number of characteristics, such as a willingness to take risks, a strong sense of self-efficacy, and persistence. An advocacy disposition is grounded in basic values of empathy, empowerment, service to others, lifelong learning, passion, and hope. Not all professionals are ready for assuming advocacy roles. Recent research on adult development and life transitions reveals that there are developmental phases in professionals' careers that dictate an individual's willingness to serve as an advocate. In addition to developmental phases, a number of other factors can foster or inhibit a professional advocacy disposition. For example, a school environment can foster the development of an advocacy disposition by establishing collaborative work relationships, arranging mentorships between inexperienced professionals and experienced professional advocates, and setting cultural norms that permit professional disagreement with school policies or practices. An advocacy disposition is further enhanced by a solid understanding of legal safeguards for speaking on behalf of a child with a disability. In a series of court cases beginning in the late 1960s, it has become well established that public employees (special education professionals) have a First Amendment constitutional freedom of expression right to comment on matters of public concern. Commentary on matters of public concern would encompass most special education advocacy disputes.

CHAPTER 3

AN ETHICAL DISPOSITION

Morality does not soar on its own wings.—Amitai Etzioni
(The Spirit of Community, *1993)*

An important component of a special education professional advocacy disposition is moral and ethical behavior in pursuing the best interests of children with disabilities and their families. Unfortunately, as noted by Etzioni above, morals or ethics are not innate human characteristics; a person learns to be moral or ethical.

According to Strike and Soltis (1992), "Ethics concerns what kinds of actions are right or wrong, what kind of life is a good life, or what kind of person is a good person" (p. 5). Ethics serve as guideposts or standards by which a professional, when confronted with a dilemma, can turn for guidance in determining an appropriate course of action (Goens, 1996). In reaching a decision, ethical judgments tell us what we ought to do and what we ought not to do (Strike & Soltis, 1992). Similarly, ethics help determine acceptable from unacceptable behavior (Heron, Martz, & Margolis, 1996). Ethics inherently involve values that discern good from bad and right from wrong, and the moral obligation owing to others (Nelson, 1994). All of these definitions emphasize the field of ethics known as *normative ethics* or *applied professional ethics,* which involves the development of principles for guiding individual behavior (Greenspan & Negron, 1994). This chapter will relate primarily to applied professional ethics. Chapter 12 will address meta-ethics and the development of philosophical and decision-making frameworks for resolving ethical dilemmas.

THE RELATIONSHIP BETWEEN LAW AND ETHICS

In special education, or any profession, law and ethics serve a similar function—to provide standards or guidelines to govern professional behavior. Since special education is rife with legal and ethical problems, it is especially urgent that well-intentioned professionals learn the relevant legal and ethical standards (Howe & Miramontes, 1992). Ideally, laws encompass ethical principles and there is a corresponding ethical obligation to abide by the law. Although both law and ethics attempt to establish behavioral parameters for professionals, there is the potential for conflict between the two sets of standards. For example, what if a law tells a professional to do something that his or her sense of ethics says is wrong? What is the right decision in such a circumstance? Whether a law is ethical and whether that same law is legally binding are two distinct questions.

Howe and Miramontes (1992) characterized the relationship between law and ethics in several ways. First, laws may be subject to criticism based on external ethical standards. For example, consider the legal requirement to provide students with disabilities a free and appropriate public education and subsequent judicial interpretations of this legal mandate (e.g., most notably the *Rowley* case, which is discussed in Chapter 5). This law may be criticized by advocates of students with disabilities whose ethical standards demand that these students receive the best educational services possible, but the law requires less than the best education possible. Second, since laws must be rather general in their construction, there is still a need for individual ethical deliberation to provide specific decision-making guidance. Third, even if a particular law is well established with no room for interpretation, the law still assumes an ethical commitment to abide the law's mandate.

Given this interface between law and ethics, it is important that special education professionals recognize that many advocacy dilemmas will require both a legal and ethical analyses. Furthermore, the decisions reached by a legal or ethical analysis may be in conflict with each other. Chapters 5 and 12 will provide in more detail legal and ethical standards to govern professionals' advocacy decision making.

PROFESSIONAL ETHICAL CODES

A key component in determining whether any occupation constitutes a "profession" is the existence of a code of ethics that governs the conduct of its members. Most professional codes of ethics include these features: training in ethics during preservice preparation programs, knowledge of ethics as a requirement for obtaining a professional license, and strict enforcement mechanisms for ethical code violations (Bayles, 1989). With these criteria in mind, Greenspan and Negron (1994) noted that the field of education has not yet received full status as a profession because (1) education codes of ethics are often incomplete when compared to other professions, (2) training in ethics is often not required as a component of preservice preparation programs nor as a credentialing requirement, and (3) enforcement mechanisms for ethical code violations are nonexistent.

Greenspan and Negron's concerns about education codes of ethics are significant and need to be addressed; the importance of establishing a code of ethics for professional educators should not be underestimated. Feeney and Kipnis (1985) defined *professional ethics* as "a shared process of

critical reflection upon our obligations as professionals" (p. 55). Professional ethical codes are important for a number of reasons. First, ethical codes articulate the values and creed of a group of professionals (Howe & Miramontes, 1992). Second, ethical codes enhance professional cognizance of the special duties and dangers inherent in their practice (Howe & Miramontes, 1992). Third, ethical codes develop out of professional self-interest in an effort to heighten a sense of professionalism. This enhanced sense of professionalism, however, demonstrates a genuine commitment to protect the interests of persons served (Jacob & Hartshorne, 1991). Finally, as noted by Jacob and Hartshorne, ethical codes show a willingness to accept responsibility for appropriate professional conduct and a commitment to self-regulation of professional members.

Despite the advantages and importance of professional ethical codes, educators must recognize the limitations of most codes. One limitation is that most ethics codes tend to be very general and purposely vague, thus providing little decision-making guidance in specific advocacy situations. Another limitation is that ethics codes are usually silent on the appropriate course of action when a professional encounters a conflict among two or more ethical principles in the same code (Howe & Miramontes, 1992).

There are a number of professional ethical codes that are relevant for a variety of school professionals. For example, the National Association for the Education of Young Children established a Code of Ethical Conduct and Statement of Commitment in 1992 (Feeney & Kipnis, 1992). The National Association of School Psychologists' Principles for Professional Ethics was revised in 1992 (NASP, 1992). Similarly, the American Psychological Association updated its Ethical Principles of Psychologists and Code of Conduct in 1992 (APA, 1992). For purposes of discussion in this chapter, the focus will be on the Code of Ethics and Standards for Professional Practice adopted by the Delegate Assembly of the Council for Exceptional Children (CEC) in 1983. The CEC is the largest professional organization in the field of special education. The purpose of the development of the code of ethics and standards was to "provide guidelines for professional etiquette, for effective interpersonal behavior, for resolution of ethical issues, and for making professional judgments concerning what constitutes competent practice" (CEC, 1983, p. 205). In the code of ethics and the standards, special education professionals identify obligations to three parties: students with disabilities, the school district employer, and the profession. The CEC Code of Ethics is comprised of the following eight principles:

I. *Special education professionals are committed to developing the highest educational and quality of life potential of exceptional individuals.*

II. *Special education professionals promote and maintain a high level of competence and integrity in practicing their profession.*

III. *Special education professionals engage in professional activities which benefit exceptional individuals, their families, other colleagues, students, or research subjects.*

IV. *Special education professionals exercise objective professional judgment in the practice of their profession.*

V. *Special education professionals strive to advance their knowledge and skills regarding the education of exceptional individuals.*

VI. *Special education professionals work within the standards and policies of their profession.*

VII. *Special education professionals seek to uphold and improve where necessary the laws, regulations, and policies governing the delivery of special education and related services and the practice of their profession.*

VIII. *Special education professionals do not condone or participate in unethical or illegal acts, nor violate professional standards adopted by the Delegate Assembly of CEC. (CEC, 1983, p. 205)*

In the CEC Standards for Professional Practice, six standards pertain to special education professional advocacy:

1.5.1   Special education professionals serve as advocates for exceptional persons by speaking, writing, and acting in a variety of situations on their behalf.

1.5.1.1   Professionals continually seek to improve government provisions for the education of exceptional persons while ensuring that public statements by professionals as individuals are not construed to represent official policy statements of the agency by which they are employed.

1.5.1.2   Professionals work cooperatively with and encourage other professionals to improve the provision of special education and related services to exceptional persons.

1.5.1.3   Professionals document and objectively report to their supervisors or administrators inadequacies in resources and promote appropriate corrective action.

1.5.1.4   Professionals monitor for inappropriate placements in special education and intervene at the appropriate level to correct the condition when such inappropriate placements exist.

1.5.1.5   Professionals follow local, state/provincial, and federal laws and regulations which mandate a free appropriate public education to exceptional students and the protection of the rights of exceptional persons to equal opportunities in our society. (CEC, 1983, p. 207)

Since advocacy responsibilities are specifically addressed in the CEC Code of Ethics and Standards for Professional Practice, there would seem to be incentive and protection for increased professional advocacy in the field of special education. In the previously described (Chapter 2) structured interviews I conducted with 27 acknowledged special education advocates, all 27 interviewees indicated they felt an ethical responsibility to be an advocate. The following are responses to the question: Do you think you have an ethical responsibility to serve as an educational advocate? Why or why not (Fiedler, 1997)?

- Believe that it is part of professional role/responsibility
- Believe that it is the right thing to do
- Feel a universal responsibility to serve people that need help
- Believe that advocacy is a method to meet the needs of children with disabilities
- Believe that advocacy helps maintain professional focus and sense of personal responsibility

- Recognize that many children and families need a spokesperson
- Recognize that professionals possess important information about a child and that they need to share that information through advocacy efforts
- Believe that advocacy maintains integrity in one's profession
- Feel that advocacy is necessary to counteract negative professional attitudes toward parents
- Believe that advocacy assists in forming an effective partnership with parents
- Feel that advocates serve as appropriate role models for other professionals

Are special education professionals knowledgeable about the CEC Code of Ethics and Standards of Professional Practice? Cobb and Horn (1989) conducted a study with a randomly selected sample of 1,000 current CEC members from around the country. Subjects were asked in a mailed questionnaire if they had a copy of the CEC Code of Ethics and Standards of Professional Practice readily available to them and if they had intentionally referred to the code since 1983 (the date of its inception) for guidance in meeting their professional responsibilities. A total of 381 (response rate of 38 percent) completed questionnaires were returned. Of the total, 51 (13 percent) of the respondents indicated they had a copy of the CEC Code and Standards and had used those documents in resolving professional dilemmas; 330 (87 percent) respondents revealed they did not have a copy of the CEC Code and Standards and therefore had never used it. The following reasons were cited for not having a copy of the CEC Code and Standards:

- I did not know of the existence of the CEC Code and Standards. (71 percent)
- The issue of professional ethics was not included in my teacher preparation program so I do not know enough about it. (47 percent)
- The standards are so closely parallel to my own values and ideals that I do not need to refer to them for guidance. (20 percent)

- As an employee, I have no input into such matters. I follow instructions. (10 percent)
- It is the responsibility of the state department of education, not special education professionals, to be advocates for exceptional persons. (4 percent)
- I disagree with the Standards as published; therefore, I do not feel bound by them. (3 percent)
- The responsibility to protect the rights of children belongs to the parents and the attorneys, not special educators. (3 percent)

The results of this study are disturbing in terms of the high percentages of CEC members who did not know of the existence of the CEC Code of Ethics and Standards of Professional Practice and had not engaged in a consideration of professional ethics in their preparation programs.

Rock, Geiger, and Hood (1992) conducted another study on CEC members' knowledge and support of the ethical standards on advocacy. From the CEC national membership list, a sample of 808 members were sent a 26-item questionnaire. A total of 530 (65.6 percent response rate) questionnaires were returned. One question this study addressed was whether special educators supported the CEC advocacy standards. On this issue, there was strong membership support for the advocacy standards, with 95 percent of the respondents indicating "strong agreement" or "agreement" with each standard. The advocacy standard of "monitor for inappropriate placements and intervene at the appropriate level" received the most support from the respondents, whereas "serve as an advocate by speaking, writing and acting on behalf of exceptional individuals" received the least support.

Another question asked respondents how frequently they engaged in specific forms of advocacy. The advocacy activities most frequently reported were "informed persons of their rights" and "spent extra time to secure rights or services." The least frequently reported advocacy activity was "testified on funding, legislation, or regulations." This study also revealed that teachers engaged in significantly fewer advocacy activities than administrators. Finally, respondents were asked about the responses of their school district employer to advocacy activities.

In general, respondents perceived high levels of encouragement for these advocacy activities: "worked with and encouraged other professionals to improve special education services" and "reported inappropriate placements." A fairly high percentage of respondents (23 percent) felt their school district would be discouraging if they "reported to supervisors/administrators inadequacies in resources." Teachers were more likely than administrators to believe that employers were discouraging advocacy activities. Although the results of this one study may be biased since all of the respondents were CEC members, there is some encouragement that educational professionals generally support the ethical advocacy standards and are actively engaged in a variety of advocacy activities on behalf of children with disabilities and their families.

A PERSONAL ETHIC OF CARING

The preceding section presented a framework for professional ethics based on the CEC Code of Ethics and Standards for Professional Practice. Although knowledge and adherence to one's professional ethics code are important dispositions, an ethical professional must also possess a personal ethical framework. As special educators demand and receive more professional empowerment and autonomy, they must recognize a concomitant increased latitude and responsibility for judgment and decision making (Goens, 1996). With this enhanced sense of professionalism, Campbell (1997) argued that issues of professionalism are largely issues of ethical significance. Indeed, many scholars maintain it is necessary for educators to regard their professional responsibilities as basic moral imperatives (Carr, 1993; Oser & Althof, 1993; Sergiovanni, 1996). A responsible person, according to Niebuhr (1963), develops the skill to discern a fitting response in a situation requiring an ethical choice. The evolution of this professional "discerning judgment" requires "a disposition to respond to novel external factors without becoming closed or defensive" (Reynolds, 1996, p. 68).

Noddings (1984) has advocated for an ethic of caring as a personal framework for moral decision making. What does it mean to care? According to Noddings:

> *Our dictionaries tell us that "care" is a state of mental suffering or of engrossment: to care is to be in a burdened mental state, one of anxiety, fear, or solicitude about something or someone. Alternatively, one cares for something or someone if one has a regard for or inclination toward something or someone.... And if I have a regard for you, what you think, feel, and desire will matter to me. And, again, to care may mean to be charged with the protection, welfare, or maintenance of something or someone. (p. 9)*

Noddings views this perspective as a caring approach grounded in receptivity, relatedness, and responsiveness. Her approach extends research on moral reasoning conducted by Gilligan (1988). According to Gilligan, when reaching moral decisions, there are two basic approaches. First, a *caring approach* focuses on showing concern for others, making personal connections with others, and protecting others from harm. Alternatively, a *rational approach* emphasizes moral decision making based on universally applied principles, such as justice and equality. Noddings favors the caring approach, which resolves moral problems by placing oneself in concrete situations and assuming personal responsibility for choices to be made. In this ethical approach, moral reasoning is not an abstract process; rather, a caring professional attempts to understand the other person's reality and what that person is feeling. Moral decision making, then, becomes a highly personal process as opposed to the more abstract rational approach based on the application of universal principles to specific dilemmas. This heightened level of empathy and commitment from an ethic of caring personalizes ethical decision making and enhances an advocacy mindset. I believe the likelihood is greater for personal involvement as a professional advocate if you can feel the pain and frustration of a child or the child's family as opposed to engaging in a purely intellectual exercise of abstract moral reasoning.

According to Noddings (1993), caring is concerned primarily with the way individuals meet and treat each other. Professionals with an ethic of caring assume advocacy responsibilities because when they see an educational problem or injustice, they experience a strong internal feeling of *I must* get involved to help this child. Although the educational advocates I interviewed did not necessarily label their advocacy motivation as springing from an ethic of caring, as I listened intently to their feelings and stories, I was struck by how each and every one of them displayed through their actions a strong sense of personal caring.

There are risks associated with operating from an ethic of caring in resolving personal and professional moral dilemmas (Noddings, 1984). First, caring special education professionals who serve as advocates for students with disabilities can easily be overwhelmed by their advocacy responsibilities. If this occurs, the caring professional is likely to cease caring and functioning as an advocate. (Professional burnout is discussed in Chapter 2.) Caring professionals must learn to nurture their caring capacity by balancing their lives and learning to appreciate and celebrate everyday life, to value "ordinary life events" (Noddings, 1984). Second, a caring professional is more vulnerable. When you try to experience another person's reality and feel their pain and frustration, you do make yourself more vulnerable. Again, a caring professional must learn when to let go of the cares and burdens of another. "We must acknowledge, then, that an ethic of caring implies a limit on our obligation" (Noddings, 1984, p. 86).

Finally, professionals risk feeling guilty in a caring relationship, especially if the relationship is long term. This guilt may spring from either a feeling that you have not done enough in your caring capacity or from a momentary lapse of caring.

Noddings (1984) argued that this guilt cannot be avoided and we need the courage to accept it without being consumed by it. I look at this type of guilt as a useful professional commodity because guilt can fuel my motivation never to become complacent and to strive for continual professional growth. An ethic of caring is an approach to ethical decision making based on relationships, caring, cooperation, and empathy (Pazey, 1995). Without a clearly articulated personal ethical framework, professionals faced with an ethical dilemma will engage in decision making fraught with confusion and anxiety (Heron, Martz, & Margolis, 1996).

CHARACTERISTICS OF ETHICAL PROFESSIONALS

Greenspan and Negron (1994) delineated several characteristics of ethical or virtuous educational professionals. They see these characteristics as likely leading to professionals who "do the right thing." The importance of these ethical/virtuous characteristics was underscored by Greenspan and Negron's statement: "One might reasonably argue that, given the difficulties in remediating deficiencies in judgment or character, that the best way to increase the likelihood that professionals will act virtuously is to place more emphasis on hiring virtuous people in the first place" (p. 194). This section will discuss the following characteristics of ethical educational professionals as identified by Greenspan and Negron: discretion, candor, competence, fairness, avoidance of dual relationships, protection, allowing autonomy, diligence, and respectfulness/humaneness.

Discretion

Ethical professionals maintain confidential information and refrain from making irresponsible comments. One mother of a child with emotional/behavioral disorders expressed her anger at finding out that her son's special education teacher had divulged information about the mother's counseling and alcohol addiction issues to other teachers who did not work with her son. After this disclosure, the mother's relationship with the teacher was irreparably damaged. The mother no longer trusted the teacher. Also, a discreet professional does not verbally attack a colleague, a parent, or a student. The amount of unethical and indiscreet talk that occurs in many teachers' lounges is appalling. Some argue that professionals are merely "venting" in such dialogues, but the need for an emotional release does not excuse negative and damaging comments. This kind of communication is victim blaming at its worst. The adage that if you cannot say anything nice about a person, say nothing at all is a good definition of professional discretion.

Candor

A candid professional tells the truth and fully informs families of all information that is relevant in making educational decisions. The law empowers parents as equal educational decision makers but this legal requirement cannot be achieved in the absence of professional candor in sharing all available information about the child and school services. Without full disclosure of relevant information, parents are placed in a subservient, dependent relationship with professionals. This is not the intended outcome of special education law nor does it reflect good professional practice.

Professionals encounter pressure to be less than candid with families in a variety of situations. For example, at multidisciplinary team or IEP meetings, often there is subtle pressure on all the professionals to present a unified front to the parents. In other words, professional disagreement and debate is often discouraged. Another example where professional candor may be deficient occurs when IEPs are developed and the school administration does not want school personnel to make recommendations for any costly related services. The school is bound to provide only the services listed on the child's IEP. If the parent is unaware of the necessity and availability of a particular service, because no professional has made a recommendation, the school can avoid legal and financial obligations. Candid professionals respect the right of families to reach their own decisions by realizing that good decision making is dependent on complete access to all relevant information.

Competence

A number of ethical issues are related to professional competence. Examples include (1) recognizing one's professional limitations and needs; (2) understanding one's professional strengths; (3) confining practice to one's competence; (4) knowing when to decline work and when to refer to competent professionals; (5) ensuring that, whenever possible, recommended interventions have an empirical basis; (6) keeping abreast of professional developments; and (7) maintaining high levels of professionalism (Corey, Corey, & Callanan, 1993; Newman, 1993). Professionals must refuse to practice beyond the bounds of their own competence. Although most professionals would agree with this assertion, adherence to this ethical characteristic is quite difficult.

The vast majority of school professionals are well meaning and sincerely want to help children with disabilities and their families. In this spirit of helpfulness, it can be difficult to refuse a parent's request for help by responding that you lack the knowledge or expertise to provide any assistance. Further, some professionals fear they might look incompetent or unprofessional if they do not have all the answers. A father of a 3-year-old son with autism reported this unfortunate incident. The father requested that the early childhood program employ the Lovaas treatment program with his young son. The early childhood director had done some reading on the Lovaas program but that was the extent of her expertise. The early childhood center had no staff who were trained and experienced in the Lovaas program or techniques. Nevertheless, the director assured the father that the center staff would incorporate the program into the child's school day. After two months of a feeble attempt to employ the Lovaas program at the center, the father confronted the early childhood staff with concerns about his son's regression in social and language behavior and increased self-injurious behavior. The director and staff finally acknowledged that they needed consultation support in developing an appropriate Lovaas treatment program. However, by this time, the father had lost his confidence in the staff and removed his son from the center.

Fairness

The principle of fairness underlies all professional ethics codes. This principle requires that professionals do not discriminate against children and their families based on characteristics such as racial/ethnic background, religious affiliation, disability, gender, or economic circumstances. Children and families are entitled to the services that they need and for which they meet eligibility criteria. I have made this statement many times to prospective special educators: "Jennifer Fiedler receives more special educational rights and services than other children with similar disabilities and needs." This is not a boastful statement; in fact, the realization of the truthfulness of the statement makes me frustrated about how unfair the educational system can be to some children and families. If the educational system was perfectly fair, children with similar needs would receive similar services as mandated by law. Instead, in my daughter's situation, since she has parents who are knowledgeable about special education legal rights and are willing to assert those rights when necessary, the educational system tends to be more responsive to the Fiedler family than to families lacking in advocacy knowledge and savvy. This is clearly not fair, but it is an unfortunate reality of special education in an era of limited resources. This reality does, however, point out the need for professional advocacy to balance the scales for some families.

Avoidance of Dual Relationships

As discussed in Chapter 2 on the dual role dilemma, professionals with an advocacy and ethical disposition must maintain a primary commitment to serving the best interests of their clients—children with disabilities. Some professionals in a dual

relationship neglect this responsibility to keep the best interests of their clients foremost in their mind, and instead use the client to meet their own needs. That is, the professional expects some personal gain or benefit from the relationship. When this conflict of interests occurs, there is some form of exploitation involved. One mother of a daughter diagnosed with depression expressed her discomfort at the special education teacher referring the mother and daughter to the private psychologist husband of the teacher. The teacher's referral may have been done with the best of intentions and with great confidence that the teacher's husband was a very appropriate professional to treat the young woman's depression. However, this does not excuse the fact that the teacher had entered into a potential dual relationship (i.e., teacher and spouse of a psychologist who may be treating the student) with her student and now the risk of not acting solely in the student's best interests was heightened.

Protection

Professionals owe a basic ethical obligation to protect children from harm. All states have mandatory reporting laws that require school personnel to report cases of possible child abuse or neglect to the local child protection and welfare agency. Since the incidence of child abuse in this country has reached epidemic proportions (1,849 children are abused every day in the United States [Simpson, 1996]), school professionals must be ever vigilant in meeting this reporting obligation.

A more difficult situation for a professional is when he or she believes that a colleague is abusing a child. DeMitchell and Fossey (1997) have complained that in many schools there is a "culture of indifference" to this kind of professional misbehavior, and many professionals do not take any actions against their colleagues. The CEC Standards for Professional Practice address this ethical responsibility in Standard 1.2.1.4: "Professionals take adequate measures to discourage, prevent, and intervene when a colleague's behavior is perceived as being detrimental to exceptional persons" (CEC, 1983, p. 206). Although this ethical directive is quite specific, consider the special education teacher who failed to report verbal and physical abuse of students with disabilities by a paraprofessional in her program. The teacher was new to the district and was afraid she would get a reputation as "somebody who was always looking for trouble." To complicate matters, the teacher considered the paraprofessional a close friend. This teacher clearly violated her legal and ethical obligations to her students.

Allowing Autonomy

Professionals must foster child and family autonomy. This means empowering children and their families to make their own decisions. Historically, many professionals have cast parents in the role of passive recipients of professionals' decisions (Turnbull & Turnbull, 1997). This is the "mere parent" syndrome, where a professional paternalistically assumes the decision-making role and the parent is merely expected to acquiesce to the professional's judgment. The individuals most affected by any decision should be the ultimate decision makers, unless they lack the mental capacity to make decisions.

Professionals can empower students with disabilities by teaching self-advocacy skills, involving students and actively seeking student input at IEP meetings. Professionals can also empower parents as educational decision makers by doing the following:

- Prepare parents in advance of upcoming school meetings. Included in this advance preparation should be (1) providing parents with the purpose and agenda for the meeting, (2) providing copies of all relevant school documents that will be discussed at the meeting, (3) providing possible questions that school professionals will ask the parents, (4) strongly encouraging parents to actively participate in educational decisions, and (5) making a positive comment about the child. Parents will be more motivated and hopeful about the upcoming meeting when

the school sets a positive tone about the meeting.
- Schedule the meeting with sufficient time for full discussion and parental participation.
- Minimize the number of professionals at the meeting so that parents do not feel "ganged up" on.
- Make the meeting as welcoming and informal as possible. One of my daughter's favorite special education teachers always had a big bowl of popcorn at every meeting. It is hard to get angry at someone when your mouth is full of popcorn!
- Encourage the parents to bring someone with them (an advocate, friend, neighbor, extended family member) if that would make them more comfortable.

Diligence

Diligent professionals go above and beyond the bare minimum requirements of their job. Such professionals embrace their role as a child advocate. I was impressed that the professionals I interviewed for this book naturally accepted their child advocacy responsibility without much conscious thought that "now I am going to be an advocate." This dedication to their job is not to impress their superiors; instead, a diligent professional has set high standards for herself or himself without regard for external expectations or rewards. Several professionals I know have told me about instances where special education "professionals" walked out of IEP meetings at 4:05 P.M., the time they were obligated by contract to stay at school. School personnel cannot expect to be treated as professionals if such unprofessional behavior is exhibited.

Respectfulness/Humaneness

Treating children with disabilities and their family members with respect and in a humane manner provides the foundation for a collaborative family/ school partnership. There are two CEC Standards that directly address this characteristic:

1.2.1.1   Professionals apply only those disciplinary methods and behavioral procedures which they have been instructed to use and which do not undermine the dignity of the individual or the basic human rights of exceptional persons. (CEC, 1983, p. 206)

1.4.1   Professionals seek to develop relationships with parents based on mutual respect for their roles in achieving benefits for the exceptional persons. (CEC, 1983, p. 207)

Despite these ethical admonitions, special education professionals are challenged in maintaining this respectful demeanor when facing personal attacks and abuse from an emotionally charged, out-of-control student or when interacting with an irrational parent. In such situations, Carl Rogers (1951) advocated "unconditional positive regard." That is, a truly supportive and ethical professional communicates acceptance and respect for another individual no matter how out of control or irrational that individual might presently be. This is the ultimate test in maintaining one's professional respect and sense of humanity.

ETHICS IN PROFESSIONAL PREPARATION PROGRAMS

As a logical outcome of the lack of attention to ethics and ethical decision making in many professional preparation programs, psychological research reveals that professionals fail to behave ethically for four distinct reasons (Rest, 1983):

- A professional may be blind to the ethical issues that arise.
- A professional may be deficient in articulating an ethically defensible course of action.
- A professional may fail to prioritize ethical concerns.
- A professional may fail in ethical matters due to an inability or unwillingness to implement an effective action plan. For ethical decision making, professionals need well-developed problem-solving and interpersonal skills as well as characteristics such as persistence and risk taking. (See Chapter 2.)

How can special education professionals develop appropriate ethical dispositions? Noddings (1984) identified three means for nurturing the ethical ideal in individuals: dialogue, practice, and confirmation. In the context of professional preparation programs, the process of *dialogue* is essential as a means to increase preservice students' awareness of ethical issues and dilemmas in the field of special education. There must be regular and ongoing discussions across the curriculum on the importance of embracing an ethic of caring.

Noddings (1984) asserted that individuals need *practice* in caring. In professional preparation programs, this practice element could be introduced as a requirement that all students preparing for careers as special educators must engage in a significant volunteer activity prior to graduation. This volunteerism could be with a professional organization, such as the Council for Exceptional Children, where members are engaged in a variety of professional advocacy activities. The volunteer activity could occur as a placement with a family in need of professional support and empowerment. The student would collaborate with the family in identifying and addressing family needs. The importance of this practice component is to instill in preservice students the value of engaging in caring activities that have an advocacy orientation.

Finally, in *confirmation,* preservice students must be allowed to interact closely with professionals in the field who can serve as models of this ethic of caring. This type of mentorship would be intensive, similar to a student teaching experience. However, this mentorship should be provided prior to a culminating student teaching or practicum experience to allow for an exclusive focus on the ethical and advocacy dimensions of the professional's day-to-day work.

SUMMARY

An ethical disposition serves special education professionals in their efforts to delineate right from wrong conduct. That is, an ethically disposed professional is likely to "do the right thing" when confronted with a dilemma. In the context of advocacy, doing the right thing is assuming the responsibility for ensuring that children with disabilities and their families receive all the educational services they are entitled.

Historically, the ethical role and responsibilities of special educators have been neglected by both professional preparation programs and professionals in the field. This neglect began to change in 1983 with the passage by the Council for Exceptional Children of its Code of Ethics and Standards for Professional Practice. The code and standards identify specific ethical and advocacy responsibilities of special educators. Professionals must be knowledgeable of both legal and ethical guidelines in establishing behavioral parameters. Although a professional code of ethics provides some behavioral guidelines, professionals still must be able to articulate a personal ethical framework. Noddings' (1984) ethic of caring is an appropriate model for making personal decisions. This perspective is not rule or principle bound; instead, the caring perspective is rooted in receptivity, relatedness, and responsiveness. A caring approach, along with adherence to the CEC code and standards, and nurturance of virtuous characteristics such as discretion, candor, competence, fairness, avoidance of dual relationships, protection, allowing autonomy, diligence, and respectfulness comprise the essential components of an appropriate professional ethical disposition.

CHAPTER 4

A FAMILY SUPPORT AND EMPOWERMENT DISPOSITION

*Research suggests that the professional and parent
partnership is a critical factor not only in helping the
child with a disability grow and learn, but also as a
means to solidify the family's ability to function as a unit.*
—*Eunice Kennedy Shriver (1997)*

Ideally, relationships between special education professionals and families of children with disabilities serve to enhance educational advocacy efforts. This professional/family partnership is dependent on several professional dispositions. First, professionals must acknowledge that the duty to work with and support the child with a disability extends beyond the child to include that child's family, as well. Quite simply, a child at risk places a family at risk and vice versa. Second, professionals must value collaborative relationships with families as a vehicle that is both beneficial to their professional growth and development and is the best means to support children with disabilities. Third, professionals must actively seek to make families less dependent on the professionals' advice and services through family empowerment strategies. And, finally, professionals must learn not to be intimidated or annoyed by families who assertively pursue their educational rights and appropriate services for their children.

The benefits of professional/family partnerships and active parent involvement in educational matters has been reported extensively (Epstein, 1992). Simpson (1996) noted, "Children's social and intellectual development is greatly influenced by their parents and families" (p. 41). Christenson and Cleary (1990), in an extensive literature review on professional/family partnerships, identi-

fied the following outcomes of active parent involvement:

- Students' academic performance improved in terms of higher grades and test scores, more homework completed, and more classroom participation.
- Schools were rated as more effective by parents.
- Teachers expressed greater job satisfaction, and parents and administrators rated them as having high interpersonal and teaching skills.
- Parents provided more learning activities at home and the communication between the family, school, and the child improved.

How can professionals support and empower families? This chapter will illustrate the meaning of professional support and empowerment of families of children with disabilities. Prior to discussing professional support and empowerment issues, however, it is critical that professionals have an understanding of family systems theory, which underlies both family support and empowerment initiatives. This chapter will also articulate family support principles and describe the necessary professional disposition for addressing the needs of families. The concept of family empowerment will then be presented. Finally, how professionals can enhance parental advocacy will be discussed, followed by some essential components of parent advocacy training. But first, before launching into family support and empowerment concepts, some historical context to professional/family relationships, including a brief discussion of some common negative professional attitudes and assumptions, will be provided.

NEGATIVE PROFESSIONAL ATTITUDES AND ASSUMPTIONS

Historically, the relations between professionals and families of children with disabilities have often been characterized by mistrust, poor communication, animosity, and adversarial attitudes and behaviors. The genesis of many troubled professional/family relationships can be traced to certain attitudes and expectations held by some professionals. Following are a sample of these pernicious professional attitudes and assumptions.

■ *Professionals assume that they know what is best for a child with a disability, that parents should gratefully and unquestionably follow the advice of the expert.* Obviously, this attitude is not conducive to establishing a partnership with families; instead, this perspective keeps the parent in a subservient and dependent position. Professional control over decision making keeps parents in a dependent role and is manifested in many ways:

■ The professional does not indicate that a decision exists.

■ The professional indicates that a decision exists, but presents no alternatives to the professional's preferred choice. That is, the professional is merely seeking parent agreement with a predetermined decision.

■ The professional links one decision with another. This tactic limits parental decision making by not allowing each decision to be made on its own merits. For example, when a school professional indicates that a child qualifies for the emotional/behavioral disorders program at Jefferson Elementary School (i.e., at a specific school), there is a linkage of the program of services with the placement site. This should not

be the case. Both of these issues should be discussed separately and decided on the merits of each.

Also, the excessive use of professional jargon, whether expressed intentionally or unconsciously, is another tactic for maintaining control over families. The result of jargon is to control access to information and to convey an "outsider" status on parents because they cannot speak the language.

■ *Judgmental professionals who possess stereotypical attitudes about certain families or are unable to suspend their judgment on family actions and lifestyles that conflict with their own prevent professionals from having empathy for a particular family's circumstance.* Without empathy, it is highly unlikely that a professional will be motivated to support or empower a family (Kerns, 1992). In addition, professional stereotypes of certain families are destructive to professional/family partnerships. For example, as noted by Brantlinger (1991), "Stereotypes of low income parents as uncaring tend to be reinforced because such parents may not have the resources to comply with school personnel's standardized views of the proper role of parents" (p. 253). An example of the impact of one professional's judgmental attitude and behavior toward low-income families is contained in Box 4.1. The special education teacher depicted in this anecdote was brutally honest in her self-evaluation. This is the first step to attitudinal changes.

■ *Professionals assume that caring, loving parents will be actively involved in their child's education; thus, those parents not actively involved must not care about their child.* Professionals need to be cognizant of the fact that more parent involvement in their child's education is not necessarily better involvement. Simpson and Fiedler (1989) acknowledged this truth when they stated, "It is a false and destructive dichotomy for educators to imply that 'good' parents are actively involved (*actively* as defined by school personnel's expectations for parents) in their child's education and that 'less than active' involvement is indicative of 'bad' parents. Expecting families to exhibit greater in-

Box 4.1 _____

Advocacy Anecdote

Perhaps the most pervasive influence on my perception of the families with whom I work is my own upbringing, which was conservative and middle class. I tend to identify with, and have a more positive attitude toward, parents who share my middle-class values of hard work, cleanliness, cooperation with authority figures, and esteem for higher education. By the same token, no matter how hard I try to banish such thoughts, I tend to be more judgmental of families who are on public assistance. This is particularly true when I find myself dealing with single mothers who have poor parenting skills.

Even though the feminist side of my nature feels a sense of solidarity with anyone who attempts the arduous task of raising a child alone, my sense of middle-class morality is outraged at the thought of a woman having children with most of the men who pass through her life. Many times in the teachers' lounge, I have heard the rhetorical question: Why is it that the ones who have the least ability to take care of kids are the ones who end up having a half dozen children? These are my thoughts exactly.

There is no doubt in my mind that the low-income mothers who finally get up the courage to enter my school building are fully aware of the appraising glances they get from my colleagues and me. I notice the missing teeth and silently speculate that some boyfriend knocked them out, although poor nutrition and lack of money for proper dental care is a more likely explanation. I notice the dirty clothes and ratty hair of the toddlers who trail behind them. I judge them, forgetting that laundromats cost money and that those babies, though dirty, are probably loved every bit as much as my children are.

My belief in the value and wisdom of planned parenthood also presents an attitudinal stumbling block when I come face to face with a woman who seems to have little control over the size of her family. Having grown up in a house with six younger siblings, I know exactly how much of an impact each new baby has on the economic, social, and emotional resources of a family. I am very judgmental, even scornful, of women who view unwanted pregnancies as just a little bad luck. I want to shake them and scream, "You deserve better than this, and so do your children!"

When I judge these mothers, I use my own experience as the mother of a 14-year-old daughter and a 12-year-old son as my measuring stick. Again, my feminist in me knows that this is an unfair comparison. I know from listening to my students' family stories that these women were not raised in the hermetically sealed "Ozzie and Harriet" environment in which I grew up. These mothers do not have the luxury of rejecting or accepting a perfectionist maternal role model. When I contrast the reality of these women's lives with my own, I am often ashamed of my knee-jerk negative response. Many of these women have no more of a conception of what it is like to live with a supportive, loving husband than I have of what it is like to be abused by a boyfriend who has recently been released from jail for drunk driving. Their children talk about relatives spending time in jail as if it were a right of passage. My kids think we are living on the edge if I set my cruise control to 67 mph instead of 65. Last summer, I was depressed because buying a house in June meant not going whale watching in Massachusetts in August. Many of my students' families face eviction on a regular basis. Sometimes they end up sleeping on the floor in a relative's house for months before finding a landlord who will rent to them. To some of the mothers whose children I teach, my life must look like the Twilight Zone or heaven.

What I need to do is look past the outward appearances and living circumstances of many of the families of my students, and look to make a very personal connection. If I keep nipping that unconscious, knee-jerk judgmental thinking in the bud, and instead search for common ground, I will be more effective in working with and supporting families. But an attitude change is not really enough. I could do more to defend disadvantaged families in the teachers' lounge.

volvement than they are able may have detrimental effects on both the child and the parents" (p. 159). Many parents, for example, are not willing or able to be therapists, teachers, and/or case managers for their children because of the inordinate demands of simply being a parent (Bailey & Wolery, 1992; Benson & Turnbull, 1986). A supportive and empowering professional approach is to individualize parental involvement by assisting parents in identifying a level of educational participation that is feasible, given their time and energy resources. Simpson and Fiedler (1989) offered several examples of potential parent involvement levels (see Box 4.2).

■ *Professionals with negative attitudes and animosity toward parents who assert their children's educational rights by functioning as an advocate reflect a disempowering attitude.* Parents who advocate on behalf of their children run the risk of, as one parent shared, being labeled by some profes-

sionals as "bitchy," "hysterical," and "overly demanding" (Pearson, 1992). Perhaps stemming from their own insecurity, some professionals are intimidated or angered by parent advocacy efforts. One group of parent advocates has created chapters of their parent support organization around the country, calling themselves a stigmatizing name they have heard all too often from professionals. Employing a tongue-in-cheek attitude, two founding members of this parent organization stated, "We are . . . a group of women who staunchly advocate for the rights of our children with disabilities. We use the name 'Mothers from Hell' because we often feel labeled as such by the systems within our society that are obliged to offer appropriate services to our children, yet seem to have a terrifically hard time doing just that" (Esperanza & Powell, 1996, p. 34).

■ *Professionals blame parents for their child's problems.* This perspective was popular during

---

Box 4.2

Advocacy Actions

1. *Attendance and approval of teacher priorities.* Parents attend IEP meetings, receive feedback about their child, and receive and approve proposed IEP goals.

2. *Sharing information.* Parents provide information to the educational staff regarding, for example, their child's current level of functioning within the family, effective and ineffective teaching strategies, preferred and nonpreferred activities.

3. *Suggesting goals.* Parents suggest specific skills or goals that they would like to see incorporated into the educational program.

4. *Negotiating goals.* When differences of opinion arise, parents and educational staff negotiate to agreement on IEP goals and implementation strategies.

5. *Collaboratively analyzing and monitoring implementation.* After reaching agreement on the IEP, parents help monitor day-to-day performance to assure achievement of goals, help include new goals when performance criteria are met, and reexamine goals that are not being met for respecification of goals or procedures.

6. *Joint programming.* Parents select specific IEP goals that they will implement in the home and/or community settings, simultaneously and in cooperation with the school's implementation of the goal.

7. *Independent programming.* Parents undertake training in the home or in the community of educational goals that are not being trained at school.

Source: From "Parent Participation in Individualized Educational Program (IEP) Conferences: A Case for Individualization" by R. L. Simpson and C. R. Fiedler in *The Second Handbook on Parent Education: Contemporary Perspectives* (p. 156) by M. J. Fine (Ed.), 1989, San Diego: Academic Press. Reprinted by permission.

the eugenics era of the early twentieth century. Basically, the eugenics movement blamed parents for the genetic inferiority of their children (Berry & Hardman, 1998; Turnbull & Turnbull, 1997). Throughout this century, parents have been blamed for causing their child's mental retardation (Scheerenberger, 1983), autism (Bettelheim, 1967), asthma (Gallagher & Gallagher, 1985), learning disabilities (Oliver, Cole, & Hollingsworth, 1991), and emotional disorders (Caplan & Hall-McCorquodale, 1985). Although some disabilities are genetically linked (e.g., Down syndrome), the vast majority of disabling conditions cannot be traced to a single cause such as "bad parenting." In particular, professionals have tended to blame parents for their children's emotional and behavioral disorders, even though there is little empirical evidence that parents are solely responsible for emotional disturbance in children (Reinert & Huang, 1987). The unfortunate consequence of professional blaming of parents for their children's problems is unnecessary guilt and stress on an already trying situation for families.

■ *Professionals tend to emphasize only the child's problems, disabilities, and other negatives when communicating with parents.* Although professionals must address the child's problems when working with a child with disabilities, it is important to maintain a balanced perspective. If excessive professional preoccupation is placed on what is "wrong" with a child, the issue of what is "right" may be overlooked (Shields, 1989). An excerpt from an article I wrote a few years ago summarizes the detrimental effects of this professional perspective and is presented in Box 4.3.

■ *Professionals take a minimalist perspective—asking "What do I have to do?" as opposed to asking "What can be done to appropriately serve the child and family?"* Professionals with this minimalist perspective lack the necessary advocacy

---

Box 4.3

Advocacy Anecdote

Many parents of children with disabilities have reported to me over the years how weary they grow from attending meeting after meeting where professionals dwell on their children's negatives, weaknesses, and deficiencies. It is not surprising that the attendance of parents at school-based meetings tends to decrease as the child with a disability gets older. Simply, parents are tired of the deficiency orientation that many professionals maintain. An alternative attitude and practice focuses on the positive aspects of individuals with disabilities. The best special education teacher that I ever knew made it a daily practice to send home a positive comment about each child every school day. Since this teacher worked with children labeled emotionally disturbed, some days it was difficult to focus on the positives. For example, if a child had a particularly troubling school day, perhaps the comment sent home that day was *"Billy accepted his timeout very well today."* This is a good example of how a negative situation, misbehaving which requires a punishment, can be changed into a positive.

I am a parent of a child with a severe cognitive disability and a principal coping strategy I employ is to actively focus on my daughter's positives. It would be very easy to dwell on all of the negatives: she is not toilet trained, she cannot feed or dress herself, she has no verbal communication skills, she does not walk, and all of the other deficiencies that professionals over the years have reminded us about. Instead, however, I choose to focus on my daughter's positives: she is very healthy, she has given me a deep appreciation for the wonder of child development, she has taught me more about individuals with disabilities than any course or instructor I have ever had, and, perhaps most importantly, as an adolescent she will never argue with me about having to wear Guess jeans as opposed to some other off-brand pair of jeans!

Source: From "Inclusion: Recognition of the Giftedness of All Children" by C. R. Fiedler, 1994, *Network, 4*(2), p. 17.

and ethical dispositions; consequently, they always take the path of least resistance in carrying out their job responsibilities. They are unwilling to fight for what is in the child's or family's best interests. This attitude prohibits the formation of advocacy partnerships between these professionals and families. As one parent succinctly put it, "This is only about one thing . . . HEART. I just want people to care about my kid" (Berry & Hardman, 1998, p.124). Examples of more appropriate professional attitudes are contained in Box 4.4.

A FAMILY SYSTEMS FRAMEWORK

Family systems theory, as applied to families with children with disabilities, has been extensively discussed in special education literature (Lambie & Daniels-Morhing, 1993; Seligman & Darling, 1989; Turnbull & Turnbull, 1997). Professionals with an appropriate family support and empowerment disposition must understand this philosophical foundation of family support and empowerment principles. Turnbull and Turnbull (1997)

Box 4.4 _____

Advocacy Actions

1. *Develop compassion.* The keys to being nonjudgmental of families are compassion and empathy. Elizabeth Boggs, one of the founders of the National Association for Retarded Citizens, referred to this human characteristic as "putting yourself in someone else's shoes." Professionals who are able to walk a mile in someone else's shoes ultimately become less judgmental and critical of families who may have different values from the professional.

2. *Surrender to the fact that life isn't fair.* All too often, well-meaning individuals feel sorry for others in difficult situations and a natural reaction is one of pity and sympathy. Most families with children with disabilities do not find public pity and sympathy helpful. Empathy is an empowering emotion; sympathy is a debilitating emotion. One mother wrote about the "cringe factor" she experiences when people shower her with pity and sympathy and tell her how wonderful and inspiring she is for raising a child with Down syndrome. She wrote, "They want to say something—anything—to make us, and themselves, feel better, so they come up with effusive platitudes. I certainly can't fault people for trying to be kind, but I cringe just the same" (Trainer, 1991, p. 136).

3. *Avoid weatherproofing.* Professionals who engage in weatherproofing are constantly on the careful lookout for what needs to be fixed or repaired in

families. With this attitude, a professional is compelled to focus on family weaknesses and pathology. The result is that the family is viewed as a client, not as a partner.

4. *Become an anthropologist.* Carlson (1997) defined anthropology as "being interested, without judgment, in the way other people choose to live and behave" (p. 111). With this level of investigation, professionals will be motivated to form partnerships with families in an effort to support and empower them. Professionals who become anthropologists will possess more compassion and patience and will be less frustrated by the actions of others.

5. *Be willing to learn from friends and family.* Professionals who see their role vis-à-vis families as the "experts" who give advice miss out on wonderful growth opportunities because they fail to see that they can learn from families. When you form a partnership with another, you expect to learn from your partner.

6. *Look for the extraordinary in the ordinary.* This strategy searches for the beauty in others, not their deficiencies. As a parent of a child with severe disabilities, I cannot trust a professional if that person does not appreciate all the gifts my daughter possesses. No parent wants a professional to view his or her child as "a bundle of deficiencies."

Source: Adapted from *Don't Sweat the Small Stuff . . . And It's All Small Stuff* by Richard Carlson, 1997, New York: Hyperion.

stressed the importance of understanding family systems theory: "Why is family systems theory important to you? Briefly, it will help you know families; and when you know families in an individual and personalized way, you can be attuned to their strengths, great expectations, priorities, and needs. In turn, the family systems approach can help you work more effectively and collaboratively with the family members who are most able to promote students' positive educational outcomes" (p. 11). As developed by Ann Turnbull and colleagues, the family systems framework comprises four major components (Turnbull, Summers, & Brotherson, 1984).

Family characteristics are the descriptive elements of the family, including characteristics of the disability (e.g., type and level of severity); characteristics of the family (e.g., sizes and forms, cultural backgrounds, socioeconomic status, and geographical locations); personal characteristics (e.g., health, intellectual capacity, and coping styles); and special challenges (e.g., poverty, substance abuse, and parents with disabilities). An understanding of family characteristics will help special education professionals assess the effects (negative and positive) that the child with a disability has on the entire family. With this knowledge, professionals will be able to determine the corresponding family resources and needs for coping with the additional demands of caring for a child with a disability.

Family interaction refers to the relationships that occur among subgroups of family members (e.g., marital, parental, sibling, and extrafamilial) and how the individuals in the family interact. In terms of family interaction, two elements are critical: cohesion (the emotional closeness or bonding of family members) and adaptability (the family's ability to cope with change and stress through effective problem solving). With knowledge of family relationships and interaction patterns, professionals can help families strike a balance between paying sufficient attention to the extra needs of the child with a disability and acknowledging that other family members have their own individual needs that must be addressed.

Family functions represent the different categories of needs the family must address to remain a viable unit (e.g., affection, self-esteem, economic, daily care, socialization, recreation, and education/vocation). Professionals must appreciate that meeting the educational needs of a child with disabilities is just one of the many functions that the family must fulfill to exist as a social entity. Placing undue educational expectations and demands on parents may seriously disrupt the delicate balance of family functioning.

Family life cycle represents the sequence of developmental and nondevelopmental changes that affect families. Change or transition usually causes stress. A change may specifically involve the child with a disability, such as when a child transitions from the elementary to secondary school programs or enters into the adult service system. Likewise, families experience transitions (e.g., when a structural change occurs in the family, such as a death or divorce or when the mother stops working outside the home). Professionals must react sensitively to families experiencing change or transition so that appropriate support can be generated to cope with the increased stress.

A FAMILY SUPPORT DISPOSITION

The concept of family support was alien to the field of special education in the beginning. At the inception of special education services in public schools, the efforts were focused on the child with a disability. The child was viewed in isolation from the family context. There was no professional appreciation for the interactional effects of the child on the family and vice versa. When schools did begin to pay some attention to families in the 1960s and 1970s, "most school services for families were designed to enhance the performance of mildly handicapped children; thus they focused on teaching parents instructional skills to reinforce what children learned in school" (Brantlinger, 1991, p. 253). That is, the role and responsibility of the parent was limited to carrying on educational programming in the home environment. There was no attention to the family's needs as a whole.

Family Support Definitions

Before defining *family support,* one first needs to define *family,* which is not an easy task in this culturally diverse society. Turnbull, Turnbull, Shank, and Leal (1995) have provided the most appropriate definition of *family* as "two or more people who regard themselves as a family and who perform some of the functions that families typically perform. These people may or may not be related by blood or marriage and may or may not usually live together" (pp. 24–25). There are a number of different definitions of *family support* and *family-centered services* in the literature. *Family centered* refers to "a combination of beliefs and practices that define particular ways of working with families that are consumer driven and competency enhancing" (Dunst, Johanson, Trivettte, & Hamby, 1991, p. 115). Family-centered services have also been described as "the provision of coordinated services based on a shared philosophy of how families are involved in every aspect of service delivery, whether it be assessment, child care, family support, therapeutic services, case management, team meetings, or consultation" (Bailey, McWilliams, Winton, & Simeonsson, 1992, p. 9).

Cheney and Osher (1997) have defined *family support* as "a constellation of services defined and determined by families. These supports (1) assist families in efforts to raise their children, (2) provide self-help groups to strengthen their parental roles, (3) maintain the integrity of the family unit, (4) inform parents of advocacy efforts, (5) provide cash assistance to families, and (6) consider the survival needs of families" (p. 40). Finally, Cooley (1994) added, "The primary goal of family support is to help individuals with disabilities and their families find balance and nourishment sufficient for them to feel fully included as citizens of their communities" (p. 119).

Family Support Principles

Family support is based on the assumption that families are experts who are best able to determine what services and supports they need (Illinois Planning Council on Developmental Disabilities, 1991). Family support is intended to build on a family's strengths. An example of implementation of effective family support principles is included in Box 4.5.

Instead of engaging in judgmental labeling of families or blaming parents for their children's problems, a professional disposition based on the following assumptions is critical in supporting families:

1. *Parenting a child with a disability is a challenging job; it can be time consuming, demanding, stressful and never ending. Supportive relationships can help reduce the stress.*
2. *Child rearing is a unique endeavor. Parents will have different goals for their children and different ways of achieving these goals. There are many right ways to parent.*
3. *Most parents want to be good parents and will work to the best of their abilities to fulfill those responsibilities. They can bring a wealth of information to professionals.*
4. *Parents are unique individuals and therefore possess varying degrees of skills and knowledge. Parents will interpret their parenting role in a variety of ways. (Stoecklin, 1994, pp. 3–4)*

The Underlying Values of a Professional Family Support Disposition

Professionals who possess family support beliefs and practices are natural advocates because they will do everything in their power to assist children with disabilities and their families in fulfilling child and family needs. To support this disposition, certain values must be subsumed into a professional's beliefs and practices framework.

The Professional Values Family Expertise

The professional recognizes that the family has much to offer the relationship. Some families may not readily present themselves as "experts," given stressful circumstances that often beset families raising a child with disabilities. Professionals may need to look beyond the surface problems and exhume the family expertise.

Box 4.5

Advocacy Anecdote

My wife and I decided when Jennifer was 10 years old that we wanted her to transition from our home at the same time that most children leave the family nest, around 18 years of age. We realized that because of Jennifer's intensive daily need for care and support services, her transition from our home would be challenging and would require long-range planning. We quickly discovered that the county agency for individuals with developmental disabilities could not provide any housing options for us. All of the county group homes were full, as were supportive services for any kind of assisted living arrangements. There was a long waiting list for services, with some individuals and their families on a waiting list for housing services for several years.

After our initial sense of panic about the lack of county housing services, we came to a realization that, ultimately, expanded our thinking into possible solutions. By not being able to rely on the county, we were not limited by traditional housing options (e.g., group home, supported apartment program, adult foster care), and that forced us to be flexible and creative.

When Jennifer turned 14 years old, we developed with the school a transition plan that contained a key goal of finding community housing for her when she turned age 18. The school professionals understood our family-determined goal and they were very supportive. The school served as a catalyst, through the transition plan, by connecting us with adult service providers and financial institutions. We, as parents, also relied on some of our strengths in working on a housing solution for Jennifer.

With my background as a former lawyer and knowledge of social security regulations and other financial support programs for people with disabilities, we were able to access supports that allowed Jennifer to finance the purchase of her own home. We accessed funds from a county low-income home ownership program, which provided assistance for a down payment on the home. In addition, we were able to secure an interest-free home rehabilitation loan (Jennifer's new home needed some remodeling and a wheelchair ramp). My wife's skills as a real estate appraiser were critical in knowing the local housing market.

We eventually found the right house for Jennifer and put together the necessary assistance. Jennifer moved into her own home six months after her 18th birthday. She has been living with two roommates in this house for over two years. She is a fully participating member of her community. Jennifer's purchase of her own home is now a model for expanding housing options for other adults with disabilities. This is a better living environment for Jennifer than some institutional or group home setting. As one of her home health aides commented, "You go into group homes, and all of people's things are labeled and it's often very institutional. This is a whole lot better. Because this is Jennifer's home, you feel more at ease and you come in with a much higher level of respect."

This goal was realized because (1) the school respected our self-determined goal, (2) we relied on some of our family strengths in reaching this goal, and (3) the school was a supportive partner in the planning process.

For example, a school psychologist working with a single mother of a 14-year-old son with emotional/behavioral disorders discovered hidden talents and expertise that had never been brought to the surface before. This mother struggled with poverty and with her own alcohol addiction. In the past, most professionals could not get beyond the mother's apparent "dysfunction." They were satisfied simply to get the mother to attend IEP meetings, which she did sometimes in a half inebriated state. The school professionals would present the mother with an already completed IEP and, as quickly as possible, get the mother's approval to the school's plan of services. The school psychologist dug beneath the surface and discovered that the mother had a lot of artistic talent. With this information, the school psychologist invited the mother to participate in some of the art therapy activities that the school was trying with her son. The art became a way for the mother to make a connection with her son and to feel involved and useful in his treatment.

The Professional Values Family Decision Making

Families and professionals will sometimes disagree. When disagreements arise, professionals must be willing to suspend their opinions and look at the issue from the family's perspective. Unless the family's decision is clearly not in the child's best interests, family self-determination should be the overriding principle.

As an example, my family and a special education teacher disagreed on the issue of including Jennifer in some general education classes. There was no clearly right answer on this issue in terms of what would be in Jennifer's best interests. The teacher argued that self-contained special education programming would be most appropriate to afford sufficient massed trial learning of functional skills. We, as her parents, argued that Jennifer could appropriately learn real-life functional skills more naturally by participating in some general education classes, plus she would experience social benefits, as well.

In situations such as this, where decisions are not so clear cut, professionals must respect family decision making by displaying a willingness to try the family's approach. In our case, the teacher could have included Jennifer on a trial basis in some general education classes. We then could have established some trial parameters to make future decision making more objective. For instance, specific behavioral objectives could have been established in advance of the trial placement, specifying the behaviors we wanted to address in the general education class—making eye contact when spoken to, following two-step directions, and using a signature stamp to sign her name. With specific behavioral objectives agreed on, the trial placement would have involved the collection of data to determine whether this was, indeed, a beneficial setting for Jennifer. Instead of an approach that values family decision making, the special education teacher in this case chose to conduct philosophical warfare with us on the detrimental effects

of inclusion. This was a lose-lose approach for both parties and, most significantly, my daughter.

The Professional Values Family Strength Enhancement as Opposed to a Deficit Approach

When families are treated as "clients," the professional approach is to employ some intervention to fix them. This is the deficit model. As an alternative, professionals should focus on building family strengths and abilities to manage and fulfill family needs.

For example, using a deficit approach, the mother of a son with multiple disabilities would probably be referred to counseling to deal with her grief feelings. Although many individuals benefit from counseling and those services are often necessary, a first-line intervention should seek to illuminate family strengths that could be employed to cope with a problem. The mother with the multiply disabled son had a well-defined sense of humor. She eventually employed that strength as a coping mechanism. She wrote, "Humor has been the most important tool that we have had. Believe it or not, we laugh a lot! Granted, the jokes are sometimes slightly warped. Although it seems obvious, it took us a while to learn that laughter can see you through rough spots. We know that there is a time to cry, but there is also a time when grief becomes debilitating. Overall, humor can make you much more productive" (Wilson, 1993, p. 29). This is an example of the family strength enhancement approach.

A FAMILY EMPOWERMENT DISPOSITION

The family support movement of the 1990s has ushered in a new paradigm of decision making between families and professionals (Summers, 1992). This new paradigm replaces the traditional model that casts professionals as the experts in total control of the decision making. Family support initiatives embrace enabling and empowering principles that promote family strength, competence, and decision making (Singer & Powers, 1993). To empower, as defined in the *Tenth Edition of the Merriam Webster's Collegiate Dictio-*

nary (1994), means (1) to give official authority of legal power to, (2) to enable, and (3) to promote the self-actualization or influence of. Empowered individuals strive for control over their lives; they take action to get what they want and need (Cochran, 1992; Dunst, Trivette, & LaPoint, 1992). Special education professionals who function as child advocates must be empowered individuals who seek to support families of children with disabilities by empowering them. This is mutual empowerment of the professional and families (Turnbull & Turnbull, 1997).

How can professionals empower families? The most comprehensive empowerment model has been proposed by Turnbull and Turnbull (1997). The identified family factors in the Turnbulls' empowerment model will be addressed here—that is, to the extent that professionals can support families to acquire certain family characteristics or factors, families will possess the tools to act "empowerfully." The basic family factors of empowerment are motivation and knowledge/skills.

For families to exert control over their lives by taking action to get what they want or need, they will need a high degree of **motivation.** This emotional component of empowerment can be fostered by professionals through the enhancement of the following five elements of motivation:

- *Self-efficacy* is the belief in your own capabilities. "Families' self-efficacy refers to their beliefs about their own ability to care for their children and to contribute to their children's positive outcomes. Teachers' self-efficacy refers to their beliefs concerning the degree to which they can make a difference in enhancing student learning" (Turnbull & Turnbull, 1997, p. 38).
- *Perceived control* is the belief that you can apply your capabilities to affect what happens to you.
- *Hope* is the belief that you will get what you want and need.
- *Energy,* according to the Turnbulls, is "what it takes to light the fire and what it takes to keep it burning" (p. 41).

- *Persistence* requires a sustained effort over time.

By itself, motivation is insufficient to act empowerfully; families also need specific **knowledge and skills.** In their empowerment model, the Turnbulls identified four knowledge/skills components:

- *Information* needs are specific to issues currently confronting families and their child with a disability. For example, a family with an 18-year-old son with mental retardation will probably require information on transition planning and services. Families of children with disabilities indicate their greatest informational needs are about (1) future services, (2) present services, (3) how to teach their child, (4) the nature of their child's disability, (5) experiences of other families with a similarly disabled child, (6) handling the emotional and time demands of parenting, (7) community resources, and (8) legal rights (Gowen, Christy, & Sparling, 1993).
- *Problem solving* is the ability to develop and execute a plan of action to resolve problems or barriers to meeting your needs or goals. There will be more discussion on problem solving in Chapter 10, which addresses conflict resolution.
- *Coping skills* allow you to handle stress in your life.
- *Communication skills* involve an interaction process in which families and professionals are able and willing to listen and learn from each other, share ideas, and be understood. Effective communication skills and strategies will be discussed in Chapter 8, which addresses interpersonal communication.

Box 4.6 presents an example of how one special education professional empowered one family.

ADVOCACY TRAINING AND SUPPORT FOR FAMILIES

As discussed in Chapter 1, parents are the first and best advocates for their children with disabilities.

Box 4.6_____

Advocacy Anecdote

Several years ago, my daughter Jennifer moved back to her home school district from a regional special education program in an adjacent district. In preparation for her enrollment in our home school district, my wife and I had several meetings with Jennifer's new special education teacher over the summer. During these meetings, we explained to the teacher our educational vision and goals for Jennifer. We stressed how important it was for us that Jennifer spend part of her school day in general education classes. We talked about the importance of community-based instruction in addressing functional skills. We indicated that Jennifer needed to have some community work experiences. Finally, we shared our hope and desire that the school would actively begin to develop peer relationships between Jennifer and students without disabilities.

As you can see, our agenda was quite full. In addition to feeling somewhat overwhelmed by us as parents of a new student, the special education teacher (as she would share with us a year later, after we had established a trusting, collaborative relationship) had doubts about some of our educational goals—especially the general education classroom inclusion. This teacher's philosophy and past experiences in working with severely disabled children was based on self-contained programming. However, the teacher knew that we were sincere in our educational vision for Jennifer, so she worked with us to implement our goals into Jennifer's IEP.

As a result, Jennifer was placed into three general education classes, the school instituted more community-based instructional services, and the special education teacher began developing community job sites. Further, after about three months in this new school, Jennifer began experiencing social interactions with nondisabled peers outside of school. Some of these social interactions turned into long-term friendships.

During this school year, as parents, we felt empowered. How did this special education teacher foster our empowerment? First, she significantly enhanced our parental motivation in the following ways:

- She respected our educational goals and thereby increased our feeling of **self-efficacy** and **perceived control.** We gained confidence that the teacher valued a close, collaborative working relationship with us. She viewed us as equal partners in educational decision making.
- The teacher instilled **hope** in us that our educational vision for Jennifer could be realized.
- By fostering our feelings of self-efficacy, perceived control, and hope, the teacher fueled our **energy** level and our **persistence** to work on our goals over the long haul.

Second, the teacher enhanced our knowledge and skills to act empowerfully in the following ways:

- The teacher provided us with a wealth of **information** on transitional and vocational programming. In addition, she linked us up with several community agency providers.
- Whenever we encountered barriers to attaining our educational vision for Jennifer, the teacher collaboratively engaged in **problem solving** with us.
- Our **coping skills** were enhanced by the mere confidence this teacher bestowed in us. She made us feel strong and knowledgeable by affirming our decisions and helping us celebrate each small victory along the way. For example, we all celebrated when the first peer called to schedule an out-of-school activity with Jennifer.
- As our relationship with this teacher grew into a partnership, our **communication skills** served as the foundation for the mutual trust we experienced.

However, many families will need professional guidance and support to fulfill their advocacy role and responsibilities effectively. Special education professionals can fulfill a vitally important support and empowerment function by assisting parents in acquiring the necessary knowledge and skills for educational advocacy. What knowledge and skills must parents possess in their desire to be effective educational advocates? Fiedler (1991) urged that professional support of parent educational advocacy efforts should focus on two broad topics: legal rights and enhancing parent participation in the IEP decision-making process.

Simpson (1996) described a model of family educational involvement that contained a component of partnership and advocacy training for parents. The parent advocacy training described consisted of three basic topics: (1) training on parent rights and responsibilities under IDEA; (2) training on participation in IEP, progress report, and other family/school conferences; and (3) training related to identifying and using school and community resources. Spiegel-McGill, Reed, Konig, and McGowan (1990) outlined an advocacy skills training program designed for parents of children with disabilities entering special education preschool programs from home-based infant special education programs. Topics covered in their advocacy skills program include: (1) the effects of transition on one's lives (emotional implications of change); (2) knowing one's child (understanding functional skill levels); (3) program options and services (placement and service options, roles and responsibilities of various professionals); (4) effective communication (describing child skills and needs, effective responding, assertive communication); (5) educational rights (legal rights with regard to assessment, placement and program planning); and (6) putting the puzzle together (preparing for team meetings, getting help from community resources and parent organizations).

Finally, Turnbull and Turnbull (1997) described the training support provided by federally funded Parent Training and Information Centers. Such centers assist families in better understanding the nature and needs of their child's disability and legal rights and procedures, provide monitoring support for children's educational programs, provide training on effective communication and how to participate fully in educational decisions, and provide information on how to access national, state, and local resources. The next section discusses advocacy training and support for families in terms of six topics: (1) legal rights of parents, (2) basic advocacy skills, (3) assertive communication, (4) parent participation in educational

(M-team) evaluation procedures, (5) parent participation in IEP decision making, and (6) parent monitoring of educational program and progress.

Legal Rights of Parents

School personnel typically inform parents of their legal rights by providing them with a written notice describing their child's educational rights. However, many parents do not receive adequate notice of their legal rights as provided by IDEA (Yoshida, Fenton, Kaufman, & Maxwell, 1978). Fiedler (1991) opined, "Perhaps part of the problem related to ensuring adequate notice to parents about their legal rights and procedures is the rather high readability level of the disseminated material" (p. 320). In fact, a nationwide survey of state departments of education revealed that materials disseminated to parents consistently had a 14th- to 15th-grade level readability rate (McLoughlin, Edge, Petrosko, & Strenecky, 1981).

About what legal rights and educational procedures should professionals ensure that parents have been sufficiently informed? This section identifies relevant informational needs of parent advocates. Chapter 5 provides specific legal answers to the questions raised in this section. Parent educational advocacy may be categorized according to the following areas: notice, consent, participation, access, verification, and oversight (South Dakota Statewide Systems Change Project, 1995). At a minimum, professionals should provide parents with information to address these areas, using the questions given here as a framework.

Notice

Parents are entitled to notice of selected proposed school actions, inactions, or changes in programs or services. Parents should be able to answer the following questions:

- What is the purpose of providing parents with notice of school actions? Must it be in writing?
- When must notice be given?
- How long before implementation of a school decision must notice be given?

- How much information must be provided in a notice?
- What is the consequence of the school's failure to provide adequate notice?

Consent

Parents are required to give their written consent prior to the initial evaluation and placement of a student in special education. Parents should be able to answer the following questions:

- Do parents need to provide their consent each year of placement or for subsequent educational evaluations?
- What happens if parents do not have sufficient information to make an informed decision?
- What does giving parental consent "voluntarily" mean?
- May parents revoke their consent? If so, when?
- What happens if parents do not consent to an initial educational evaluation or special education placement?

Participation

Parents are entitled to participate fully in the referral and evaluation procedures and in the development, monitoring, and revision of a child's individual education plan. Parents should be able to answer the following questions:

- How does the school find children who need special education? Who may make a referral for special education services?
- How does the multidisciplinary team (M-team) do its evaluation? How can parents participate in the evaluation?
- What happens after the M-team makes its report?
- What happens after the IEP is finished?
- May parents contribute educational goals and objectives?
- What does "least restrictive environment" mean?
- What related services will be given at the school besides classroom teaching?
- How will those services be delivered?

- May parents bring someone such as an advocate to an M-team or IEP meeting?
- Can the school conduct an M-team or IEP meeting in the parents' absence?

Access

Parents are entitled to inspect and review their child's educational records. Parents should be able to answer the following questions:

- What educational records are subject to parents' inspection? How soon after parents request an inspection of records must the school comply?
- Must the school provide explanations and interpretations of records?
- Must the school provide parents with copies of educational records?
- May parents request an amendment of educational records if they believe there is inaccurate or misleading information? What happens if the school refuses to amend the records?
- What are the school's confidentiality obligations to parents in terms of educational records?

Verification

Parents are entitled to obtain an independent educational evaluation if they disagree with the M-team report. Parents should be able to answer the following questions:

- Who pays for the cost of an independent educational evaluation? Are there any qualifications for who may conduct an independent educational evaluation?
- Do school personnel have to consider independent educational evaluations in their decision making?
- May a due process hearing officer order an independent educational evaluation at public expense?

Oversight

Parents are entitled to disagree formally with school decisions by initiating and participating in a due process hearing. Parents should be able to answer the following questions:

- On what school decisions may parents request a due process hearing?
- What due process hearing rights do parents have? Who pays for the costs of a due process hearing? May parents seek reimbursement for their costs of hiring an attorney?
- What due process hearing rights does the school have?
- What is the role and responsibility of the due process hearing officer? What format does a due process hearing follow? What are the procedures?
- When a due process hearing has been requested, what happens to the child's educational placement and services?
- How do parents appeal a decision after the due process hearing?
- Are there any dispute resolution alternatives to a due process hearing? How do parents write a letter of complaint or a request for a due process hearing?

Basic Advocacy Skills

Although a more in-depth discussion of advocacy skills will be presented in Chapter 11, this section will briefly review some of the basic advocacy skills parents must possess. Pardeck (1996) identified the following advocacy skills that are necessary for parents to advocate effectively for their children with disabilities:

- *Parents must believe in their rights.* Parents must appreciate the full meaning and responsibility of being an "equal partner" in educational decision making.
- *Parents must have a clear vision.* Parents must be able to clearly articulate what they want for their children. They must be realistic and optimistic about what services their children need and be able to recognize what is appropriate for their children.
- *Parents must have good organizational skills.* Parents must know how to file information, and how to keep track of records and other important educational information. Clearly orga-

nized materials will facilitate effective parental decision making.
- *Parents must be able to prioritize.* Parents must be able to decide what are the most important issues related to their children's educational program. Advocacy efforts should focus on priority goals and needs.
- *Parents must possess a good understanding of their children's disabilities.* Parents must learn as much as possible about their children's disability condition(s). This includes learning about the typical characteristics, medical and educational implications, prognosis, support groups, and necessary services. Parents often know more about their child's disability than professionals, so this knowledge becomes an important avenue for parental sharing of information with professionals.
- *Parents must know the laws.* When it comes to exercising legal rights, knowledge is power. By knowing relevant special education laws, parents will be better able to advocate for their children's rights.
- *Parents must follow the chain of command.* Effective advocacy means that parents should start with the teacher before going to higher authorities with complaints and concerns. By knowing the school chain of command for decision making, parents will be able to pursue their recourse if they are dissatisfied at any one level.
- *Parents should be informative.* Parents must be able to help professionals understand the needs of their children. Any information that will enhance the child's learning experience should be conveyed to school personnel. This includes information on what motivates the child, particular likes and dislikes of the child, and instructional approaches that have worked well in the past.
- *Parents should offer solutions.* Parents need creative problem-solving skills. The ability to seek win-win solutions is essential in effective advocacy.
- *Parents must be principled and persistent.* Parents must be able to stand firm in their advocacy

efforts and to muster the strength and effort to maintain their advocacy over the long haul if necessary. By being principled, parents attempt to advocate by building collaborative partnerships with professionals, not by fostering adversarial relations through aggressive tactics.

- *Parents must learn to communicate effectively.* Some important communication skills include building trust and rapport, good listening, asking questions when one is uncertain about something, being honest, and saying what one really means. In addition, nonverbal communication is as important as verbal communication. Therefore, maintaining a relaxed nondefensive posture will facilitate interactions with professionals.

- *Parents must let others know when they are pleased.* It is important that parents express satisfaction and excitement when their children are making progress. That is, professionals should not just hear from parents when there are problems. Parents must be effective at reinforcing professionals for a job well done.

- *Parents must develop endurance.* Advocacy often extends over a long period of time; indeed, parenting and advocating for their children are lifelong responsibilities. Parents must develop resilience to withstand and overcome the inevitable failures and obstacles they will encounter as educational advocates.

- *Parents must follow through.* Effective advocacy requires constant vigilance and monitoring to ensure services promised are appropriately provided.

- *Parents need a sense of humor.* A sense of humor will help lighten some of the burdens incurred by advocacy. Humor is an effective coping mechanism for many families.

Assertive Communication

Chapter 8 will discuss interpersonal communication skills at length. This section will focus on the importance of assertive communication during advocacy. Parents experiencing frustrations or concerns relative to their children's education often behave in problem personalities at polar extremes. At one extreme is the parent who becomes angry and aggressive in fighting the injustices of the educational system. At the other extreme is the parent who easily is intimidated by professionals and consequently is afraid of making waves by challenging professionals' decisions. Obviously, both extremes result in ineffective advocacy. Specific advocacy problem personalities are discussed by Stoecklin (1994, p. 31):

The policeman personality. From the time a meeting begins, this parent makes sure everyone knows that he or she is up to date on all laws. During the meeting, the parent spends most of the time looking for legal technicalities. Since most of the parent's energies are spent on "catching the district," the needs of the child take a backseat.

The lawyer personality. The lawyer personality is also caught up in legal rights, only this parent's focus is on "taking the district to court." Whenever there is a problem, the threat is to take the district to due process. Because legal threats are used so often, no one takes this person's threats or even good ideas seriously.

The dictator personality. The dictator is always well prepared but has no desire to work as part of any team. This parent enters every meeting angry and takes control by demanding things. Most sentences begin with "You will" and "I want." People dislike working and even communicating with such a person. Because of the way this parent acts, professionals avoid communication as much as possible and just move the child along so their interactions with the parent are kept to a minimum.

The Mickey/Minnie Mouse personality. This parent knows his or her rights, shows up at every meeting, but never asks a question or disagrees with anyone. Even though the parent knows the child's program is inappropriate, he or she goes along with things for fear someone will "take it out on the child." Everyone in the district likes this parent, describing him or her as one of the easiest parents with whom to deal.

To avoid these advocacy problem personalities, parents and professionals need to exercise appropriate assertiveness. Assertive communicators are confident, positive, and forceful yet respectful in advocating for their rights.

Parent Participation in Educational Evaluation (M-Team) Procedures

Parent/professional collaboration should begin during the evaluation process. Winifred Anderson, Stephen Chitwood, and Diedre Hayden (1997, pp. 41–45) outlined specific "parent action-steps for evaluation" during each of the four phases of the evaluation process. The four phases include:

1. Giving or refusing permission to evaluate
2. Activities before evaluation
3. Activities during evaluation
4. Activities after evaluation

The parent action-steps for each of these four phases are summarized here.

Giving or Refusing Permission to Evaluate

- *Action 1: Explore one's feelings about this evaluation by* (1) talking to a spouse, a friend, or a professional; and (2) if the child has been evaluated previously, recall what was difficult and what was helpful in previous evaluations.
- *Action 2: Learn more about the local evaluation process by* (1) asking the director of special education or the school principal to identify the person in the school system most responsible for the child's evaluation; (2) obtaining all relevant written policies and procedures from the person responsible for the evaluation; (3) obtaining parent handbooks and pamphlets on evaluation; (4) making a list of questions; and (5) meeting with a knowledgeable person such as an experienced parent, a school professional, or an advocate to discuss evaluations.
- *Action 3: Learn more about the evaluation planned for one's child by* (1) requesting in writing from school officials the reasons for this evaluation; and (2) requesting a detailed

plan for evaluation, including the areas to be evaluated, tests to be used, reasons for selecting tests, qualifications of persons giving tests, and a statement as to how the evaluation will be adapted to compensate for the child's suspected disability.

- *Action 4: Assess the appropriateness of the tests by* (1) consulting a knowledgeable person such as another parent or an independent school professional; and (2) reviewing the literature on special education evaluation.
- *Action 5: Explore the independent evaluation alternative by* (1) learning about one's right to an independent evaluation; (2) learning the school's procedures for providing independent evaluations; (3) talking with parents whose children have had independent evaluations; and (4) consulting a special education professional in private practice.
- *Action 6: Explore the consequences of refusing evaluation by* (1) talking to the principal and teachers about alternatives to special education at the school; (2) discussing concerns with the person in charge of the evaluation; (3) learning the school's procedures when parents refuse evaluation; and (4) talking with knowledgeable professionals about the child's learning needs and the reasons for considering refusing the school's evaluation.

Activities before Evaluation

- *Action 1: Anticipate the child's needs in this evaluation by* (1) talking with school professionals about how the child handles evaluations and the following factors related to evaluation: reaction to strangers, tolerance for testing demands, ability to sit still for long time periods, fatigue threshold (i.e., how long until the child gets too tired to work at his or her best), need for an interpreter if the child is non-English speaking or is a user of sign language, and high and low points in the day; (2) reading pamphlets or articles on children and evaluations; and (3) talking with the child about prior evaluation experiences and thoughts about the new evaluation.

- *Action 2: Prepare for this evaluation by* (1) talking to other parents about their experiences; (2) seeking tips on rough spots and how to work around them from an organization for parents of children with disabilities; (3) listing practical concerns about the evaluation, such as schedules, costs, child care, transportation, and obtaining an interpreter; (4) learning the evaluation staff's expectations for parental involvement; and (5) choosing among various parental roles for one's child, such as observer, supporter, and information source.
- *Action 3: Plan for the child's evaluation with a representative of the school by* (1) arranging for a meeting or a phone conference; (2) preparing for this meeting by listing questions and concerns in priority order; (3) requesting information on, or clarification of, the evaluation process; (4) sharing one's plans for parental involvement; and (5) raising concerns over keeping the experience positive for one's child.
- *Action 4: Prepare the child for the evaluation by* (1) talking together about the reasons for, and process of, this new evaluation; (2) giving the child opportunities to express feelings and ask questions; (3) visiting the place where the evaluation will be conducted so the child will be familiar with the people and the surroundings; and (4) planning together for a special activity when the evaluation is completed.

Activities during Evaluation

- *Action 1: Ease the child into the situation by* (1) allowing the child to become familiar with the areas in which the testing will occur; (2) introducing the child to the people who will be giving the tests; (3) reviewing the evaluation plan; (4) reassuring the child of the parent's availability at all times; and (5) encouraging the child to ask questions and share worries.
- *Action 2: Monitor the evaluation process by* (1) requesting that the evaluation start on time; (2) inquiring as to any changes in personnel or tests to be used; (3) observing testing of the child whenever appropriate; (4) recording impressions of one's child's performance; and

(5) recording impressions of each evaluator's interactions with one's child.
- *Action 3: Monitor the child's performance by* (1) keeping an eye on the child's fatigue and stress levels; (2) staying with the child during any medical procedures; and (3) asking for explanations of unexpected procedures.

Activities after Evaluation

- *Action 1: Help the child round out the experience on a positive note by* (1) encouraging the child to review the evaluation experience; (2) discussing with the child the people and activities he or she liked and disliked; (3) sharing the parent's own feelings and perceptions of the experience; and (4) informing the child of the evaluation results and what was learned about strengths and needs.
- *Action 2: Help complete the experience by* (1) recounting the experience to a friend or parent support group; (2) checking the actual evaluation experience against what one had planned or anticipated; and (3) writing a letter to the school describing one's sense of the strengths and needs of the process.
- *Action 3: Prepare for the conference with the evaluation team by* (1) reading through the child's previous evaluation records; (2) reviewing the information and notes on this evaluation; (3) asking the evaluation case coordinator for the individual evaluation reports; (4) analyzing the school records by identifying the child's strengths and problems in academic and social/behavioral areas; (5) noting concerns in the form of questions to be asked at the evaluation conference; and (6) asking someone to go with the parent to the evaluation conference.

Parent Participation in IEP Decision Making

Professionals should involve parents to the maximum extent possible in IEP decision making, while at the same time acknowledging the parents' rights to choose minimal participation. (See Box 4.2 as an example of various parent participation levels ranging from low to high involvement.)

Adhering to the family systems perspective, professionals should tolerate and encourage a range of parent participation options matched to the needs and interests of each family. Parent participation in IEP decision making is critical because the IEP identifies what is "special" about special education.

A poorly written and/or implemented IEP results in the denial of an appropriate education for a child with a disability. As Barb Buswell, the mother of Wilson, a young child with a disability, stated, "Thinking of myself as Wilson's 'case manager' makes it easier for me to ask for the things he needs. When I think I can't ask for something else for Wilson because they'll think, 'She's a pushy mother,' I remember, 'I'm the manager; it's my job to ask'" (Simons, 1987, p. 54). This section will briefly identify several considerations and strategies for successful parent participation in IEP decision making.

Anderson and colleagues (1997) have provided a helpful checklist (see Box 4.7) of questions to ensure that an IEP contains all of the legally required information and that serves as a useful educational planning document. Another useful IEP planning tool is Bateman and Linden's (1998) three-step process for developing educationally useful IEPs. This planning process is especially family friendly because active parent input is solicited from the very beginning. The three steps are:

1. Professionals and family members brainstorm and list the student's educational needs and characteristics. After completing this list, the needs and characteristics are clustered.
2. Professionals and family members identify what the school will do to meet each need/characteristic cluster (e.g., special education programming, related services, general classroom modifications, etc.).
3. Professionals and family members determine what changes in the student's behavior will indicate if the service the school is providing is effective.

An example of how this three-step process leads to IEP goals and objectives is provided in

Box 4.8. This IEP development process is family friendly in that the first brainstorming step immediately acknowledges parental expertise in contributing information on their child's educational needs and characteristics. This brainstorming session is less intimidating for parents and solicits active parent participation right at the outset of the IEP planning process. Another feature of Bateman and Linden's IEP process is that the second step clearly places the responsibility on the school to provide services in an attempt to enhance a student's educational experience. Some IEPs are poorly (and illegally) written in placing responsibility for behavioral change solely on the student or the family. Finally, the third step of Bateman and Linden's IEP development process ensures school accountability and leads directly to the drafting of IEP goals and objectives.

The research on professional/parent partnerships in developing IEPs is not encouraging. Most studies conclude that IEPs tend to function as legal formalities where a previously developed IEP is merely presented to the parents for their information and acquiescence (Goldstein, Strickland, Turnbull, & Curry, 1980; Harry, Allen, & McLaughlin, 1995; Vaughn, Bos, Harrell, & Lasky, 1988). One strong reason for parent dissatisfaction in IEP meetings is the insufficient amount of time devoted to planning and discussing goals and objectives (Witt, Miller, McIntyre, & Smith, 1984). These findings reinforce Turnbull and Turnbull's (1997) conclusion: "The dominant theme of all the research and testimony is that schools try to comply with legal mandates and procedures but do not make an effort to foster empowerment through collaboration" (p. 231).

An alternative to traditional IEP meeting practices, one which supports and empowers families of children with disabilities, is the Making Action Plans (MAPS) (Falvey, Forest, Pearpoint, & Rosenberg, 1994; Vandercock, York, & Forest, 1989). MAPS was originally used for students with severe disabilities in an effort to foster more school and community inclusion. I believe that MAPS has a much broader utility and can assist professionals and families in articulating a future

Box 4.7

Advocacy Actions

CHECKLIST OF IEP REQUIREMENTS

1. Description of child's present level of educational performance in all areas, including specific student strengths.
2. Statement of measurable annual goals and short-term objectives for each of those goals.
3. Statement of the special education and related services to be provided to meet each of the goals and objectives, including supplementary aids and services to support general education class participation if appropriate.
4. Statement of the extent to which the child will participate in general education programs.
5. Statement of transition services for a student 14 years or older.
6. Modifications in the administration of state- or districtwide student performance assessment.
7. Projected dates for starting services and the anticipated duration of the services.
8. If the child's behavior is a problem, a positive behavior intervention plan should be included.
9. Consideration of assistive technology and services must be documented.
10. Statement of the objective criteria, evaluation procedures and schedules for determining, on at least an annual basis, whether the child is achieving his or her short-term objectives.

CHECKLIST FOR DETERMINING THE APPROPRIATENESS OF THE IEP

1. Does the IEP accurately and fully describe the child's present level of educational performance in all areas?
2. Do the annual goals describe the skills the parent would like the child to develop within the next year?
3. Are annual goals written to build on the child's present level of educational performance?
4. Is there at least one annual goal and short-term objective for each related service the child will receive?
5. Are goals and objectives written as positive, measurable statements?
6. Do goals and objectives contain the five essential parts of who will do what, how, where, and when?
7. Do the annual goals and objectives meet the priorities the parent has established as essential for the child?
8. Are all special education and related services clearly identified, along with projected dates for beginning services and the anticipated duration of the services?
9. Does the IEP clearly describe the extent to which the child will participate in general education programs?
10. Are necessary transition services described?
11. Does the IEP include appropriate and understandable criteria and evaluation procedures and schedules for determining, at least on an annual basis, whether the instructional objectives are being achieved?
12. Is there agreement among all teachers and therapists who are providing services to the child with the IEP and do they agree to provide these services?

Source: From *Negotiating the Special Education Maze: A Guide for Parents and Teachers* (pp. 109–110) by Winifred Anderson, Stephen Chitwood, and Diedre Hayden, 1997, Bethesda, MD: Woodbine House. Reprinted by permission.

Box 4.8 _____

Advocacy Actions

JOHN'S NEEDS/CHARACTERISTICS

- Enjoys interaction with people
- Enjoys motion
- Enjoys music
- Is susceptible to "down time"
- Has difficulty attending to a task
- Needs to have more control over his environment
- Needs to be out of his chair more
- Is unable to dress himself
- Needs hand over hand assistance in eating
- Needs friends
- Enjoys the outdoors

STEP 1: NEEDS/CHARACTERISTICS

John needs friends.

STEP 2: SCHOOL WILL DO/PROVIDE

1. *Organize a Circle of Friends.*
2. *Provide training for general education students on how to interact with John.*

3. *Encourage more extracurricular activities for John and nondisabled peers.*

STEP 3: CHANGES IN STUDENT'S BEHAVIOR (TO BE OBSERVED)

IEP GOAL

John will have more social interaction opportunities with nondisabled peers.

IEP OBJECTIVES

1. *Within one month, the school will conduct a Circle of Friends activity in at least three 8th-grade general education classes and attempt to organize a Circle of Friends for John.*
2. *Within two months, John will have at least three positive interactions per day with nondisabled peers.*

---

vision and educational goals for any student with disabilities. As a parent, I have participated in a MAPS process for my daughter, Jennifer. The MAPS session was conducted about two weeks prior to the annual IEP meeting. In attendance at the MAPS session were Jennifer, my wife and I, Jennifer's sister (Lindsay), special education teachers, general education teachers, related services personnel, community vocational agency personnel, and several friends without disabilities. The meeting was conducted by a facilitator who guided us through seven key questions:

- *What is Jennifer's history?* We, as parents, shared background information on Jennifer, including her educational history, triumphs, challenges, and key milestones in her life.
- *What are your dreams for Jennifer?* Everyone shared their great expectations and dreams for Jennifer's future. It was surprising how much similarity there was in everyone's dreams for

Jennifer. These dreams included living in a house in the community, having a job, socializing with friends, and participating in a variety of community activities.

- *What are your nightmares?* Although this question was difficult for us as parents to contemplate, it is essential that families identify and face potential barriers to the realization of their dreams for their children with disabilities. This question allows the planning participants to identify the necessary supports. For my family, our greatest nightmare has always been that Jennifer would not have friends who freely choose to spend time with her.
- *Who is Jennifer?* Everyone was asked to think of words that describe Jennifer. After we developed a lengthy list, the facilitator asked us to choose the words that best described Jennifer: *good listener, joyful, music lover, vocal,* and *always there for you.*

- *What are Jennifer's strengths, gifts, and talents?* Too often, educational planning meetings for students with disabilities dwell on negatives, deficits, and what the student cannot do. All of the participants were asked to discuss what Jennifer can do, what she likes to do, and what she does well. This established a positive atmosphere for the session and fueled our sense of hope and optimism.

- *What are Jennifer's needs?* This question required the participants to consider what it would take to make everyone's dreams and expectations for Jennifer's future come true. After we identified several needs, the facilitator asked us to prioritize those needs. Identifying those needs served as the basis for developing Jennifer's educational program.

- *What is Jennifer's plan of action? What would Jennifer's ideal school day look like?* This question encouraged the participants to identify the specific steps that needed to happen in order to accomplish our goals. Specific school services and supports were identified. The plan of action involved specific tasks, time lines, resources, and personal responsibilities to implement Jennifer's plan.

After addressing these seven questions, the facilitator concluded the session by asking each participant to describe, in one word, the MAPS process. The words contributed by Jennifer's MAPS participants were *exhausting, exciting, hopeful, focused, eye-opening, helpful, horizons, overwhelmed, vision, team, ecstatic,* and *joyful.* The MAPS process served as a helpful prelude to the IEP meeting that occurred two weeks later. Educational priorities and necessary services were clearly identified prior to the IEP meeting. MAPS is a positive, empowering process that actively involves families in educational decision making.

Parent Monitoring of Educational Programming and Progress

If a trusting and effective professional/parent partnership has been established by the time the IEP is developed, the parent monitoring role should be easily accomplished and successful. The law envisions parents as the primary enforcers of school compliance with special education mandates and procedures. In their monitoring capacity, parents must focus on two central issues concerning implementation and appropriateness of the educational plan: (1) Is the educational plan being carried out? Is the classroom instruction following the IEP? Are the required related services being provided? and (2) Is the plan working well for the child? Is the classroom setting truly appropriate for the child's needs? Is the child making educational progress in school? (Anderson, Chitwood, & Hayden, 1997, p. 199). The following useful techniques for monitoring IEPs were cited by Anderson and colleagues (1997):

- *Holding conferences.* Whenever a parent is concerned about any aspect of a child's education, he or she should consider requesting a conference with the professionals involved. An IEP can be changed at any time; furthermore, the law only establishes a minimum of at least one IEP meeting per year. If requested, parents and professionals can conduct as many IEP conferences as necessary to ensure an appropriate educational experience for a student with a disability. When parents meet with professionals about their educational concerns, it is important to keep a written record of the dates of meetings, topics discussed, and outcomes.

- *Making classroom observations.* Parents can gather firsthand information in relation to their concerns or questions by visiting their child's classroom. Most parents have a keen sense of what type of an educational setting will best meet their child's instructional and learning needs. For example, parents generally know what kind of classroom atmosphere is most conducive to their child's learning, or whether their child benefits from cooperative learning activities or one-to-one instruction, or whether a highly structured instructional approach or more independent learning activities are most beneficial. Many of these classroom environment factors can be assessed through a focused classroom observation.

- *Exchanging a notebook.* Professionals and parents can share daily comments, suggestions, observations, and concerns with each other via a notebook that the child carries to and from school. If the parents are particularly concerned about the child's social skills progress, a checklist can be devised to solicit daily feedback from school personnel on social skills performance. Similar checklists or behavioral monitoring sheets can be developed for any IEP objective about which the parents are concerned.

- *Talking with one's child.* Parents can gain relevant monitoring information from their child by spending some time each day reviewing the day's activities and homework. Instead of asking general and vague questions such as "How did school go today?" parents should focus on specific IEP goals and objectives when seeking feedback from their child. For example, if one of the IEP objectives is to teach the student how to use and manage an assignment notebook for better tracking of assignment due dates, the parents should ask the student to show them the assignment notebook. As another example, if an IEP goal is to increase the student's oral reading rate and accuracy, the parents should ask the student to orally read a few paragraphs from one of his or her textbooks. Parents could keep track of reading rate and accuracy by periodically taking 3- to 5-minute oral reading samples. The work of being a parent advocate is a never-ending responsibility. One of the most important parent advocacy duties is to monitor educational services to ensure the delivery of an appropriate education for the child.

SUMMARY

A professional disposition that values family support and empowerment is essential in establishing respectful, collaborative professional/family partnerships. Educational advocacy efforts on behalf of children with disabilities are enhanced when professionals and parents join forces. Empowered families possess the requisite motivation, knowledge, and skills to function as effective advocates for their children. Professionals foster family empowerment by understanding family needs and strengths from a family systems perspective. In addition, professionals support and empower families by addressing advocacy training needs, including information on legal rights, basic advocacy skills, effective assertive communication, and strategies for parental participation in evaluation, IEP development, and educational monitoring procedures.

CHAPTER 5

KNOWLEDGE OF SPECIAL
EDUCATION LAW

Knowledge is of two kinds. We know a subject ourselves,
or we know where we can find information upon it.
—Samuel Johnson

This chapter addresses both kinds of knowledge noted by Samuel Johnson. First, it is imperative that special education professionals possess a solid working knowledge of special education law if they aspire to function as effective advocates. Knowledge of special education law is even more essential considering the Council for Exceptional Children (CEC) Standards for Professional Practice 1.4.1.5, which states that special education professionals should inform parents of the educational rights of their children and of any proposed or actual practices that violate those rights (CEC, 1983). Following a brief discussion of the four sources of law (constitutional law, statutory law, regulatory law, and case law), this chapter organizes the knowledge of special education law according to the six major legal principles: (1) zero reject, (2) nondiscriminatory evaluation, (3) free and appropriate education, (4) least restrictive environment, (5) procedural due process, and (6) parent participation (Turnbull, 1993). A question-and-answer format will be used in presenting the six major principles of special education law.

Second, this chapter also addresses the sources of special education law and briefly describes some basic legal research tools and strategies. Thus, professionals can develop skills to find information about special education statutes and regulations. Professionals desiring a more thorough understanding of special education law than is provided in this chapter should consult any of the textbooks solely devoted to that topic (see Figure 5.1).

Given the importance of law in governing everyday activities and relations among people, and especially given the prominent place held by legal rules and regulations in securing educational rights for children with disabilities, why are so many nonlawyers intimidated by the law and legal procedures? Riley (1976) noted that the three ancient "learned professions"—law, medicine, and divinity—have a mystique about them. This mystique, unfortunately, makes the law remote to most nonlawyer parents and professionals. Professionals and parents are often mystified and intimidated by the law and legal procedures, and therefore see themselves as unable to take action to correct educational injustices. However, law is too important to leave understanding and access to it in the hands of a small minority of individuals (i.e., lawyers). Of course, it is unrealistic for nonlawyers, after reading only one chapter on the subject, to become legal experts on special education law. It is feasible, however, for nonlegally trained professionals to develop what Postman and Weingartner (1969) referred to as effective "crap-detecting" skills. That is, if a professional or parent possesses a basic understanding of the six major principles of special education law, he or she ought to be able to detect

FIGURE 5.1   Special Education Textbooks

Garfinkel, L. (1995). *Legal issues in transitioning students*. Horsham, PA: LRP Publications.

Gorn, S. (1996). *What do I do when . . . The answer book on special education law*. Horsham, PA: LRP Publications.

Grzywacz, P., & Vandegrift, K. (1998). *Early childhood law and policy: 1998 desk book*. Horsham, PA: LRP Publications.

McEllistrem, S., Roth, J. A., Cox, G. (Eds.). (1998). *Students with disabilities and special education* (15th ed.). Rosemount, MN: Date Research, Inc.

Osborne, A. G. (1996). *Legal issues in special education*. Boston: Allyn and Bacon.

Pitasky, V., & Grzywacz, P. (1998). *The special educator: 1998 desk book*. Horsham, PA: LRP Publications.

Rothstein, L. F. (1995). *Special education law* (2nd ed.). New York: Longman.

Ruesch, G. (Ed.). (1997). *Special education law and practice: A manual for the special education practitioner*. Horsham, PA: LRP Publications.

Turnbull, H. R. (1998). *Free appropriate public education: The law and children with disabilities* (5th ed.). Denver: Love Publishing.

Underwood, J. K., & Mead, J. M. (1995). *Legal aspects of special education and pupil services*. Boston: Allyn and Bacon.

Yell, M. L. (1998). *The law and special education*. Upper Saddle River, NJ: Merrill/Prentice-Hall.

---

violations of legal mandates. With this knowledge, effective advocacy activities may result in legal compliance.

Two additional issues contribute to the law's mystique and inaccessibility to nonlawyers. First, Kauffman (1984) expressed concern about the overlegalization of special education. He was sharply critical of the special education profession's tendency to turn over questions of ethical judgment or educational programming to attorneys and the legalistic methods of the due process hearing system. By applying a solid understanding of special education law and by exercising their advocacy responsibilities, special education professionals can assume leadership in shaping educational policy and practice instead of allowing attorneys to possess that control. This issue will be discussed more fully in Chapter 6.

The second issue relates to a fundamental assumption that the U.S. adversarial legal system is based on the notion that justice will prevail in an adversarial legal system where the two opposing sides are relatively equal in strength and resources (Riley, 1976). What this means with respect to formal legal disputes in special education is that both sides—the school district and parents of children with disabilities—must have equal access to the due process hearing procedures to ensure that justice will prevail.

The reality is that equal access to the special education due process hearing system does not exist in this country. Families face significant financial burdens in accessing the due process hearing system (Fiedler, 1993). In due process disputes, school districts are either represented by an attorney or by trained school personnel who present the district's case with backup legal assistance available if required. In such a scenario, parents usually feel compelled to have legal representation, yet many cannot afford such representation. Research findings have consistently revealed that the due process hearing system is accessible to middle- and upper-socioeconomic families and parents who are Caucasian and highly educated (Budoff & Orenstein, 1981; Goldberg, 1989; Strickland, 1983).

Parental access to the due process hearing system may have improved with the passage of the Handicapped Children's Protection Act (HCPA) in 1986 (this statute is discussed later in the section on procedural due process and parent participation principles), which allows parents to be reimbursed for their attorney fees if they are the prevailing party in a special education dispute. However, even with the possibility of reimbursement as provided by the HCPA, parents still assume financial risks, which may serve as barriers to due process hearing access. For example, parents receive no reimbursement for their attorney fees if they lose the dispute. Further, as a result of the IDEA Amendments of 1997, parents may not be reimbursed fees for their attorney's participation in the IEP process or in mediation sessions prior to filing of a due process hearing. Therefore, this basic lack of equal access denies adequate due process rights of minority parents and families from lower socioeconomic backgrounds (Salend & Zirkel, 1984).

Professionals who possess a basic knowledge of special education law and function as child and family advocates can help restore more equal status and access to the due process hearing system by informing parents of their legal rights and of the procedures for enforcing those rights. In addition, special education professionals can collaborate with and refer families to a variety of organizations designed to advocate for the rights of children with disabilities. These organizations include Parent Training and Information Programs, state protection and advocacy agencies, parent support groups, legal services agencies, and a multitude of state and national disability organizations. For a listing of many of these organizations see *Negotiating the Special Education Maze: A Guide for Parents and Teachers* (1997) by Anderson, Chitwood, and Hayden.

SOURCES OF LAW AND LEGAL RESEARCH TOOLS

There are four sources of law that comprise special education legal mandates and procedures: constitutional law, statutory law, regulatory law, and case law. Each of these four sources exist on both the federal and state levels. The relationships between these four sources of law are succinctly explained by Yell (1998):

> The supreme laws are contained in federal and state constitutions (i.e., constitutional law), and these constitutions empower legislatures to create law

> *(i.e., statutory law). Legislatures in turn delegate lawmaking authority to regulatory agencies to create regulations that implement the law (i.e., regulatory law). Finally, courts interpret laws through cases, and these interpretations of law accumulate to form case law. (p. 2)*

This section will address the four sources of law.

Constitutional Law

The supreme law of the land is the Constitution of the United States. The Constitution establishes the basic parameters of our federal system of government and allocates power and responsibility among the legislative, executive, and judicial branches of government. All federal and state statutes, administrative regulations, and judicial decisions establishing case law are subject to the provisions of the U.S. Constitution. Statutes, administrative regulations, or governmental practices in conflict with the Constitution may be declared by a court to be unacceptable (i.e., unconstitutional). For example, in the famous case in 1954, *Brown* v. *Board of Education,* the U.S. Supreme Court determined that state action in segregating children by race in public education violated (was unconstitutional) the equal protection clause of the Fourteenth Amendment.

Although the U.S. Constitution does not specifically guarantee a right to a free public education, the Constitution bears directly on the rights of children with disabilities. Providing an education to the public is a matter left to the states via the Tenth Amendment to the Constitution. All state constitutions have public educational mandates. Once a state guarantees its citizens a public education, the state must do so in a manner that is in accordance with the principles established by the U.S. Constitution. Specifically, primarily through the equal protection clause of the Fourteenth Amendment, states must not discriminate against children with disabilities in the provision of public educational services. That is, children with disabilities have the same equal right to participate in public education as children without disabilities.

Statutory Law

The U.S. Constitution bestows Congress with the authority to make laws. The laws enacted by Congress and state legislatures are called *statutes*. Federal and state statutes are the most direct and influential source of law affecting the delivery of educational services to children with disabilities. Statutes tend to be broad and general in scope and language. The primary federal statute mandating educational services for children with disabilities is the Individuals with Disabilities Education Act (IDEA) originally passed in 1975 and, most recently, reauthorized and amended in 1997. States also have statutes mandating educational services for children with disabilities. State statutes must be compatible with constitutional principles and requirements in IDEA.

Federal statutes are organized by topic and published in a series of volumes called the *United States Code (U.S.C.)*. Each title of the *U.S.C.* contains the statutes that cover a specific subject. For instance, Title 20 contains education statutes, including IDEA. Title 29 contains labor statutes, and that is where one would find another important federal law for individuals with disabilities: Section 504 of the Rehabilitation Act of 1973. The Americans with Disabilities Act (ADA) is published in Title 42, which contains public health and welfare statutes. Every statute is referenced by a citation, which is how one finds a particular statute. For example, the legal citation for the Individuals with Disabilities Education Act is: **20 U.S.C. Sec. 1401 (20).** Using this legal citation, you can locate the IDEA statute by looking in Title 20 of the *United States Code* and turning to section 1401. The text of IDEA begins at section 1400 and ends at section 1485. The (20) after 1401 refers to a subsection of that particular section. Each volume of the *U.S.C.* has a table of contents where one may locate page numbers for particular statutory sections. Yell's (1998) book, cited in Figure 5.1, contains excellent chapters on legal research and legal research on the Internet, which includes lists of discussion groups and websites related to special education law.

Regulatory Law

Since statutes are broad and general in scope and language, Congress and state legislatures designate authority to the appropriate governmental administrative agencies to promulgate specific regulations to implement the statutes. These agencies operate in the executive branch of government. At the federal level, any statute pertaining to education (e.g., IDEA) is administered by the U.S. Department of Education, which is the regulatory agency responsible for developing and implementing rules and regulations. Administrative regulations have the force of law.

In addition to promulgating regulations to implement statutes, administrative agencies also function in a quasi-judicial capacity by monitoring state (monitored by the U.S. Department of Education) and local education agency (monitored by state departments of education) compliance with special education statutes and regulations and by making rulings interpreting specific statutory and regulatory mandates. In the U.S. Department of Education, the Office of Special Education and Rehabilitation Services (OSERS) and the Office of Special Education Programs (OSEP) rule on special education matters. The Office of Civil Rights (OCR) investigates and rules on violations of Section 504 of the Rehabilitation Act of 1973.

Federal administrative regulations are published in a multivolume series of books called the *Code of Federal Regulations (C.F.R.)*. The *C.F.R.* is organized by subject. Each *C.F.R.* title covers a general subject area. Regulations pertaining to education are located in Title 34 of the *C.F.R.* With each *C.F.R.* title, there is a reference to the statute that authorized the regulation. Like the statutes, regulations have legal citations to assist in locating a particular regulation. For example, **34 C.F.R. Sec. 300.500(a)(1)** is a reference to the IDEA regulations. These regulations are located in Title 34 of the *Code of Federal Regulations,* beginning at section number 300. There is a general subject index to the *C.F.R.* to locate specific regulations by topic area.

Case Law

Case law is the product of published judicial decisions resulting from litigation involving families and school districts. There is a federal court system and a state court system. There are three levels in the federal court system: United States district courts (trial courts; every state has at least one federal district court), United States courts of appeals (11 circuits, the District of Columbia, and one dealing with special patent and copyright issues), and the United States Supreme Court. Generally, the federal court system is used when a dispute involves a constitutional issue or a federal statute, although the basis for determining which court to use is a most complex issue (Turnbull, 1993). The state court systems vary; however, many states have a judicial structure similar to the federal system. Case law is based on the English tradition of common law and is ever evolving as courts decide new issues every day. The scope and influence of a court decision is based on two factors: (1) the place in the judicial hierarchy of the court (U.S. Supreme Court cases have more influence than lower court cases) and (2) the cumulative influence established through a series of decisions that when considered together establish a trend or precedent.

Published decisions of the U.S. District Courts are collected in a reporter called the *Federal Supplement.* An example of a district court case citation is **Stuart v. Nappi, 443 F. Supp. 1235 (D. Conn. 1978).** This citation provides a lot of information. It indicates that this is a federal district court case, because it is published in the *Federal Supplement* (abbreviated *F. Supp.*), from Connecticut, and the case was decided in 1978. The text of the court's decision is located in volume 443 of the *Federal Supplement* reporter series beginning on page 1235.

Published decisions of the U.S. Courts of Appeals are collected in a reporter called the *Federal Reporter,* which is now in its third edition. An example of a court of appeals court case citation is **Daniel R.R. v. State Board of Education, 874 F.2d 1036 (5th Cir. 1989).** Based on this legal citation, it is apparent that this is a federal circuit court of appeals case, because it is published in the *Federal Reporter* second series (abbreviated *F.2d*). This case was decided by the Fifth Circuit Court of Appeals in 1989. The text of the decision is located in volume 874 of the *Federal Reporter* second series beginning on page 1036.

Judicial decisions of the U.S. Supreme Court are published in three different sources. The official reporter of Supreme Court decisions is the *United States Court Reports* (abbreviated *U.S.*). The other two reporters are the *Supreme Court Reporter* (abbreviated *S.Ct.*), published by West Publishing Company, and *Supreme Court Reports, Lawyers' Edition* (abbreviated *L.Ed.*), published by Bancroft-Whitney/Lawyers' Cooperative. An example of a U.S. Supreme Court case citation is **Board of Education of the Hendrick Hudson School District v. Rowley, 458 U.S. 176 (1982).** This case citation signifies it is a 1982 U.S. Supreme Court decision, because it is published by the *United States Court Reports (U.S.)* and is located in volume 458 of the *United States Court Reports* beginning on page 176.

The intent of this section was to outline briefly the four sources of law, to show the relationship between the three branches of government, and to identify some legal finding tools for federal statutes, administrative regulations, and court cases. There are many excellent resources on how to do legal research, including the use of computers (see Figure 5.2). Finally, it is critical that special education professionals serving as advocates have access to updated information on legal issues. Figure 5.3 contains some examples of law-related resources, including websites, that provide updated information on special education legal issues.

ZERO REJECT PRINCIPLE

The zero reject principle of special education law is philosophically premised on the democratic notion that every person is valuable and should be afforded equal opportunities to develop their full potential (Burgdorf, 1980). The constitutional foundation for zero reject is the equal protection

FIGURE 5.2   Legal Research Resources

Cohen, M. L., Berring, R. C., & Olson, K. C. (1989). *How to find the law* (9th ed.). St. Paul, MN: West Publishing Company.

Cohen, M. L., & Olson, K. C. (1992). *Legal research in a nutshell.* St. Paul, MN: West Publishing Company.

Elias, S., & Levinkind, S. (1992). *How to find and understand the law* (3rd ed.). Berkeley, CA: Nolo Press.

Jacobstein, J. M., & Mersky, R. M. (1990). *Fundamentals of legal research* (5th ed.). Mineola, NY: Foundation Press.

Johnson, N. P., Berring, R. C., & Woxland, T. A. (1991). *Winning research skills.* St. Paul, MN: West Publishing Company.

FIGURE 5.3   Resources for Updated Information on Special Education Legal Issues

Print Resources

West's Education Law Reporter
Journal of Law and Education
Index to Legal Periodicals
Individuals with Disabilities Education Law Reporter
The Special Educator (published by LRP Publications)
Special Education Law Update (published by Data Research, Inc.)

Internet Websites

Axis Disability Rights Website
(http://www.island.net/~axis)
Contains articles related to advocacy, inclusion, and other special education issues.

Council for Disability Rights
(http://www.disabilityrights.org/)
Contains information on the Americans with Disabilities Act (ADA) and a parent's guide to special education.

Disability Resources on the Internet
(http://www.geocities.com/~drm/)
Contains information on Supplemental Security Income (SSI) and legislative updates.

Disability Rights Activist
(http://www.teleport.com/~abarhydt/index.html)
Contains lots of information to foster advocacy on behalf of individuals with disabilities.

Internet Law Library (http://law.house.gov/102.htm)

National Parent Network on Disabilities
(http://www.npnd.org/boutnpnd.htm)
Contains the Friday Fax, which addresses current disability issues, as well as the Monday Memos, which provides updated information. Links to IDEA legal issues and parent training and information centers.

Technical Assistance Alliance for Parent Programs
(http://www.taalliance.org)
Contains legislative updates.

EdLaw (http://www.access.digex.net/~edlawinc/)
Contains special education statutes and regulations, links to disability law on the Internet, and provides analysis on special education legal issues.

Thomas Legislative Information
(http://thomas.loc.gov/)
Maintained by the Library of Congress to provide access to a number of federal databases, including bills introduced in Congress, the Congressional Record, and U.S. Government Internet resources.

The Council for Exceptional Children
(http://cec.sped.org/home.htm)
Contains links to the ERIC Clearinghouse on Disabilities and Gifted Education, the National Clearinghouse for Professions in Special Education, and legislative information.

The National Center for Children and Youth with Disabilities (http://www.aed.org/nichy/)
Contains information on a variety of disability and law issues and information searches.

The Special Ed Advocate (http://www.wrightslaw.com)
The Special Ed Advocate is a free online newsletter about special education legal issues, cases, tactics and strategy, effective educational methods, and Internet links.

Advocating for the Child (http:/www2.crosswinds.net/washington-dc/~advocate/)
Contains a wealth of information on special education legal rights, responsibilities, and procedures.

clause of the Fourteenth Amendment, which provides that no state may deny to any person within its jurisdiction equal protection of the laws (Turnbull, 1993). Therefore, if a free public education is provided to children without disabilities, access to the same public service must be provided to children with disabilities. This means that *all* students with disabilities eligible for services under the IDEA are entitled to a free appropriate public education.

According to zero reject, the state must ensure that all students with disabilities ages birth to 21 in need of special education and related services are identified, evaluated, and educated. Through "child find" activities, local education agencies are affirmatively responsible, even if the parents fail to notify the school district, to locate, identify, and evaluate children birth to age 21 who are suspected of having disabilities (Gorn, 1996). As indicated by Yell (1998), "A school district's child find system can take many forms. One method is the general public notice. . . . Additional methods that may be used to locate and identify children with disabilities include referrals, public meetings, door-to-door visits, home and community visits, brochures, speakers, contacting pediatricians, contacting day care providers, kindergarten screening, and public awareness efforts" (p. 76).

In interpreting the zero reject principle, the courts have encountered a variety of legal issues. Relevant legal issues decided by the courts according to the zero reject principle include basic eligibility provisions, educability, residential and private school placements, minimum competency testing, and disciplinary sanctions including suspension and expulsion.

Who is eligible for special education services under the IDEA? The determination of student eligibility for special education and related services is made on an individual basis by the multidisciplinary team in accordance with the categorical eligibility criteria in the law. Students are eligible for special education and related services (1) if they meet one or more of the 13 categorical disability criteria: autism, deaf-blindness, deafness, hearing impairment, mental retardation, multiple disabilities, orthopedic impairments, other health impaired, emotional disturbance, specific learning disability, speech or language impairment, traumatic brain injury, and visual impairment, including blindness; and (2) if the student's disability has an adverse impact on their education and they therefore require special education services.

States have an absolute obligation to provide special education to qualified students with disabilities between the ages of 6 to 17. Most states provide special education services to students with disabilities between ages 3 to 5 and ages 18 to 21. In addition, Part C of IDEA provides incentive grants to states to operate a system of early intervention services for infants and toddlers with disabilities from birth through age 2. Infants and toddlers are eligible for early special education services if they are diagnosed as "developmentally delayed" (meaning a developmental delay in one or more of these areas: cognitive development, physical development [including vision and hearing], language and speech development, psychosocial development, and self-help skills).

A school district's obligation to provide special education services to qualified students with disabilities terminates when the student (1) graduates with a diploma, (2) successfully completes an appropriate IEP leading to graduation, or (3) voluntarily drops out of school. Graduation, however, cannot be used as a means to terminate the school's obligation to provide special education services. In such situations, school districts can be required to supply compensatory educational services beyond the age of 21.

Are some children so severely disabled that they are totally ineducable and therefore not entitled to protection of the IDEA? In *Timothy W.* v. *Rochester, New Hampshire School District* (1989), a U.S. Circuit Court of Appeals ruled that a severely disabled student (Timothy W. was a 13-year-old boy who was blind and deaf, profoundly mentally retarded, had cerebral palsy, was spastic with frequent convulsions, had no communication skills, lacked carotid tissue, and was described as operating "at the brainstem level") was entitled to special education and related services under the IDEA without any exception. In fact, as noted by the court, students with the most severe disabilities were actually given priority under the law. This case strongly reaffirmed the basic tenets of the zero reject principle.

Are school districts obligated to pay for residential placements of students with disabilities?   In many cases, courts have found that residential placements were necessary to provide a free appropriate public education (FAPE) and required the school district to pay the costs (including nonmedical care and room and board) associated with those placements. In such cases, the courts have viewed the residential placement as a related service (the concept of a related service is discussed more fully later in this chapter) that is necessary for a student with a disability to receive benefit from special education. However, if an appropriate educational program exists in the public school system, the school district will not be obligated to pay for a residential placement.

There has been no clear judicial decision when the residential placement consists primarily of psychiatric services. Some courts have viewed such services as medical services, which are excluded related services, and the school district was not obligated to fund those services. Some courts have attempted to separate educational costs of residential placements from the noneducational costs and to hold the school district liable for only the educational costs. Most cases involving residential placements where the school district was obligated to pay the costs involved students in need of intensive care for severe emotional and behavioral disorders.

Are public school districts obligated to provide special education services to students with disabilities whose parents enroll them in private schools?   Case law clearly dictates that when parents unilaterally place their children with disabilities into a private school in an attempt to receive an appropriate education, if the court finds

that the public school district failed to provide an appropriate education, the parents are entitled to tuition reimbursement for the costs of the private school placement (*Burlington School Committee v. Department of Education,* 1985). If a private school student is eligible for special education, the public school district must develop an IEP that provides a FAPE and provide an opportunity for equitable participation in special education (Mentink, 1991). The IDEA Amendments of 1997 clarified that school districts are not required to pay for private school placements if a FAPE has been made available to a student in the public school setting.

A separate question is whether public schools must provide special education services to private school students onsite at the private school, at a neutral site, or at the public school. This issue of location of special education service delivery is a matter of interpreting what is meant by the legal requirement to "provide an equitable participation in special education." On this issue, the courts are presently divided.

Does the Constitution permit public schools to use funds for special education services to students with disabilities attending private parochial (church-affiliated) schools?   This question raises the issue of the establishment clause of the First Amendment and required governmental neutrality in relation to religious groups. If special education services are made available to students in parochial schools, such services may be construed as aid to a particular religious group in violation of the First Amendment.

Prior to 1993, as a result of U.S. Supreme Court rulings in *Lemon* v. *Kurtzman* (1971) and *Aguilar* v. *Felton* (1985), public schools provided special education services to parochial school students (1) by transporting those students to a local public school for a portion of the school day or (2) by providing special education services at a neutral site off the grounds of the parochial school. These actions were permissible under the establishment clause of the First Amendment. It was deemed unconstitutional to provide public-paid teachers or personnel to directly provide special education services onsite at the parochial school.

In 1993, in *Zobrest* v. *Catalina Foothills School District,* the Supreme Court ruled that there was no general prohibition against providing special education services onsite at parochial schools. In *Zobrest,* the Supreme Court authorized the public school funding of a sign language interpreter for a deaf high school student attending a parochial school. The Court ruled that the student, not the parochial school, was the primary beneficiary of the public school's funds; therefore, the First Amendment was not violated. In allowing the provision of an interpreter onsite at the parochial school, the Court left open the issue of whether other support services could be provided by public funded personnel, such as teachers or counselors.

The impact of the *Zobrest* decision was seemingly expanded in 1997 when the Supreme Court reversed the *Aguilar* decision; thus permitting federally funded programs and personnel that provide supplemental and remedial instruction to disadvantaged students to do so onsite at parochial schools (*Agostini* v. *Felton*). The Court held that the primary beneficiaries of the public funded services were the parochial students, not the religious affiliated school. Further, the Court noted there were sufficient safeguards in place to ensure that the public employees would not inculcate their religious beliefs on the parochial students. It is, however, still somewhat unclear the exact extent to which the public funded special education support services can be constitutionally provided onsite at parochial schools.

Do school districts who deny graduation diplomas to special education students who fail to pass the state's minimum competency test (MCT) deprive such students of a free appropriate education? With increasing frequency in the past 10 years, most states require, as a condition of receiving a high school diploma, that students pass a minimum competency test (MCT). The use of MCTs has been spawned by demands for greater school accountability for student learning and as an effort to restore some significance to the receipt of a high school diploma. Courts have consistently ruled that the denial of a diploma to a special education student who fails a MCT does not constitute a denial of FAPE (*Brookhart* v. *Illinois State Board of Education,* 1983).

Schools are required to provide reasonable accommodations to allow students with disabilities to take a MCT; however, this does not require school districts to substantially modify the content of a MCT to the point of negating the purpose of this requirement. The IEP meeting is the appropriate venue for determining whether a student with a disability requires any testing accommodations, and, if so, those accommodations (e.g., student response accommodations, changes in the test setting, allowing for more time, etc.) should be listed in the IEP (Ysseldyke, Thurlow, McGrew, & Vanderwood, 1994). Further, if the IEP committee decides that the student should not participate in the MCT, the IEP must include a statement of why the MCT is inappropriate and how the student will be alternatively assessed.

What are the basic rights of students faced with disciplinary sanctions of school suspension or expulsion? The due process clause of the Fifth and Fourteenth Amendments to the U.S. Constitution provides that the state may not deprive any person of "life, liberty or property without due process of law." In the context of school disciplinary sanctions, the U.S. Supreme Court has held that due process applies to all students, with and without disabilities, when they are threatened with suspension or expulsion (*Goss* v. *Lopez,* 1975). In *Goss,* the Court ruled that a student's entitlement to a public education (right to attend school) is a property interest that is protected by the due process clause of the Fifth and Fourteenth Amendments. This due process protection requires the school to adhere to certain procedural protections prior to imposing a short-term (less than 10 days) school suspension:

— Written or oral notice of the charges (the misbehavior or conduct for which the school is threatening suspension)

- Opportunity for the student to respond to the charges (which may occur in either a formal or informal meeting)

When threatened with a long-term suspension (more than 10 days) or expulsion, since this disciplinary sanction is more severe than short-term suspensions, students are accorded more extensive and formal due process protections, including the following:

- Written notice specifying the charges
- Notice of the evidence, witnesses, and substance of their testimony
- A formal hearing (usually conducted by the school board) with an advance notice of the time, place, and procedures to be followed
- The right to confront witnesses and present their own witnesses
- A written or taped record of the hearing proceedings
- The right of appeal

Once the school district has adhered to these procedural protections, if a decision is rendered finding a student committed the charged misbehavior, and if school officials decide that suspension or expulsion is an appropriate punishment, the school may implement its suspension or expulsion punishment. (Specific IDEA protections for students with disabilities threatened with long-term suspension or expulsion are discussed on page 75.) Two caveats are important here: (1) brief in-school sanctions (e.g., after-school detention or in-school suspension) do not require due process procedures; and (2) dangerous students may be immediately removed from school with the due process procedures subsequently applied.

What disciplinary sanctions are legally permissible and do not require due process procedural protections? If a disciplinary sanction is relatively minor and unobtrusive, part of the school district's discipline plan, commonly used with all students, and does not result in a change of educational placement or a denial of FAPE for students with disabilities, courts allow school officials to employ those sanctions. Examples of permitted

disciplinary sanctions include contingent observation procedures where the student is temporarily removed to a classroom location where the student can observe but not participate in class activities, detention, exclusionary timeout, verbal reprimands, response cost procedures where students lose points or privileges for misbehavior, restriction of privileges, warnings, the temporary delay or withdrawal of activities such as recess or lunch, and emergency procedures such as physical restraint.

What disciplinary sanctions are legally permissible provided the school practices appropriate procedures in implementing such sanctions? The disciplinary sanction of seclusion/isolation timeout requires a student to leave the classroom and spend a brief amount of time in a separate timeout room. If a school excessively uses timeout procedures for long periods of time, courts have held that a student's right to an education is violated in such situations. However, if the school follows established policies that outline timeout procedures, if behavior management plans specifying the use of timeout are incorporated into IEPs, and if school officials document the use of timeout, courts permit the application of timeout as a disciplinary sanction.

In-school suspension (ISS) sanctions are legally permissible if the school district (1) has a written policy informing students and parents what specific behaviors may result in an ISS, (2) provides students with a warning prior to imposing an ISS sanction, (3) informs parents when their children are placed in ISS, (4) supervises students in ISS with a teacher or paraprofessional, (5) documents the use of ISS, and (6) continues to provide students in ISS with an appropriate education (meaning students with disabilities are engaged in appropriate academic work addressing IEP goals and objectives).

What is the legal status of corporal punishment as a form of discipline? Although the U.S. Supreme Court in *Ingraham* v. *Wright* (1977) held that public schools may use corporal punishment without violating any constitutional provisions, slightly more than one-half of the states now have statutes that prohibit the practice of corporal punishment in public schools. Even in states where corporal punishment is legal, it must be applied in a reasonable manner. Corporal punishment that is brutal or excessively demeaning has been held by many courts to be a violation of a student's due process rights.

Can a student with a disability be suspended on a long-term basis or expelled from a public school? Courts view long-term suspensions (more than 10 school days) and expulsions of students with disabilities as a change of educational placement and schools are legally prohibited from unilaterally making placement changes. Therefore, prior to any attempt to expel or suspend a student with a disability on a long-term basis, schools would need to convene an IEP team meeting to consider such action. If the IEP team (including the parents) concluded that the student's misbehavior and disability were not related and the student received an appropriately implemented IEP, long-term suspensions and expulsions are legal. However, as noted later on this page, school districts are required to continue special education services to legally suspended or expelled students with disabilities.

The process of conducting this IEP team review of any relationship between the student's misbehavior and his or her disability is called a *manifestation determination*. This manifestation determination is now required by the 1997 IDEA amendments. The manifestation determination is based on the notion that students should not be denied special education services because of misbehavior that is caused by their disability (Dagley, McGuire, & Evans, 1994). A legally correct manifestation determination should address the following questions (Yell, 1998):

- *Is the IEP appropriate?*
- *Is the IEP being implemented as written?*
- *Did the disability prevent the student from understanding the impact and consequences of behavior?*
- *Did the disability prevent the student from controlling the behavior? (p. 335)*

If the IEP team determines that either a relationship between the student's misbehavior and disability exists, or that the IEP was inappropriate or not appropriately implemented, the student may not be expelled or suspended on a long-term basis. However, school officials are permitted to initiate change-of-placement procedures and seek a more restrictive educational placement.

Are schools required to continue special education services during long-term suspension or expulsion? Yes, the 1997 IDEA Amendments require that special education services be continued to legally suspended or expelled students with disabilities. If schools do not continue services, students will be denied their right to a FAPE. The effect, therefore, of a legally valid long-term suspension or expulsion decision is to restrict the location (i.e., the public school) of where a student with disabilities receives special education services, not the total denial of special education services. Special education services may, however, be discontinued for short-term (less than 10 days) suspensions.

What are legally permissible procedures for schools to use when dealing with students with disabilities who present a danger to themselves or others? First, school officials can legally implement an emergency suspension for up to 10 days without having to conduct a manifestation determination. Second, the IEP team may be convened to seek a change of placement to a more restrictive setting. Third, if the parents refuse a more restrictive educational placement, school officials may seek an injunction from a due process hearing officer to remove a student from the school environment to a more restrictive setting.

In *Light* v. *Parkway School District* (1994), a U.S. Court of Appeals established a two-part test to determine the appropriateness of issuing an injunction to remove a dangerous student from school to a more restrictive setting: (1) whether maintaining the student in the current educational setting is likely to result in injury to the student or others, and (2) whether the school district made reasonable attempts to minimize the risk of injury. If the school can establish these two points, an injunction is appropriate.

Finally, as a result of 1997 IDEA Amendments, schools may unilaterally place special education students who bring weapons to school or who possess or sell illegal drugs in a more restrictive setting. This unilateral placement is to an interim alternative educational setting for up to 45 days. This interim alternative educational setting must be determined by the IEP team and the student must continue to work on IEP goals and objectives, including the behaviors that caused the new placement.

Does the IDEA provide any disciplinary protection to students not yet determined eligible for special education?   The IDEA Amendments of 1997 provide that students not yet eligible for special education may assert IDEA protection if school district personnel had knowledge that the student had a disability *before* the behavior that led to the disciplinary sanctions. This means that the student's parents made a written request for special education services, or the student's behavior indicated a need for special education or the parents or a teacher requested an evaluation for special education services.

What are the requirements under IDEA for including behavior management plans in IEPs?
According to the IDEA Amendments of 1997, special education students who frequently misbehave must have behavior goals and objectives, including a discipline plan, as part of their IEP. This behavioral intervention plan must be based on a functional behavioral assessment, including proactive positive behavioral supports and interventions.

NONDISCRIMINATORY EVALUATION PRINCIPLE

Due to concerns over the quality of school district evaluation procedures for determining eligibility for special education services, the IDEA contains specific evaluation protections to ensure fair and comprehensive educational evaluations. The importance of accurate, fair, and comprehensive educational evaluations is viewed from a domino perspective. That is, if the eligibility evaluation is flawed, the placement and resulting special education services are likely to be inappropriate. Yell (1998) summarized the evaluation procedures required by IDEA:

- *Tests are provided and administered in the child's native language or mode of communication.*
- *Standardized tests must have been validated for the specific purposes for which they are intended.*
- *Standardized tests are administered by trained personnel in conformity with the publisher's instructions.*
- *The evaluation is tailored to assess the child's specific areas of educational need, including information provided by the parent that may assist in determining disability and the content of the IEP.*
- *Evaluators must use technically sound instruments that assess multiple areas and factors.*
- *No single procedure is used as the sole criterion for determining the presence of a disability, the student's program, or placement.*
- *The evaluation team is comprised of a multidisciplinary team or group of persons, at least one of whom has knowledge in the child's suspected area of disability.*
- *The child is assessed in all areas related to the suspected disability. (p. 78)*

Is parental consent required for a preplacement special education evaluation?   Yes. The school district must notify the parents in writing of its intent to conduct a preplacement evaluation a reasonable amount of time prior to conducting the evaluation. Parents must be informed of their due process rights and the evaluation procedures must be described. If the parents fail to give their written consent for the preplacement evaluation, the school may either (1) abide by the parents' decision and not conduct the evaluation or (2) seek to override the parents' refusal by requesting a due process hearing on this issue.

Schools frequently engage in screenings to determine whether a more comprehensive assessment is necessary. When screenings are conducted on all students in a school, and not selectively on just a few students, the IDEA preplacement evaluation requirements do not apply and parental consent is not required.

What is the effect of prereferral evaluations and interventions on the IDEA preplacement evaluation requirements? Prereferral evaluations and interventions are conducted in general education classrooms in an effort to remediate a student's problem(s) prior to referral for special education. Since prereferral evaluations and interventions are typically informal, the formal preplacement evaluation requirements of IDEA are not mandated. Prereferral interventions, however, may not act to delay the referral of a student for special education (Bateman & Linden, 1998).

Can a school ignore a special education referral or decide not to conduct an IDEA preplacement evaluation? The school cannot simply ignore a special education referral; the referral and accompanying information must be reviewed by school personnel. After reviewing the referral information, however, the multidisciplinary evaluation team (M-team) may decide not to conduct a preplacement evaluation if there is no reasonable basis to suspect that a disability exists. If the school does not conduct an evaluation, the parents must be notified of the reasons for the school action and informed of their due process rights (OSEP Policy Letter, 1994). Parents may appeal this decision by requesting a due process hearing.

Who is required to be a member of the multidisciplinary evaluation team (M-team)? The M-team must include at least one teacher or specialist in the area of the student's suspected disability. Parent participation is allowed but not required (OSEP Policy Letter, 1993). If the student is suspected of having a learning disability, the M-team must also include the student's general education teacher or a person qualified to teach students with learning disabilities, in addition to a person qualified to conduct an individual diagnostic evaluation of the student. All of the M-team's assessment personnel must be qualified in evaluating students with disabilities.

Can IQ tests be used in making special education placement decisions of minority students? A federal district court in California prohibited the use of standardized IQ tests in placing African American students in classes for students with mental retardation (*Larry P.* v. *Riles,* 1979) because the tests were found to be racially and culturally biased. Subsequent court cases, most notably *PASE* v. *Hannon* (1980), ruled that schools could use standardized IQ tests in making special education placement decisions of minority students so long as the IQ tests were not the sole basis for making the placement decisions. Finally, in 1994, a U.S. Court of Appeals lifted the *Larry P.* ban on using IQ tests for placing minority students in special education (*Crawford* v. *Honig*).

What are the multidisciplinary evaluation team's decision-making responsibilities? In deciding special education eligibility, the M-team first determines if, based on all of the information collected and reviewed during the evaluation process, the student meets the criteria for one of the disability categories covered by IDEA. Second, the M-team must determine if, as a result of the disability, the student requires special education and related services. In addition, the M-team must (1) rely on information from a variety of sources, including aptitude and achievement tests, teacher recommendations, physical condition, social or cultural background, and adaptive behavior; (2) carefully document and consider the evaluation information; (3) ensure that decisions are made by a team including a person knowledgeable about the student, the meaning of the evaluation data, and placement options; and (4) ensure that the placement decision is made in compliance with least restrictive environment requirements.

What are the reevaluation requirements for students in special education?   The IDEA requires that special education students be reevaluated at least every three years or more frequently if necessary or if requested by the student's parents or teacher. When a parent requests a reevaluation, the student must be reevaluated unless the school requests a due process hearing to challenge the reevaluation request (Tinsley, 1990). As a result of the IDEA Amendments of 1997, parental consent is now required for a school to conduct a reevaluation. Further, the 1997 Amendments place more emphasis on collecting reevaluation information that is useful in learning how to most effectively teach a student with disabilities, as opposed to merely reaffirming, in many cases, an obvious continuing eligibility decision. If the IEP team decides that additional reevaluation data is unnecessary, the parents must be notified of their right to request a full evaluation.

FREE AND APPROPRIATE PUBLIC EDUCATION (FAPE) PRINCIPLE

Since the advent of special education law, the notion of what constitutes an appropriate education for students with disabilities has proven to be one of the most dynamic and evolving principles of the law. The constitutional bases for free and appropriate public education can be found in the principles of substantive due process under the Fifth and Fourteenth Amendments and on equal protection under the Fourteenth Amendment. Constitutional principles of due process and equal protection are violated when students with disabilities are either (1) totally excluded from the opportunity to receive a public education (see zero reject principle) or (2) functionally excluded from a meaningful educational experience. Functional exclusion is an education that lacks meaning or significance for a student, which is tantamount to no education at all.

The term *special education* is defined in IDEA as "specially designed instruction, at no charge to the parents or guardians, to meet the unique needs of a child with a disability" (IDEA, 20 U.S.C. Sec. 1404(a)(16)). The FAPE requirement has both procedural and substantive components (Guernsey & Klare, 1993). First, there are numerous procedural protections to ensure parent and student participation in educational decision making. Second, the substantive right to a FAPE consists of "special education and related services which (A) have been provided at public expense, under public supervision and direction, and without charge, (B) meet standards of the state educational agency, (C) include an appropriate preschool, elementary, or secondary school education in the state involved, and (D) are provided in conformity with the Individualized Education Program" (IDEA, 20 U.S.C. Sec. 1401(18)(C)).

Numerous issues have engaged the courts in interpreting the requirements of the FAPE mandate. The issues discussed in this section include cost considerations, FAPE standards, procedural requirements, choice of teaching methods, extended school year programming, IEP requirements, parent participation in IEPs, related services, and third-party billing for related services.

Are costs of providing a student with a FAPE a relevant factor in educational decision making? It is clear that schools may not refuse to provide special education services to an eligible student because of the costs of those services. Costs may enter into educational decision making when school personnel are deciding between more than one option or service, all of which will provide a FAPE. In such situations, the school may legally opt for the least costly, yet appropriate, choice. Courts are becoming more conscious of cost considerations.

Is the IEP a legally binding contract? The IEP is not legally binding in terms of guaranteeing that a student will achieve all of the listed goals and objectives by the end of the school year. That is, schools and school personnel cannot be held liable if a student fails to attain specified IEP goals and objectives. The IEP does, however, legally commit the school district to provide the listed special education and related services and to make a good faith attempt to achieve the identified goals and objectives.

What is the Rowley standard for determining a FAPE?   In 1982, the U.S. Supreme Court decided its first-ever case under special education law. In *Board of Education of the Hendrick Hudson School District* v. *Rowley,* the Supreme Court announced a two-part test for determining whether a student with disabilities is receiving a FAPE.

Amy Rowley was a moderately hearing impaired young child whose IEP provided for education in a general education classroom, use of a hearing aid, instruction from a tutor for deaf children for an hour daily, and speech therapy three hours per week. In addition, Amy's parents requested a sign language interpreter for all of Amy's classes. The school refused to provide the sign language interpreter, arguing such services were not necessary in providing Amy with a FAPE. The parents argued that a sign language interpreter was a necessary related service to afford their daughter with a FAPE. The parents requested a due process hearing and the case, ultimately, came before the U.S. Supreme Court.

The Supreme Court developed a two-part test to determine whether a school district has fulfilled its obligation to provide a FAPE to students with disabilities. The first question asks whether all of the procedural requirements of the law have been complied with in developing an IEP. The second question inquires whether the IEP developed through adherence to all of the law's procedural requirements is reasonably calculated to enable the student to receive educational benefits.

In Amy's case, the Supreme Court ruled the school district did adhere to all of the procedural requirements and Amy did receive educational benefits, primarily, as noted by the Court, because she was promoted from grade to grade. She was receiving an appropriate education in the absence of a sign language interpreter. Therefore, Amy was not entitled to a sign language interpreter. The Court clearly announced in *Rowley* that an appropriate education does not mean providing a student with disabilities the "best education" possible.

Cases subsequent to *Rowley* have held that special education services must confer meaningful benefits to the student, not merely minimal or trivial benefits.

What is the effect of a procedural violation in developing a student's IEP on the receipt of a FAPE?   If the procedural violation of the law is technical and causes no harm to the substantive quality of the student's education, courts generally see no reason to grant any judicial relief. In the law, this would be referred to as a *harmless error*. The amount of harm caused to the student's educational experience, then, is the critical factor in determining the impact of any procedural violation. Specifically, courts have invalidated IEPs for procedural violations when the error (1) diminished the student's right to an appropriate education, (2) resulted in the exclusion of the parents from the IEP decision-making process, or (3) caused the student to be denied substantive educational rights.

Is there a denial of a FAPE when the parents object to a particular instructional approach or methodology?   Most courts have held that parents have no authority under the IDEA to compel schools to choose a particular instructional approach or methodology. Therefore, such disagreements do not rise to the level of a denial of a FAPE. In such cases, courts grant considerable discretion to professional judgments because courts are reluctant to involve themselves in second guessing professional decisions. Courts have been consistent in declaring that as long as the school provides an appropriate educational program, the choice of instructional approach or methodology lies within the school's discretion.

There have been a number of recent cases where parents of young children with autism have pressured schools to use the Lovaas treatment program. In situations where the parent can prove that the school's current programming is not producing any educational benefits, and the Lovaas program has documented educational progress, courts have been willing to order that the schools use the

Lovaas program. The key factor is whether there is any educational benefit to the school's program. When the answer has been yes, parents have not been successful in forcing the school to employ a particular instructional approach or methodology.

Are some students with disabilities entitled to extended school year programming?   In cases where a student with disabilities' educational programming is interrupted by summer vacation and the student suffers a severe regression of skills and is likely to experience great difficulty in recouping those lost skills once educational programming resumes after the summer, courts have consistently ruled that extended school year programming (over the summer) is a necessary component of providing such students with a FAPE. In these situations, courts recognize that extended school year programming is necessary to prevent this regression/recoupment problem. Most of the cases where extended school year programming has been mandated by the courts have involved students with severe disabilities who suffer functional skill loss (performance of daily living skills) when they encounter a long break in educational programming, although courts have held that regression may be in a number of areas such as academics, emotional or behavioral performance, physical skills, self-help skills, or communication.

What are the IDEA requirements for placement decision making in providing a FAPE?   Placement decisions identify the educational settings in which a FAPE will be delivered. The IDEA Amendments of 1997 require that placement decisions be made by the IEP team, after the IEP has been written. A variety of factors enter into placement decision making, including parental hostility to the school's proposed placement. A recent U.S. Court of Appeals case opined that parental hostility could seriously undermine the proposed placement; therefore, the school district was obligated to consider the negative effects of parental hostility on the school's responsibility of developing an IEP reasonably calculated to benefit the student (*Board of Education of Community Consolidated*

School District No. 21 v. *Illinois State Board of Education,* 1991). The U.S. Department of Education, Office of Special Education and Rehabilitative Services, has acknowledged that parental hostility to a proposed placement is an important consideration in the placement decision making, but it is not the most important factor (Burton, 1991).

According to the IDEA, the school district must address the following requirements in determining the educational placement:

- The placement must be based on the student's IEP and be designed as the most appropriate setting where the required special education and related services can be delivered (IDEA Regulations, 34 C.F.R. Sec. 300.552(a)(2)).
- The educational placement must be determined at least annually (IDEA Regulations, 34 C.F.R. Sec. 300.552(a)(1)).
- The placement must comply with the least restrictive environment requirement (IDEA Regulations, 34 C.F.R. Sec. 300.553(a)(4)).

Who are the required IEP team members?   The IDEA regulations list the required IEP team members (34 C.F.R. Sec. 300.344(A)(1)-(3)):

- A representative of the educational agency
- The student's special education teacher
- The student's general education teacher
- The student's parents or guardians
- A person who can interpret the instructional implications of the evaluation results
- The student, when appropriate (*note:* the student is required for developing a transition IEP)
- Related services personnel
- For a transition IEP, a representative of the agency that is likely to provide or pay for the transition services
- Other persons, at the discretion of parents or the educational agency

The representative of the local education agency (LEA) must have authority to commit on a districtwide level all of the resources designated in the IEP. The LEA representative may be the principal, special education administrator, or any person designated by the principal or administrator, with the exception of the student's teacher. Furthermore, the representative must be qualified to supervise the provision of special education services and be knowledgeable about the general education curriculum. It is important to note that school officials may not change decisions made by the IEP team (OSEP Policy Letter, 1991a; OSEP Policy Letter, 1991b). The requirement that the student's general education teacher participate in the IEP team was added by the IDEA Amendments of 1997. When a secondary special education student has multiple general education teachers, only one teacher is required to attend the IEP meeting.

What are the parental participation requirements in developing the student's IEP? The IDEA envisions an active parent role in educational decision making. In pursuit of that goal, the school district has some specific obligations in trying to ensure parental participation in the IEP meeting. The school district (1) must notify the parents of the IEP meeting a reasonable time prior to the meeting date (there is no specific number of days for this advance notice); (2) must schedule the meeting at a *mutually* agreeable time and place (this means, for example, the school cannot arbitrarily schedule all IEP meetings on Wednesdays at 3:30 P.M. at the school); (3) must indicate the purpose, time, and location of the meeting and who will be in attendance; (4) must also invite the student and name any additional community agency representatives who are invited in the case of a transition IEP; (5) must use other methods to ensure parental participation (e.g., conference telephone calls, fax) in the event that neither parent can attend; and (6) must give the parent a copy of the IEP. IEPs developed without a legitimate opportunity for parental input have been repealed (*New York City School District Board of Education,* 1992). The parent is not required to sign the IEP, nor does it indicate agreement with its content; a parental signature merely indicates the parent was present at the IEP meeting.

Can the school district conduct an IEP meeting in the parents' absence? Yes. Provided the school has made a reasonable attempt to involve the parents in the IEP decision-making process, the school may proceed with the IEP conference. If the parents choose not to attend the IEP meeting, it is important that the school adequately document its attempts to arrange a mutually convenient IEP meeting. This documentation should include records of telephone calls, copies of any correspondence sent or received from the parents, and records of any visits to the parents' home or place of employment.

What happens when the parents do not agree with the IEP? If possible, the school and parents should attempt to agree to an interim plan for services and continue to work on resolving their IEP differences. The IEP may be implemented in the areas of agreement with the parents. If the school and parents cannot resolve their IEP differences, the parties should seek mediation prior to a request for a due process hearing. While waiting for a mediation or due process hearing resolution, the old IEP (if there is one) remains in effect.

School personnel may prepare a draft IEP prior to the meeting in an effort to stimulate discussion, but it is clear that the school cannot simply present the parents with a completed IEP at the meeting. If this was allowed, it would defeat the law's intent of parental participation in educational decision making.

Does the public school district have any IEP responsibilities for students the district places in private schools? Yes. Prior to placement, the public school district must conduct an IEP meeting that includes a representative of the private school. The IEP legally remains the responsibility of the public school district.

What are some of the substantive requirements of an IEP that courts have scrutinized in judging the legal validity of an IEP? Courts have invalidated IEPs that have not been written with the required elements. A list of the required elements of an IEP can be found in Chapter 4 by referring to Box 4.7. The following IEP substantive concerns have been addressed by the courts:

- IEPs must be individualized to appropriately address the needs of the student. IEPs should not be written to merely reflect the services available. Further, schools cannot use standard IEPs that are designed by a particular disability or by categorical educational programming (IDEA Regulations, 34 C.F.R. Sec. 300 Appendix C).
- The description of the student's present level of educational performance should include academic and nonacademic areas. A label (e.g., learning disabled) is not an adequate description for present educational performance. All areas of educational performance where the student has deficiencies should have corresponding goals and objectives.
- At least one goal should be written for each identified area of need. An appropriate goal statement should not be unrealistically ambitious nor should a goal be so easy to achieve that student attainment will not result in meaningful improvement.
- All supplementary aids and services that are provided as part of a student's special education must be listed in the IEP (IDEA Regulations, 34 C.F.R. Sec. 300 Appendix C:48). The IEP team must determine the special education supplementary aids and services and related services that a student needs, and not base decisions on what services are available. In fact, if specific services that have been determined necessary by the IEP team are not available, the school district must contract for those services with other agencies.
- The IEP team must determine the extent to which the student with disabilities will participate in general education classes. The IEP statement addressing general education participation must not be a mere conclusion that the team has determined a particular educational setting as representing the least restrictive environment for the student. Instead, the statement should describe the student's ability or inability to participate in a general education program (*Thorndock* v. *Boise Independent School District,* 1988).
- The 1997 IDEA Amendments require that students with disabilities, in most cases, participate in state- and districtwide assessments of student performance as students without disabilities. If the student requires any assessment modifications, the IEP needs to list those modifications. If the IEP team determines that a student cannot be adequately assessed with modifications, the IEP must contain a statement expressing why the assessment is not appropriate and what alternative assessments will be used.
- Parents of children with disabilities must be informed about their children's progress as regularly as are parents of nondisabled children.
- The IEP must contain measurable goals and objectives as well as contain specific evaluation procedures to be used to document progress.
- If the student is not making any progress over time, the IEP needs to be reviewed and revised.

What are the IDEA requirements for revising IEPs?   The IEP cannot be revised unless the parents are notified of the proposed change and the reasons for the change. The IEP must be reviewed at least annually, although it can be reviewed and revised as often as the parents or school deem necessary. An IEP review must be conducted when (1) the student has shown a lack of progress in relation to goals and objectives, (2) reevaluation findings need to be considered, (3) the parents provide additional information about the student, (4) the student's needs are expected to change, or (5) other considerations occur as deemed necessary. Although parent notification is required, parental consent is not required for IEP revisions. If parents disagree with any revision, they have the right to request a due process hearing.

Are there any potential legal consequences if a teacher decides not to abide by the contents of the IEP in terms of goals, objectives, and services provided?   As mentioned previously, the IEP is a legal commitment by the school district to make every good faith effort to address all of the goals and objectives as well as to provide the listed services. Any school professional who is working with a student who has an IEP is entitled to review information in the student's IEP and educational record. In fact, the school has an affirmative obligation to inform all staff working with a student with disabilities of any requirements in the IEP.

In *Doe* v. *Withers* (1993), a high school student with learning disabilities had an IEP that required a number of general education classroom modifications. The student's general education social studies teacher refused to abide by one of the IEP modifications that required oral testing instead of written essay examinations. Even after several school personnel—including the special education teacher, principal, and special education director—ordered the teacher to comply with the IEP required modifications, the teacher still refused.

Finally, the parents sued the teacher and school under a federal statute, Section 1983 of the Civil Rights Act of 1871. Section 1983 authorizes private individual lawsuits in which injunctive or monetary relief or both are sought when governmental officials (e.g., school employees) violate a federal statutory or constitutional right. All of the defendants—except the general education social studies teacher, Mr. Withers—were dismissed from the lawsuit. A jury found that Mr. Withers did violate the student's federal statutory rights under the IDEA and that, under Section 1983, liability was assessed against the teacher in the amount of $5,000 in compensatory damages and $10,000 in punitive damages. This case is significant in reinforcing the importance of school personnel compliance with IEP requirements.

What is the IDEA definition of **related services** *and what are listed related services under the law?*   *Related services* are defined as "services that may be required to assist the child with a dis-

ability to benefit from special education" (IDEA, 20 U.S.C. Sec. 1401(a)(17)). The IDEA listed related services include assistive technology, audiology, counseling, early identification and assessment, medical services (for diagnostic purposes only), occupational therapy, orientation and mobility services, parent counseling and training, physical therapy, psychological services, recreation, rehabilitation counseling, school health services, social work services, speech pathology, transportation, and transition services. For many students with disabilities, related services are essential in ensuring they receive a FAPE. Section 504 of the Rehabilitation Act of 1973 also requires the provision of related services if needed to ensure a FAPE, even if special education services are not provided for students with disabilities who are deemed ineligible under IDEA (Zirkel, 1993). Once a related service is listed on a student's IEP and becomes part of that child's appropriate education, the school must provide the service at no cost to the parents.

What is the U.S. Supreme Court's criteria for determining whether a service qualifies as a "related service" that the school is legally obligated to provide?   The leading case in which a school's obligation to provide related services was analyzed is *Irving Independent School District* v. *Tatro* (1984). In *Tatro,* the U.S. Supreme Court decided that a child with spina bifida was entitled to receive a procedure known as clean intermittent catheterization (CIC) in order to be provided with a FAPE. The CIC was determined by the Court to be a related service, not an excluded medical service. The Supreme Court reached its decision by balancing the interests of the child in receiving the service versus the school's interests in containing costs and making only "reasonable accommodations." The Court noted that in the absence of the CIC as a related service, the child could not attend school and thus could not benefit from special education.

Conversely, when inquiring into the school's interests, the Court noted that the cost to the school in providing the service was minimal because it is a simple procedure that can be performed by a nonmedical person with minimal training. In addition, the Court noted the existence of school nurses, who were qualified to render this service or train others to safely perform the CIC procedure. Since schools have long employed nurses, the schools would not be required to make an "unreasonable accommodation" in providing the CIC.

Yell (1998) identified the Court's analysis in *Tatro* as setting forth a three-part test in determining whether a particular service is a required related service. First, the student must be eligible for special education services under the IDEA or require a particular related service as a reasonable accommodation if the child is eligible under Section 504. Second, the service must be necessary to assist the student to benefit from special education services. Third, related services are only required when the service can be provided by a nurse or qualified person, not if the service could only be performed by a physician. In the third scenario, the service would be deemed a medical service, not a related service. Schools are only obligated to provide medical services for diagnostic purposes.

How have courts decided on other specific requests for "related services"? The issue of whether a service is a required related service under the IDEA has sparked much litigation because the requested services are often very costly. The following is a brief summary of judicial responses to specific requested services.

Transportation

Transportation to and from school and the necessary equipment to transport students with physical disabilities, such as buses with lifts and ramps, are clearly required related services. Courts have ordered that parents be reimbursed by the school for expenses incurred in transporting their child with disabilities to school when the school was not providing the required service. In terms of other transportation related issues, courts have ruled that if a student with disabilities loses instructional time from the school day because of transportation, there is likely to be a finding of discrimination in

that the student with disabilities experiences a reduced school day compared to students without disabilities. Although there are no regulations on the length of a student's time in transit, some courts have held that an excessively long commute to and from school may constitute a denial of a FAPE.

School Health Services

School health services are provided by school nurses or other qualified persons. What constitutes a required school health service can be broadly interpreted to include simple procedures (e.g., administering medication) to services requiring some level of training (e.g., catheterization), to fairly sophisticated procedures requiring extensive training (e.g., tracheotomy care) (Lear, 1995). If a health service must be provided by a physician, courts view such services as medical in nature, and the schools are not obligated to provide medical services. When some health services are required to be provided "under physician supervision," the determining factor is whether the physician can provide indirect supervision or physically needs to be present when the service is provided. If the physical presence of the physician is required, the service is medical and therefore excluded under the IDEA. Also, most courts have held that drug treatment programs are excludable medical services for which the schools are not responsible.

Complex Health Services

The courts are not uniform in deciding whether certain health-related services to medically fragile students are excluded medical services or required school health services. Given the diversity of judicial decisions on the provision of complex health services to medically fragile children, it is impossible to state any general legal guidelines. These requests must be decided by the school on a case-by-case basis. The IEP team should be the group that makes these local decisions. Yell (1998) offered some decision-making factors that should enter into an IEP team's determination: (1) ask if the procedure is required to assist the student in benefiting from special education, (2) consider the cost of the service, (3) judge the level of expertise needed to perform the service, (4) review state laws concerning the provision of health and medical services, (5) determine the complexity of the procedure, and (6) evaluate the risk of providing the service.

Assistive Technology

The 1990 Amendments to IDEA incorporated definitions used in the Technology-Related Assistance for Individuals with Disabilities Act (1988). An *assistive technology device* is "any item, piece of equipment, or product system, whether acquired commercially off the shelf, modified, or customized, that is used to increase, maintain, or improve the functional capability of children with disabilities" (IDEA Regulations, 34 C.F.R. Sec. 300.5). An *assistive technology service* is "any service that directly assists a child with a disability in the selection, acquisition, or use of an assistive technology device" (IDEA Regulations, 34 C.F.R. Sec. 300.6). Assistive technology devices or services may be required as a special education service, a related service, or in the general education classroom as a supplementary aid or service. Schools are not obligated to provide assistive technology if it is for medical reasons. If assistive technology may be necessary for a student, a person qualified to conduct assistive technology evaluations must be on the IEP team.

Examples of common assistive technology devices that schools have been ordered to provide include calculators, FM auditory training systems, computers, closed-circuit televisions, and computerized communication systems. If the IEP team decides that a student must have access to an assistive technology device at home also, the school must provide for this home use. The school district retains ownership of the device, however. Finally, it is permissible for school districts to seek alternative funding sources such as medical assistance and private insurance to cover the costs of assistive technology.

Counseling and Psychological Services

Courts usually conclude that counseling and psychological services, if required to assist the student in benefiting from special education, is a required related service. Specific types of psychological services, such as psychotherapy, have also been held to constitute a related service, provided the psychotherapy was not intended to correct behaviors occurring solely outside of school. There must be a direct connection between the service and its ability to assist a student in benefiting from special education. Another form of counseling that is a legitimate related service is *parent counseling and training,* which is defined as "assisting parents in understanding the special needs of their child and providing parents with information about child development" (IDEA Regulations, 34 C.F.R. Sec. 300.13(b)(6)).

Is it legally permissible for school districts to seek reimbursement from third-party payers for the cost of related services?   The IDEA does not prevent schools from attempting to have third-party payers meet their obligations to provide for certain related services. In 1988, the Social Security Act was amended to specifically allow school districts to bill Medicaid for services provided to students with disabilities. Medicaid provides a variety of services, such as early and periodic screening, diagnosis, physician services, physical and occupational therapy, speech and language pathology, audiology, and physiological services. Eligible recipients of Medicaid services include families on public assistance, persons over age 65, disabled individuals, and individuals receiving Supplemental Security Income (SSI). Schools may not, however, make the provision of a required related service contingent on Medicaid funding. Schools may also access private insurance proceeds, provided there is no financial disadvantage to the family and the family has given their consent to use their private insurance.

LEAST RESTRICTIVE ENVIRONMENT (LRE) PRINCIPLE

Least restrictive environment requires that

> to the maximum extent appropriate, children with disabilities, including children in public or private institutions or other care facilities, are educated

with children who are not disabled, and that special classes, separate schooling, or other removal of children with disabilities from the regular educational environment occurs only when the nature or severity of the disability is such that education in regular classes with the use of supplementary aids and services cannot be achieved satisfactorily. (IDEA, 20 U.S.C. Sec. 1412)

To many individuals with disabilities and their families, the LRE principle is a civil rights mandate attempting to ameliorate over 200 years of segregation of individuals with disabilities from the societal mainstream. The LRE principle is rooted in the constitutionally based doctrine of the least restrictive alternative. Turnbull (1993) noted, "This doctrine states that even if the legislative purpose of a government action is legitimate (e.g., promoting public health, regulating commerce, or providing education), the purpose may not be pursued by means that broadly stifle personal liberties if it can be achieved by less oppressive restrictive means" (p. 158). In other words, it is a legitimate exercise of governmental authority to compel local education agencies to provide free and appropriate public education to students with disabilities. However, in meeting that valid governmental purpose, students with disabilities should experience the least restrictive educational means, and have the same rights of access to their environment as students without disabilities enjoy. This notion of *restrictiveness* was defined by Champagne (1993) as "a gauge of the degree of opportunity a person has for proximity to, and communication with, the ordinary flow of persons in our society" (p. 5).

As a piece of civil rights legislation, it should not be surprising that "no requirement of the right-to-education movement and the federal law that codified the cases was as likely at the outset to generate as much heat as light as the requirement that children with disabilities be educated in the least restrictive placement" (Turnbull, 1993, p. 157). Much of the public controversy and debate over the LRE requirement has occurred in the judicial system. Indeed, how to interpret and apply the LRE mandate to individual cases is one of the most litigated issues in the IDEA. A number of judicial

standards of review have been articulated by the courts in their attempts to interpret the LRE principle. This section will describe several of these judicial standards for determining the extent of the right of students with disabilities to be educated with nondisabled peers in general education classrooms.

Are the terms* mainstreaming *and* inclusion *legal concepts in the IDEA? No. The IDEA states only that children with disabilities shall be educated with peers without disabilities to the maximum extent appropriate. The terms *mainstreaming* and *inclusion,* although often used synonymously, are two different educational placement practices. *Mainstreaming* refers to the earlier special education practice of initially removing children with disabilities from general education classrooms and providing segregated special education programming. At some future point, if the student with disabilities progressed, that student was a candidate to be mainstreamed back into one or more general education classrooms with the expectation that he or she would be able to perform at grade level academically and behaviorally in the class(es).

In contrast, *inclusion* refers to the more recent educational philosophy and practice that seeks to provide what ever support a student with disabilities needs to function successfully in the general education environment. Further, under the practice of inclusion, even students with severe disabilities may legitimately be educated in general education classrooms with no expectation or requirement that they perform at grade level.

What is the relationship between the legal principles of LRE and FAPE? The LRE principle establishes a presumption that students with disabilities should be educated with students without disabilities in general education environments. However, this presumption is rebuttable, meaning if a student with disabilities cannot be successfully educated while receiving appropriate support services in the general education classroom, removal to an alternative special education setting is required (Turnbull, 1993). Therefore, the FAPE principle takes priority over the LRE presumption in situations where the student with disabilities cannot receive an appropriate education in the general education classroom. Clearly, the school's primary obligation is to provide the student with disabilities a FAPE. The result of these two legal principles is that school districts must provide a full continuum of educational placements to allow school personnel to choose from a number of options in determining the LRE that is appropriate for the student. Further, a school district may not refuse to place a student with disabilities in a LRE because it lacks the appropriate placement option (Tucker & Goldstein, 1992).

Are school districts legally required to educate students with disabilities in their neighborhood schools?   The IDEA regulations require that "unless the IEP requires otherwise, students with disabilities should be educated in the school they would attend if they were not in special education" (IDEA Regulations, 34 C.F.R. Sec. 300.552(a) (3)). The controlling factor is what constitutes an appropriate educational placement to render a FAPE (Huefner, 1994). If a FAPE can be provided in the student's neighborhood school, that is where the student should be placed. However, placement in a student's neighborhood school is not an absolute right. That is, the preference for a neighborhood placement is not an absolute entitlement. However, if the student with disabilities cannot be appropriately educated in the neighborhood school, the student should be placed as close to home as possible.

Does the LRE requirement apply to nonacademic settings and programming?   Yes. The IDEA regulations extend the LRE mandate to extracurricular activities, meals, recess, counseling services, athletics, transportation, health services, recreational activities, and special interest groups or clubs sponsored by the school (IDEA Regulations, 34 C.F.R. Sec. 300.553). This application of the LRE principle to nonacademic areas is even more critical for a student with disabilities who is presently being educated out of general education classrooms.

What are some of the most significant judicial standards enunciated by the courts for determining the extent of the right of students with disabilities to be educated with nondisabled peers in general education classrooms?   Yell (1998) identified four key cases enunciating judicial standards interpreting the LRE requirement. The first case is *Roncker* v. *Walter* (1983), where the Sixth Circuit Court of Appeals set forth the so-called *portability test*. The *Roncker* portability test addressed two issues: (1) Can the educational services that make a segregated placement superior be feasibly provided in a nonsegregated setting? and (2) If so, the placement in the segregated setting is inappropriate.

The second significant LRE case is *Daniel R.R.* v. *State Board of Education* (1989). In *Daniel R.R.,* the Fifth Circuit Court of Appeals established a two-part test for determining the LRE rights of students with disabilities: (1) Can education in the general education classroom with supplementary aids and services be achieved satisfactorily? and (2) If a student is placed in a more restrictive setting, is the student integrated to the maximum extent appropriate?

The Ninth Circuit Court of Appeals, in *Sacramento City Unified School District* v. *Rachel H.* (1994), enunciated a four-factor test in its interpretation of the LRE mandate. All of these factors should be considered in school placement decision making: (1) the educational benefits of the general education classroom with supplementary aids and services as compared to the educational benefits of the special education classroom; (2) the nonacademic benefits of interaction with students without disabilities; (3) the effect of the presence of the student with disabilities on the teacher and on the other students in the classroom; and (4) the cost of including the student with disabilities in the general education classroom.

Finally, the Fourth Circuit Court of Appeals, in *Hartmann* v. *Loudoun County Board of Education* (1997), most recently announced a three-part test in its LRE interpretation. The court ruled that including students with disabilities in general education classrooms is not required, under the LRE mandate, when (1) the student would not receive any educational benefit from the general education placement; (2) any marginal benefit from including the student in general education classrooms would be outweighed by benefits that could only be provided in a separate special education setting; and (3) the student with disabilities is a disruptive force in the general education classroom.

An analysis of the recent LRE rulings reveals some elements that school personnel should consider in their LRE placement decision-making process. First, school personnel should consider potential nonacademic benefits (such as social/behavioral and language modeling) that occur from placing a student with disabilities in a general education classroom. This factor legitimately opens the general education classroom door to students with even severe disabilities. Second, the school's obligation to provide supplementary aids and services to a student with disabilities requires more than a mere token gesture to accommodate the student in a general education setting. The extent of this obligation is determined on a case-by-case basis and is practically determined by individual educator attitudes.

Third, most courts find placement out of the general education setting is appropriate when the student with disabilities (1) is overly disruptive, (2) requires an inordinate amount of the teacher's time and attention, or (3) requires an extensively adapted curriculum to the point that the grade level curriculum is totally inapplicable (this is the most controversial of these out-of-general-education-classroom placement considerations, since this might obviate the need to place students with severe disabilities in general education classrooms). Fourth, if the IEP team decides that placement out of the general education mainstream is most appropriate and required, every attempt needs to be made to provide for out-of-class interaction opportunities between the student with disabilities and nondisabled peers. Fifth, if the placement is justified out of the general education mainstream, the IEP

must reflect goals and objectives that could eventually lead to an appropriate placement in general education classrooms.

PROCEDURAL DUE PROCESS AND PARENT PARTICIPATION PRINCIPLES

These final two principles of special education law are discussed together because they work in tandem to ensure that schools comply with the requirements of the IDEA. The IDEA ensures that parents are equal participants in the special education decision-making process through the multitude of procedural safeguards in the law. This section will address procedural safeguards and parent participation in terms of notice and consent requirements, access to student records, appointment of surrogate parents, independent educational evaluations, voluntary mediation, and due process hearings.

What are the notice requirements in the IDEA?
The IDEA requires that written notice be provided to parents prior to the school proposing to initiate or changing the identification, evaluation, educational placement, or provision of a FAPE to a student with disabilities or prior to the school refusing to make such changes (IDEA Regulations, 34 C.F.R. Sec. 300.504-505). The purpose of these notice requirements is to allow the parents equal participation in educational decision making to ensure their children's rights (Osborne, 1995).

When is parental consent required?   The school district must obtain the parents' voluntary and informed consent prior to (1) a preplacement special education evaluation, (2) the initial placement in special education, and (3) reevaluation, unless the school can demonstrate that it tried to secure the parents' consent but was unsuccessful. If the parent refuses to give consent at any of these junctures in the process, the school may continue to pursue evaluation or placement by employing the mediation or due process hearing procedures. The parent may revoke consent so long as the activity for which consent was initially given is still taking place (Williams, 1991).

What access rights do parents have to their children's educational records?   Schools must permit parents access to their children's educational records. Once a parent requests to inspect his or her child's educational record, the school must comply with the request within 45 days. If the parent requests assistance from school personnel in having any record information interpreted or explained, the school must respond to those requests. Parents are entitled to copies of their child's educational records and, if they cannot afford copies themselves, the school must provide copies free of charge. Finally, if a parent believes that information in the educational records is inaccurate or misleading, the parent may request that the school amend that information. If the school refuses to amend the record, the parent may request a due process hearing on this issue.

The IDEA also requires that educational records on students be kept confidential. Only school personnel who work with a student with a disability have access to that student's educational record. The school must keep a record of individuals obtaining access to any student's educational record, including the person's name, date, and purpose of the record inspection.

What is a "surrogate parent" and when must the school district appoint one?   If a child does not have a parent, the parent cannot be found, or the child is a ward of the state, the IDEA requires that a surrogate parent be appointed. The responsibility of the surrogate parent is to serve as the child's educational advocate. In this capacity, the surrogate parent assumes all the rights bestowed by the IDEA to natural parents or guardians. To serve as a surrogate parent, an individual must have no conflicts of interest, must have the requisite knowledge and skills to ensure that the child is adequately represented, and may not be employed by the school district charged with the responsibility of providing the child a FAPE. School districts do not have any authority to appoint a surrogate

parent when the biological parents or guardians are located but take no interest in the child's education or have even acted in bad faith in the special education process (*Board of Education of Northfield High School District 225* v. *Roy H. and Lynn H.,* 1995).

What are the IDEA independent educational evaluation (IEE) requirements?   When parents disagree with the school's evaluation, they have the right to request an independent educational evaluation (an evaluation conducted by a qualified professional not employed by the school district) at any time during their child's education. Parents may request information from the school on where to obtain an IEE and the school must provide that information. The school district is obligated to pay for the cost of the IEE unless the school maintains their evaluation is appropriate and requests a due process hearing. The IEE results must be considered by the school in its decision making, although the school is not obligated to accept or agree with the IEE findings or recommendations. School districts, in an effort to protect themselves from excessive and unreasonable IEE expenses, may establish a reasonable fee structure that the parents may not exceed (OSEP Policy Letter, 1995).

Does the IDEA provide for mediation when parents and school districts are in dispute over a student's special education?   The IDEA Amendments of 1997 included a provision that voluntary mediation be available to the parties experiencing a special education dispute. Mediation seeks a non-adversarial resolution of the dispute by directly engaging the parties involved in a collaborative problem-solving process led by an impartial mediator (Dobbs, Primm, & Primm, 1991; Goldberg & Huefner, 1995). Mediation must be a voluntary option that both parties agree to try; it cannot be used to delay or deny a parent's right to a due process hearing. If an agreement is reached by the parties at mediation, the agreement is put in writing. Any information shared during a mediation session is confidential and may not be used as evidence in a subsequent due process hearing. More information on typical mediation procedures will be discussed in Chapter 6.

What is a due process hearing and when may it be requested?

The ultimate procedural safeguard for parents when they are dissatisfied with their child's education is the right to request a due process hearing. The purpose of the due process hearing is to allow an impartial hearing officer to hear both sides of a dispute and render a decision (Anderson et al., 1997). The school district also may request a due process hearing in an effort to reverse a parental decision, such as refusal to consent to an initial evaluation or special education placement. The due process hearing is modeled after the regular adversarial court system. Parents may request a due process hearing to contest a school's identification, evaluation, educational placement, or provision of a FAPE (IDEA Regulations, 34 C.F.R. Sec. 506(a)).

What are the parents' basic due process hearing rights?

The IDEA regulations (34 C.F.R. Sec. 300.508) contain the following due process hearing rights. Parents may:

- Be accompanied and advised by counsel and by individuals with special education expertise.
- Present evidence and confront, cross-examine, and compel the attendance of witnesses.
- Prohibit the introduction of any evidence at the hearing that has not been disclosed to the other party at least five days prior to the hearing.
- Obtain a written or electronic verbatim record of the hearing.
- Obtain written findings of fact and decisions.
- Have their child present at the hearing.
- Open the hearing to the public.

What is the Handicapped Children's Protection Act (HCPA)?

The HCPA, passed in 1986, amended the IDEA to allow parents to be reimbursed for their attorney fees if they are the prevailing party (meaning they are successful on a significant issue they raised) in a special education dispute at the administrative hearing or judicial levels (HCPA, 20 U.S.C. Sec. 1415). The HCPA prohibits parents from being reimbursed their attorney fees if they rejected a properly made settlement offer by the school district. Finally, the IDEA Amendments of 1997 restrict awarding the parents attorney fees for their attorney's participation in the IEP process or in mediation sessions prior to the filing of a due process hearing.

What happens to the student's educational placement during the pendency of the due process hearing?

The IDEA provides that during the pendency of the due process hearing or any judicial proceeding, the student remains in his or her present educational placement (IDEA Regulations, 34 C.F.R. Sec. 300.513). This is the *stay put* provision of the law. The parents and school may, however, agree to a temporary educational placement.

What is the role of the due process hearing officer?

"The primary duties of the hearing officer are to inform the parties of their rights during the hearing, allow all parties the opportunity to present their cases, conduct the hearing in a fair, orderly, and impartial manner, and render a decision in accordance with the law" (Yell, 1998, p. 281). In other words, the hearing officer functions very much like a trial judge. The hearing officer, however, does not enjoy the same powers to grant certain remedies as a judge (Guernsey & Klare, 1993). This individual may order an independent educational evaluation at the school's expense, or award the parents reimbursement for educational expenses or compensatory education, but he or she cannot award attorney fees. Further, the hearing officer has no authority to issue orders over agencies other than the local education agency (Yell, 1998). Finally, the hearing officer must render a decision within 45 days after the written request for the hearing. The decision of the hearing officer is final unless the parties appeal.

What are the due process hearing appeal rights of the parties?

In a one-tier state, an appeal of the due process hearing officer's decision is commenced by either party (i.e., parents or school district) filing a civil action in either a state or federal court. Prior to the filing of a civil law suit, the parties must have exhausted all administrative options, unless an administrative hearing would be futile or inadequate. In a two-tier state, an appeal proceeds to the state education agency for an independent review and decision. The state education agency's decision is final unless the parties appeal by filing a civil action in either a state or federal court. When an appeal of a due process hearing officer's decision is filed, the next level of review usually renders a decision based on the facts and evidence established by the record in the hearing. In some situations, the state education agency or court may accept additional evidence, but it is important for the parties to submit all their relevant evidence at the initial hearing. State laws specify time lines for appealing from a due process hearing officer's decision.

SECTION 504 OF THE REHABILITATION ACT OF 1973

Section 504 is a federal statute designed to prohibit discrimination against individuals with disabilities in programs receiving federal financial assistance (29 U.S.C. Secs. 706(8), 794, 794a). This means that Section 504 is applicable to all public school districts. In many respects, Section 504 establishes similar rights and procedures for students with disabilities and their parents as secured by the IDEA: (1) nondiscriminatory evaluation and placement procedures; (2) periodic reevaluation of students with disabilities; (3) educational services that meet individual educational needs; (4) educational services equal in quality to those provided for students without disabilities; (5) to the maximum extent possible, the education of students with disabilities along with students without disabilities; and (6) due process procedures that ensure parent participation in evaluation and placement decisions that provide for an impartial hearing with parent representation by counsel.

Section 504 protects *students with disabilities,* defined as "any person who (i) has a physical or mental impairment which substantially limits one or more of such person's major life activities, (ii)

has a record of such an impairment, or (iii) is regarded as having such an impairment" (29 U.S.C. Sec. 706(7)(B)). Section 504 protects many students with disabilities who are not deemed eligible for special education under the IDEA, since the definition of *disability* under Section 504 is broader than that under the IDEA (Zirkel, 1996). Section 504 applies beyond students with disabilities in the public school system to cover any eligible individual with a disability in postsecondary educational settings, in employment settings, and parents and school employees who are disabled.

Schools are required, under Section 504, to provide "reasonable accommodations" to otherwise qualified students with disabilities. This means that a student with disabilities is entitled to various school modifications (curricular, instructional, behavioral, and environmental) to enable that student to have the same opportunity to receive an appropriate public education as is afforded students without disabilities. The question of what constitutes a reasonable accommodation is determined on a case-by-case basis. Courts generally rule that if the accommodation causes an undue financial burden to the school or requires a fundamental alteration in the program, such accommodations are "unreasonable" and the school is not legally obligated to provide such accommodations.

Section 504 is an important legislative companion to the IDEA and protects many students with disabilities who fall through the relatively rigid categorical eligibility gaps of the IDEA (i.e., students who do not qualify for special education services). If a student meets the eligibility requirements under both Section 504 and the IDEA, generally the major source of rights protection is found in the IDEA, which is a more specific and extensive law for special education services.

SUMMARY

The importance of a fundamental knowledge of special education law for professionals serving as educational advocates for children with disabilities and their families cannot be overstated. Without such knowledge, professionals will be unable to effectively challenge school district policies and practices that prevent students with disabilities from receiving a free and appropriate public education as required by law. Back in 1982, Bateman issued this concern: "Lack of legal knowledge is rapidly becoming a major concern for all special educators, from the director of the large school district struggling with complex budget issues to the teacher feeling the pressure to describe children's needs only in terms of already available services. Until very recently, the courts left the daily operation of schools almost totally in the hands of professional educators and school boards" (p. 58).

As discussed in this chapter, the courts no longer give schools and educators unlimited pro-fessional discretion in how educational decisions are rendered and implemented. In fact, in some professionals' opinions, the judicial scrutiny seems unrelenting. Professionals who possess ample knowledge of special education law and who take seriously their role and responsibility as a child advocate, can minimize some of this "unrelenting judicial scrutiny" by doing a better job of policing schools to ensure adherence to all of the legal rights and procedures accorded to children with disabilities and to their parents.

CHAPTER 6

KNOWLEDGE OF DISPUTE RESOLUTION MECHANISMS IN SPECIAL EDUCATION

As a litigant, I should dread a law suit beyond
almost anything else short of sickness and of death.
—Judge Learned Hand

The incorporation of parent participation rights and procedural safeguards in the IDEA (discussed in Chapter 5) reflects a congressional intent of fostering participatory democracy and collaboration between parents and school professionals in an effort to provide children with disabilities a FAPE (Turnbull, 1993). Establishment of the right to request a due process hearing as a formal mechanism to resolve special education disputes was based on a congressional assumption that an adversarial process was the best way to achieve accuracy in fact finding and fairness (Goldberg & Kuriloff, 1991). Unfortunately, all too often, the litigants in due process hearing disputes, both parents of children with disabilities and school professionals, experience the same feelings of dread expressed by Judge Learned Hand in the quote above. Indeed, as declared by Goldberg and Kuriloff and many others, the legal model, as typified in the due process hearing, is ill suited to resolving educational disputes and creates unnecessary antagonisms between parents and school personnel.

What is the alternative to the adversarial due process hearing model in effectively resolving special education disputes? The shortcomings and negative consequences of participating in due process hearing disputes are significant; however, it is important that the constitutional right of due pro-

cess be available to both parents and school officials. The key, according to Goldberg and Kuriloff (1991), is to alleviate the need for due process in the first place: "The question then, is really not of doing away with due process, but of finding ways to prevent disputes between parents and schools from landing in court" (p. 554).

In their advocacy efforts, special education professionals must possess the interpersonal interaction skills (communication, collaboration, conflict resolution, advocacy methods, ethical analysis) to effectively resolve disputes between parents and schools in the most collaborative, nonadversarial manner possible. However, effective advocacy also requires knowledge of the formal dispute resolution mechanisms in place in special education. Without this latter knowledge, special education professionals will be unable to pursue their advocacy efforts when a dispute impasse has been reached. In addition, knowledge of the dispute resolution mechanisms in special education is necessary in order to engage in an informed cost-benefit analysis to determine whether to pursue the advocacy issues in the formal dispute resolution arena (i.e., via a due process hearing).

This chapter discusses the current dispute resolution mechanisms that exist in special education. First, as required in the 1997 IDEA Amendments, voluntary mediation must now be available to parents and school officials experiencing a special education dispute. This chapter examines the process of special education mediation, including goals and principles, procedures and rules, models, instances when mediation is not appropriate, a comparison of mediation and due process hearing models, and research on the effectiveness of mediation. Second, the due process hearing system is reviewed, with attention to typical procedures, elements of procedural fairness, school errors causing due process hearings, factors to consider prior to requesting a due process hearing, and concerns/limitations of resolving parent and school special education disputes via the due process hearing model. Third, alternative dispute resolution strategies in special education are considered. Finally, various additional special education enforcement and dispute resolution mechanisms are reviewed. This review includes (1) the IDEA complaint process, (2) the Section 504 complaint process, (3) the Family and Educational Rights and Privacy Act (FERPA) complaint process, and (4) state and federal compliance monitoring procedures.

MEDIATION

The National Institute for Dispute Resolution defines *mediation* as "a process in which a neutral third party skilled in identifying areas of agreement assists disputants in reaching a negotiated settlement of differences on their own rather than having outsiders impose a settlement" (Ahearn, 1994, p. 2). A similar definition is offered by the Justice Center of Atlanta, Inc., describing *mediation* as "a confidential dispute resolution process to determine the appropriate individual and collective outcomes via the able assistance and skills of a trained, impartial third party with no vested interest in the decisions which result" (Primm, 1988, p. 1). The key elements of mediation include (1) it is a nonadversarial process, (2) it engages the involved parties in a collaborative problem-solving process, and (3) the process is led by an impartial third party (Dobbs, Primm, & Primm, 1991).

The Principles and Goals of Mediation

Mediation rests on several principles (Lane County Direction Service, 1996):

- *Voluntary.* The parents and school must both voluntarily agree to enter into mediation. The parties enter freely into any agreement reached in mediation and they have the right to withdraw from mediation at any time.
- *Informed.* The parties have a right to information describing the mediation process, including dispute resolution options and resources before consenting to mediation or agreeing to the terms of any agreement.
- *Self-determined.* This principle recognizes that the parties to the dispute have the ability and the right to define their own issues, needs, and solutions.
- *Impartial.* This principle affirms the parties' right to a fair process facilitated by a mediator who refrains from any bias or favoritism.
- *Confidential.* This principle ensures that all information shared during mediation will remain confidential and not be shared with anyone outside of the two direct parties. Further, information shared during mediation may not be used as evidence in a subsequent due process hearing.

In addition to these listed principles, the following goals are inherent in mediation. First, the mediation process is collaborative. The parties must work together to create solutions that meet their respective and mutual interests and needs. Second, mediation empowers the parties to function as the ultimate decision makers. The mediator has no decision-making authority over the parties. Third, mediation fosters acceptance of mutually determined solutions by not focusing on blame and fault. Instead, the focus is on communication, collaborative problem solving, and reaching mutually acceptable solutions. Fourth, mediation seeks to foster greater trust and respect between the parties by engaging in nonjudgmental communication and solution finding. Finally, mediation is future oriented in that the past is only used as a guide and background for developing agreements about future interactions between the parties. The parties do not spend time and energy arguing about past events and perceptions in which they may never find any agreement (Engiles, Peter, Baxter Quash-Mah & Todis, 1996).

Mediation Procedures and Rules

Although mediation is less formal and adversarial than due process hearings, there is a structure and set of common procedures that most special education mediation systems follow (Engiles et al., 1996; Lane County Direction Service, 1995; Schrag, 1996b). This section discusses the following mediation phases: the opening, fact finding/identifying the issues, understanding interests, collaborative problem solving, and concluding the mediation.

Opening
In this first phase of the mediation process, the mediator(s) introduces himself or herself and explains the ground rules and responsibilities of the participants. During the opening phase, the following information should be provided: both parties introduce themselves and their representatives, the purposes of the mediation are reviewed by the mediator, the mediator's role is described, the subsequent steps in the mediation process are outlined, the due process rights of the parties are reviewed, the implications and impact of reaching a settlement agreement are explained, and the basic ground rules for the mediation session are established. The main intent of the opening is to put the parties at ease and to provide a safe environment to discuss freely the issues in dispute. Schrag (1996b, p. 35) suggests that the following mediation rules should be established by the mediator:

- The mediator is an impartial third party.
- The mediator has no authority to compel any action by either party.
- Mediation participants for both parties must include individuals who possess the authority to act on behalf of the student and the school district.

- Mediation requires the full participation and commitment of both parties and can only begin or continue when the parties agree.
- The mediation session is not recorded by any means. The only record that is maintained of the mediation session is the mediation agreement (if there is one).
- Discussions at mediation sessions will not be admissible at subsequent due process hearings except for the purposes of indicating that mediation occurred and stating the terms of any agreement reached by both parties.
- The mediator shall terminate the mediation session at any point, in the opinion of the mediator or either party, no resolution of the disagreement(s) is likely.
- The number of participants for each party shall generally be limited to two or three persons.
- A reasonable time limit should be set from the initiation of the mediation process to a resolution or impasse point. This time limit could be extended by mutual agreement of both parties.
- The mediator will facilitate all mediation sessions with due respect for the rights and responsibilities of both parties.
- The content of all mediation sessions is confidential and shall not be shared with outside parties.
- The mediation session will be present and future oriented; past problems will not be the focus of the mediation.
- The mediation will be conducted with respect accorded to all of the participants (e.g., no name calling or interruptions will be tolerated).
- A copy of the final agreement will become part of the student's school records.
- Both parties agree to demonstrate good faith and commitment to implementing the final agreement.

Fact Finding/Identifying the Issues
In this phase, both parties are allowed to make an uninterrupted statement where they can articulate their concerns, perspectives, and proposals for resolving the disagreement. After each party's

statement, the mediator may ask clarifying questions for the purpose of seeking an understanding and identification of the issues that need to be addressed during mediation. The mediator summarizes the points raised in each party's statement and validates any efforts made by the parties to resolve their dispute. In addition to identifying the issues needing resolution, it is important for the mediator to inquire about the feelings the parties are experiencing as a result of the dispute in order to assess how "ready" the parties are to engage in a dialogue.

The mediator can move the process to the next phase if there is a clear understanding of the issues in dispute for each party, and if the parties are ready and able to talk to each other. As a starting point for the next phase, it is recommended that the parties begin discussion of (1) a point on which they are already near agreement; or (2) a common background, experience, or shared concern; or (3) the most manageable of the issues that have been identified; or (4) the issue that must be addressed in order for the other issues to be resolved (Lane County Direction Service, 1995).

Understanding Interests

During this phase of the mediation process, the parties are instructed to talk directly to each other. The goal of this phase is for each party to be heard and understood by the other. The party who is listening is directed not to interrupt or to respond to what the other party is saying. Instead, each party attempts to view the issues in dispute from the perspective of the other party. In fact, the mediator asks each party to paraphrase what they heard the other party say. The mediator's role is to keep the discussion on track by focusing on only one issue at a time. The discussion during this understanding interests phase can progress to the next stage in the mediation process when both parties appear to understand each other's main concerns and also demonstrate a willingness to trust each other enough to work together on a mutual resolution to the dispute.

Collaborative Problem Solving

In the collaborative problem-solving mediation phase, the discussion is oriented to brainstorming possible solutions to each of the issues in dispute. The mediator facilitates the brainstorming by ensuring that any initial attempts to evaluate proposed solutions are not permitted because, at this stage, creativity should be encouraged and the goal is to get as many potential solutions on the table as possible. At the conclusion of the problem-solving brainstorming session, the mediator assists the parties in carefully considering each proposed solution from each party's perspective.

The mediator also facilitates a discussion of potential obstacles to proposed solutions by (1) assisting the parties to be specific about the exact details of their commitments, (2) testing each proposed solution against what is realistic for each party to do, (3) acting as a devil's advocate by voicing barriers which may threaten the implementation of the mediation agreement, and (4) helping the parties decide what to do if one or the other does not comply with the agreement (Engiles et al., 1996).

During this collaborative problem-solving phase, as proposed solutions are being generated and discussed, either one or both parties may have a need to caucus. During a caucus, the parties meet separately, with the mediator acting as a facilitator who clarifies specific concerns and determines what each party is willing to consider as a solution. It may be necessary for the parties to caucus several times. The mediator should ensure the parties prior to a caucus that whatever is said during a caucus is confidential (i.e., is not shared with the other party).

Concluding the Mediation

There are three possible outcomes of mediation: (1) the parties reach an agreement about all of the issues in dispute, (2) the parties remain firm in their positions and further mediation time would not produce a mutual agreement, or (3) both parties agree to reconvene later after gathering and/or considering additional information (Schrag, 1996a). If the parties reach a mutual resolution of their dispute, the mediator assists the parties in drafting a written agreement. The mediation agreement should be specific, clear about deadlines, balanced in terms of obligations and concessions from both parties, positive, realistic, clear and simple, and signed by both parties (Arizona Department of Education, 1993). In addition, Schrag (1996b) offers the following mediation agreement writing recommendations:

- Use simple and understandable language in drafting the agreement. Avoid legalese and educational jargon.
- Refer to the parties by name, not by some legal term such as *complainant* or *respondent*.
- Use short paragraphs when writing the agreement.
- Be as specific as possible in terms of describing the obligations of both parties. For example, if one of the agreements is to provide a particular educational service to the student with a disability, specify by name or by title who will provide that service, where that service will be provided, when that service will be provided, and how that service will be provided.
- Use the parties' word choices whenever possible if that serves to enhance clarity and understanding.
- Attempt to balance the written agreement by alternating the concessions made so that it appears that each party won something during the mediation.
- Focus on future actions and avoid language that places blame for past problems or dissatisfaction.
- Schedule an IEP meeting to incorporate those components of the agreement that are pertinent to the student's IEP.

If the parties are at an impasse, the mediator must review their due process hearing rights at the conclusion of the mediation session. If the parties have decided to reconvene at a later date after gathering and/or considering additional information, the mediator needs to set a specific date and time for the next session and clarify what should be accomplished by that next session. If the parties have reached and signed an agreement, the mediator may suggest that the parties establish a periodic review schedule to meet and discuss the ongoing implementation of the mediation agreement.

Mediation Models

Although the 1997 IDEA Amendments provided for greater uniformity among the states and provided a model for the states that had not yet implemented mediation, most states had already adopted some form of mediation prior to the 1997 amendments (Yell, 1998). The IDEA does require that special education mediators be knowledgeable about special education law and trained or qualified to conduct mediation sessions. Further, the mediator cannot be an employee of the local school district involved in the mediation or the state education agency. A final requirement of mediators is that they not have any personal or professional conflicts of interest.

State mediation models vary in the way mediators are selected and/or assigned, in the scheduling of the sessions, in the way local school districts can request or obtain the services of a mediator, in the amount of time for a mediation session, and in the presence, absence, and extent of the follow-up involvement of the state education agency (Schrag, 1996a; Symington, 1995). In her review of mediation in special education, Schrag (1996a) identified three distinct state mediation models: the single mediator model, the co-mediator model, and the panel mediator model. The majority of states use the single mediator model in special education disputes. Individuals who serve in the single mediator role are hired and paid in a variety of ways. For example, some states contract with a private organization to provide qualified mediators. Other states rely on trained volunteers to serve as mediators (Ahearn, 1994). In the co-mediator model, two individuals serve as mediators. In the third model, panel mediators, typically three or four individuals facilitate the mediation process.

Situations When Mediation Is Not an Appropriate Dispute Resolution Mechanism

Special education professionals serving as advocates must appreciate the limitations of mediation as a dispute resolution mechanism. That is, there are certain situations where it is inadvisable to pursue mediation. Engiles and colleagues (1996) outlined four situations where mediation may not be appropriate for resolving special education disputes: (1) one or both parties require a legal interpretation of the IDEA or other applicable law; (2) the parents' goal is a personnel change; (3) any of the parties in the dispute are unwilling to participate in a collaborative problem-solving process; or (4) there is an imbalance between the parties in their abilities to negotiate and problem solve which cannot be remedied by the mediator. Such a situation exists, for example, if one of the parties of a dispute is suffering from an illness that diminishes his or her mental capacity.

Comparison of Mediation and Due Process Hearings

Most legal scholars maintain that the due process hearing system is ill suited to resolving special education disputes and advocate for alternative dispute resolution strategies, including mediation (Fiedler, 1993; Goldberg & Huefner, 1995; Goldberg & Kuriloff, 1991; Maloney, 1993; Schrag, 1996a; Symington, 1995; Turnbull & McGinley, 1987; Vitello, 1990; Zirkel, 1994). The presumed dispute resolution advantages of mediation compared to due process hearings are revealed in the following discussion of the differences between these two procedures (Schrag, 1996a, 1996b; Vitello, 1990; Whelan, 1996).

Procedural Qualities

As has been stated, mediation is a nonadversarial process that emphasizes collaborative problem solving by the parents and school personnel. Due process hearings are adversarial by nature, often polarizing the two parties in the dispute because there is a level of contentiousness. In mediation sessions, the atmosphere is informal, emphasizing brainstorming, discussion, and negotiation. In contrast, due process hearings are quite formal, with many of the procedural trappings (e.g., direct and cross-examination of witnesses, formal presentation of documentary evidence, adherence to judicial rules of evidence, transcription of testimony by a court stenographer) of a court trial. Although attorneys are often present at mediation sessions, their role is reduced in comparison to the participation of attorneys at due process hearings.

Past or Future Orientation

A due process hearing is past oriented as witnesses recollect events that have already occurred. This focus on the past is usually fault oriented in an effort to establish blame on the school district. In contrast, mediation discourages levying blame on either party and, instead, emphasizes the future and what needs to be done to provide the student with a FAPE.

Emphasis on Winning

A win-win philosophy is inherent to mediation in the fact that the parties in dispute must *mutually* agree to an acceptable solution of their differences. There is no "loser," because neither party is forced to agree to a proposed solution unless they are satisfied and comfortable with the proposal. In comparison, due process hearings, as is the nature of litigation, are win-lose contests. That is, the hearing officer will render a decision that will result in one party's position prevailing while the other party loses.

Communication

A skilled mediator can effectively reestablish communication between the parents and school personnel as those parties learn to trust and listen to each other, appreciate each other's perspective, and collaboratively problem solve. In due process hearings, the parties typically stop communicating with each other as their attorneys take over the communication responsibility. This emphasis on attorney communication makes the dispute resolution process more formal and adversarial.

Decision-Making Authority

In mediation, the parties have control over the decision and its implementation. The mediator is a facilitator, not a decision maker. This aspect of empowerment and self-determination positively affects the parties' satisfaction with the dispute resolution process and their willingness to comply with the mutually derived agreement. In contrast, the parents and school district lose their decision-making authority in a due process hearing, as the hearing officer is now empowered to render the decision. This lack of self-determination in adversarial proceedings often contributes to continuing conflict, even after the hearing (Folberg & Taylor, 1984). In these situations, neither the parents nor the school may feel inclined to abide by a decision imposed on them by an outside authority (i.e., the hearing officer), especially if both parties feel they did not have an adequate opportunity to shape the parameters of the decision.

Costs

The financial and emotional costs of participating in mediation are substantially lower than the costs associated with due process hearings. Estimates of the financial costs of mediation sessions range from $150 to $400, whereas the cost of a due process hearing could be $25,000 or higher (Schrag, 1996b). Further, as noted by Fiedler (1993), "Perhaps the emotional trauma and distress experienced by parents and school personnel over the course of meetings, preparation for due process hearings, and the hearings themselves is more debilitating than the financial expenditures" (p. 267).

Flexibility and Responsiveness of the Decision-Making Mechanism

The claim that the due process hearing model is ill suited to resolving educational disputes is based primarily on the lack of certainty, predictability, and inability to agree on the "true facts" of special education disputes (Goldberg & Kuriloff, 1991; Vitello, 1990). Thus, it is difficult, if not impossible, to base special education decision making on accurate fact finding. The indeterminate nature of

the facts leads school personnel and parents to legitimately disagree on what educational approaches are best for a particular child. In reality, the acknowledgment that there is often more than one appropriate educational approach that could be utilized should cause parents and schools to seek more flexible, responsive, and experimental decision-making mechanisms.

The due process hearing model is quite inflexible once a decision is rendered by the hearing officer. The parties are obligated to abide by the hearing officer's decision and if experience proves that the services mandated by the hearing officer are not enhancing the child's educational progress, the parties must seek further modifications from the hearing officer or a court. This process can be quite cumbersome. The mediation process is more flexible and conducive to applications of proposed solutions on a trial basis. As argued by Vitello (1990), "Decisions arrived at between professional educators and parents should be considered flexible and experimental. Time should be allowed to test the efficacy of a particular educational program. If the program doesn't work there should be a renegotiation and reconsideration of alternative approaches" (p. 10). The problem-solving process initiated during mediation is based on trial implementation of proposed solutions, review of the child's educational progress, and reconsideration of other proposals if the child's progress is insufficient.

Research on the Effectiveness of Mediation

The presumed advantages of mediation over the adversarial due process hearing system have been discussed. There have been a few studies that have investigated the effectiveness of mediation procedures. Turnbull and McGinley (1987) conducted a survey of 89 parents who had participated in mediation, a due process hearing, or both. The purpose of their study was to determine the effectiveness of mediation as an alternative dispute resolution process by investigating parental satisfaction with the due process hearing and mediation systems, and parental satisfaction with the outcomes of these two processes. Some of their more relevant findings were that (1) the quality of interpersonal relationships between parents and school personnel was a critical factor in determining parent satisfaction with either conflict resolution process, (2) the emotional costs associated with parent participation in mediation were significantly lower than participation in due process hearings, (3) mediation did not significantly lower the financial costs of conflict resolution nor did mediation improve the interpersonal relationships between the parents and school personnel, and (4) there were no significant differences in parental satisfaction with either the processes of mediation or due process hearings or with the outcomes of either process.

Vitello (1990) conducted a survey study of 104 special education cases (53 cases were successfully mediated, 20 cases resulted in settlement at the due process hearing stage, and 31 cases required a due process hearing decision) in New Jersey. As noted, 53 percent ($n = 53$) of the studied cases resulted in a mediation agreement. This finding is consistent with other studies indicating a 50 percent settlement rate using mediation (Budoff, Orenstein, & Sachitano, 1987; Singer & Nace, 1985). There was no significant relationship between the type of special education dispute (e.g., eligibility and identification, appropriateness of special education services, related services, or placement) and the process (e.g., mediation or due process hearing) used to resolve the dispute. In the cases that proceeded to a due process hearing, the schools prevailed in 55 percent of those hearing decisions.

Conversely, the parents' interests were secured in 75 percent of the cases which reached a mediation settlement. Similar to the Turnbull and McGinley (1987) study, parents reported that participation in a due process hearing was more emotionally draining than mediation procedures. Finally, although there was no significant relationship between the presence of an advocate representing the parents and the outcome of the dispute, parents did prevail in more cases when they had an advocate.

Symington (1995) investigated mediation in five states (Connecticut, Massachusetts, New Hampshire, New Jersey, and Pennsylvania) during 1993. She found that mediation was very successful in reaching a settlement agreement and averting a due process hearing. In Connecticut, 90 percent of the mediation cases reached a settlement, in Massachusetts 85 percent were settled, in New Jersey there was a 64 percent settlement rate during mediation, and in Pennsylvania 81 percent of the mediation cases were settled prior to a due process hearing. There were no data on the percentage of settled mediation cases in New Hampshire. These settlement rates are considerably higher than the 50 percent settlement figure reported by Vitello (1990) and others.

Finally, Ahearn (1994) reported on a 1994 National Association of State Directors of Special Education study of mediation in the 39 states that had a formal special education mediation process at that time. Two significant findings merit attention. First, although no specific data were provided, Ahearn indicated that almost all of the states surveyed reported that it was common to have attorneys and advocates representing the parties at mediation sessions. Second, the percentage of mediation cases that did not reach an agreement ranged from 0 to 55 percent across the 31 states reporting these data. As speculated by Ahearn, the wide range of responses may be due to data collection issues and irregularities.

DUE PROCESS HEARINGS

The due process hearing model is based on certain elements designed to ensure accuracy in fact finding and to provide equitable treatment to the parties in dispute. Goldberg (1989) identified these required elements of "fair hearings:" (1) the hearing officer must be unbiased, (2) participants must receive adequate notice regarding the hearing, (3) participants must have ample opportunity to respond, (4) participants have the right to call witnesses on their behalf, (5) the decision must be based on evidence presented at the hearing, (6) participants have the right to legal representation,

(7) a record of the proceedings must be kept, (8) a statement of the reasons for the decision must be provided, and (9) public attendance must be permitted. Specific procedural safeguards and due process hearing rights were discussed in Chapter 5. This section briefly outlines the format of a due process hearing.

The hearing officer opens the hearing with an introductory statement, which typically includes a statement of the legal authority for the hearing, an explanation of the purpose for the hearing, an explanation of the hearing officer's role, an introduction of all persons present, information on the parties' due process rights, and general instructions on the decorum, structure, and hearing procedures (Shrybman, 1982). Following this introductory statement, the hearing officer usually inquires as to whether there are any questions, objections, or requests from the parties.

Following these matters, each party is allowed to make an opening statement outlining their case. Opening statements do not constitute evidence. After the parties' opening statements, the formal presentation of the evidence begins. Since the school district bears the burden of proof as to the appropriateness of the education provided to the child involved, the school presents its case first. The formal rules of evidence applied by courts are not followed in the more informal due process hearing, although the hearing officer is responsible for ensuring the relevance and reliability of evidence presented at the hearing (Guernsey & Klare, 1993).

In presenting its case, the school district will introduce documents (e.g., evaluation reports, IEPs, behavioral reports) and testimony to support its position. The parents may cross-examine the school's witnesses after their direct examination testimony. The hearing officer may also ask questions of any of the witnesses. After the school completes the presentation of its case, the parents present their case. In a similar format to the school's case presentation, the parents present documents and witness testimony to support their position. The school may cross-examine any witness testifying in support of the parents' case. When the parents finish the presentation of their case, both parties may conclude with a closing statement that summarizes their positions. The hearing officer closes the hearing by explaining the timelines for issuance of a written decision, explaining the appeal rights and procedures and adjourning the hearing.

School District Errors Leading to Due Process Hearings

With all of the inherent limitations/problems associated with participation in a due process hearing and the corresponding criticism of due process procedures, it is incumbent on school districts to minimize the necessity of resolving special education disputes via the due process hearing mechanism. Due process hearings have been criticized as being too expensive (both financially and emotionally), time consuming, and excessively adversarial (Goldberg & Huefner, 1995; Maloney, 1993; Zirkel, 1994). These concerns and limitations/problems will be discussed in greater detail later in this chapter.

Maloney (1993) identified seven common errors, or the "seven deadly sins" as she called them, that school districts commit which typically lead to due process hearings. These errors are likely to result in the parents prevailing at a due process hearing or subsequent court action, and may possibly lead to school district liability.

Maloney's first identified error is procedural violations of the IDEA, which are the most common mistakes committed by school districts. The most common procedural violations are (1) insufficient notice of proposal or refusal to change placement; (2) failure to obtain parental consent; (3) denial of the right to an independent educational evaluation; (4) incomplete or insufficient IEPs, especially in regard to transition services, graduation, and assistive technology; (5) improper or incomplete evaluations; (6) procedurally deficient IEP committees (not having in attendance all of the IEP members required by law); (7) unilateral change of placement (without parental notice and participation); (8) inadequate provision of parental access to and opportunity to examine student educational records; (9) illegal student suspensions or expulsions; and (10) failure to implement due process hearing orders. These procedural errors are significant since courts have ruled that such violations can constitute a denial of a FAPE and lead to school district liability for damages, compensatory education, or tuition reimbursement (Yell, 1998).

The second common school district error is when parents are told that an educational service or program is appropriate for their child but the school cannot afford such services. This error is a clear violation of the law, because schools cannot deny appropriate services based solely on cost factors.

The third error committed by school districts is the result of rigidity in their approach to providing appropriate educational services to students with disabilities. This rigidity is manifested whenever the school district fails to conduct a case-by-case analysis and decision on the necessary services that an individual student requires to receive a FAPE and, instead, relies on blanket statements or policies that automatically exclude or prohibit certain kinds of actions, services, or programs. For example, some school districts have been sued for failing to provide extended school year services to any student with disabilities or for adhering to policies that fail to evaluate students with attention deficit disorders for special education eligibility.

The fourth error identified by Maloney (1993) is the result of school districts acquiescing to the demands of parents, even when school personnel believe the parents' demands will not provide the student with a FAPE. The right to a FAPE is guaranteed to the child with disabilities, not the parents. In instances where the school is convinced that the parents are not making decisions that will provide their child with a FAPE, the school district must seriously consider requesting a due process hearing to fulfill its legal obligation of providing a FAPE.

The fifth common error, according to Maloney (1993), is when a school district acts on the basis of principle rather than reason. This kind of behavior is often stimulated by frustration in working with a particular family or in an effort to prove a

point. Yell (1998) offered the example of the school's actions in *Rapid City School District* v. *Vahle* (1990) as illustrative of this fifth common error. In the *Vahle* case, the parents were dissatisfied with the amount of occupational therapy services provided by the school district. The parents purchased independent occupational therapy (OT) services and sought reimbursement from the school district for their bill of $861. Although the school agreed that more OT was necessary and would provide those services, the school refused to reimburse the parents. Over the principle of not reimbursing these parents for a $861 OT bill, the school district lost in federal court and suffered legal fees of over $30,000.

The sixth common school district error involves the issue of burden of proof. Typically, most due process hearing officers and courts require the school to prove it has met its legal obligation of providing a FAPE to a student with disabilities. Often, school districts fail to give this burden of proof issue sufficient consideration prior to embroiling themselves in a due process hearing dispute.

The final error committed by school districts is the failure to act promptly to provide the IEP recommended services. This school procrastination has led to hearing and judicial decisions holding the school district liable for compensatory educational services and, in extreme cases, potentially liable for damages if there is a finding that the failure to act promptly constituted intentional bad faith or misconduct by the school district.

Factors to Consider Before Requesting a Due Process Hearing

Before requesting a due process hearing, parents and special education professionals must recognize that certain conflicts are not resolvable through due process hearings because (1) the presented issues do not relate to issues of law for which there can be a legal interpretation and decision, (2) the parental concerns over staffing and instructional approaches fall within the discretion of school professionals' decision-making authority, and (3) the law is ill equipped to resolve personality problems. Anderson, Chitwood, and Hayden (1997) identified the following examples as inappropriate issues for due process hearing resolution:

- The parents want a particular teacher for their child, but school officials state there are other teachers with similar qualifications.
- The parents want a teacher to use a specific teaching approach with their child, but the teacher uses another approach considered equally effective by professionals.
- The parents are dissatisfied with how they are treated by school personnel. Specifically, parents have claimed that school personnel are condescending to them and sometimes abrasive to work with.
- The parents want their child moved to another class because they feel there is a personality conflict with the teacher. The school refuses to make a change because the teacher is competent and appropriately addressing the educational needs of the child.
- The parents want the school officials to move faster in evaluating and placing their child in special education. However, the school does comply with the time lines imposed by state law.

In addition to recognizing the kinds of parent/school disputes that are inappropriate for due process hearing resolution, there are a number of factors that parents and advocates should consider before making the decision to request a hearing. Box 6.1 lists some relevant issues to consider when weighing the advantages/disadvantages of participating in a due process hearing.

Negative Consequences and Limitations of the Due Process Hearing Model

As stated at the beginning of this chapter, the issue is not the elimination of parents' or schools' rights to invoke a due process hearing to settle their disputes. In fact, there are a number of potential benefits to due process hearing participation

(Turnbull, 1993; Turnbull & Strickland, 1981). These include:

- The provision of a new forum for parents and school professionals to articulate their educational concerns
- The opportunity to legitimize educational decisions and the process by which they are made
- A means by which issues are brought to public and state education agency attention
- The opportunity to assess the school's needs, as well as the needs of the child
- A preliminary means of clarifying issues that lack legal interpretation
- The opportunity to provide consumers and school professionals with feedback on whether their interests are mutually consistent
- A method of sanction in the event that the rights of any party are abused
- The opportunity for increased communication and decreased misunderstanding
- The opportunity to increase the competence and impartiality of the decision-making process

The issue, then, is not to eliminate due process. However, given the inherent problems and limitations of the due process hearing model in resolving parent/school disputes, the issue is how to minimize reliance on this mechanism for dispute resolution. This section frames the context for a discussion of alternative dispute resolution mechanisms and strategies by identifying a number of negative consequences and limitations resulting from parent/school participation in a due process hearing, including (1) the excessively adversarial nature of due process hearings, (2) the perceived unfairness of the hearing process, (3) the time-consuming nature of hearings, (4) the financial and emotional costs to both parents and school personnel, (5) the removal of the decision-making authority from the parties in dispute, (6) the inaccessibility of the hearing system, (7) the overlegalization of the hearing system and special education, and (8) the negative effects on the child with disabilities whose parents participate in a due process hearing.

Box 6.1 _____

Advocacy Actions: Factors to Consider Before Requesting a Due Process Hearing

1. The parents must clearly understand the school district's position regarding the education of their child. The parents must consider and evaluate the evidence (e.g., facts, reports, professional testimony) the school will present to support its position.

2. The parents must be clear as to what they believe is wrong with the school district's decisions or actions regarding their child's education. Further, the parents must be able to present evidence that the school's actions were incorrect/illegal.

3. The parents must be able to articulate exactly what services, placement, or other actions the school should take to provide their child with a FAPE. The parents need to be prepared to present professional evidence supporting the appropriateness of their educational recommendations.

4. The parents should weigh all of the evidence supporting their position against all of the evidence supporting the school's position. Whose position is more credible and convincing?

5. The parents must consider where their child should be placed during the pendency of the due process hearing. Normally, according to the stay put rule, the child would remain in his/her existing educational placement during the course of the due process hearing. If this is an unsuitable arrangement for the parents, they must consider alternative temporary educational settings.

6. The parents must consider who will represent them at a due process hearing. If the parents hire an attorney to represent them, they must estimate the costs in advance. Even though the law provides for reimbursement of the parents' attorney fees if they prevail, the parents will pay their own legal fees if the school district prevails.

7. The parents must consider and weigh the potential benefits of requesting a due process hearing and winning versus the potential costs of resolving their dispute with the school via this adversarial process. Win or lose, will the parents still be able to work with school personnel in planning an appropriate education for their child?

Source: Adapted from *Negotiating the Special Education Maze: A Guide for Parents and Teachers* (pp. 41–45) by Winifred Anderson, Stephen Chitwood, and Deidre Hayden, 1997, Bethesda, MD: Woodbine House. Used with permission.

The Adversarial Nature of Due Process Hearings
The due process hearing is an overly adversarial legal proceeding (Goldberg & Huefner, 1995; Turnbull & McGinley, 1987; Vitello, 1990; Zirkel, 1994). The inherent problem of an adversarial process is that the parties are forced to oppose each other and to function within a win-lose environment (Folberg & Taylor, 1984). This resultant preoccupation with winning causes communication breakdown between the parents and school, leading to antagonism and alienation, and undermining cooperation (Beekman, 1993; Goldberg & Huefner, 1995; Symington, 1995). In this dispute resolution environment, the parties lose sight of planning for the educational future of the child (Budoff & Orenstein, 1982; Weisenstein & Pelz,

1986). These adversarial outcomes of due process hearings damage the long-term relationship between the parents and school personnel (Fiedler, 1993). In fact, the hearings widen the gulf between parents and schools and thus make it more difficult for both parties to cooperate in future educational planning for the child.

Perceived Unfairness of the Hearing Process
As noted by Fiedler (1993), "The fairness and efficiency by which parent-school disputes are handled can be an important ingredient in either losing or restoring public confidence in school systems" (p. 268). Although due process hearings guarantee impartiality and fairness, parents often report their perceptions that the hearing process is unfair

(Goldberg, 1989; Goldberg & Kuriloff, 1991). Unfortunately, due to parental perceptions of unfairness, the due process hearing system has weakened support for public education among parents who had once considered themselves as proponents of public education (Budoff & Orenstein, 1982).

School personnel report greater satisfaction with hearing fairness. According to Goldberg and Kuriloff (1991), the perception of due process hearing fairness is highly correlated with the hearing outcome. That is, those parties who prevailed at the hearing tended to express greater satisfaction with procedural fairness. In the Goldberg and Kuriloff study, the schools won more of the hearings than the parents. Since perceptions of procedural fairness are highly correlated with the hearing outcome, it is important to note the findings in another study by Kuriloff (1985). He studied the effectiveness of each party's use of the due process hearing procedures toward affecting the outcome. The findings revealed that parents who called more witnesses, offered more exhibits, presented their cases more effectively, and cross-examined the school's witnesses more thoroughly won their cases more often than parents who used these procedures less effectively.

The Time-Consuming Nature of Hearings

Zirkel (1994) asserted that the due process hearing system has become unduly time consuming and open ended. Hearings and subsequent appeals to court can delay appropriate educational placements and services for years (Goldberg & Huefner, 1995). Even though the IDEA requires that a due process hearing must be held and a final decision by the hearing officer must be reached within 45 days of the request for a hearing, it is not unusual for hearings to extend well beyond this 45-day limit (Zirkel, 1994). Further, it is not unusual for a case to return to the hearing stage several times prior to any final resolution of the dispute (Zirkel, 1994). For many children with disabilities being deprived of appropriate educational services, justice delayed is tantamount to justice denied.

Financial and Emotional Costs

Due process hearings are financially and emotionally costly to both parents and school personnel (Fiedler, 1993; Goldberg & Huefner, 1995; National Council on Disability, 1989; NASDSE, 1993; Symington, 1995; Turnbull & McGinley, 1987; Vitello, 1990; Zirkel, 1994). Many professionals have complained that excessive preoccupation with legal compliance has absorbed an inordinate amount of the time and resources of school personnel, hampering substantive efforts to improve educational programs and services (NASDSE, 1993). As an example of the financial costs to school districts, Zirkel (1994) cited one due process hearing where the cost of the transcript was $27,000 and the hearing officer's fees amounted to $20,000. These fees do not include other costs, such as the school's attorney's fees, the instructional time lost by staff having to testify at a hearing, and the potential reimbursement costs for the parents' attorney if the parents prevail. Parents also incur financial costs, including their attorney's fees (if they lose, those costs are not reimbursed by the school district), time away from work, or, in a few extreme situations, loss of a job due to repeated absenteeism necessitated by preparation for the due process hearing (Fiedler, 1993).

The emotional costs experienced by parents and school professionals participating in due process hearings may be more significant than the financial costs (Fiedler, 1993). For example, in their study of due process hearings, Budoff and Orenstein (1982) reported that 56 percent of the parents interviewed indicated that their participation in a hearing was "extremely upsetting" and 70 percent of the parents agreed with the statement that "the emotional costs of using the hearing system are high." School personnel also experience emotional trauma and anxiety as a result of their due process hearing participation (Budoff & Orenstein, 1982). Due process hearings can have a damaging effect on school staff morale and confidence because special educators' self-image as advocates for more humane treatment of children with disabilities within their school systems is often under attack at a due process hearing (Fiedler, 1993).

Removal of the Decision-Making Authority from the Parties in Dispute

This limitation was previously mentioned when comparing the mediation process with the due process hearing model. When the parties in dispute lose their self-determination and must rely on the decision of a third party (hearing officer), they feel less inclined to abide by a decision imposed on them by an outside authority (Fiedler, 1993). These feelings often lead to further hostility escalation by both parties. After studying the hearing system and interviewing parents, school officials, and hearing officers, Budoff and Orenstein (1982) identified these inherent limitations in the decision-making authority of hearing officers: hearing officers cannot usually change attitudes; they cannot change theoretical or methodological disputes rampant among special education experts; the quality of one party's representation may be as influential to the hearing officer as the actual merits of the case; the hearing officer usually will not deal with hidden agendas and motivational issues; and the hearing officer cannot resolve social-policy issues (e.g., a claim that children with disabilities should be entitled to the best educational services possible).

Inaccessibility of the Hearing System

Research findings have consistently shown that the due process hearing system is accessible primarily to parents in the middle- and upper-income levels (Fiedler, 1993). As stated by Goldberg (1989), "There is some evidence that parents who are especially knowledgeable about the legal procedures and those with greater financial resources have disproportionate access to the system's benefits" (p. 449). Further, Goldberg contended that few parents appeal denial of their children's rights in a large bureaucracy (such as a school district) because parents who have low incomes are not able to afford legal representation, they may be ignorant of the system's requirements, or they fear

school retaliation against their child. In reality, the fiscal burdens associated with due process hearing participation abridge the rights of parents from lower socioeconomic backgrounds (Salend & Zirkel, 1984).

The Overlegalization of the Hearing System and Special Education

The hearing system has been criticized as representative of the special education profession's tendency to turn over questions of ethical judgment or educational programming to attorneys and the legal procedures of due process (Kauffman, 1984). In fact, given the increase in litigation over the past decade, it is apparent that school professionals and parents are allowing attorneys, hearing officers, and judges to shape educational policy and practice that should rightfully be shaped by educators and parents (Audette, 1982).

Negative Effects on the Child with Disabilities

When the due process hearing system works as well in reality as it is supposed to in theory, and when both parents and school personnel willingly comply with the hearing officer's decision, the hearing process can be expected to benefit children with disabilities. However, parents' due process hearing participation may entail several possible negative effects on their children with disabilities (Fiedler, 1993). For example, many parents reported that their children's attitude toward school deteriorated during the hearing process (Budoff, 1976). Another negative consequence of due process participation may be undue harshness or indifference toward the child at school (Strickland, 1982). The educational experience for the child whose parents have filed for a due process hearing may be altogether unpleasant. Further, parents may impose undue pressure on their children while preparing them to testify at a hearing. These negative emotional effects on the child undoubtedly depend on the child's age and the parents' effort to shield the child from anxieties associated with the educational dispute (Fiedler, 1993).

ALTERNATIVE DISPUTE RESOLUTION STRATEGIES IN SPECIAL EDUCATION

With the previous discussion of the potential negative consequences and limitations of parent/school participation in due process hearings, both parties ought to have sufficient incentive to consider alternative dispute resolution strategies. An ideal dispute resolution process would have, at a minimum, these elements:

- *The process addresses mutual concerns without doing additional harm to individuals and their relationships.*
- *The process allows parents and schools to make constructive, ongoing contributions to resolutions that affect them.*
- *The process values time and money as precious resources and uses them as sparingly as possible.*
- *The process is responsive to the needs of diverse populations. (Engiles et al., 1996, p. 1)*

Zirkel (1994) proposed a five-step solution to improving the due process hearing system. First, similar to grievance arbitration in labor law, he recommended that the due process hearing be the final stage for most special education cases. The hearing decision would be binding on both parties, with judicial review only available in a limited number of cases where there is a purely legal issue in dispute. This recommendation would require an amendment to the IDEA to delete the option of a second tier appeal process. The single tier would be at the state level to remove the possible influence of the school district paying the hearing officer. In this model, the selection, training, and payment of hearing officers would become the responsibility of an independent state agency.

Second, Zirkel proposed that the hearing officer have expertise in special education, as opposed to being an attorney. Third, the hearing's format and structure would change from an adversarial focus to a problem solving model. The hearing officer would facilitate this problem-solving process by engaging the active participation of both parties. Zirkel's fourth recommendation reinforces the deemphasis on an adversarial hearing

model by limiting attorney fees to the judicial stage and precluding school districts from being represented by attorneys at the hearing unless the parents are represented by an attorney. Finally, Zirkel would limit hearings in routine cases to one full day. This recommendation addresses the time consuming and financial cost concerns of the current due process hearing system.

Schrag (1996a) identified several examples of alternative dispute resolution strategies in special education that are being used around the country. The following examples will be briefly discussed: independent ombudsperson, impartial reviews, prehearing conferences, advisory opinion process, neutral conferences, and resource parents.

Independent Ombudsperson

An independent ombudsperson is available to parents to provide information about special education and how to access necessary services. The ombudsperson works with parents and school personnel before and during IEP development and implementation. He or she is independent of the school district and serves as an objective neutral party in working with parents and the school to find solutions to disagreements. One function of the ombudsperson is to engage in fact finding when the parties have tried unsuccessfully to settle an issue. The purpose of the fact finding conducted by the ombudsperson is to gain an understanding of the issue(s) in dispute and to offer recommendations to the parties in an effort to resolve their differences.

Impartial Reviews

As Schrag (1996a) stated, "An impartial review team is two or three impartial/knowledgeable professionals who spend one full day or two half days on site to review the situation in conflict and render a written second opinion" (p. 13). Although this second opinion is nonbinding on the parties, it can be introduced as evidence at a subsequent hearing. The impartial review allows both parties an opportunity to review the merits of their positions prior to committing to an adversarial due process hearing. In some cases, the opinions rendered by the impartial review team enhances the parties' motivation to continue efforts at mutually resolving their dispute.

Prehearing Conferences

Many states have legal provisions authorizing due process hearing officers to conduct prehearing conferences. The purposes of a prehearing conference are to (1) offer the parents and school one final opportunity to mutually resolve their dispute; (2) clarify the issues needing resolution at the hearing; and (3) identify whether the parties are willing to stipulate to any facts, thus alleviating the need to establish those facts via documentary evidence or testimony at the hearing. During my eight years as a due process hearing officer, I presided over approximately 20 due process cases. At the prehearing conference, the parties were able to mutually resolve their differences in about 75 percent of those cases. The hearing officer must be careful, however, not to impair his or her impartiality while conducting a prehearing conference in the event the parties do not resolve their dispute and proceed to a due process hearing.

Advisory Opinion Process

The advisory opinion process occurs between mediation and a due process hearing. During this process, the parents and school officials are each allowed one hour to present their case to a hearing officer. The parties may call witnesses to testify and present documents to the hearing officer. At the conclusion of this two-hour period, the hearing officer issues an oral nonbinding advisory opinion. This case assessment process allows the parties to reassess their respective positions. This reassessment may cause the parties to elect to settle their differences, go back to mediation, or proceed to a full due process hearing with a different hearing officer.

Neutral Conferences

In this alternative dispute resolution process, a neutral individual functions like an arbitrator to review the facts and merits of a special education case. Both parties present their cases to the neutral arbitrator who renders a nonbinding decision. The neutral conferences are similar to the impartial review process, with the exception that a single individual serves in the advisory opinion capacity.

Resource Parents

Resource parents, who are trained in mediation and conflict resolution, work on relationship building between parents and school personnel. Resource parents also provide these services to parents embroiled in a dispute with their child's school: "parent-to-parent consultation," assistance in identifying options, help in finding resources from other agencies, and linking parents with other parents with similar issues and concerns. Resource parents also attend IEP meetings as the parents' advocate.

ADDITIONAL SPECIAL EDUCATION ENFORCEMENT AND DISPUTE RESOLUTION MECHANISMS

This section reviews several administrative agency procedures available to parents and special education professionals who are dissatisfied with the educational services provided to children with disabilities. The federal Department of Education and state departments of education have administrative responsibility to enforce compliance with special education laws and regulations. An effective advocate will seek to "make the educational system work" by invoking the appropriate administrative enforcement mechanisms. These administrative enforcement mechanisms are discussed: the IDEA complaint process, the Section 504 complaint process, the Family and Educational Rights and Privacy Act (FERPA) complaint process, and the state and federal compliance monitoring procedures.

The IDEA Complaint Process

An individual or organization may file a signed written complaint with the state department of education, alleging a special education procedural or substantive violation under the IDEA (Suchey & Huefner, 1998). From 1980 to 1990, the state complaint procedure existed within the Department of Education's newly created General Administrative Regulations (EDGAR) (U.S. Department of Education, 1980). In 1990, when the federal special education law was renamed from the Education of the Handicapped Act to the IDEA, the state complaint procedure was incorporated into the Department's IDEA regulations (U.S. Department of Education, 1992).

Under the IDEA complaint process, the state department of education must investigate and resolve a complaint within 60 days. The state agency issues a written decision with its findings and conclusions. Appeals of the state agency's complaint decision may be taken to the Office of Special Education Programs of the U.S. Department of Education. Any individual or organization may file a complaint if it is believed a school district responsible for providing special education has violated a state or federal law or regulation. "The complaint may be based on an alleged violation affecting one child or a group of children; it may allege an incident that is a violation or a systemic violation throughout the agency" (Underwood & Mead, 1995, p. 155). If a violation is found, the state department of education will require the local school district to submit a corrective action plan detailing how the district will correct the violation(s).

Suchey and Huefner (1998) have argued that the state IDEA complaint process has several potential advantages over mediation and hearings. These advantages include (1) the scope of a complaint can cover the full range of substantive and procedural issues that can be addressed in a due process hearing (OSEP, 1994); (2) the costs of the complaint process are borne by the state agency, not the local school district or parents; (3) attorneys do not usually participate as representatives

for the parties in the complaint process; and (4) orders of the state education agency in a complaint decision are enforceable in court, similar to due process hearing decisions.

In a survey of IDEA complaint managers within the 50 state departments of education (35 states responded to all or a portion of the survey), Suchey and Huefner (1998) discovered that the number of complaints filed with 23 state departments of education had increased an average of 29 percent over the three years that data was collected (1992–1994). In another pertinent finding, a majority of the state respondents favored mediation over the complaint process and due process hearings in terms of both cost effectiveness and effectiveness of outcomes for students. Finally, Suchey and Huefner were not surprised to find that educators file only a small percentage of the complaints. They stated, "To challenge one's own school district, no doubt, is uncomfortable, and requires careful thought" (p. 540). I agree with this sentiment but, at the very least, special education professionals must be aware of the state complaint process regardless of whether they file the complaint or encourage the parents to file. See Box 6.2 for an example of an IDEA complaint letter format.

The Section 504 Complaint Process

As discussed in Chapter 5, Section 504 of the Rehabilitation Act of 1973 closely parallels the special education rights and procedures under the IDEA. Section 504, similar to the IDEA, has an administrative complaint process. Any individual or organization who believes a school district or school officials have violated students' or parents' rights under Section 504 may file a formal complaint with the regional office of the Office of Civil Rights (OCR) of the U.S. Department of Education. (See Figure 6.1 for a list of regional OCR offices.) Section 504 complaints must be filed within 180 days of the alleged discriminatory actions. OCR will investigate the circumstances of the complaint and issue a written Letter of Finding. The Letter of Finding may exonerate the school district by concluding there was no viola-

Box 6.2 _____

Advocacy Actions: IDEA Complaint

To: State Department of Education

Date: _____

From: _____

Address: _____

_____

Phone: _____

Relationship to the child involved in the complaint: _____

Child's name: _____   Date of birth: _____

Disability: _____   Age: _____

School Superintendent: _____

School District: _____

Address: _____   Phone: _____

_____

List the names and positions of each person mentioned in this complaint.

Name   Position

_____

_____

_____

_____

_____

_____

_____

_____

Box 6.2   Continued _____

Name of the school in which the child is enrolled now (if the alleged violation occurred in a different

 school, point that out in your complaint): _____

Name of the principal of that school: _____

School Address:_____   Phone: _____

                        _____

Describe the complaint. (Make the description as specific as possible by using dates of events, names of people involved, and names of places where the events happened. Consider listing the events and dates in chronological order to facilitate recollection and investigation of the complaint.) Include additional pages if necessary.

Assistance needed from the State Department of Education. (Describe the assistance sought in the complaint—for example, *Please assist this school district in writing IEPs that more accurately reflect individual student needs.* Another example, *Please assist this school district to provide the necessary related services for individual students.*)

Other concerns and considerations. (Here it would be important to mention if you are concerned that the school district may not follow through on an issued corrective action plan or if you are worried that the school may retaliate against the child.)

(continued)

BOX 6.2   Continued _____

Statement from the child named in the complaint (if appropriate).

How many additional pages have been included? _____

Signature of person filing the complaint: _____ Date: _____

Signatures of persons supporting this complaint (if appropriate).

Name	Position	Date
_____		
_____		
_____		
_____		

Include copies of any documents that will support the complaint. Keep the original. Send only copies.

Source: Parent Education Project of Wisconsin, Inc., 1998, 414-328-5520. Reprinted by permission.

---

tion or OCR may identify specific violations and the corrective actions required of the school district. OCR will rarely investigate alleged violations of individual placement or other educational decisions. Instead, OCR investigates claims of discriminatory treatment by school districts or officials (Anderson et al., 1997). See Box 6.3 for a listing of information that should be contained in a Section 504 complaint.

The FERPA Complaint Process

The access rights of parents to their children's educational records, including confidentiality protections and amendment rights, were discussed in Chapter 5. The main federal law granting parental rights to their children's educational records is the Family and Educational Rights and Privacy Act (FERPA). A failure to comply with FERPA provisions for access to educational records and confidentiality may be prosecuted by the parents' filing a written complaint with the FERPA Office, Family Policy Compliance Office, U.S. Department of Education (Anderson et al., 1997; Fiedler & Prasse, 1996).

After the U.S. Department of Education investigates the complaint, if there is a finding that the school district did not comply with FERPA provisions, the school district can be ordered to take corrective actions. If the school district does not voluntarily comply with the department's corrective order, the Secretary of Education may withhold federal funds to the school district (Fiedler & Prasse, 1996).

State and Federal Compliance Monitoring Procedures

State departments of education and the U.S. Department of Education have administrative responsibility for ensuring compliance with special education laws and regulations. The state departments

FIGURE 6.1 U.S. Department of Education, Office of Civil Rights (Regional Offices)

Region I (Connecticut, Maine, Massachusetts, New Hampshire, Rhode Island, Vermont)

Office of Civil Rights, Region I
John W. McCormack POCH
Post Office Square, Room 222
Boston, Massachusetts 02109
(617)223-9662; TTY (617)223-9695

Region II (New Jersey, New York, Puerto Rico, Virgin Islands)

Office of Civil Rights, Region II
26 Federal Plaza–33rd Floor
New York, New York 10278
(212)264-4633; TTY (212)264-9464

Region III (Delaware, District of Columbia, Maryland, Pennsylvania, Virginia, West Virginia)

Office of Civil Rights, Region III
Gateway Building
3535 Market St., Room 6300
Philadelphia, Pennsylvania 19104-3326
(215)596-6791; TTY (215)596-6794

Region IV (Alabama, Florida, Georgia, Kentucky, Mississippi, North Carolina, South Carolina, Tennessee)

Office of Civil Rights, Region IV
101 Marietta Tower–27th Floor
P.O. Box 1705
Atlanta, Georgia 30301
(404)331-2959; TTY (404)331-7803

Region V (Illinois, Indiana, Minnesota, Michigan, Ohio, Wisconsin)

Office of Civil Rights, Region V
401 South State Street–7th Floor
Chicago, Illinois 60605
(312)353-2520; TTY (312)353-2540

Region VI (Arkansas, Louisiana, New Mexico, Oklahoma, Texas)

Office of Civil Rights, Region VI
1200 Main Tower Building–Suite 2260
Dallas, Texas 75202
(214)767-3936; TTY (214)767-3315

Region VII (Iowa, Kansas, Missouri, Nebraska)

Office of Civil Rights, Region VII
P.O. Box 901381
10220 N. Executive Hills Blvd.–8th Floor
Kansas City, Missouri 64190-1381
(816)891-8026; TTY (816)374-7607

Region VIII (Colorado, Montana, North Dakota, South Dakota, Utah, Wyoming)

Office of Civil Rights, Region VIII
1961 Stout Street, Room 342
Denver, Colorado 80294
(303)844-5695; TTY (303)844-3417

Region IX (Arizona, California, Hawaii, Nevada, Guam, Trust Territory of the Pacific Islands, American Samoa)

Office of Civil Rights, Region IX
221 Main Street–10th Floor
San Francisco, California 94105
(415)227-8020; TTY (415)227-8124

Region X (Alaska, Idaho, Oregon, Washington)

Office of Civil Rights, Region X
2901 3rd Avenue, Room 100
Seattle, Washington 98121-1042
(206)442-1636; TTY (206)442-4542

select a percentage of local school districts each year and conduct onsite monitoring compliance reviews. Although the administrative compliance monitoring provisions vary from state to state, typically state agency personnel will conduct a review of a sample of local school district's special education documents (e.g., evaluation reports, IEPs, student educational records, parental notice and con-

sent documents, etc.) to monitor for procedural compliance with state and federal special education laws.

In addition, state agency personnel conduct onsite interviews with local school district officials, teachers, related services personnel, and parents. The purpose of these interviews is to determine if there are any systemic issues or prob-

Box 6.3_____

Advocacy Actions: Components of a Section 504 Complaint Letter

A complaint based on an alleged Section 504 violation should include:

- The name, address, and telephone number of the person(s) making the complaint
- The name, address, and telephone number of the student(s) whose rights are being violated
- The nature of the student's disabling condition
- The name, address, and telephone number of the school and officials who are violating the student's rights
- A description of the violations in terms of Section 504
- The date(s) of the violation(s) occurrence(s)
- Other children with disabilities who are also affected, if known
- The names, addresses, and telephone numbers of persons who can be contacted for further information
- Other attempts to solve the problem (e.g., meetings)
- A request that OCR keep the complainant informed of any action taken, including copies of any written findings

Source: From *You, Your Child, and "Special" Education: A Guide to Making the System Work* by B. C. Cutler, 1993, Baltimore: Paul Brookes Publishing Company, P.O. Box 10624, Baltimore, MD 21285-0624. Reprinted by permission.

lems in complying with special education laws and procedures. Local school districts who are found to be out of compliance with legal provisions must submit corrective action plans to the state department of education. These corrective action plans detail the local school district's actions to remediate the legal violations they have been cited for by the state agency. The state agency will then monitor to ensure the local school district fulfills its corrective action plan obligations.

Similar to state department of education compliance monitoring of local school districts, the Office of Special Education Programs (OSEP), U.S. Department of Education, engages in state compliance monitoring. Each state must submit a state plan of special education to the U.S. Department of Education, outlining how the state will comply with the IDEA and its regulations. Personnel from OSEP review the state plan and other relevant state special education documents. OSEP personnel also conduct on-site state compliance reviews in a manner similar to state agency monitoring of local school districts.

OSEP schedules several public meetings around the state as part of its compliance monitoring. The purpose of these public meetings is to gather oral and written comments on issues, concerns, or problems that have an impact on the effectiveness of the state education agency's systems for supervision of special education compliance by local school districts. Any interested individual can request a copy of the state's plan of special education services and may submit input at public compliance monitoring meetings. If a state is found to be out of compliance with the IDEA or its regulations, OSEP will work with the state agency to develop a state corrective action plan.

SUMMARY

The intention of the parent participation provisions of the IDEA is to empower parents to serve as equal educational decision makers with school professionals regarding their children. Although the collaborative process envisioned by the IDEA works well in many instances, it is to be expected that closer parent/school decision making collaboration often inevitably leads to differences of opinion and disagreement between parents and school professionals. The manner in which parent/school disagreement or conflict is managed can make the difference between constructive resolution of the dispute or a destructive escalation of conflict. Although the due process rights afforded parents and school districts under the law are necessary as an ultimate dispute resolution system, most parents and professionals agree that nonadversarial dispute resolution mechanisms like mediation must serve as the primary means for parent/school dispute resolution.

CHAPTER 7

KNOWLEDGE OF SCHOOL CHANGE ISSUES AND STRATEGIES

To cope with a changing world, any entity must develop the
capability of shifting and changing, of developing new skills
and attitudes; in short the capability of learning . . . the
essence of learning is the ability to manage change by
changing yourself - as much for people when they grow up as
for companies when they live through turmoil.
—*A. de Gues* (The Living Company, *1997*)

In addition to knowledge about special education law (Chapter 5) and knowledge about dispute resolution mechanisms in special education (Chapter 6), an effective advocate needs an understanding of school change issues and strategies. Special education advocacy is essentially a problem-solving endeavor where an advocate attempts to improve a student's educational situation. Such change requires that an individual, the advocate, identify an essential need that is unmet for a student in the current educational environment and commit himself or herself to advocating for a change (Ryndak, 1994a).

As noted in Chapter 1, advocacy actions, by definition, seek a change in the status quo. Change, whether positive or negative, however, is inherently stressful for both individuals and institutions. Because of this stress, as recognized by family systems (Turnbull & Turnbull, 1997) and school reform literature (Gersten, Vaughn, Deshler, & Schiller, 1997), change is often slow, anxiety producing, and resisted by those who are expected to alter their attitudes and behaviors. Change typically involves a level of discomfort in moving from the "known" of the status quo to the "unknown" of a new situation. Special education advocacy affects change for students with disabilities at three

levels: intrapersonal change (occurring within the individual professional), interpersonal change (involving relations between the individual professional and others, (such as, colleagues, administrators, and family members), and systems change (involving change in the way schools and the people in them do business).

Individuals who are affected by change are referred to as *stakeholders* (Karasoff, 1991). Not only are stakeholders affected by change but they also fulfill various roles and responsibilities. Specifically, there are four key stakeholders in the change process as it relates to special education: (1) students with disabilities and their families, (2) the change initiators, (3) the power sources, and (4) the change agents (Ryndak, 1994a). Students with disabilities and often their families are the catalyst for advocacy to bring about change. Ryndak (1994a) pointed out that change efforts are initiated because of a student's unmet needs, continue until those needs are met to the satisfaction of all stakeholders, and are evaluated for the effectiveness of the advocacy in meeting the student's needs.

A second stakeholder in the change process is the change initiator. The change initiator is the individual who identifies an unmet need and resolves to advocate for change until that need is addressed (Ryndak, 1994a). An internal change initiator is one who works within the school district as a professional (i.e., teacher, related services person, administrator, etc.). Also, given their legally prescribed role as educational decision makers, parents can be considered as internal change initiators. Examples of external change initiators include parent advocates, advocacy organizations (e.g., state protection and advocacy organizations, parent training and information centers), attorneys, professional organizations (e.g., Council for Exceptional Children), university experts in special education and related fields, and local citizens. By identifying discrepancies between educational services provided and best practices, external change initiators may create the requisite motivation among internal change initiators to form an advocacy partnership with the external change initiators in bringing about necessary educational change.

Power sources represent another key stakeholder in the change process. These are individuals with the capacity for facilitating change in either a positive or negative manner (Ryndak, 1994a). Typically, individuals in administrative positions (e.g., school board members, superintendents, directors of special education, and principals) are considered to be the power sources, as they can initiate or thwart school change efforts. Although any administrator may indeed be a crucial power source, other power sources are often overlooked. These individuals possess their "power" because they are (1) highly respected in the school building or the district; (2) most immediately affected by the proposed change; or (3) most influential in changing the opinions or attitudes of others (Ryndak, 1994a).

Therefore, a number of individuals have the capacity to function as power sources, including general and special education teaches, related services personnel, paraprofessionals, school support personnel, parents, and students themselves. Ryndak (1994a) asserted that each power source may function as an ally (who actively assists in facilitating the desired change), or an adversary (who actively hinders change efforts), or a cooperative (who takes a "wait and see" approach, allowing the change to occur and then deciding if they will support or oppose the change).

Finally, change agents are critical stakeholders in the change process. "Change agents are individuals who actually conduct the activities through which the desired change will occur" (Ryndak, 1994a, p. 255). Change agents facilitate school change by providing (1) information on the rationale for the proposed change, (2) support and assistance to promote change efforts, and (3) training and technical assistance to implement the change. Change agents may be internal or external to the school district. Effective school change is dependent on all of these key stakeholders. A professional who functions as an effective advocate must fulfill one or more of the roles of a change initiator, a power source, or a change agent.

ADVOCACY SCENARIOS

The issues that a professional must consider prior to engaging in advocacy on behalf of a student with disabilities are multifaceted and complex, involving at least three levels of consideration: intrapersonal, interpersonal, and systems changes. In this section, important questions to be addressed by advocates, at each level of change, will be identified.

In terms of **intrapersonal change,** professionals must address issues involving (1) the boundaries of their professional roles and responsibilities, (2) whether they possess sufficient knowledge and skills to competently advocate, (3) their ethical obligations, (4) potential personal consequences of their advocacy efforts, (5) whether they possess the required time and energy to advocate, and (6) whether they can emotionally tolerate being unsuccessful in their advocacy efforts.

In regard to **interpersonal change,** professionals must be able to (1) identify their potential allies and adversaries in the change process, (2) identify the impact that their advocacy is likely to have on relations with colleagues and administrators, and (3) contemplate their advocacy responsibility if the parents are unwilling to advocate for the necessary change.

Finally, on a **systems change** level, professionals must consider (1) the likelihood of changing school district values and/or priorities, (2) whether there are adequate resources to implement the change, (3) whether the school district will commit to providing staff with the required training and technical assistance support to implement the change, (4) the level of administrative support for staff who speak out to identify deficiencies in an effort to improve services, and (5) whether it is necessary to invoke administrative agency enforcement mechanisms to effect the necessary change.

Following is a brief review of the four advocacy scenarios presented in Chapter 1. I pose some potential questions/issues that each professional may have to address in his or her advocacy efforts at each of the three levels affected by school change efforts: intrapersonal, interpersonal, and systems changes. By engaging in this kind of analysis, I hope to illuminate some of the important considerations and factors that must be addressed by professionals prior to embarking on their "advocacy mission." Although the individual professionals in each of the advocacy scenarios will not be able to resolve all the issues by themselves (especially the systems change issues), the questions posed do represent critical issues that must be addressed in order to bring about successful and long-lasting school change.

Mary Kinney

As the only speech and language clinician in a small rural school district, Mary Kinney is faced with an advocacy challenge. She is informed that her school district has no intention of hiring a second speech and language clinician, even though an increasing number of children are in need of such services and Mary is unable to meet those children's needs because her caseload is full.

Intrapersonal Change Issues

Does Mary accept the obligation to advocate for students who are not her direct responsibility because they are not on her caseload? Is Mary suf-

ficiently knowledgeable about special education law to inform parents of their rights and options to secure appropriate educational services for their children? What is Mary's ethical obligation in this situation? Does her professional code of ethics provide any guidance in this case? Will Mary be considered by the administration as insubordinate if she meets with the parents and discusses her concerns with them?

Interpersonal Change Issues

Can Mary find any allies among her professional colleagues to support her advocacy actions? Should Mary inform the director of pupil services that she intends to meet with parents to inform them of their educational rights? What should Mary do if none of the parents are willing to challenge the school's denial of speech and language services for their children? Should Mary turn to potential external allies (e.g., parent organizations, advocacy agencies, professional organizations) to support this advocacy effort?

Systems Change Issues

Is the school district budgeting process sufficiently open to the public for comment and input? How might the school board and administration react if Mary documented the need for a second speech and language clinician and presented this information at a school board meeting? Should Mary file an IDEA complaint with the state department of education? Can Mary organize the delivery of her services in another way to address the speech and language needs of more students (e.g., employ a transdisciplinary model of service delivery or utilize a speech and language therapy aide)?

Steve Kern

The high school students with emotional/behavioral disorders taught by Steve Kern are, in his opinion, receiving an inappropriate education. Specifically, these students are being provided with inadequate vocational/career services, poor transitional planning and services due to the lack of community agency involvement, and the school is employing excessively punitive disciplinary sanctions. The school district administration has not been receptive to Steve's expressed concerns about these inadequate services.

Intrapersonal Change Issues

Is Steve confident that the IEPs he has written for his students adequately document the need for vocational/career and transitional services? Do his students with behavioral problems have specific behavior management plans written in their IEPs, which include goals and objectives based on a functional behavioral assessment and include positive behavioral supports and interventions? Is Steve willing to commit considerable time and energy to advocate for students who are the least liked and appreciated in the school? What is Steve's ethical duty in this situation?

Interpersonal Change Issues

Do any of Steve's professional colleagues agree that his students are receiving inadequate educational services? Will any colleague stand with Steve in challenging the administration on this issue? Will any parents of his students take up this advocacy issue? Are there any community agency personnel who are dissatisfied with the relationship between their agency and the school district?

Systems Change Issues

What are the specific training needs of school district staff in regard to transition planning and programming and positive behavior management techniques? Will Steve and other school staff receive sufficient time to collaboratively plan for appropriate transition services and behavioral interventions? Will the state department of education adequately monitor the implementation of new regulations on vocational services and transition programming? Are the university teacher education institutions in the state devoting sufficient curricular attention to the transition planning/ programming and positive behavior management competencies needed by special educators?

Karen Snyder

As principal of Wilson Elementary School, Karen is confronted with the problem that many of the teachers in her building are not complying with all of the IEP requirements of students with disabilities who are included in general education classrooms. Specifically, many of the IEP listed accommodations are not being implemented by the general education teachers.

Intrapersonal Change Issues

Is Karen knowledgeable about the legal consequences if a teacher does not abide by the contents of an IEP in terms of goals, objectives, and services provided? (This relates to the *Doe* v. *Withers* case discussed in Chapter 5.) Are the students with disabilities being appropriately placed into general education classrooms according to relevant least restrictive environment (LRE) decision-making criteria? After informing the teachers of their legal obligation to adhere to IEP requirements, is it Karen's responsibility to serve as a monitor to ensure teacher compliance?

Interpersonal Change Issues

Will Karen's rapport and relations with her teachers suffer as a result of her hard line stance on this IEP compliance issue? What responsibility do the special education teachers have to ensure that students' IEP accommodations are being implemented? Should Karen inform parents of this problem at her school? Would other principals in this school district act similarly to Karen on this matter? Will central administrators support her?

Systems Change Issues

Does the school staff need any inservice training on LRE legal requirements, IEP and appropriate education legal requirements, and effective accommodations to enhance the learning of students with disabilities in general education classrooms? Does the staff need inservice training on professional collaboration models and strategies? Will the school be able to commit sufficient collaborative planning time for special and general education teachers? Should an IDEA complaint be pursued with the state department of education?

Miguel Hernandez

As a school counselor, Miguel Hernandez has taken an active interest in the education and family life of Susie Ortiz, a seventh-grader with learning disabilities. Miguel is concerned that Susie's mother is stressed and overwhelmed in meeting Susie's needs at home and at school. The mother states that she is dissatisfied with Susie's education and does not trust school staff. The mother is also a single parent trying to raise five children on limited financial means.

Intrapersonal Change Issues

How involved should Miguel get in Susie's home situation? Is Miguel functioning more as a social worker instead of a school counselor or does that not even matter? Can a school professional make a positive impact on a student's home situation? In becoming so close to Susie, will Miguel be able to emotionally handle disappointment if Susie's school and home situations do not improve?

Interpersonal Change Issues

How will Miguel's colleagues at school react to his encouraging Susie's mother to demand educational changes and seek the assistance of an advocate? Will the school administration view Miguel as a troublemaker? What will Miguel do if Susie's mother does not follow through on advocating for more appropriate educational services? What is Miguel's responsibility if Susie's mother does not follow through on trying to improve the home situation?

Systems Change Issues

Does the school district value family support and empowerment principles? Should the school district attempt to function as a community resource by offering a variety of services (e.g., food pantry, parenting classes, after school programs for latch key children) to families? Does the school district view the involvement of an advocate as potentially beneficial to home/school relations or as an unwanted intrusion into school decisions? Does the school administration encourage staff to speak out when they identify a problem or deficiency?

BARRIERS TO SCHOOL CHANGE

Perhaps the greatest obstacle to school change efforts is the attitudes of the individuals who must implement the change initiative (Smith & Rose, 1993). Smith and Rose identified several such attitudinal barriers. First, there are "turf issues," which can derail the change process. These turf issues often surface when the change effort necessitates redefining the roles and responsibilities of general and special education teachers. The inclusion movement, which is heavily dependent on changing roles of both general and special educators, is a prime example of where turf issues have often stymied change efforts due to the resistance encountered from educators in changing their professional roles and responsibilities.

A second attitudinal barrier relates to teacher preparedness and professional collaboration. This attitudinal problem arises when professional collaborative relationships are not based on parity and respect for each professional's area of expertise. For example, in a relationship where a special education teacher views his or her role as that of the "expert" when working with a general education teacher, this kind of relationship is bound to foster attitudes that are not conducive to collaboration.

Awareness issues represent a third attitudinal barrier. That is, some education professionals lack adequate information and sensitivity to the needs of students with disabilities. Professionals who are insensitive to the needs of students with disabilities may be unwilling to cooperate in meeting those students' needs. This attitude results in an educational philosophy that creates obstacles to educating students with disabilities in the least restrictive environment by fostering the belief that the education of students with disabilities is solely the responsibility of special education teachers.

A final attitudinal barrier is the "someone will lose" mentality. This attitude is fostered by a belief that some students will suffer as a result of the change initiative. On the surface, this attitude seems perfectly reasonable and, indeed, compassionate by expressing concern for the needs of students. This kind of healthy skepticism becomes negative, however, when the person maintaining this attitude refuses to try out new ideas to determine whether there are any adverse consequences.

A substantial literature base on the issue of change in schools has identified several factors associated with unsuccessful attempts to change educational practice (Fullan, 1993; Fullan & Hargreaves, 1991; Hargreaves, 1997; Louis & Miles, 1990; Sarason, 1990). These factors are:

- *Rationale.* The reason for the change is poorly conceived and articulated. The change initiators are unable to clearly identify how the change will benefit students.
- *Scope.* The change initiative is either too broad or too narrow in scope. If the change is too broad, education professionals are overwhelmed with trying to work on too many issues at once. If the scope of the proposed change is too narrow, professionals and parents may not see much change at all and may become disillusioned.
- *Pace.* The change is too fast for individuals to cope with or so slow that everyone becomes bored and disinterested.
- *Resources.* The resources to implement the change effort (e.g., training support, planning time, materials) are inadequate or withdrawn too soon after the change effort is initiated. If the change efforts are to continue, educators must bear the brunt by taking on additional duties without sufficient support.
- *Commitment.* Initial change efforts will invariably experience setbacks, failure, and frustration. If there is not a long-term commitment to carry out the change process in the face of such adversity, the change initiators and agents will become disillusioned and disinterested.
- *Key staff.* Power sources in implementing the proposed change are either not sufficiently committed to the change process or are overinvolved to the exclusion of other professionals who must cooperate in the change effort. The result of either scenario is resentment and resistance from those staff who must carry out the change initiative.
- *Parents.* Parents of children with disabilities and without disabilities are not directly involved in planning and implementing the change initiative. Successful school change is heavily dependent on parent support.
- *Leadership.* There is a lack of effective leadership for the change effort because the leaders are either too autocratic, or ineffective, or lacking in long-term commitment.
- *Relationship to other initiatives.* The proposed change is too isolated and not compatible with other innovations, which diffuses the focus of educators who must implement the change.

How can advocates circumvent these barriers to school change? Advocates must respond in a systematic, mindful manner that carefully considers school change issues, barriers to change, and strategies to facilitate change. Advocates must "go deeper" (Hargreaves & Fullan, 1998) by engaging in hard thinking and soul searching about their fundamental values and purposes as an education professional. This requires the sort of analysis demonstrated by Mary Kinney, Steve Kern, Karen Snyder, and Miguel Hernandez. Going deeper requires probing school change issues and implications on intrapersonal, interpersonal, and systems change levels.

INTRAPERSONAL CHANGE

Advocating for school change on behalf of students with disabilities starts at the intrapersonal level. Advocacy is difficult and demanding work that requires professionals to understand clearly their reasons and competencies for serving as an advocate. This clarity of understanding comes from self-reflection about one's values and purposes as an education professional. This level of intrapersonal reflection is necessary to become a transformative intellectual who constantly questions the propriety of the status quo, asserts the rights of children with disabilities and their families, and actively works to promote change (Freeman, 1991).

As a component of self-reflective thinking, transformative change agents must consider their ability to deal with the inevitable criticism that comes with advocacy and to recognize that they probably already have some self-advocacy experience that is relevant. Hines (1987, pp. 11–12, 16–17) enumerated several self-reflective questions to "go deeper" on these two issues. The advocate should ask himself or herself:

- Do I believe that people should have the right to give opinions, to disagree, and to try to change conditions?
- Do I believe in the goals for which I will advocate? Do I care about the people for whom I will advocate?
- In the situations I may face, who might not like my advocacy? How many people are involved? How important is it to please these people? How hard do these people try to please me?
- Are there people or other resources that can help me take risks?
- What have been some situations where I advocated for myself?
- How did I feel about the outcome of my self-advocacy efforts? Are there reasons for my feelings? What are they?
- Recall all the steps I went through in deciding what to do and in carrying through with my advocacy plans. How did I feel during this process? Did I want more information, assistance, or resources during that process? Did I feel in control of the process? What worked and what did not work? If I had the chance, what would I change? Did the process take a long time? Could the same end have been accomplished in less time or with less stress on me?

- What strengths do I bring to the advocacy process? What areas do I want to work on in order to improve my advocacy skills?

A professional's intrapersonal reflective thinking should also consider the supports available to maintain sufficient personal resilience in the face of change. Skynner and Cleese (1993) observed that three kinds of support contributed to personal resilience: good relationships, connections in the community, and a transcendent value system. *Good relationships* in one's private and work lives are essential in supporting change efforts (Hargreaves & Fullan, 1998). Without the support of solid personal relationships with loved ones and friends, professionals engaged in advocating for school change are at risk for becoming consumed by their work and losing the necessary balance between their work and private worlds. This is a prescription for professional burnout. Good relationships are needed with one's professional colleagues because advocating for school change is a synergistic process. The change process is likely to be more successful if the change agent is working in an environment of collaborative support from colleagues. In the absence of collegial support, change agents are prone to either zealotry or withdrawal and escapism. This is another prescription for professional burnout.

The second support system, *connections in the community,* involves professional networking. I know that my advocacy work on behalf of my daughter, Jennifer, has been greatly enhanced through my professional networking in the disability field. For example, I served for several years on the board of directors of the state protection and advocacy agency. I have often used my personal connections with staff at the protection and advocacy agency to solicit advice on how to proceed on an advocacy concern regarding my daughter's education. This support system gave me confidence to advocate for necessary educational changes for my daughter.

The third support contributing to personal resilience, according to Skynner and Cleese, is a *transcendent value system*. The requisite transcendent values are hope, passion, and purpose (Hargreaves & Fullan, 1998), which were discussed in Chapter 2.

INTERPERSONAL CHANGE

The four advocacy scenarios initially presented in Chapter 1 and analyzed earlier in this chapter, demonstrate examples of professionals fulfilling the role and responsibility as an advocate for children with disabilities and their families. The professionals in these four scenarios are functioning as change initiators and change agents. With all of their commendable dedication to advocacy and school change, and their positive intrapersonal attributes, none of these four advocates can accomplish their advocacy goals by themselves. In other words, in every advocacy situation, the desired change will require interpersonal collaborative relations with others. Therefore, the second level in the school change process involves interpersonal change. How can advocates successfully foster interpersonal change? This section discusses two approaches for promoting interpersonal change: (1) the six thinking hats and (2) the Concerns Based Adoption Model (CBAM).

The Six Thinking Hats

De Bono (1985) warned that institutional change is often restricted because there is a natural human tendency to surround oneself with like-minded individuals, especially during difficult times when an organization is struggling with the uncertainty of change. According to De Bono, this "birds of a feather, all flocking together" approach does not foster the interpersonal conditions that promote creativity and change. Instead, De Bono recommended that a collaborative team that is planning and implementing change be as diverse as possible. Through this interpersonal diversity, the team will gain more insight into the potential issues and problems surrounding their change initiative. The change process is enhanced by interpersonal rela-

tions, which include the "six thinking hats" (i.e., six diverse perspectives and personalities):

1. The *white hat* represents the individual who can remain unemotional during impassioned times (good and bad) and is constantly requesting the facts. For example, the white-hat person in a team would not be impressed with all the philosophical arguments about how beneficial (or detrimental) inclusion is for students with disabilities. Instead, the white-hat thinker would want to see the evidence. This person would ask questions such as: Has the academic performance of students with disabilities included in general education classrooms improved? Has the social/behavioral performance of students with disabilities improved as a result of general education classroom inclusion? What about the academic and social/behavioral performance of students without disabilities in inclusive school programs?

2. The *black hat* is the pessimist in the group. This person is constantly arguing that the change is not possible; it will never work. Although sometimes annoying, this perspective causes the entire team to address the difficult implementation issues head on. By doing this, the change process can be more proactive instead of reactive to potential problems.

3. The *blue hat* is the highly skilled planner and organizer of the team. This individual can break large, long-term goals down into manageable short-term tasks that can be assigned to individuals in an effort to keep everyone involved in the change initiative.

4. The *red hat* represents the emotional individual on the team who fuels the team's energy with passion. Educational change for children with disabilities must be based on both the head and the heart—the head to remain rational and analytical in one's decision making and the heart to provide the change agents with the necessary dedication and commitment to maintain the change initiative over the long term.

5. The *green hat* stimulates the team's thinking and problem solving by being the creative member through his or her abilities to envision potential solutions and to stimulate the thinking of others.

6. The *yellow hat* counterbalances the black hat's pessimism by being eternally optimistic. The optimist can help the team weather the difficult times and failures that school change efforts will inevitably encounter.

The six thinking hats are a useful approach for encouraging diverse attitudes and perspectives when planning and implementing school change efforts. The value of this approach lies in the respectful interpersonal interactions it can foster. Interpersonal change is more likely to occur in an environment that values and encourages diverse opinions, while maintaining the dialogue amongst the individuals holding these different points of view. As an example of how interpersonal change can occur, read Box 7.1, which describes one of my experiences with a school change initiative.

Box 7.1_____

Advocacy Anecdote

Several years ago, I consulted on a year-long basis with an elementary school that was initiating the first year of its inclusion of students with mild/moderate mental retardation to a greater extent in general education classrooms. There were 11 students with mental retardation at the fifth- and sixth- grade levels who were being included in general education classrooms for an average of approximately 80 percent (the previous year they were included 25 percent of their school day.

My role as a consultant was to evaluate the effectiveness of the first year's inclusion efforts from the perspectives of all relevant stakeholders: special and general education teachers, administrators, parents of students with disabilities, parents of students without disabilities, the students with mental retardation who were being included to a greater extent in general education classrooms, and the students without disabilities in those general education classrooms. The inclusion effort was voluntary in terms of staff participation. The two special education teachers involved worked with three fifth- and sixth- grade general education teachers on the inclusion change initiative. As part of my consulting responsibilities, I met every week with the five participating teachers (the inclusion team) to collaboratively plan and problem solve concerns.

I learned many valuable lessons during that year, but one of the most important lessons I learned came at the last meeting of the year with the inclusion team. One of the fifth-grade general education teachers chose not to participate in the inclusion effort. In fact, this teacher was so philosophically opposed to inclusion that, at the beginning of the year, he threatened to purchase T-shirts for the rest of the staff and inscribe the shirts with an anti-inclusion slogan. Although this teacher was opposed to inclusion, he attended most of the weekly meetings of the inclusion team. I think he was simply curious about the change initiative and he probably wanted to keep a close watch on the "enemy."

At the last meeting of the inclusion team, the participating teachers were discussing plans for the next year and how they were going to expand their efforts. At the end of this meeting, the anti-inclusion teacher stood up and announced that he wanted to participate in next year's inclusion efforts. I was stunned. I never expected this teacher to change his opinion on the issue of inclusion. After the meeting, I went up to the teacher and asked if he had some sort of a religious conversion. (I wanted to approach the subject of his changed perspective on a light-hearted note!) He proceeded to explain that he wanted to participate in the inclusion effort because over the course of the year he had become jealous as he saw firsthand how excited his colleagues were as they collaborated and problem solved together. He saw his colleagues trying new ideas and being energized by this change project. He finally decided that he wanted some of this professional development action for himself.

This was a profound lesson on interpersonal change. I learned that collaboration cannot be forced on anyone. I learned that significant change can occur through rather low key interpersonal interactions. I learned to never underestimate the power of personal and professional development. And, finally, I learned the true value of collegial relationships.

The Concerns Based Adoption Model

A major useful approach to overcoming personal resistance to change is the Concerns Based Adoption Model (CBAM) developed in the early 1970s at the University of Texas Research and Development Center for Teacher Education (Hall, Loucks, Rutherford, & Newlove, 1975; Hall & Hord, 1987). CBAM is a systematic approach for finding and fixing barriers to change in school by helping users become actively and effectively engaged in implementing innovations, beginning with gaining access to information and leading, step by step, to operational use. CBAM has proved effective in helping people understand and control many of the factors that stimulate or stifle school change. This approach empowers people to make change while addressing their needs during the change process. CBAM is a tool for bringing people together to deal with change as an organized team.

The CBAM conceptualizes the change process in schools as proceeding through stages of concern that affected individuals possess about the change initiative. The first step in the change process is to know what concerns individuals have, and the second step is to respond to those concerns (Roger, Gorevin, Fellows, & Kelly, 1992). The CBAM assists change initiators, change agents, and power sources in identifying the concerns of individuals and in appropriately responding to those concerns. The CBAM stages of concern are:

- *Awareness.* Individuals express no concern about the proposed change because they have no information about it.
- *Informational.* Individuals need information about the change initiative.
- *Personal.* Individuals want to know how the change will affect them.
- *Management.* Individuals start to worry about how they will manage to cope with the change in their work environment.
- *Consequence.* Individuals think about how the school change will affect students and how they can have a positive impact on the change process.

- *Collaboration.* Individuals are thinking about how they can relate what they are doing to what others are doing.
- *Refocusing.* Individuals start thinking about ideas that might make the change initiative even better.

The CBAM recognizes that individuals confronting school change will have different concerns. Effective school change efforts must address those different concerns if the individuals who are expected to implement the change initiative are going to possess the required commitment. This approach facilitates interpersonal change by acknowledging and respecting the different informational and support needs of individuals. Examples of strategies for addressing concerns at each stage are presented in Box 7.2.

SYSTEMS CHANGE

Intrapersonal change is often necessary to motivate education professionals to function as change initiators or change agents. Interpersonal change facilitates school change efforts by promoting collaboration. However, broad-based school change efforts generally require organizational and structural changes in school districts. This third level of school change—systems change (reform)—is the focus of this section. (Specific advocacy strategies for initiating systems change will be discussed in Chapter 11.)

Key Factors in Systems Change Efforts

Changing the manner in which a school district is organized and conducts its business is a complex endeavor (Villa & Thousand, 1992). This section summarizes the key factors promoting successful systems change efforts: (1) positive attitudes and values, (2) a clear mission, (3) a school culture and climate conducive to change, (4) increasing participant ownership of the change effort, (5) a long-term commitment, (6) an outcomes-based orientation, (7) acquisition of necessary technical

Box 7.2 _____

Advocacy Actions: Example of Strategies for Addressing Concerns at Each of the CBAM Stages (Source: Roger, Gorevin, Fellows, & Kelly, 1992)

AWARENESS CONCERNS

- Involve educators in discussions and decisions about the change initiative.
- Share information to arouse interest, but not too much to avoid overwhelming people.
- Indicate that a lack of awareness is expected and reasonable and encourage questions about the change initiative.
- Encourage unaware individuals to talk with more knowledgeable colleagues.

INFORMATIONAL CONCERNS

- Provide clear and accurate information about the proposed change.
- Share information in a variety of ways amongst individuals, small and large groups.
- Arrange visits to schools that have successfully engaged in a similar change initiative.
- Assist educational staff in recognizing how many of their current practices relate to the proposed change.

PERSONAL CONCERNS

- Legitimize the existence and expression of personal concerns.
- Use personal notes and conversations to encourage and reinforce feelings of personal competence.
- Connect concerned educators with others whose concerns have subsided and will be supportive.
- Demonstrate how the change initiative can be implemented one step at a time instead of leaping full scale into the change.

MANAGEMENT CONCERNS

- Clarify the steps toward and components of the change initiative.

- Provide answers that address the specific "how to" issues that cause concerns.
- Demonstrate specific and practical solutions to management concerns.

CONSEQUENCE CONCERNS

- Encourage individuals with consequence concerns to attend conferences pertaining to the change initiative.
- Find opportunities for individuals with these concerns to share their skills with others.
- Share results from other schools who have adopted a similar change initiative.

COLLABORATION CONCERNS

- Provide opportunities for educators to develop skills in working collaboratively.
- Help collaborators establish reasonable expectations and guidelines for their collaborative efforts.
- Do not force collaboration on those who are not interested.

REFOCUSING CONCERNS

- Respect and encourage the interest shown by educators in finding better ways.
- Encourage these educators to act on their concerns for program improvement.
- Help these educators to access the resources they need to refine their ideas and implement them.

Source: From *Schools Are for All Kids: School Site Implementation—Level II Training* by B. Roger, R. Gorevin, M. Fellows, and D. Kelly, 1992, San Francisco: California Research Institute, San Francisco State University. (ED 365 052). Reprinted by permission.

knowledge, (8) ongoing professional growth, (9) collaboration, (10) a preventive orientation, and (11) initiatives that continue to evolve.

Positive Attitudes and Values

Participants in systems change efforts respond to new initiatives based on attitudes and values they have formed through prior experiences and knowledge (Hanline & Halvorsen, 1989). "Many attempts to improve educational services for students with disabilities are met with comments by stakeholders that reflect attitudes and values about the students, their value to and role in society, and their right to equal access to effective educational services" (Ryndak, 1994b, p. 270). If stakeholders maintain negative attitudes toward students with disabilities and do not value their future potential contributions to society, systems change efforts will be difficult. Negative attitudes can be counteracted by change agents providing positive information about the developmental potential of students with disabilities as well as power sources having direct experiences in interacting with students with disabilities.

Villa and Thousand (1992) identified other attitudes and values that may influence the degree to which advocacy for systems change is effective. Some stakeholders may react negatively to change efforts if (1) the change idea was not their own; (2) the change proposed is to address an aspect of educational services for which they had been influential in establishing; or (3) they perceive the change initiative as meaning they are not providing the best services for students.

A Clear Mission

Stakeholders must clearly understand the mission and goals of the systems change initiative (Hargreaves & Fullan, 1998). All of the stakeholders should be involved in developing the mission statement of the systems change project. Without this clear understanding, confusion and loss of commitment to the change process are the likely outcomes. As an example, systems change for inclusion of students with disabilities in general education classrooms has often been hampered because of a failure to clearly define the concept of *inclusion.*

For some educators, *inclusion* is synonymous with *full inclusion,* which means that students with disabilities spend 100 percent of their school day in general education settings. If stakeholders in the inclusion systems change initiative believe that the mission of the change effort is to fully include students with disabilities in general education settings, many stakeholders (both special and general education teachers) will resist such efforts as too radical and not in the best interests of the students.

School Culture and Climate

Research has shown that school culture and climate are an integral component in the success or failure of systems change efforts (Fullan, 1991; Gersten, Vaughn, Deshler, & Schiller, 1997; Kaufman & Adema, 1998; Sarason, 1990). The culture of the school system includes norms (behaviors that will be rewarded and punished) and roles (expectations that others have for the behavior of individuals within the system) (Arends & Arends, 1977). Change the norms and roles, and the system is changed. For example, consider inclusion of students with disabilities in general education classrooms as a common systems change issue. If the norms and roles of special education and general education teachers in the system are successfully changed so that (1) special and general educators have a shared responsibility for educating students with disabilities, and (2) special and general educators collaborate in providing educational services to students with disabilities, the systems change effort will likely succeed.

Increasing Participant Ownership of the Change Effort

Research on educational systems change has demonstrated that increasing the amount of ownership of a reform effort increases the likelihood of its success (Fullan, 1991; Sarason, 1990). The significance of this factor in facilitating successful systems change can be viewed from a historical perspective by reviewing the two most recent educational reform movements in this country (DeMitchell & Fossey, 1997).

The first educational reform wave focused on academic content and higher performance standards for teachers and students. This reform movement took the form of state mandates that increased the bureaucratic control of public schools (Elmore, 1990). This top-down strategic approach, characterized as the *excellence in education* movement (First, 1992), failed to cultivate broad-based ownership by the stakeholders who were directly responsible for implementing the policies and practices of the change initiative (teachers and building-based administrators).

Disenchantment with the outcomes of this excellence in education movement led to a second reform movement known as *restructuring* (DeMitchell & Fossey, 1997). The restructuring movement proceeds from the bottom-up, decentralizing educational decision making and empowering teachers (Darling-Hammond, 1988). This movement pushed for greater professional control over education by reducing bureaucratic regulations and shifting the locus of management decision making to the school site. That is, this second systems change approach consciously cultivated participant ownership by empowering teachers as the key educational decision makers. Amongst educational reformers, there is more optimism that this restructuring movement has a greater chance for successful substantive improvement in the quality of educational services to all students than the excellence in education movement (DeMitchell & Fossey, 1997).

A Long-Term Commitment

Hargreaves and Fullan (1998) noted that most systems change efforts that make a difference in the classroom take five years or more to yield results. The problem is this time frame does not fit with that of politicians who are typically involved in educational systems change decision making by passing legislative mandates or providing financial inducements for new program initiatives.

Unfortunately, political decision making is usually short term to coincide with election cycles. Educational reform efforts are constantly at risk of premature termination because of political impatience and the public's appetite for a "quick fix." The solution to this problem was simply stated by Hargreaves and Fullan: "Governments must put educational investment beyond their own needs for political survival. By showing such integrity they may paradoxically gain greater political support" (p. 122).

An Outcomes-Based Orientation

This factor establishes credibility and accountability of the systems change process by maintaining the focus on the desired outcomes (Rainforth, York, & Macdonald, 1992). Evidence of this outcomes-based orientation is present if the school district regularly conducts student performance evaluations, program evaluations, and evaluations of personnel training efforts. Every systems change activity should ask these questions: (1) What were the desired outcomes? (2) Were those desired outcomes achieved? and (3) If the desired outcomes were not achieved, what alternative activities should be implemented to achieve those outcomes? (Villa & Thousand, 1992).

Acquisition of Technical Knowledge

The educators responsible for implementing the systems change initiative must possess the knowledge and skills to achieve the desired change effectively, or at least be willing to acquire that knowledge and those skills (Ryndak, 1994b). Without the requisite knowledge and skill bases, educators will become frustrated and demoralized by the systems change effort. The school district must be committed to providing opportunities for educators to gain the requisite knowledge and skills. Systems change efforts have lived or died by the amount and quality of technical assistance the change implementors received once the change process was initiated (Huberman & Miles, 1984). For example, many general education teachers have initially expressed a willingness to teach students with disabilities in their classrooms, only to later recant their willingness to work with such students because of a lack of inservice training support and ongoing consultation support from special education teachers.

Ongoing Professional Growth

This factor is closely related to the previous one on acquisition of technical knowledge. In order for the school district to grow and evolve, the same staff who are responsible for implementing the change activities must be provided with growth opportunities. Ryndak (1994b) noted the importance of this factor: "When stakeholders are consistently aware of changes in best practices, change in their services becomes less threatening and is personalized much less frequently. Thus, the more stakeholders are involved in ongoing professional growth activities, the more prepared they are to understand, accept, and implement changes" (p. 272).

Collaboration

The need for collaborative support from one's colleagues was previously mentioned in this Chapter as a critical support system fostering intrapersonal change. Regular collaboration with professional colleagues is also an important factor in enhancing systems change efforts (Gersten et al., 1997; Hargreaves & Fullan, 1998). Professional isolation produces conservatism and resistance to change (Lortie, 1975). Conversely, a collaborative culture facilitates an individual's commitment to change and improvement (Fullan & Hargreaves, 1991).

The power of collaboration is that individual professionals experience an increased commitment to continuous improvement and an increased sense of self-confidence and efficacy, while experiencing a decreased sense of powerlessness and uncertainty about their job (Fullan & Hargreaves, 1991). I know, from personal experience, when I changed professions from law to education, the most difficult aspect of the transition was going from a highly collaborative work environment (as a lawyer, I regularly reviewed cases and strategies with my colleagues) to a highly isolated work environment (as a first year teacher, I primarily worked behind my closed classroom door with very little professional interaction with other teachers).

A Preventive Orientation

Educational change that responds to external pressures to correct problems and deficiencies of a school system is likely to be fraught with anxiety and expedient solutions. This reactive perspective is based on the hope of finding a quick fix to the problems to alleviate the external pressure and criticism (Schorr, 1997). Alternatively, systems change that is based on a proactive and preventive approach to projected future issues and problems is more likely to be carefully planned and implemented because the external pressure is absent. A preventive approach is also politically appealing because change proponents can point to good returns for each dollar of public investment in prevention-oriented services. This preventive orientation is one of the explanations for the dramatic increase in early childhood special education services in the past decade. Research has documented the long-term benefits of investing in early childhood services as a way of reducing the impact of an infant's or toddler's disability (Hargreaves & Fullan, 1998).

Change Initiatives That Continue to Evolve

With an outcomes-based orientation and regular data collection for accountability as components of the systems change process, the change initiative has a built in capacity to evolve over time as the need dictates (Schorr, 1997). If the change process becomes static, the systems change effort will be unable to adequately respond to changing needs and unable to make the necessary midcourse corrections when the desired outcomes are not being achieved.

SUMMARY

The effectiveness of one's advocacy efforts is primarily judged by whether the desired change(s) occurred to address unmet educational needs. An understanding of school change issues and strategies promotes informed professional analysis and decision making about the likelihood of advocacy success. In essence, the professional engages in a cost-benefit type of analysis. Utterly futile advocacy (i.e., where there is no chance of success) serves no legitimate purpose for anyone. Professional advocacy is a limited resource that must be used wisely.

This chapter identified some change factors that should be considered in a professional's advocacy cost-benefit analysis. First, successful advocacy is dependent on intrapersonal change factors such as whether the professional possesses sufficient knowledge and skills to competently advocate, whether the professional possesses the required time and energy commitment, and whether the professional can cope with potential personal consequences of advocacy. Second, successful advocacy is dependent on interpersonal change -issues such as an identification of potential allies and adversaries in the advocacy situation and the impact advocacy is likely to have on relationships with professional colleagues.

Finally, successful advocacy must involve a systems change analysis. This analysis considers issues such as the likelihood of changing school district values, policies, and practices, and whether there are adequate resources to implement the necessary change. The role of serving as an advocate for students with disabilities includes the responsibility to make reasoned decisions on whether advocacy in a given situation is a justifiable expenditure of a professional's limited time and energy resources.

CHAPTER 8

INTERPERSONAL COMMUNICATION SKILLS

If I were to summarize the single most important principle I have learned in the field of interpersonal relations, it would be this: Seek first to understand, then to be understood. *This principle is the key to effective interpersonal communication.* —Stephen Covey (The 7 Habits of Highly Effective People, *1989*)

The advocacy efforts of special education professionals occur in the context of interpersonal communicative interactions. The four advocacy scenarios introduced in Chapter 1 have a common element: Each advocate (Mary Kinney, Steve Kern, Karen Snyder, and Miguel Hernandez) must engage in a variety of interpersonal interactions to initiate the desired educational changes for their students and families. The likelihood of experiencing a successful advocacy outcome in each scenario will be significantly dependent on the quality of interpersonal interactions each advocate establishes with parents and family members of students with disabilities, professional colleagues, and administrative superiors. Further, the quality of those interpersonal interactions will be almost totally dependent on each advocate's effective use of interpersonal communication skills.

Interpersonal communication involves sending and receiving messages between two or more individuals (Turnbull & Turnbull, 1997). The importance of effective interpersonal communication in special education advocacy was noted in Chapter 6 in the finding that a common theme in family/school conflict is a breakdown in communication between the two parties and a resultant deterioration of relations. Families involved in conflicts

with schools have reported patterns of unresponsive, condescending, and misleading communication in their interactions with school personnel (Fiedler, 1986). Similar negative sentiments have been expressed by school personnel in regard to their communicative attempts with family members.

The goals of effective interpersonal communication are varied. Examples of common interpersonal communication goals that are relevant to successful special education advocacy include:

- To establish interpersonal trust in a relationship. There is trust in a relationship when the individuals believe that each person will behave in a mutually beneficial manner (Berry & Hardman, 1998; Fisher & Ellis, 1990).
- To create a relationship of mutual acceptance and respect (Berry & Hardman, 1998; Wisniewski, 1994). This goal, along with trust, fosters risk taking which is essential in educational change efforts.
- To convey empathy for another person's concerns. This goal focuses on an understanding of how the other person thinks, feels, and what it is like to "see the world from their perspective" (Wisniewski, 1994).

- To establish rapport by creating the conditions for a comfortable and unconditional relationship between the individuals (Rogers, 1969).
- To set an atmosphere for mutual problem solving (Krehbiel & Kroth, 1991).
- To establish a collaborative relationship (Winton & Bailey, 1993).
- To provide individuals with a catharsis by relieving tension, frustration, and anxiety and, in the process, lead to greater insight (Shea & Bauer, 1991).
- To influence the attitudes and behaviors of another person (Shea & Bauer, 1991).

This chapter addresses key variables influencing the quality of interpersonal interactions between families and school professionals. In that discussion, emphasis is placed on effective interpersonal communication skills, including effective communication characteristics, nonverbal communication skills, verbal communication skills, and influencing skills. Finally, the chapter examines some specific interpersonal communication issues, such as communicating with culturally diverse families, interpersonal interactions with angry or upset individuals, and effective interpersonal communication in reaching win-win solutions.

VARIABLES INFLUENCING THE QUALITY OF INTERPERSONAL INTERACTIONS

Fiedler (1986, 1993) identified several variables influencing the quality of interpersonal interactions between families of students with disabilities and school professionals. The key interpersonal interaction variables included (1) different assumptions and expectations concerning the student's present abilities and future needs, (2) objectivity, (3) different opinions of the student's educational progress, (4) flexibility, (5) trust, and (6) effective and open communication. Although Fiedler's study investigated family/school personnel interpersonal interaction variables, these variables are equally relevant in fostering effective professional interactions between colleagues and with administrative superiors.

Different Assumptions and Expectations Concerning the Student's Present Abilities and Future Needs

Fiedler (1993) suggested that "establishing substantial agreement between parent and school concerning the child's strengths, weaknesses, and educational needs primarily determines whether the parents will be satisfied with the appropriateness of their child's education" (p. 272). Different assumptions and expectations concerning the student with disabilities can arise between teachers and parents, between professional colleagues, and between school professionals and their administrative superiors.

For example, parents have particular expectations for their children, which are largely tied to hopes and dreams of what their children will become when they grow up. Whereas teachers hold universal expectations for their students, which are based less on personal aspirations (as with parents and their children) and more on comparisons with other students of similar abilities. That is, quite naturally, there is much less emotional investment in the universal expectations that teachers hold of their students (Canady & Seyfarth, 1979). Diamond (1981), who grew up as a child with a disability, related that her parents and teachers were often adversaries because of their different expectations about what she could and could not do.

Several barriers hinder parents and school personnel from maintaining similar assumptions and expectations concerning the student's abilities and future needs. First, the parents and school personnel may have different values and attitudes regarding the implications of the child's disability (Mesibov & LaGreca, 1981). Parents who tend to be overprotective may have unrealistically low expectations of their children's capabilities. Conversely, parents struggling with denial and acceptance issues may possess unrealistically high expectations of their children's future potential. Second, parents may question whether the school has committed adequate attention to their concerns. To a large extent, parents consider their child's needs are met if school personnel listen and respond to their concerns about their child's educational needs (Simpson, 1996). Third, conflict over educational assumptions and expectations can arise when parents believe that their child's assessment was inaccurate or inadequate.

Objectivity

Objectivity is the ability to refrain from personalizing a dispute and to concentrate on resolving a problem using facts and data without distorting information with personal feelings or prejudice (Fiedler, 1986). Interpersonal communication involving participants who are unable to remain objective in resolving their differences is characterized by defensiveness and blame-casting behaviors by both parties. In fact, such negative communication behaviors pervade due process conflict between parents and school personnel (Budoff & Orenstein, 1982; Strickland, 1982).

When attempting to resolve differences of opinion regarding a student's educational characteristics and needs, school professionals must be objective and as data based as possible to document unmet needs, instead of relying merely on subjective feelings of "what ought to happen" for the student (Simpson, 1996). As Fiedler (1993) observed, "Decisions and recommendations that are based on objective data force educational planners to articulate the basis for such decisions" (p. 274).

In the advocacy scenarios from Chapter 1, Mary Kinney must objectively document the number of students she has evaluated that are in need of speech and language services and the extent of each student's educational needs. Mary must also objectively document how much time she is currently spending on each student on her caseload. This kind of systematic documentation can clearly indicate why Mary is unable to adequately address the needs of the newly referred students and serve as a justification for hiring a second speech and language clinician.

Similarly, in the Karen Snyder advocacy dilemma, a data collection system should be established to measure student academic and behavioral progress while receiving the various IEP accommodations in the general education classrooms. If these accommodations are indeed necessary, the data should document student progress. With this objective information, Karen will be in a better position to change the attitudes and behaviors of her teaching staff.

Different Opinions of the Student's Educational Progress

Advocacy by either professionals or parents is precipitated by dissatisfaction with the level of educational progress demonstrated by a student with disabilities. In the four advocacy scenarios, the advocacy initiatives by Mary Kinney, Steve Kern, Karen Snyder, and Miguel Hernandez were incited by each advocate's dissatisfaction with the educational progress experienced by the students involved and their disenchantment with the appropriateness of the educational programming. In each scenario, the advocates will have to contend with different opinions maintained by their colleagues and school administration on the issue of student progress.

A recurrent theme in the Budoff and Orenstein (1982) study of due process conflict is that school personnel tended to defend the effectiveness of current programming while ignoring parental unhappiness with its results. If interpersonal interactions between advocates and school personnel are characterized by such irrational allegiance to current educational programming, there will be very little basis for engaging in mutual problem solving. The most effective tactic when an advocate encounters such educational intransigence is to objectively document the lack of student progress. Conversely, it is critically important that school personnel instill confidence and trust in parents by accurately and adequately describing students' educational progress. In Box 8.1, Stephens and Wolf (1980) recommend several steps in describing a student's educational progress.

Box 8.1 _____

Advocacy Actions
(Stephens & Wolf, 1980)

STEPS IN DESCRIBING A STUDENT'S EDUCATIONAL PROGRESS

1. Organize information into broad categories.
2. Begin with positive information.
3. Cite specific examples related to informational categories.
4. Relate the information to the student's IEP.
5. Encourage parents/advocates to discuss each point in need of clarification.
6. Provide examples of the student's work.
7. Explain how student progress is evaluated.
8. Emphasize how instruction is individualized.

Flexibility

Flexibility refers to a person's receptiveness to change, new ideas, and alternatives, and a willingness to compromise. "A flexible educator or parent is open to alternative ideas and suggestions, is willing to compromise to meet the concerns and needs of both parties, and is amenable to trying different educational strategies or methods" (Fiedler, 1993, p. 275). One inherent limitation of being an advocate is also one of an advocate's greatest strengths—unyielding dedication and commitment to advancing the child's best educational interests.

This dedication and commitment to the educational rights of children with disabilities fuels an advocate's desire to "make a difference." However, advocates must be careful not to turn this strength into a deficit by being inflexible during discussions and meetings regarding the student's education. For example, Mary Kinney might have to compromise when the school administration offers to hire a part-time speech and language clinician, even though Mary ideally believes a full-time clinician is justified. Steve Kern may have to be flexible by agreeing to employ an in-school suspension (ISS) program, even though he feels his

students need more behavioral supports and positive interventions. Steve realizes that, at least, using ISS, as opposed to out-of-school suspensions, represents an improvement and is keeping his students in school.

A common source of due process conflict between families and school is related to parental beliefs that school personnel came to educational planning meetings with the student's IEP already written, and that school personnel were inflexible and unwilling to change the IEP (Budoff & Orenstein, 1982). When school professionals behave in an inflexible manner, parents feel impotent in their legitimate attempts to have input in the educational decision-making process. This causes feelings of frustration and engenders future conflict between families and school. An unwillingness to consider different perspectives, new ideas, or alternatives forecloses the possibility of compromising in an attempt to find a mutually satisfactory solution for both parties. Fisher and Ury (1991) warned that such inflexibility is marked by either/or thinking and a tendency to bargain over positions rather than addressing the particular concerns of both parties.

Trust

The development of a collaborative and problem-solving relationship between parents and school professionals will largely depend on the establishment of trust (Simpson, 1996; Turnbull & Turnbull, 1997). Without trust in a relationship, interpersonal communication is significantly impaired. The importance of trust in family/school relationships was noted by Turnbull and Turnbull (1997): "When you have trusting and respectful relationships with families, you can practically ensure that collaboration and empowerment will be enhanced. By the same token, when families trust professionals, they create opportunities for all sorts of otherwise unattainable results" (p. 73).

Interpersonal trust is a characteristic of every successful decision-making relationship (Fisher & Ellis, 1990). Fisher and Ellis have advised that a trusting relationship takes time to develop; "it emerges from the relationship after it has endured for some time" (p. 28). Other interpersonal relationship conditions that foster the development of trust include sharing similar objectives; recognizing that a commonly shared goal can best be accomplished by working together, not separately; and believing that the other person in the relationship possesses the requisite ability to perform the behaviors appropriate to the situation (Fisher & Ellis, 1990).

Simpson (1996) suggested a trusting relationship involves three basic components: an atmosphere in which a shared feeling of safety exists; reassurance and modeling of risk-taking behavior; and reinforcement of both parties for risk-taking efforts. Several other factors associated with the development of a trusting and collaborative relationship include (1) a willingness to contribute to a common cause, (2) an acknowledgment that both parties have a commitment to children, (3) assertive advocacy on behalf of children, (4) a positive outlook, (5) a willingness to both reinforce and confront one another, (6) a sensitivity to each other's needs, (7) a feeling of wanting to trust one another, (8) a relationship based on parity, (9) opportunities for mutual development of goals and outcomes, (10) honesty, and (11) an attempt to use a noncompetitive problem-solving process (Simpson, 1996).

Effective and Open Communication

Fiedler (1986) stated, "Effective and open communication involves an interaction process in which parents and school are able and willing to listen and learn from each other, share ideas, and be understood" (p. 4). Effective and open communication significantly contributes to cooperative working relationships between parents and school personnel and minimizes the probability of conflict that rises to the level of a due process hearing dispute (Budoff & Orenstein, 1982; Strickland, 1982). This section discusses common barriers to effective communication and effective communication skills.

BARRIERS TO EFFECTIVE COMMUNICATION

Berry and Hardman (1998) classified three types of barriers to an effective communication process between parents and professionals: professional, family, and system. In terms of *professional barriers,* Berry and Hardman noted that many professionals lack experience in working with families of children with disabilities. They call for more personnel preparation program attention to providing preservice professionals with experiences in working with families through practicum and intern experiences and mentoring with veteran professionals. A second professional barrier to effective family/professional communication is negative attitudes on the part of professionals toward parents. (Some typical negative professional attitudes and assumptions toward parents were discussed in Chapter 4.) The final professional barrier discussed by Berry and Hardman is communication differences, including language and cultural differences and professional jargon.

Family barriers to effective communication with professionals include the parents' lack of knowledge about their child's special education needs and how to meet those needs, lack of family resources (especially time and money) leading to professional frustration when families do not follow their programming advice, and parental emotions that can impair the communication process (Berry & Hardman, 1998).

System barriers involve school district policies and procedures that do not sufficiently value family/school communication because insufficient time is devoted to meetings and home visits, and practices dictate that parent/school personnel interactions take place in school settings that are convenient for professionals but may be inconvenient or intimidating for parents. The importance of allocating sufficient time for family/school meetings was verified by research that identified *allowing enough time* as the most important factor in parent satisfaction with team meetings (Witt, Miller, McIntire, & Smith, 1984). The other system barrier discussed by Berry and Hardman

(1998) is lack of necessary educational resources, which results in undermining parent confidence in the educational system and demoralizing well-intentioned professionals who are frustrated by resource constraints.

Poor listening behavior is a common barrier to communication between individuals (Covey, 1989; Kroth, 1985; Simpson, 1996; Turnbull & Turnbull, 1997; Wolfe, Petty, & McNellis, 1990). In fact, as noted by Simons (1987), "Not being treated like an individual—not being listened to—is parents' greatest complaint about professionals" (p. 47). Kroth (1985) conceptualized four types of general listening behavior: passive nonlistening, active nonlistening, passive listening, and active listening. "Two types of listening behavior work counterproductively to the parent-professional relationship. The passive nonlistener tends to 'hear' but not to listen. If asked, the passive non-listener could repeat back what is said but does not engage in any verbal or nonverbal feedback that shows interest. The active nonlistener, by talking excessively and not following the thoughts of the speaker, never lets the other person get to the point" (Krehbiel & Kroth, 1991, p. 104).

Covey (1989) has maintained that most individuals listen with the intent to reply, not to listen with the intent to understand. Poor listeners are "filtering everything through their own paradigms, reading their autobiography into other people's lives" (p. 239). Covey has criticized "listening autobiographically" in any of these four ways: (1) when individuals *evaluate* their focus is on either agreeing or disagreeing with the speaker; (2) when people *advise* their interest is in giving the speaker advice based on their experiential wisdom; (3) when autobiographical listeners *probe* they ask the speaker questions from their own frame of reference; and (4) when individuals *interpret* they are intent on analyzing the speaker's motives and behaviors based on their own motives and behaviors. According to Covey (1989), these four autobiographical ways of listening are ineffective because the listener is not first trying to understand the speaker. Instead, the listener is being judgmental, wanting to rush in with advice to solve the speaker's problem, playing 20 questions, or engaging in amateur psychoanalysis.

INTERPERSONAL COMMUNICATION SKILLS

The significance of effective interpersonal communication in developing collaborative, advocacy-oriented relationships between families and professionals was acknowledged by Simons (1987): "Good communication is the key. 'Put it at the top of the list!' they said. A group of parents was discussing techniques they had used to deal with the pressures of raising a child with a disability. There was no debate about the most important one: good communication. Good communication has to take place on three levels they felt: between husband and wife, between parents and pros, and between the head and the heart" (p. 75).

As noted earlier, interpersonal communication involves sending and receiving messages between two or more individuals. Every communicative message contains two dimensions: a content dimension and a relationship dimension (Fisher & Ellis, 1990). The content and relationship dimensions of communication are inseparable. "Whenever communication occurs, the communicators are dealing with information at the same time that they are developing a social relationship" (Fisher & Ellis, 1990, p. 94). Effective interpersonal communication skills facilitate advocacy efforts by accurately conveying and receiving the content information of a message while developing a collaborative, supportive relationship between the communicators. This section addresses interpersonal communication skills in terms of effective communication characteristics, nonverbal communication skills, verbal communication skills, and influencing skills (see figure 8.1).

Effective Communication Characteristics

Rapport
When special education professionals' advocacy brings them in contact with an individual with whom they have no prior relationship (i.e., a

---

FIGURE 8.1   Interpersonal Communication Skills

I. Effective Communication Characteristics
   - Rapport
   - Genuine
   - Concrete
   - Confront
   - Self-Disclosure
   - Immediacy
II. Nonverbal Communication Skills
   - Physical Attending
   - Empathic Listening
III. Verbal Communication Skills
   - Door-Opening Statements/Furthering Responses
   - Paraphrasing/Restating Content
   - Reflecting Affect
   - Clarifying Statements
   - Questioning
   - Summarization
IV. Influencing Skills
   - Providing Information
   - Providing Support
   - Focusing Attention
   - Offering Assistance

---

parent or family member, another professional, a school administrator), effective interpersonal communication requires establishing rapport as an initial interaction goal. Establishing rapport facilitates a positive and collaborative working relationship (Simpson, 1996). In the development of an initial relationship, rapport between two individuals typically develops in a patterned manner (Krehbiel & Kroth, 1991).

In the context of an initial interaction over an advocacy-related concern, the other individual is likely to be somewhat apprehensive and uncertain. After all, the person, at this point, does not know whether the advocate will be critical of his or her actions, make demands on him or her, or impugn his or her character in any manner. The advocate's attempt to initially build some rapport can ease the other person's tension and anxiety. This rapport building can involve taking time for getting acquainted with the person or sharing a positive comment.

For example, if a professional is interacting with a school administrator in regard to an advocacy concern, the professional might attempt to build some rapport by this comment: "I have heard many positive comments about your personal commitment to ensuring that students with disabilities receive quality educational services." A professional should never make such a comment, however, unless the sentiment can be expressed sincerely as a truthful statement. Another example of a special education teacher building rapport with parents of her students was offered in Chapter 4 (Box 4.3).

According to Krehbiel and Kroth (1991), this initial sense of apprehension and uncertainty is followed by a brief period of exploration, where the parties observe each other, trying to discover what the other person is like and what they want to hear. Advocates can foster rapport at this stage by clearly articulating their position and what they would like to see happen in a nonaccusatory manner. If the first two stages of the rapport building process have been successfully navigated, the interpersonal communication can move to the third stage of rapport, which is cooperation between the two individuals who have both learned what to expect of each other. This level of cooperation does not mean that both parties are necessarily going to be in agreement on every issue, but rather that the parties are committed to seeking a mutually satisfactory resolution to the concerns presented. This stage of cooperation then leads into the final stage of participation, where the parties are engaged in collaborative problem solving.

Finally, as an example of the importance of building rapport in parent/professional relationships, see Box 8.2. I describe an initial meeting my wife and I had with several professionals when our family moved to a new school district. The importance of making a good first impression in any relationship is the lesson of this anecdote. People only get one chance to make a good first impression.

Genuine

Communicators who are genuine do not use a lot of professional jargon in their communications,

Box 8.2 _____

Advocacy Anecdote

Several years ago, we moved to another state when I accepted a new university faculty position. At the time, our daughter Jennifer was 9 years old. Knowing that the new school district would need to do a considerable amount of advance planning to address Jennifer's special education needs, we sent the new school district a complete set of her educational records three months prior to the beginning of the school year. We moved during the summer. In early August, my wife and I went to a school meeting to plan for Jennifer's new school year, which would start in three weeks.

At this school meeting, we were introduced to a large number of professionals, including two special education teachers, the director of special education, the building principal, the school psychologist, an occupational therapist, a physical therapist, a speech and language pathologist, and a school counselor. Needless to say, we had not memorized everyone's name by the end of the meeting. As soon as we sat down in our chairs, the various professionals started grilling us with questions about Jennifer's disability, her previous educational program, her developmental and medical history and assorted other topics. It is important to note that most of the information we were questioned about was contained in the educational records we had sent to the school district three months prior.

This information gathering activity went on for over an hour. Then the meeting ended rather abruptly. My wife and I sat stunned for a couple of minutes at the course of these events. Finally, one of the special edu-

cation teachers came up to us and reintroduced himself (everyone had quickly introduced themselves at the beginning of the meeting). This teacher engaged in some "get acquainted talk" with us. He asked how our move went, how we liked our new city, and similar topics. The teacher told us a little bit about himself, why he became a special education teacher, and how long he had been teaching. Then he offered to give us a tour of Jennifer's new school and her classroom.

When we got home after this meeting, my wife and I discussed the experience. Our most significant lingering feeling was rather negative about the meeting that had just transpired. We felt like the school professionals treated us merely as "clients" and not as collaborators in developing an appropriate education for our daughter. When we analyzed why we felt this way, we realized it was because the school professionals failed to establish any sense of rapport with us. They proceeded right into the "business at hand" by grilling us with one question after another. The only professional we had any positive feelings about was the special education teacher who interacted with us at the end of the meeting. He attempted to establish rapport with us and he treated us as human beings, not just as clients.

Based on this negative initial meeting with school personnel, we began the school year with very little confidence and trust in the new school district. It took us almost an entire year to restore our trust and confidence in working with the school on our daughter's education.

---

especially when interacting with parents. Limited understanding of professional jargon severely restricts the communication process. One parent described sitting in a meeting with several school professionals who were conversing with a lot of jargon and acronyms (e.g., LEA, SEA, WISC, TOWL, LRE, FAPE) and she described that experience as being in a foreign country where you do not speak the native language. Many parents feel intimidated by jargon, especially in large, formal meetings where they feel surrounded by profes-

sionals (Skinner, 1991). Excessive use of jargon is usually a signal to parents that the school has no real interest in forming a collaborative partnership with them.

The importance of avoiding excessive use of jargon also holds true for interactions between professionals. For example, a special education teacher using a lot of jargon in communicating with a general education teacher will probably not be able to establish a parity-based collaborative relationship. The general education teacher will be alienated by all of the jargon and feel that the special education teacher is trying to project himself or herself as the "expert" in the relationship.

Concrete

Effective communicators are concrete or specific when describing situations or concerns to another person. Concrete communication leaves less room for misunderstanding and future problems. For example, in the Mary Kinney advocacy scenario, Mary would not be very concrete in her communication with parents if she described her concern in this manner: "I have evaluated your children and determined that they qualify for speech and language services. I am the only speech and language clinician in this district and I have been informed that the district has no intention of hiring a second speech and language clinician." Although this message is technically true, Mary has poorly communicated her concern to the parents that their children will be denied free and appropriate special education services due to the district's failure to provide sufficient staffing resources to meet all of the students' needs. Without this kind of a concrete communicative message, the parents will not be adequately informed of educational practices that violate their children's rights.

Confront

Confronting the other person during an interpersonal interaction may be constructive, especially if the person being confronted reflects on questions, reconsiders issues of concern, or modifies his or her attitudes or behavior (Wisniewski, 1994). Wisniewski identified three confrontation strategies: didactic confrontation, experimental confrontation, and calling the game.

In *didactic confrontation,* the person doing the confronting provides feedback about the other person's behavior. This strategy must provide corrective feedback that is descriptive and perceived as important to the individual being confronted. A second confrontational strategy, *experimental confrontation,* occurs when the confronter notes a discrepancy between the other person's verbal behavior and actions. As an example, in the Karen

Snyder advocacy scenario, Karen will probably have to use experimental confrontation in pointing out the discrepancy in the general education teachers' verbal behaviors when they agree to implement the accommodations discussed at IEP meetings and their subsequent actions in failing to implement the listed IEP accommodations.

The third strategy is *calling the game.* This strategy may be appropriate in interpersonal interactions in which a hidden agenda distorts true intentions in the relationship. If one is engaged in an interpersonal interaction where it is suspected that there is a hidden agenda, by calling the other person's game, an attempt is made to move from a hidden agenda to an intentional discussion of the real issues. Suppose in the Steve Kern advocacy scenario, Steve suspects that the school administration's hidden agenda is to keep some of his most disruptive students out of school for as long as possible by using repeated suspension sanctions. By calling the administration's game and exposing this hidden agenda, Steve can force, at the very least, a discussion of his concerns of inadequate educational services and unnecessarily punitive disciplinary measures. He can further start to respond directly to the administration's concern about the students' disruptive behaviors by getting this issue in the open.

Self-Disclosure

Effective communicators interact with people on a personal level by not being afraid to disclose some of their own feelings or experiences. Professionals who approach interpersonal interactions from an aloof, objectively detached posture are not successful in developing the level of rapport and trust required for a collaborative relationship.

The positive influence of self-disclosure on interpersonal interactions was evidenced by a special education teacher at an initial special education evaluation meeting. At this evaluation meeting, the professionals diagnosed the 8-year-old boy they had evaluated as attention deficit hyperactivity disordered (ADHD). This diagnosis devastated the mother, who began crying. At this point, the special education teacher disclosed that she had a son who was diagnosed with ADHD a year ago. The teacher proceeded to inform the mother that her son was doing well in school as a result of medication and a highly structured behavior management program. This self-disclosure was highly supportive and empathic to the mother who was confronted with this new bit of information.

Immediacy

Effective communicators keep the interpersonal discussion focused on the present and the future by not allowing the other person to dwell on past events that cannot be changed and that have only an indirect relationship to the current situation. For example, in the Miguel Hernandez advocacy scenario, when Miguel meets with Mrs. Ortiz, he will want to direct the discussion to an identification of community services that are available to address the family's needs and how Mrs. Ortiz can receive advocacy assistance by contacting the parent advocacy center. If Mrs. Ortiz wants to talk about all of her past problems in raising five children as a single mother or how school personnel do not listen to her, Miguel must politely bring the discussion back to the present and discuss what actions Mrs. Ortiz can take now to improve her family's future situation and Susie's future educational program.

Nonverbal Communication Skills

Nonverbal communication involves communication other than by oral or written word. Communication experts estimate that only 10 percent of interpersonal communication is represented by spoken words, 30 percent is represented by sounds, and 60 percent by nonverbal communication such as body movements, gestures, facial expressions, posture, physical proximity to others, and voice volume and inflections (Covey, 1989).

Fisher and Ellis (1990) categorized nonverbal communication behavior into three types: proxemic behavior, kinesic behavior, and paralinguistic qualities. *Proxemic behavior* involves the communicative use of space and how people are affected by spatial and distance orientations. For example, in group discussions, it is easier to interact with people who are seated opposite to you than it is to interact with individuals on either side of you. Research on proxemic behavior during team meetings reveals that people at the corners of the table will contribute least to the discussion and people at the head of the table will contribute the most. *Kinesic behavior* involves body motion, including gestures, body posture, eye contact, and facial expressions. Finally, *paralinguistic qualities* include loudness, pitch, tone, and rate of speech.

Nonverbal communication assists listeners in interpreting a message. Fisher and Ellis (1990) discussed four functions of nonverbal communication: (1) clarification, (2) control, (3) emotional states, and (4) interpersonal relationships. People tend to clarify the messages they receive by relying more on vocal cues and body movements than the spoken words. To enhance one's control and persuasiveness when interacting with others, Fisher and Ellis suggested these control techniques:

- Maintain a solid physical presence by steady eyes, calm hands, and a comfortable body posture.
- Be appropriately animated to denote strong feelings about an issue, but do not use animated movement excessively.
- Speak in a low, soft voice to make a sensitive or emotional point.
- Speak fluently to increase one's credibility with listeners.
- Speak authoritatively by varying voice intonation to emphasize certain points and speaking slightly more loudly and rapidly than normal. Varying one's vocal intonation maintains listeners' attention.
- Use voice inflections and body language to communicate approval during interpersonal interactions and to signal confidence and authority.

Facial expressions are key indicators to emotional states and feelings. As noted by Fisher and

Ellis (1990), "The face is a source of emotional leakage. That is, even when we are trying not to express emotions, certain feelings leak out of the face. The eyes, mouth, and forehead portray people's responses and inner feelings. Even when people are trying to control their emotions, their faces often give them away" (p. 115). The voice is also an indicator of a person's emotional state. For example, anger is most easily identified by the tone of voice employed by a person.

The fourth function of nonverbal communication discussed by Fisher and Ellis is interpersonal relationships. They identified four types of information about interpersonal relationships that are conveyed by nonverbal communication. First, whether a person is considered included or excluded from an interaction is communicated nonverbally. Eye contact or lack of it usually conveys group inclusion or exclusion. Second, people nonverbally communicate support or disapproval of others' ideas. For example, smiling, nodding one's head, and leaning forward communicates approval of the other person. The last two types of information about interpersonal relationships are control messages and emotional messages discussed previously.

Physical Attending

As I indicated earlier, physical attending consists of body movements, gestures, facial expressions, posture, physical proximity to others, and voice volume and inflections (Covey, 1989). Physical attending skills communicate respect for and interest in what the other person is saying (Wisniewski, 1994). Hepworth and Larsen (1982) identified the following as desirable physical attending skills: making direct eye contact, displaying an appropriately varied and animated facial expression that conveys warmth and concern, having your body leaning slightly forward in the direction of the speaker, and using moderate speech tempo with your voice modulated to reflect nuances of feeling and the emotional tone of the speaker's message.

Empathetic Listening

Simpson (1996) noted that educational professionals are generally more adept at talking than listen-

ing. In terms of interpersonal communication, Simpson highlighted the importance of good listening skills, "Listening, and the attention that accompanies the process, offers a primary means of facilitating a feeling of acceptance and trust in another person" (p. 118). For a self-assessment of your effective listener behaviors, see Box 8.3.

Empathy is an important component of effective listening. The word *empathy* is Greek for "suffering in." The ability to be empathic enhances the listening process by increasing one's acceptance of another person's perspective and by facilitating understanding of the other person's emotions (Simpson, 1996). Covey (1989) advocated empathic listening as one of his seven habits of highly effective people: "When I say empathic listening, I mean listening with intent to *understand*. I mean *seeking first* to understand, to really understand. It's an entirely different paradigm. Empathic listening gets inside another person's frame of reference. You look out through it, you see the world the way they see the world, you understand their paradigm, you understand how they feel" (p. 240).

Verbal Communication Skills

The effective communicator, in addition to displaying the nonverbal communication skills of physical attending and listening, must also possess specific verbal communication skills to facilitate interpersonal communicative interactions. Examples of effective verbal communication skills include (1) door-opening statements/furthering responses, (2) paraphrasing/restating content, (3) reflecting affect, (4) clarifying statements, (5) questioning, and (6) summarization.

Door-Opening Statements/
Furthering Responses

Door-opening statements and furthering responses are similar verbal communication skills designed to demonstrate an interest and willingness to listen, while encouraging the other person to continue talking (Simpson, 1996; Turnbull & Turnbull, 1997). This skill, as noted by Simpson, can be especially beneficial in professional interactions with family members, because a door-opening

Box 8.3 _____

Advocacy Actions: Behaviors of an Effective Listener

Choose the one response that most accurately represents your behavior.

1	2	3	4
Most of the time	**Sometimes**	**Occassionally**	**Rarely**

1. Give the othe person a chance to talk.
   1   2   3   4

2. Remove distracting stimuli by eliminating interruptions and physical barriers.
   1   2   3   4

3. Ask the appropriate questions.
   1   2   3   4

4. Use door opening statements which invite another to talk.
   1   2   3   4

5. Make encouraging statements which lead the speaker to add new information such as
   "Tell me more . . . , How do you feel about that? . . . , Can we talk about that further . . . "
   1   2   3   4

6. Make affirmative reinforcing statements which encourage the speaker to continue such as
   "Yes . . . , I hear you . . . , That's interesting . . . , Go on . . . "
   1   2   3   4

7. Face the speaker, sit in an upright but relaxed position, and lean forward.
   1   2   3 .   4

8. Use positive and responsive facial expressions and head movements.
   1   2   3   4

9. Use appropriate eye contact, comfortably focusing on the speaker and looking away occasionally.
   1   2   3   4

10. Attend to content, not delivery.
    1   2   3   4

11. Listen to the complete message before beginning to formulate your evaluation or response.
    1   2   3   4

12. Listen for the main ideas.
    1   2   3   4

13. Effectively deal with emotionally charged language.
    1   2   3   4

14. Identify areas of common experience and agreement.
    1   2   3   4

15. Deal effectively with blocks to listening.
    1   2   3   4

16 Practice listening in a variety of listening situations with different types of listening materials.
    1   2   3   4

Source: From *Special Training for Special Needs* by B. L. Wolfe, V. G. Petty, and K. McNellis, 1990, Boston: Allyn and Bacon. Copyright © 1990 by Allyn and Bacon. Reprinted by permission.

statement breaks a typical family expectation that the professional will do all of the talking during the meeting. Further, a door-opening statement or furthering response communicates to families that the professional is not the expert dispensing advice to solve the family's problems; instead, this interaction will be a mutual process to stimulate both parties' problem-solving skills. Examples of door-opening statements and furthering responses are encouraging responses such as "Oh?" "OK," "Then what?" "I see," or questions and comments such as "Can you tell me about . . . ?" "How do you feel about . . . ?" and "That's interesting." Nonverbal communication skills such as a smile or a head nod can also serve to encourage the speaker to continue talking.

Paraphrasing/Restating Content

To paraphrase means to state in one's own words what they thought someone just said. Simpson (1996) indicated that paraphrasing/restating content enhances listening by: (1) demonstrating to the speaker that the listener is hearing what is being spoken and is interested in an elaboration, (2) allowing the speaker an opportunity to hear what they are saying through the interpretation of another individual, and (3) providing the participants to the conversation with an opportunity to correct any misunderstanding.

Examples of paraphrasing/restating content include: "What I hear you saying is . . . ," "In other words . . . , " "So, basically how you felt was . . . ," "Let me understand, what was going on for you was . . . ," "What happened was . . . ," "Do you mean. . . . " Turnbull and Turnbull (1997) maintained that "Paraphrasing is an extremely useful technique in clarifying content, tying a number of comments together, highlighting issues by stating them more concisely, checking one's empathic understanding, and—most important—communicating interest in and understanding of what the family member is saying" (p. 66). Professionals must be careful, however, that their use of paraphrasing does not become excessive and tantamount to "parrot-phrasing" which is very annoying to the speaker.

Reflecting Affect

Similar to Covey's (1989) concept of empathic listening, the nonverbal communication skill of reflecting affect involves the ability to sensitively perceive the other person's underlying feelings and to communicate understanding of those feelings (Turnbull & Turnbull, 1997). Benjamin (1969) noted that "reflection consists of bringing to the surface and expressing in words those feelings and attitudes that lie behind the interviewee's words" (p. 117). In many advocacy-related interpersonal interactions, one or more of the participants will be experiencing strong emotions. Effective communication is augmented by a communicator's ability to expose those emotions as a legitimate component of the issues that must be discussed. For example, school professionals will be unable to appreciate the depth of parental concerns regarding their children's education unless both content and emotions of the parents' messages are accurately perceived.

Reflecting affect serves a similar purpose to restating content: to communicate to the speaker that his or her feelings are being understood, to provide the speaker with an opportunity to hear his or her feelings expressed by another person, and to determine the accuracy of the listener's perceptions (Simpson, 1996). As with any communication skill, Simpson warns against the indiscriminate and excessive use of reflecting affect.

Clarifying Statements

As discussed previously in this chapter and in Chapter 6, a common characteristic of family/school due process conflict is miscommunication and failed relationships. The use of clarifying statements serves to minimize miscommunication by ensuring that the listener accurately understands the intent of the speaker's message. When a listener is not sure he or she understands the speaker, or when the listener requires additional information, a clarifying statement such as "What do you exactly mean?" or "Could you elaborate?" facilitates accurate communication. By seeking clarification, the listener wants more background information or to know more about the circumstances of a particular situation. Clarifying statements help the listener focus to hear more than vague generalities. The listener hears events in the context of what someone thought and felt. Clarifying also lets the other person know that the listener is interested in the communicative interaction.

In the course of an advocacy interaction, one of the parties might make a concession or agree to take an action that is favorable to the interests of the advocate and the child with disabilities. In that situation, a clarifying statement such as "It is my understanding that you have agreed to . . . . Is that correct?" solidifies the accord that has been reached.

Questioning

There are two types of questions: close-ended and open-ended questions (Turnbull & Turnbull, 1997). *Close-ended questions* are useful in seeking specific factual information. The response to a close-ended question is usually limited to a few words or a yes or no. For example, the principal/advocate Karen Snyder might need to ask these close-ended questions to the general education teachers in her building: Do you meet regularly with the special education teacher to discuss IEP accommodations? How many students with disabilities do you have in your class? or Do you have a copy of the IEPs of every student with disabilities in your class?

Turnbull and Turnbull (1997) have warned that overuse of close-ended questions can make an interaction seem like an interrogation. This is an especially important admonition because advocacy interactions are often conducted in the context of a problem situation where one party might be feeling somewhat defensive already. If the conversation proceeds like an interrogation, the interrogee (the person being questioned) might feel like an accused person and any sense of cooperation and mutual problem solving is unlikely to occur.

Open-ended questions invite more discussion. The open-ended questions might be very general and open the conversation to anything that is on the mind of the other person. For example, when Karen Snyder interacts with a general education

teacher, she could ask: How is the school year going for you so far? Or Karen could ask a more structured open-ended question to a teacher: How do you feel about working with students with disabilities in your classroom?

There are three general ways to pose an open-ended question (Hepworth & Larsen, 1982):

1. *Ask a direct question:* "How is Seth (a student with a disability included in a third grade general education class) doing in reading in your class?"
2. *Give a polite request:* "Would you please elaborate on your feelings of frustration regarding classroom accommodations for students with disabilities?"
3. *Use an embedded question:* "I'm interested in learning more about your classroom accommodations for students with disabilities."

Turnbull and Turnbull (1997) cautioned about using a particular form of an open-ended question: "We encourage you to be cautious about *why* questions. The word *why* can connote disapproval, displeasure, blame, or condemnation and evoke a negative or defensive response from the person with whom you are speaking" (p. 67).

Summarization

A final effective verbal communication skill is summarization. Summarizing statements attempt to restate/review the critical components of an issue or concern during a conversation (Wisniewski, 1994). This technique communicates interest in what the other person is saying and a genuine desire to understand both content and affect of the message (Simpson, 1996). Summarizing statements may also signal closure on a particular topic of discussion and serve as a transition to another topic (Wisniewski, 1994). Karen Snyder could employ summarization in her interactions with a general education teacher: "To summarize, it appears to me that you have three major concerns about having a student with disabilities in your classroom." Summarizing statements focus the parties' attention on the heart of the issue in an effort to foster mutual problem solving.

Influencing Skills

A final set of effective interpersonal communication skills involves influencing skills (Turnbull & Turnbull, 1997). In large respect, the act of advocating seeks to influence another person to take actions or make changes deemed necessary by the advocate. Therefore, effective advocates must possess influencing skills in their communicative interactions. This section presents four types of influencing skills: (1) providing information, (2) providing support, (3) focusing attention, and (4) offering assistance (Walker & Singer, 1993).

Providing Information

As change initiators or change agents, advocates must be prepared to provide relevant information to assist decision makers (e.g., power sources) in making the necessary changes to enhance educational services for students with disabilities. In each of the four advocacy scenarios, the advocates must address several informational needs of other individuals:

- *Mary Kinney:* Mary must provide her school administrators with information on the number of newly referred students in need of speech and language services, the extent of each student's service needs, the number of students currently on Mary's caseload list and the amount of time devoted to each student, and the amount of additional time required of a speech and language clinician to address the appropriate educational needs of all of the eligible students. In addition, Mary needs to provide parents of the newly referred students with information on their special education rights and options for exercising those rights.
- *Steve Kern:* Steve needs to provide his school administration with the following information: the legal requirements related to transition planning and services for students with disabilities; the documented needs of his students in terms of transition services, including vocational/career services and community services; the documented lack of community agency participation in transition planning; and information on behavioral management alternatives to punitive disciplinary sanctions such as out-of-school suspension.
- *Karen Snyder:* Karen must address her teaching staff's informational needs for the legal requirements of educating students with disabilities in the least restrictive environment, the legal requirements for providing students with disabilities educated in general education classes with supplementary aids and services, the legal obligations of school personnel to make good faith efforts to provide all of the services listed in an IEP, the potential legal consequences if a school professional does not abide by the contents of the IEP in terms of goals, objectives, and services provided, and general and special education teacher collaboration models.
- *Miguel Hernandez:* Miguel must address the informational needs of Mrs. Ortiz for a list of community agencies to assist the Ortiz family in meeting functional needs in the areas of economic, daily care, socialization, and education. In addition, Mrs. Ortiz needs information on her legal rights of parent participation in educational decision making, including her right to assist in developing Susie's IEP.

Providing Support

Turnbull and Turnbull (1997) identified two methods of providing support: social support and affirming support. *Social support* is critical in educational advocacy activities because it is easier to take risks and seek change when one has the support and assistance of other individuals. In the Miguel Hernandez advocacy scenario, Miguel is providing Mrs. Ortiz with social support by referring her to a parent advocacy center that can provide an advocate to assist Mrs. Ortiz in advocating for changes in Susie's IEP.

Affirming support enhances interpersonal communication by showing appreciation for a person's willingness and commitment to engage in mutual problem solving to bring about necessary educational changes. An advocate also demonstrates affirming support by expressing compliments and indicating the valuable contributions that others make to improving educational services for students with disabilities. Affirming support fosters good will between individuals who may initially perceive themselves as adversaries on an issue. By generating interpersonal good will, an advocate establishes a communicative atmosphere that is conducive to collaborative problem solving.

Focusing Attention

An advocate must be able to focus others' attention on issues that require change. Advocates can focus attention on educational concerns by clearly articulating what the problems are with the status quo, and indicating what corrective actions need to be taken. Examples of potential problems that advocates may need to focus attention on include inadequate or inappropriate educational services, a student with disabilities who is not progressing as expected, or a school district that is out of compliance with special education legal rights and procedures. (Focusing attention on a problem will be discussed further in Chapter 11.)

Offering Assistance

Effective advocacy not only identifies a problem that requires change but it also offers possible solutions to the identified problem. As an interpersonal communication skill, when an advocate offers assistance to resolving a problem, the best method is to do so by presenting options rather than directives (Turnbull & Turnbull, 1997). Issuing directives such as "You should," "You must do," "You ought to," or "You are really making a mistake by . . ." tend to engender defensiveness and resistance in the person who has been issued such a directive.

SPECIFIC INTERPERSONAL COMMUNICATION ISSUES

This final section addresses considerations and skills during specific interpersonal communication interaction situations, including communicating with culturally diverse families, interacting with angry or upset individuals, and making pre-

sentations or arguments seeking win-win solutions.

Communicating with Culturally Diverse Families

Establishing productive relationships between school professionals and culturally diverse families is dependent on effective verbal and nonverbal communication (Misra, 1994). The importance of cultural sensitivity in interpersonal communication with diverse families was underscored by Misra: "Verbal and nonverbal communications styles, which differ from those prevalent in the dominant culture may create barriers when culturally diverse people meet. Ignorance, lack of acceptance, or lack of sensitivity about different forms of communication are common reasons for barriers" (p. 155).

In an effort to avoid communication barriers with culturally diverse families, school professionals should consider the common verbal and nonverbal communication patterns of different cultural groups. In Box 8.4, several relevant verbal and nonverbal communication considerations for the following cultural groups are presented: Hispanic Americans, African Americans, Asian Americans, and Native Americans. Professionals must be careful to remember that these considerations represent generalizations about culturally diverse groups. Individual communication patterns may vary from these group patterns.

Interpersonal Interactions with Angry or Upset Individuals

Advocacy interpersonal interactions often evoke strong emotions in the participants. For family members, they may be frustrated with what they perceive as the lack of appropriate educational services for their children with disabilities. In this state of frustration, family members may display anger toward school professionals. Conversely, a school professional being confronted by an angry parent or advocate is likely to feel "emotionally charged." During interpersonal interaction crises, such as communicating with an angry or upset

Box 8.4 _____

Advocacy Actions: Communication Patterns of Culturally Diverse Families (Misra, 1994; Seligman & Darling, 1989; Shea & Bauer, 1991)

CULTURAL GROUP	VERBAL COMMUNICATION	NONVERBAL COMMUNICATION
Hispanic American	- May be hesitant to participate in meeting - Do not question authority figures - Possible language barriers	- Physical contact during conversation is acceptable - Required distance between people not maintained or expected
African American	- Direct in stating their opinions - Active participation during discussions - Feel restricted by turn taking - Less likely to verbally reinforce or acknowledge what is said	- Much use of body language and gestures - Eye contact avoided as sign of respect
Asian American	- Relatively passive during discussions to avoid attention to self - Avoid confrontation in favor of harmony; do not actively assert rights - Courteous and respectful to authority - Voluntarily expressing opinions or discussing personal matters is avoided	- Eye contact avoided with elders and authority figures - Comfortable with more distance during conversation - Dislike pointing at someone and physical contact
Native American	- Taking turns and mutual respect emphasized during discussion - Cooperation, rather than individualism is stressed - Embarrassed by praise or compliments - Dislike lots of questions	- Prefer a gentle handshake - Silence during a discussion is acceptable - Prefer eye movements and gestures rather than verbal communication

Note: Portions of the above are from "Partnership with Multicultural Families" by A. Misra in *Families of Students with Disabilities: Consultation and Advocacy* by S. K. Alper, P. J. Schloss, and C. N. Schloss (Eds.), 1994, Boston: Allyn and Bacon. Copyright © 1994 by Allyn and Bacon. Adapted by permission.

individual, professionals are advised to take the perspective advocated by Turnbull and Turnbull (1997): "Rather than bemoan a crisis, you can embrace it as a unique opportunity for relationship enhancement" (p. 72).

The risk and goal of effective interpersonal communication with angry individuals was articulated by Simpson (1996):

Failure to contend with parent and family anger effectively can result in reduced cooperation and willingness to collaborate, exacerbated suspicion,

and eventual destruction of good communication. On the other hand, conferencers who contend with anger effectively and convert these situations into opportunities for joint problem solving can enhance feelings of trust and value in parents, families, and educators cooperatively searching for solutions to problems." (pp. 290–291)

Simpson (1996) and Turnbull and Turnbull (1997) offer a number of relevant considerations when interacting with angry or upset individuals:

- Allow the angry/upset individual to express her feelings and concerns without interruption.

- Record the concerns of the angry/upset individual and show him the recorded list to ensure that it is complete.
- To ensure that the communication focuses on the most critical issues or concerns, assist the angry/upset individual in prioritizing her concerns. This is an important consideration because often irate individuals do not express the most critical issues during their emotional venting.
- Once the angry/upset individual calms down, ask for his suggestions on how to solve any of the issues or concerns expressed and write those suggestions down.
- Concentrate on keeping a low voice tone, a relaxed posture, and avoid defensive or intimidating gestures. As the angry/upset individual speaks more loudly, speak more softly in response.
- Avoid arguing with an angry/upset individual. Similarly, do not become defensive or discount the person's feelings or concerns.
- Request clarification on any statements that are not understood.
- Avoid attempts to engage the angry/upset individual in collaborative problem solving. Let the person vent her feelings and calm down prior to engaging in rational problem solving.
- Avoid responding to generalized accusations (e.g., "You are incompetent") or threats (e.g., "I'm going to call my lawyer").
- Avoid promising the angry/upset individual something that may not be possible to produce or accomplish.
- Recognize that most anger can be translated into energy to motivate collaborative problem-solving efforts.

Making Presentations or Arguments Seeking Win-Win Solutions

In making effective presentations or arguments, as advocates must be able to do, Covey (1989) stated that reaching a win-win solution is dependent on this interpersonal interaction sequence: ethos, pathos, and logos. *Ethos* refers to one's personal

credibility, the trust other people have in an individual's integrity and competence. *Pathos* is the emotional, empathic component of interpersonal communication. Finally, *logos* is the logic, the reasoning part of the presentation or argument.

According to Covey (1989), most people make interpersonal presentations or arguments by proceeding directly to the logos and trying to convince other people of the validity and logic of one's position or ideas. This presentation/argument style, by not proceeding first with ethos and pathos, will be unsuccessful in securing win-win solutions to problems. Instead, an effective presentation or argument should proceed by first, ethos (establishing one's character); second, pathos (fostering an empathic relationship with the other person); and, finally, logos (emphasizing the logic of one's argument).

As an example of this interpersonal interaction sequence of making win-win presentations or arguments, consider, again, the Karen Snyder advocacy scenario. In seeking a win-win solution with the general education teachers in her building on the issue of implementing the necessary IEP accommodations for students with disabilities attending general education classes, Karen's presentation/argument should use ethos, pathos, and logos in that sequence.

First, Karen's interpersonal interactions with her general education teachers will be greatly facilitated if she, through previous interactions, has established her own credibility with these teachers. That is, it is important that the teachers in her building trust and respect Karen's integrity and competence. Karen can start her interaction with ethos, by ensuring the teachers that she would never require them to engage in teaching activities that were not feasible, legally mandated, and educationally necessary to benefit students with disabilities.

Second, Karen can continue her presentation to the general education teachers by employing pathos in demonstrating empathy for their concerns and a genuine commitment to understanding the teacher's feelings. For example, Karen can indicate to the teachers that she appreciates their concern about the need for adequate collaborative planning time with special education teachers. From this expression of empathy, Karen can proceed to the logos part of her presentation by (1) reminding the teachers of the legal requirement of educating students with disabilities in the least restrictive environment, (2) emphasizing the legal requirement of providing students with disabilities appropriate accommodations in general education classes, (3) discussing the consequences of failure to abide by IEP listed services and accommodations, and (4) ensuring that sufficient collaborative planning time and support from special education teachers will be made available.

SUMMARY

Advocacy on behalf of students with disabilities engages special education professionals in innumerable interpersonal interactions with family members, professional school colleagues, professionals from various community agencies, and school administrative superiors. A key factor in determining the quality of those interactions, and ultimately the success or failure of one's advocacy efforts, is the degree to which the advocate is skilled in interpersonal communication.

This chapter identified several crucial factors influencing the quality of interpersonal interactions between advocates and other individuals, including (1) different assumptions and expectations concerning the student's present abilities and future needs, (2) objectivity, (3) different opinions of the student's educational progress, (4) flexibility, (5) trust, and (6) effective and open communication. In terms of effective interpersonal interactions, advocates must be proficient in using nonverbal communication skills (e.g., physical attending and empathic listening), verbal communication skills (e.g., door-opening statements/furthering responses, paraphrasing/restating content, reflecting affect, clarifying statements, questioning, and summarization), and influencing skills (e.g., providing information, providing support, focusing attention, and offering assistance). Finally, advocates must be able to effectively communicate with culturally diverse families, with angry and upset individuals, and with the goal of reaching win-win solutions to problems.

CHAPTER 9

COLLABORATION SKILLS

A wry observer of the current scene is reported to have said, "Collaboration is an unnatural act between two nonconsenting adults." —William Morse (1996)

The above comment serves as an appropriate admonishment that collaboration between two or more school professionals, as well as between professionals and families of children with disabilities, can be difficult, frustrating, and unfamiliar work. Although there are substantial challenges associated with collaboration, successful collaboration can be one of the most rewarding aspects of an educator's work. Professionals engaged in advocacy on behalf of children with disabilities must possess collaboration skills to successfully fulfill their advocacy responsibilities. Collaboration involves working together cooperatively with others (i.e., professional colleagues, family members) for a common goal (Cheney & Osher, 1997). In the context of this chapter, the common goal is advocacy that is successful in bringing about necessary educational changes to address the needs of students with disabilities.

Each of the previously discussed essential advocacy competencies for special education professionals contributes to the requisite collaboration skills. An advocacy disposition (see Chapter 2) fosters risk-taking behavior, which is essential for successful collaboration. In addition, an advocacy disposition is dependent on "interactive professionalism" (Fullan & Hargreaves, 1991), which promotes collaboration as a necessary support mechanism for professionals who serve as special educational advocates. Special education professionals with the requisite ethical disposition (see Chapter 3) foster collaboration with families by enhancing the educational decision making autonomy of family members, and by fulfilling professional ethical code obligations to work collaboratively with colleagues and families to improve special education services.

Professionals who maintain a family support and empowerment disposition (see Chapter 4) possess the motivation to establish collaborative partnerships with families by acknowledging parental expertise and educational decision making rights. Professionals with sufficient knowledge of special education law (see Chapter 5) recognize that the legal provisions of the IDEA cannot be implemented by individuals in isolation; collaboration between various school professionals and between professionals and family members is essential in addressing the educational needs of students with disabilities (Fishbaugh, 1997). Knowledge of dispute resolution mechanisms in special education (see Chapter 6) advances willingness to collaborate due to the professional's understanding of the limitations and negative consequences associated with adversarial dispute resolution processes (i.e., due process hearings) versus the potential benefits of collaborative dispute resolution mechanisms such as mediation.

Knowledge of school change issues and strategies (see Chapter 7) enhances a professional's comprehension of the value of establishing collaborative relationships in an effort to facilitate both interpersonal change and systems change through advocacy. Finally, proponents of collaboration acknowledge that school professionals must possess effective interpersonal communication skills (see Chapter 8) (Dettmer, Dyck, & Thurston, 1996; Fishbaugh, 1997; Friend & Cook, 1996; Tiegerman-Farber & Radziewicz, 1998).

This chapter examines several aspects of school professional collaboration. First, a context for understanding school collaboration issues is presented by addressing common collaboration characteristics, factors precipitating an increase in professional collaboration, and barriers to collaboration. Second, the necessary skills for effective collaboration to augment advocacy efforts are presented. Finally, group decision-making skills that are essential to effective collaboration efforts are discussed. These professional skills for enhancing group decision making include building group cohesiveness, improving group decision-making processes, and collaborative leadership.

A CONTEXT FOR UNDERSTANDING SCHOOL COLLABORATION ISSUES

Collaboration Characteristics

Friend and Cook (1996) define *collaboration* in this way: "Interpersonal collaboration is a style for direct interaction between at least two coequal parties voluntarily engaged in shared decision making as they work toward a common goal" (p. 6). In support of this definition, Friend and Cook have identified several common characteristics for effective collaboration:

- *Collaboration is voluntary.* Effective collaboration between school professionals or with families cannot be legislatively nor administratively mandated. Collaboration requires a disposition that values cooperative partnerships.
- *Collaboration requires parity among participants.* Parity means that each participant's contribution to the collaborative relationship is equally valued and each participant has equal decision-making power.

- *Collaboration is based on mutual goals.* This characteristic does not ensure that all the collaborative participants will agree on the same goals or strategies for goal attainment. However, in the context of advocacy for children with disabilities, the participants must agree on a shared goal of advocating for the best interests of the student(s) with disabilities to maintain the motivation to continue collaborating. There may be different perspectives among the participants on what constitutes the "best interests" for a particular student with disabilities, but this shared standard or goal serves as the incentive for committing the necessary time and energy to collaborate.
- *Collaboration depends on shared responsibility for participation and decision making.* Successful collaboration does not require that all participants share equally in completing the various tasks associated with an advocacy effort on behalf of a student with a disability. Rather, all collaborators have participated in making the necessary advocacy decisions, even though the collaborators have different responsibilities for various advocacy tasks.
- *Collaborators share their resources.* As was discussed in Chapter 7, professional advocacy is a precious and limited resource. Given scarce time and resources, advocacy participants are wise to pool their available resources. For example, some participants may have more time to carry out certain advocacy tasks. Another participant may have specialized knowledge that is critical to the advocacy effort. A third participant may have access to other individuals or agencies that could benefit the advocacy effort. This sharing of individual resources is more efficient and effective than one individual attempting to acquire the diverse knowledge and skills to handle all of the advocacy tasks.
- *Collaborators share accountability for outcomes.* As acknowledged in previous chapters, advocacy work is often stressful and intimidating due to multiple factors, such as the apprehension in seeking educational change, possible negative job repercussions, the potential for

damage to collegial relationships, and time and energy demands. The necessary risk-taking behavior that fosters educational advocacy is bolstered by a commitment from *all* the collaborative participants to accept accountability for the advocacy outcomes.

- *A collaborative interpersonal style is valued.* The adage that "two heads are better than one" functions as the primary belief underlying professional collaboration. Collaborators believe that their advocacy efforts are likely to be more successful and significant when they collaborate as opposed to solely individual efforts.
- *Collaborators must trust one another.* Chapter 8 discussed the importance of trust in fostering interpersonal relationships. Trust is both a prerequisite for effective collaboration and an outcome of successful advocacy collaboration.
- *A sense of community evolves from collaboration.* This evolving sense of community builds group cohesiveness. Friend and Cook (1996) noted the power of an evolving sense of community in collaborative relationships: "When collaborative efforts result in higher levels of trust and respect among colleagues, and working together results in more positive outcomes for both students and professionals, the risks taken seem small in comparison to the rewards" (p. 11).

Factors Precipitating an Increase in Professional Collaboration

A number of societal, school, and family factors have caused a heightened interest and increase in professional collaboration. In terms of societal trends, Toffler (1990) has maintained that collaboration is fundamental to an organization's survival in this information age. To manage the information explosion, organizations such as schools have had to rely increasingly on collaboration. That is, the information explosion has become so complex that it is impossible for individuals to know everything they must know to function effectively in their job responsibilities (Cook & Friend, 1991). Collaboration and reliance on others is necessary to accomplish both individual and collective goals. Modern life is characterized by increasing interdependence of countries, companies, and individuals. The concept of the rugged individualist, which was romanticized in the history of the settlement of the United States, is an anomaly in this interdependent world. In truth, even those so-called rugged individualists of frontier America relied on others for survival. Friend and Cook (1996) recognized this societal trend: "As a psychological support, we are turning as did the pioneers to collaboration and reliance on others to accomplish our goals" (p. 13).

There are several school factors driving this increased collaboration trend. First, as noted in Chapter 7, the most recent educational reform movement, known as *restructuring,* emphasizes decentralized decision-making structures and empowering school professionals by granting them greater control over educational decisions (Audette & Algozzine, 1997; DeMitchell & Fossey, 1997). The decision-making structures supported by this educational reform movement favor collaborative decision making. Second, there is an increased effort in schools and in human services in general to empower clients by involving them in decisions about their service needs (Cook & Friend, 1991). As an example of this trend, Chapter 5 noted the increased educational decision-making rights bestowed on families in the 1997 IDEA Amendments.

Third, schools are expected to educate an increasingly diverse student population with complex needs. To adequately address these diverse and complex student needs, school professionals require specialized knowledge from many disciplines, along with collaborative working relationships in which expertise is shared among school professionals. As recognized by Cook and Friend (1991):

Schools are now serving children with a wider range of handicapping conditions than ever before. One new and challenging group of students with special needs consists of children of parents who abused drugs; another includes students whose disabilities are so severe that they probably would not have survived infancy in the past. The already growing num-

ber of students who would benefit from specialized assistance but who may not qualify for special education service means that we will probably need new approaches to educate them. No single group of professionals will have the expertise to accomplish this; it will require collaborative relationships in which each professional contributes expertise so that an appropriate set of options can be generated." (p. 26)

Finally, as advocated by several noted educational change strategists, an effective mechanism for enhancing professionalism as well as continued professional development of educators is collaboration that promotes collegiality (Cook & Friend, 1991; Hargreaves & Fullan, 1998).

Also contributing to an increased interest in school collaboration is the area of family issues and concerns (Williams-Murphy, DeChillo, Koren, & Hunter, 1994). One set of concerns centers on families' long-standing dissatisfaction with educational services provided to their children. In an attempt to assuage these feelings of dissatisfaction, families have demanded greater collaborative decision-making authority with school professionals. Another family factor resulting in increased collaboration with professionals grew out of parents' feelings of alienation and isolation from the professionals providing services to their children with disabilities. Parents often felt such alienation from service providers due to perceived professional blaming of parents for their children's problems (see Chapter 4).

A third factor that has resulted in increased family/professional collaboration is a general heightened sense of consumerism. This consumerism translates into demands by parents for greater authority and control over what happens to their children in school. A fourth factor that has had an impact on family/professional collaboration is the reality of shrinking educational resources and the resultant need for schools to access the resources and expertise of other community human service agencies (e.g., mental health centers, vocational service providers, juvenile correction services, family support agencies) in the provision of services to students with disabilities.

Barriers to Collaboration

Although the previously mentioned societal, school, and family factors have created an increased interest in and need for collaboration between school professionals and with family members, professionals must be cognizant of numerous barriers to their collaborative efforts. Many school professionals lack sufficient training and preparation in the knowledge and skills to engage in effective collaboration (Fishbaugh, 1997; Kagan, 1992; Kerns, 1992). Also, some school professionals are philosophically opposed to collaboration, preferring the more traditional and independent educator work environment (Fishbaugh, 1997).

In addition, Nevin, Thousand, Paolucci-Whitcomb, and Villa (1990) identified a number of school organizational constraints operating as barriers to collaboration: (1) lack of sufficient collaborative planning time; (2) lack of a common knowledge base among school professionals; (3) hierarchical relationships among school professionals and with families; (4) lack of responsibility or ownership by all collaborative participants; (5) excessive caseloads, which prevent professionals from taking the time to collaborate; and (6) lack of adequate funding to support professional collaboration activities.

Families also experience barriers to collaborative partnerships with school professionals. For instance, poverty and parental work schedules make it difficult for many families to engage in collaborative activities (Dettmer, Dyck, & Thurston, 1996). As recognized by Voltz (1994), "Parents who find themselves economically challenged and struggling for survival may not have as much time and energy to devote to home-school relationships as would be desired, or, perhaps expected" (p. 289).

A second area where family characteristics may function as a barrier to collaboration with school professionals is family diversity and the competence of educators to successfully interact with families from diverse cultures (Dettmer, Dyck, & Thurston, 1996; Voltz, 1994). School professionals must accept, honor, and respect family cultural differences; otherwise, those families will experience discomfort in interacting with educators. Cultural differences exist with respect to families perceived causes of their children's disabilities, how families react to accessing professional services, how families interact with perceived "authority figures" (see Chapter 8), and how families assert their educational rights (Arcia, Keyes, Gallagher, & Herrick, 1992; Sontag & Schacht, 1994).

Finally, families' attitudes and their own past educational experiences may function as barriers to effective collaboration with school professionals (Dettmer, Dyck, & Thurston, 1996). Some parents harbor fear, suspicion, and mistrust toward educators because of their own negative experiences as students (Voltz, 1994). Further, past negative experiences with other professionals may make some parents leery of establishing trusting relationships with educators (Dettmer, Dyck, & Thurston, 1996). In a study by Williams-Murphy and colleagues (1994), families of children with disabilities and professionals rated barriers to family/professional collaboration. Families and professionals agreed that the three most frequent barriers to collaboration were (1) professionals' lack of sufficient time to spend with families, (2) high caseloads, and (3) families' prior negative experiences with professionals. Box 9.1 provides a checklist to assess the degree to which family collaborative partnerships are valued at a given school.

COMPETENCIES FOR EFFECTIVE ADVOCACY ORIENTED COLLABORATION

As indicated at the beginning of this chapter, previous chapters have established a foundation for many of the requisite competencies for effective professional and family collaboration to foster advocacy efforts on behalf of children with disabilities. This section focuses on the identified competencies that promote effective advocacy oriented collaboration (Carter, 1996; Robinson &

Box 9.1 _____

Advocacy Actions: A Checklist to Assess Whether Your School Values Collaborative Partnerships with Families

- How do teachers and administrators keep families informed about what is going on?
- Are families welcomed into the school?
- Does your school offer information about family education programs?
- Are there opportunities for families and educators to collaborate in providing services for a child with disabilities? in program planning, policy formation, and evaluation? in training and education? in teambuilding? in inservice training?
- Do educators share complete information? demonstrate respect for families? honor family choices? appreciate cultural differences?
- Are there opportunities for educators to learn directly from families about their perspectives and support needs?
- Are meeting times and locations scheduled at times that are convenient for families?
- Do preservice and inservice training programs provide instruction in these areas: effective communication skills and methods for working collaboratively with families? skills in working collaboratively as a team member with educators and related services personnel?
- Are families invited to participate in inservice programs?

Source: South Dakota Statewide Systems Change, South Dakota Deaf-Blind Project. Reprinted by permission.

Fine, 1994; Simpson, 1996; Tiegerman-Farber & Radziewicz, 1998). These competencies are categorized as either dispositions or skills.

Collaboration Dispositions

Effective collaboration with professional colleagues or with families requires the following dispositions.

Demonstrates genuine empathy and sensitivity to the needs and perspectives of families. As noted by Simpson (1996), families of children with disabilities encounter a variety of issues and stressors: "These issues may include social isolation and feelings of guilt and embarrassment, financial strain, limitations on recreational options, pessimistic perceptions of the future, household routine delays and disruptions, and interference with other family members' needs and gratification" (pp. 30–31). As discussed in Chapter 2, empathy is necessary to fuel professional motivation to commit the time and energy to care about the personal circumstances of children with disabilities and their families. A special education professional who does not expend the energy to understand families' unique needs and circumstances will be unwilling and unable to function as an advocate.

Displays interest in and sensitivity to people. Collaboration requires interpersonal interaction with others. Simpson (1996) recognized that "individuals who expect to adequately serve the needs of parents and families must possess a genuine interest in people and a willingness to invest time and energy in seeking solutions to needs and problems" (p. 28). I am reminded of the importance of this disposition when I think about a colleague who was a brilliant researcher and writer but who eschewed collaborative activities because he lacked sufficient interest in other people. He was totally consumed by his own research activities, and he therefore did not value collaborative interactions with others. As a result, he was an "outsider" within his own professional work environment. Such "outsider status" does not facilitate professional collaboration, and consequently it is more difficult to function as an effective advocate in this kind of work environment.

Understands one's own values. When professionals are drawn into close collaborative interpersonal proximity with colleagues and family members, there is a greater likelihood of personal conflicts over values. A professional advocating for changes on behalf of a child with disabilities may value inclusionary educational practices more than a colleague or that child's family. When confronted with value differences, an effective collaborator must be respectful of other's values and seek "common ground" by emphasizing any areas of agreement.

As an example, a parent told me of an advocacy situation where value conflicts were evident. The parent and her child's special education teacher wanted more general education classroom participation for the elementary-aged child with disabilities. However, they were encountering resistance from a third-grade general education teacher who questioned the appropriateness of such a placement, as she did not feel the child would be able to do third-grade level academic work. From this initial educational values conflict, the parent and the general and special education teachers were able to collaborate for change by reaching an initial agreement that the development of social relationships was an important educational goal for the child with disabilities.

Once this educational goal was clearly articulated, the initially reluctant general education teacher was able to identify the possible advantages of inclusion into her third-grade classroom. Previously, the general education teacher had focused solely on perceived academic issues in educating the child with disabilities in her classroom. With this new "common ground" on the value of social relationships, the general education teacher was now motivated to include the child with disabilities in her classroom. Once the general education teacher started seeing the benefits of inclusion from a social relationship perspective, she became more willing to collaborate with the special education teacher in making necessary modifications in the curriculum and instruction to enhance academic benefits for the child, as well.

Displays an ability to learn from others. There will be no motivation or desire to collaborate if a professional does not believe that he or she can learn from other colleagues or families. One of the common characteristics that I have noted in interviewing educators who served as child advocates was their excitement over the prospect of learning from others in their professional interactions. This disposition is important for two reasons. First, this attitude fosters the value of lifelong learning and continuous professional growth and development. Effective professionals are constantly reflecting on and improving their knowledge and skills in an effort to be more effective advocates. Second, this attitude engenders a willingness to truly listen to the perspectives of another person. This dispositional characteristic instills flexibility in interpersonal communication (see Chapter 8) and a concomitant willingness to change one's own perspective or to compromise when necessary and appropriate.

Exhibits an ability to respect other's input, opinions, and criticisms.   At the very least, in every collaborative interpersonal interaction, the participants must feel that their ideas and opinions are respected, even though the participants may disagree with each other. As revealed in Chapter 6, one of the major limitations of adversarial due process hearings is the inability of both parties in the dispute (school personnel and parents) to remain respectful in their interpersonal communication. This leads to a complete breakdown in communication and reluctant reliance on the due process hearing system to resolve disputes as opposed to the use of a more collaborative process such as mediation.

Presents self as a professional ally of families.
An advocate is an ally—a person who is willing to challenge the educational system to address the needs of children with disabilities. How does a professional communicate this ally perspective to families? As a parent of a child with a disability, these are the indicators that I look for in determining whether professionals are interested in being my educational allies: (1) a demonstrated understanding of the uniqueness of my child and her needs; (2) a willingness to listen to and respect my concerns; (3) active involvement in professional organizations devoted to protecting rights of and improving services for individuals with disabili-

ties; (4) a willingness to express their own concerns when educational services are perceived as inadequate; and (5) a strong character, displayed by a desire to fulfill their professional ethical and advocacy obligations.

Is willing to take risks and make mistakes in order to learn.   The ability to function as a risk taker was discussed at length in Chapter 2. The act of collaboration exposes oneself to second-guessing, disagreement, and possible criticism from others. A risk-taking attitude is necessary in order to focus on the long-term potential for professional growth as a result of interpersonal interactions with individuals representing diverse perspectives.

Models and promotes self-reflection.   Collaborators who engage in advocacy activities will undoubtedly experience interpersonal interactions where their motives and actions are challenged. In such instances, the natural tendency is to respond in a defensive and aggressive manner. This behavioral style will alienate colleagues and family members, polarize diverse positions, and increase the adversarial and competitive nature of any advocacy situation. Instead, effective advocacy collaboration requires self-reflection whereby professionals can demonstrate a willingness to change their views and positions when confronted with alternative ideas/suggestions.

Demonstrates an ability to support the viewpoints of others.   Effective collaboration requires a belief that good decision making emerges from a process where all diverse and competing viewpoints are freely aired for everyone's consideration. Professionals who are effective collaborators work from this assumption by assisting their colleagues and families in completely articulating their views. This can be accomplished through the use of many of the verbal communication skills discussed in Chapter 8, such as clarifying statements, furthering responses, restating content, reflecting affect, questioning, and summarizing.

Collaboration Skills

Effective collaboration with professional colleagues or with families requires the following skills.

Ability to practice constructive conflict resolution. Chapter 10 will discuss constructive conflict resolution at length. Professionals engaged in advocacy-oriented collaboration with colleagues and families will inevitably encounter conflict in the pursuit of their advocacy goals. As Dettmer, Dyck, and Thurston (1996) noted, "Conflicts are a part of life. They occur when there are unreconciled differences among people in terms of needs, values, goals, and personalities. If conflicting parties cannot give and take by integrating their views and utilizing their differences constructively, interpersonal conflicts will escalate" (p. 166). Gordon (1977) and many others have recommended

that conflict resolution attempts seek a win-win outcome.

A constructive conflict resolution outcome is promoted by the use of collaborative problem-solving techniques that are characterized by (1) effective communication processes; (2) friendly, helpful, and unobtrusive interpersonal interactions; (3) coordination of effort and task completion; and (4) a high level of confidence in each individual's ideas for reaching a mutually satisfactory resolution. Collaborative problem solving is particularly beneficial when the parties respond creatively. Creative problem solving is enhanced by an appropriate level of motivation to solve the problem, development of conditions that permit reformulation of the problem once an impasse has been reached, and the availability of diverse ideas that can be flexibly combined into novel patterns. As an example of creative problem solving, see Box 9.2.

Box 9.2

Advocacy Anecdote

A parent of a child with severe physical disabilities told me about a bitter conflict she had become embroiled in with her son's school over the amount of physical therapy the school district would provide each week. The parents maintained that their son required daily interventions from the physical therapist. The school district insisted that they did not have enough physical therapists to provide daily services and offered physical therapy twice a week.

The family and school personnel engaged in several conflict resolution discussions but they had reached an impasse, primarily due to a lack of creative problem solving. Both parties were stuck in the mindset of looking at the conflict as a situation where the family wanted five sessions of physical therapy each week and the school was willing to provide only two sessions per week. With this mindset, the likely outcome would be to seek a compromise at three or four physical therapy sessions per week. However, when the parties agreed to bring an independent mediator into their conflict resolution process, the mediator brought a creative problem-solving perspective.

The mediator suggested that the parties change their definition of the "conflict" from the issue of number of units of therapy provided by a physical therapist per week to an issue of service delivery. That is, instead of providing therapeutic services in a traditional pull-out interdisciplinary model, where the physical therapist removes the child from the classroom and works independently with the child, a transdisciplinary model of service delivery allowing the physical therapist to share her expertise with other school staff could be utilized. Thus, appropriate therapy could be integrated into the child's school day and be provided by the classroom teacher and paraprofessionals on a daily basis.

In this transdisciplinary model of service delivery, the physical therapist becomes a consultant who establishes an intervention program, trains staff in implementing the program, and supervises the services provided. This creative change in the problem-solving process allowed both parties to find some common ground that adequately addressed mutual interests and ensured appropriate educational services for the child with disabilities.

Ability to listen. The importance of this particular nonverbal communication skill was addressed in Chapter 8. Effective collaboration requires active listening by all of the participants; listening to understand both the content and the emotion underlying another person's communicative interaction. Dettmer, Dyck, and Thurston (1996) recognized the importance of good listening skills during collaborative interactions when emotions can run high: "Listening establishes a common intent and develops a starting attitude. Listening to one who is upset helps that person focus on a problem rather than an emotion. Listening lets people cool down" (p. 168).

Ability to establish trust and rapport. These skills were also discussed in Chapter 8. In terms of advocacy-oriented collaboration, trust and rapport facilitate the necessary risk taking and build an esprit de corps, which is defined as "the common spirit existing in the members of a group and inspiring enthusiasm, devotion, and strong regard for the honor of the group" (*Merriam-Webster Collegiate Dictionary,* 1994). To withstand the travails of educational advocacy, professionals must be able to seek refuge within a collaborative work environment as a means of maintaining the necessary energy, commitment, humor, and resilience.

Ability to communicate clearly. Effective communication skills were presented in Chapter 8. In the context of advocacy-oriented collaboration, effective communication means asserting your ideas, feelings, and opinions in a persuasive manner. An example of assertive and effective communication was shared by a school psychologist regarding his experience at a recent IEP meeting. During the meeting, the parents of a tenth-grade boy with learning disabilities requested testing modifications (oral instead of written essay exams) and classroom note-taking services as general education accommodations. Whenever the parents addressed this request, one of the teachers or the principal began talking about the impor-

tance of maintaining academic integrity and rigorous educational expectations, and that students with disabilities should strive to be as independent as possible. None of the educators at the meeting directly responded to the parents' request for general education accommodations.

Finally, the school psychologist said, "Mr. and Mrs. Warren have expressed their desire that John's IEP include two general education classroom modifications: oral testing and note-taking services. We must consider this request and decide whether this is an appropriate educational modification that will allow John to be educated in the least restrictive environment. How many of you think that John requires these two modifications to be successful in his general education classes?" The school psychologist was functioning as an advocate by assertively expressing the parents' desires in a manner that the rest of the IEP committee members could no longer avoid addressing. Box 9.3 summarizes effective communication skills for responding to resistance and conflict during collaborative interactions.

Ability to employ problem-solving processes. Chapter 10 will discuss problem-solving approaches and strategies in greater detail. Robinson and Fine (1994) acknowledged the importance of a problem-solving process in fostering effective collaboration: "The main theme of a solution-oriented approach is for the persons involved to reach agreement on what they want to happen and what needs to occur to achieve that goal. Taking the steps through a problem-solving process can keep the discussion more on task and offer greater assurance of the participants' reaching resolution" (p. 13). Robinson and Fine also identified the following six steps in a problem-solving process:

1. The collaborators must identify their purpose for coming together as a group.
2. The collaborators listen to each others' perspectives on a situation or problem.
3. The collaborators reach a common understanding on what constitutes the problem and the desired goal or outcome.

Box 9.3 _____

Advocacy Actions: Skills for Responding to Resistance and Conflict during Collaborative Interactions

I. Responsive Listening
- Has assertive posture
- Use appropriate nonverbal listening
- Do not become defensive
- Use minimal verbals in listening
- Reflect content
- Reflect feelings
- Let others do most of the talking
- Use only brief, clarifying questions

II. Assertiveness
- Do not use roadblocks such as giving advice
- Use "I" messages
- State wants and feelings

III. Recycled the Interaction
- Use positive postponements
- Do not problem solve before emotions were controlled
- Summarize
- Set time to meet again, if necessary

Source: From *Consultation, Collaboration, and Teamwork for Students with Special Needs* by P. A. Dettmer, N. T. Dyck, and L. P. Thurston, 1996, Boston: Allyn and Bacon. Copyright © 1996 by Allyn and Bacon. Reprinted by permission.

---

4. The collaborators review options (e.g., brainstorming activities) for resolving the problem.
5. The collaborators agree on a specific plan of action, including specification of each person's role and responsibility, a timetable for carrying out activities, and criteria to determine whether the plan has been successful.
6. The collaborators evaluate the success of the plan that was implemented.

Ability to introduce ideas noncompetitively. Collaborative interactions that take on a competitive nature quickly turn adversarial and reflect a win-lose mentality. Alternatively, effective collabora-

tors are skillful in acknowledging the strengths or value of others' ideas before introducing their own suggestions (Robinson & Fine, 1994). This approach reduces the sense of competitiveness and fosters the goal of working together toward a common goal. Robinson and Fine further recommended "It can also be useful to present ideas or suggestions in a nonpersonalized way. For example, a teacher stating, 'Here's a suggestion that was useful in a situation we worked on last year,' involves less ego than, 'I've got an idea that I know will work'" (p. 13).

ENHANCING GROUP DECISION-MAKING PROCESSES

The goal of collaboration is effective group decision making. This final section focuses on critical issues and factors associated with collaborative decision making, including (1) promoting group cohesion, (2) improving processes for effective group decision making, and (3) developing collaborative leadership skills.

Promoting Group Cohesion

The effectiveness of a collaborative group and its level of cohesion are interdependent factors. Rudestam (1988) recognized this interdependence: "Basically, the more effective a group is in meeting needs that attract people, the more cohesive it will be.... When a group is cohesive, there is an atmosphere of acceptance, support, and a sense of belonging" (p. 115). A starting point for understanding how group cohesion develops is to delineate the characteristics of a group. Fisher and Ellis (1990) identified these five characteristics of a group: (1) it is comprised of a relatively small number of individuals so that every one is aware of their interactions with and reactions to each other, (2) there is a mutually interdependent purpose where the success of each individual is dependent upon the success of others, (3) there is a sense of belonging or membership with the other individuals of the group, (4) oral interaction occurs, and (5) there are established norms and procedures for group behavior that are accepted by all members.

A group's effectiveness in making decisions and accomplishing tasks is heavily dependent on the group's ability "to get along," or its cohesiveness. *Cohesiveness* was described by Fisher and Ellis (1990) as "that powerful appeal which attracts group members to one another and creates a collective identity, so that the success of the group means the success of the individuals" (p. 38). To promote group cohesion, Fisher and Ellis suggest the following strategies:

1. *Encourage external threats*. When group members perceive an external threat to their existence or security, there is a psychological tendency to "band together" to combat the common "enemy." For example, I know of an instance where a group of teachers in the same building increased their cohesiveness when a new school district administrator threatened to change decision-making processes from site based to a centralized model.

2. *Create history*. As a group remains together over time sharing the same experiences, this common "group history" draws the members closer together. This history can be especially effective in establishing cohesion if the group has experienced some success in accomplishing difficult tasks. My wife and I experienced this sense of group history as we collaborated with our daughter's special education teacher and human services agency case manager over the course of three years to accomplish the task of finding a home in the community for our daughter. We still get together periodically and reminisce about the obstacles we had to overcome to accomplish our goal.

3. *Establish interdependent goals*. "The goals of a group must be in the interest of all members and, more important, should be goals that require coordination and contribution from everyone in the group. As group members increase their reliance on one another, they increase their need and desire for cohesiveness. There is no need for unity when a job can be done by one person" (Fisher & Ellis, 1990, p. 39). Most of us have had the experience of serving on some group where one or two individuals dominated the meetings and unilaterally made all of the decisions. Under these conditions, the group never develops cohesiveness.

4. *Accomplish something*. Newly formed groups should initially set easily attainable goals to experience a sense of accomplishment in their efforts. I served on the board of directors for a local disability organization that constantly endured one crisis after another, without achieving much success. Our meetings became an exercise in frustration and futility, largely because the members lost confidence in their ability to accomplish the group's goals. Predictably, membership on the board dwindled over time.

5. *Develop relationships and shared norms*. An obvious but important point is that groups are more cohesive when members like each other. Relationship-building activities such as group retreats or social events are useful strategies during the initial formation of a group. The group should also develop common norms and behavioral expectations. Group cooperation and cohesion are easier to achieve when there are shared norms. Special education professionals can employ this strategy by always beginning every IEP meeting with introductions of everyone present and having each person share some positive comment about the student whose IEP is being developed.

6. *Promote acceptance for group members*. As Fisher and Ellis (1990) wrote, "Secure group members are cohesive group members" (p. 40). It is critical that each member of the group know that her contributions are valued by the group. This admonition is especially critical in fostering more active parent participation in educational decision making groups. Many parents feel threatened and intimidated by all of the professionals at IEP meetings. Professionals should reinforce parents for their comments and suggestions at IEP meetings and ensure parents that their expertise about their children is valued by the school.

Another element of group cohesion is the extent to which members are satisfied with their group experiences (Fisher & Ellis, 1990). Marston and Hecht (1988) identified six factors that are associated with group members' satisfaction. First, members must feel like they are allowed to *participate* equally with everyone else. All members must feel that they are included in the group discussions. Further, member satisfaction is enhanced when others direct comments to them during group discussions.

Second, the *quality of messages* that are communicated during a group discussion is an important determinant of member satisfaction. Any kind of *negative communication* (e.g., personal criticism) or *ambiguous communication* that creates confusion contributes to dissatisfied members. Alternatively, *orienting communication* promotes satisfaction with the group by focusing and clarifying the discussion.

A third factor associated with group members' satisfaction is *feedback*. Group members must provide feedback (both positive and negative) to each other. The most effective way of delivering negative feedback to another member is to be descriptive of the person's behaviors and to describe the impact of that behavior by using "I-messages." Further, Haslett and Ogilvie (1988) suggest that effective feedback in group discussions is characterized by (1) specifying the behaviors of concern or praise; (2) supporting observational comments with evidence; (3) separating the issues from the people; (4) softening negative messages; (5) interspersing negative messages between positive messages; (6) posing the situation as a mutual problem, not solely the responsibility of one person; (7) using good timing; and (8) using a proper manner of delivery being as nonconfrontational and as supportive as possible.

A fourth factor contributing to enhanced satisfaction amongst group members is *interaction management*. This refers to the regulation and flow of communicative interactions during a group discussion. Effective interaction management establishes and enforces turn taking by all members.

Fifth, group members tend to be satisfied when they are comfortable with the hierarchy of *status* relationships in the group. In most groups, it is unrealistic to expect that all group members will have equal status, although to ensure parity, each member's contributions are valued and each member has an equal vote on decisions. Therefore, groups will have some status differential. Individuals who emerge as leaders of a group will contribute to satisfaction levels of the other members so long as the high-status leaders are respected and accepted in their roles by the other group members.

Finally, group members' satisfaction is dependent upon a high level of *motivation* to be involved in and contribute to the group discussion. Group members should be enthusiastic about participating in group discussions and display that enthusiasm by asking questions, seeking information, requesting clarification, and maintaining focus on interactions during the discussion.

Improving Processes for Effective Group Decision Making

Several researchers have identified factors associated with effective group functioning and decision making (Glaser & Glaser, 1985; Huszczo, 1990; Ysseldyke, Algozzine, & Mitchell, 1982). The following factors contribute to successful group decision making:

- *Consensus decision making.* Ensuring that all group members understand the decision to be made and contribute to the decision-making process
- *Clarity of goals.* Ensuring that the group's goals and the process for determining whether the goals have been met are clearly understood by all members
- *Operating processes.* Employing group procedures and rules for directing problem solving, conflict resolution, and decision making
- *Organization.* Specifying members' roles and responsibilities
- *Interpersonal relationships.* Developing procedures for instilling trust among all group members
- *Intergroup relations.* Facilitating cooperation with other groups working on similar goals

- *Talent.* Ensuring that the group members possess the requisite knowledge and skills necessary to accomplish the group's goals
- *Reinforcement.* Ensuring that group members acknowledge and appreciate each others' contributions to the group

As noted earlier in this chapter, collaborative groups encounter task-related and social problems. Group decision making is enhanced to the degree that group members successfully approach their tasks and get along with each other. In an effort to facilitate effective group functioning and decision making, Fisher and Ellis (1990) delineated several *task roles* that individual members might fulfill to move the group toward its goal, and

several *group building and maintenance roles* for individual members to improve interpersonal relations in the group. In some situations, when a group is struggling in terms of effective decision making, it may be necessary to formally designate certain individuals with some of these specific roles. Ideally, individuals in effective groups will automatically fulfill most of these roles during the course of group interactions. Further, these roles may be fluid, with group members fulfilling multiple roles in one meeting and/or more than one member fulfilling the same role and function. See Box 9.4 for descriptions of these task roles and Box 9.5 for social (i.e., group building and maintenance) roles.

A final issue that is relevant to a discussion of effective group decision making is the phenomenon of groupthink. *Groupthink* is defined by Fisher and Ellis (1990) as "what happens when a group avoids conflict and reaches consensus without criticizing and evaluating ideas" (p. 218). Effective group decision making is dependent on critical thinking and constructive conflict. Fisher

---

Box 9.4

Advocacy Actions: Task Roles

- *Initiator-Contributor.* Initiates new ideas and directions.
- *Information Seeker.* Seeks information, clarification, and evidence.
- *Opinion Seeker.* Checks the opinion and agreement or disagreement of other group members.
- *Information Giver.* Contributes important and relevant information.
- *Elaborator.* Explains, extends, and clarifies the ideas of others.
- *Coordinator.* Shows relationships between ideas and facts.
- *Orienter.* Keeps the group on task and progressing toward the goal.
- *Evaluator-Critic.* Comments on group information and applies critical standards in an effort to evaluate proposed recommendations.
- *Energizer.* Stimulates the group to action.
- *Procedural Technician.* Deals with procedural tasks (e.g., scheduling, copying handouts, distributing the agenda, etc.) to facilitate smooth operation of the group process.
- *Recorder.* Takes the minutes of group meetings.

Source: From *Small Group Decision Making: Communication and the Group Process* by B. A. Fisher and D. G. Ellis, 1990, New York: McGraw-Hill. Copyright © 1990 by McGraw-Hill. Reprinted by permission of The McGraw-Hill Companies.

Box 9.5

Advocacy Actions: Group Building and Maintenance Roles

- *Encourager.* Accepts and reinforces the ideas of other group members.
- *Harmonizer.* Keeps the peace and resolves tensions in the group, often by employing humor or sarcasm.
- *Compromiser.* Tries to offer ideas and solutions that satisfy everyone.
- *Gatekeeper and Expediter.* Tries to encourage equal participation of all group members.
- *Group Observer.* Makes generalized comments about the behavior of the group as a whole.
- *Follower.* Goes along easily with the trends in the group.

Source: From *Small Group Decision Making: Communication and the Group Process* by B. A. Fisher and D. G. Ellis, 1990, New York: McGraw-Hill. Copyright © 1990 by McGraw-Hill. Reprinted by permission of The McGraw-Hill Companies.

and Ellis identified four norms that contribute to groupthink:

1. *Mindless cohesion.* A group can become ineffectively optimistic when it dismisses challenging ideas that may temporarily disrupt the group harmony. As an example, a parent shared the experience of being involved in a parent advocacy group that was seeking increased inclusion into general education classrooms for their children with mental retardation. This group was extremely cohesive; all of the parents felt strongly that their children's education was inappropriate because of a lack of inclusive educational experiences.

When two new parents joined this advocacy group, the group's cohesion was threatened. These new parents were cautious about moving too quickly to force inclusion on their children's school. Although these two parents recognized some potential benefits to inclusion for their children, they had some concerns, as well. The majority of parents in this advocacy group dismissed these two parents' concerns and proceeded with their plan to force the inclusion issue on the school. The end result of this parent group's advocacy was relatively unsuccessful because many of the teachers rejected the parent group imposing inclusion on them. As it turned out, the two cautious parents raised a number of valid issues about teacher preparedness and attitudes, which the advocacy group failed to acknowledge in their groupthink mindset.

2. *Pressuring nonconformists.* If group members feel pressure to conform to the will of the majority, the free expression of ideas and opinions is compromised. Under these conditions, creativity is stifled and groupthink emerges.

3. *Failing to reward critical thinking.* Groups engage in groupthink when they feel invulnerable and when strong group leaders demand support and discourage conflict and critical thinking. Honest opposition to ideas must be stimulated in group decision making.

4. *Tendency to justify what they have done.* The limitation of this group norm was recognized by

Fisher and Ellis (1990): "Groups make poor decisions when they discount information because it is inconsistent with an established position. Groupthink decisions emerge from rationalizations. The group blindly believes that what it has done in the past is best. They reject new information and reaffirm the inherent 'correctness' of their own group. This leads to a false sense of consensus" (pp. 219–220). This groupthink norm was also evident in the example of the parent advocacy group cited in item 1.

Developing Collaborative Leadership Skills

Special education professionals who function as advocates within collaborative groups must be prepared to serve as leaders in three domains: group procedures, task requirements, and social needs (Fisher & Ellis, 1990). An effective leader establishes group procedures that ensure efficient operation of meetings and decision-making processes. Some of the tasks associated with establishing group procedures include planning the meeting agendas, handling routine administrative matters (such as taking attendance, calling the meeting to order, and making announcements), and preparing for the next meeting. Examples of leadership skills in fostering task requirements and social needs were identified in Boxes 9.4 and 9.5. Finally, a tool for engaging in a self-assessment of one's own leadership skills is provided in Box 9.6.

SUMMARY

Educational advocacy is generally most effective when it is pursued as a collaborative activity by a group of dedicated professionals and family members. Advocacy-oriented collaboration amongst professionals and with families creates synergistic effects on behalf of children with disabilities. For reasons identified in this and in earlier chapters, special education professionals do not have the option of refusing to engage in collaborative activities on behalf of children with disabilities. Special

Box 9.6 _____

Advocacy Actions: Understanding Your Leadership Actions Questionnaire

Directions: Each of the following items describes a leadership action. In the space next to each item write **5** if you **always** behave that way, **4** if you **frequently** behave that way, **3** if you **occasionally** behave that way, **2** if you **seldom** behave that way, and **1** if you **never** behave that way.

When I am a member of a group:

_____ 1. I offer facts and give my opinions, ideas, feelings, and information in order to help the group discussion.

_____ 2. I warmly encourage all members of the group to participate. I am open to their ideas. I let them know I value their contributions to the group.

_____ 3. I ask for facts, information, opinions, ideas, and feelings from the other group members in order to help the group discussion.

_____ 4. I help communication among group members by using good communication skills. I make sure that each group member understands what the others say.

_____ 5. I give direction to the group by planning how to go on with the group work and by calling attention to the tasks that need to be done. I assign responsibilities to different group members.

_____ 6. I tell jokes and suggest interesting ways of doing the work in order to reduce tension in the group and increase the fun we have working together.

_____ 7. I pull together related ideas or suggestions made by group members and restate and summarize the major points discussed by the group.

_____ 8. I observe the way the group is working and use my observations to help discuss how the group can work together better.

_____ 9. I give the group energy. I encourage group members to work hard to achieve our goals.

_____ 10. I promote the open discussion of conflicts among group members in order to resolve disagreements and increase group cohesiveness. I mediate conflicts among members when they seem unable to resolve them directly.

_____ 11. I remind the group about the practicality and workability of ideas, evaluate alternative solutions, and apply them to real situations to see if they will work.

_____ 12. I express support, acceptance, and liking for other members of the group and give appropriate praise when another member has taken a constructive action in the group.

Scoring: In order to obtain a total score for **task actions** and **maintenance actions,** write the score for each item in the appropriate column and then add the columns. The higher your score in either column, the more you tend to function as a leader (Maximum score = 30; Minimum score = 6).

_____ 1. Information and Opinion Giver	_____ 2. Encourager of participation
_____ 3. Information and Opinion Seeker	_____ 4. Communication Facilitator
_____ 5. Direction and Role Definer	_____ 6. Tension Reliever
_____ 7. Summarizer	_____ 8. Process Observer
_____ 9. Energizer	_____ 10. Interpersonal Problem Solver
_____ 11. Reality Tester	_____ 12. Supporter and Praiser
_____ Total for Task Actions	_____ Total for Maintenance Actions

Source: From "Understanding Your Leadership Actions Questionnaire" in *Joining Together: Group Therapy and Group Skills*, 6th ed. by D. W. Johnson and F. P. Johnson, 1997, Boston: Allyn and Bacon. Copyright © 1997 by Allyn and Bacon. Reprinted by permission.

education processes for evaluation, IEP development, and placement decision making are inherently collaborative group decisions. Within the
context of these group decisions, professionals
encounter numerous opportunities to function as
an advocate to ensure appropriate educational services for children with disabilities. This chapter
reviewed relevant skills for effective collaboration
and discussed considerations and strategies for
improving group functioning and decision making.

CHAPTER 10

CONFLICT RESOLUTION SKILLS

An eye for an eye and we all go blind. —Mahatma Ghandi

Ghandi's ageless wisdom concerning conflict is important to heed in special education professionals' advocacy work on behalf of children with disabilities and their families. A competitive, win-lose approach to interpersonal conflict leads to hostile, adversarial, vindictive, and ineffective relationships between professionals and family members who must work together cooperatively in planning and implementing appropriate educational services for students with disabilities. *Conflict* is defined as "any situation in which one person or group perceives that another person or group is interfering with his, her, or their goal attainment" (Friend & Cook, 1996, pp. 198–199).

Friend and Cook (1996) cited several reasons why educational conflict is on the rise. First, school professionals have traditionally avoided conflict and were successful in their avoidance tactics because school culture emphasized isolated working environments for most teachers. In today's schools, however, professional isolation has slowly given way to increasing collaboration (see Chapter 9) with professional colleagues and families. Professionals are more likely to experience conflict under conditions of closer proximity in their working relationships. Further, as Friend and Cook opined, "When professionals from several disciplines with different frames of reference are making decisions about student needs, they are likely to differ occasionally about desired outcomes" (p. 199).

Second, schools are becoming more nurturing environments for students and staff (Lee & Barnett, 1994). As school culture encourages the expression of individual needs, conflict is a likely result because, with limited resources, it is impossible to adequately meet everyone's needs. In effect, individuals and groups are in competition with each other for needs satisfaction in an arena of significant resource constraints. Finally, school decision-making practices are changing from centralized, administrative directive models to site-based, participatory decision-making approaches (Thurston, Clift, & Schacht, 1993). When more individuals participate in decision making, there are more opportunities for conflict (Budoff & Orenstein, 1982; Deutsch, 1973; Fiedler, 1993; Simpson, 1996).

Disagreement and conflict between and among professionals and families is often inevitable, natural, and healthy (Brock & Shanberg, 1990; Fiedler, 1993; Shields, 1989; Simpson, 1996). Indeed, Simpson recognized this reality when he stated,

> Normal disagreement among parents, family members, and professionals should be viewed as indications of open communication, interpersonal maturity, a willingness to collaborate, and the basis for meeting the individualized needs of children and adolescents with exceptionalities most effectively. Consistent with this perception, the educator should not actively seek strategies for avoiding healthy conflicts but rather ways for arbitrating differences and selecting mutually satisfying and collaborative solutions to problems. (p. 326)

In fact, as discussed later in this chapter, professionals who possess skills in resolving conflict constructively will yield a number of potential benefits and results from conflict situations.

To realize the potential benefits of conflict and to avoid unnecessary special education litigation, professionals must possess competence in group processes, listening, trust building, problem solving, and knowledge of their ethical and legal obligations (Heron, Martz, & Margolis, 1996). This chapter addresses conflict in the context of special education advocacy and the skills and strategies required to engage in constructive conflict resolution. First, the causes of conflict in special education advocacy are presented. Next, characteristics of destructive and constructive conflict resolution are examined. Then, different conflict resolution approaches are reviewed, including competition, accommodation, avoidance, compromise, and collaboration. And, finally, specific constructive conflict resolution skills and strategies are discussed.

CAUSES OF CONFLICT IN PROFESSIONALS' ADVOCACY EFFORTS

As advocates on behalf of students with disabilities, special education professionals will inevitably encounter conflict—conflict with other school personnel, conflict with family members, and conflict with personnel from other agencies and organizations providing services to students with disabilities. What are the causes of this advocacy-related interpersonal conflict? This section discusses several factors associated with the development of interpersonal conflict.

A variety of factors affect the development of conflict between special education professionals and families, including parental characteristics for waging conflict, the prior family/professional relationship, the nature of the conflict and its perceived importance, the social environment within which the conflict occurs, interested audiences to the conflict, and the willingness of the participants to compromise or concede to the demands of the other party (Deutsch, 1973; Fiedler, 1993; Simpson, 1996).

Parental Characteristics for Waging Conflict

Interpersonal conflict between professionals and families of children with disabilities is affected by certain characteristics of the parents for entering

into and waging conflict. The most relevant parental characteristics are financial resources to hire legal representation in pursuing due process remedies (see Chapter 6), knowledge of legal rights and procedures in the education of children with disabilities (see Chapter 5), and time and energy to initiate a legal action.

Financial Resources

As discussed in Chapter 6, the financial and emotional costs of participating in formal conflict in special education (e.g., a due process hearing) are significant for both school personnel and families. Research has revealed that the vast majority of parents who pursue the due process hearing option are well educated and from the middle to upper socioeconomic levels (Budoff & Orenstein, 1982; Strickland, 1983). The significance of adequate parental financial resources for waging conflict was noted by Fiedler (1993): "In considering the financial costs associated with pursuing a due process hearing, it can be surmised that financial ability to afford legal representation is an important determinant of whether or not a parent resorts to legal processes in an effort to resolve a conflict with the school" (p. 259).

Knowledge of Legal Rights and Procedures

Parents of children with disabilities who are not well versed in special education legal rights and procedures will be more willing to accept less than satisfactory solutions to their educational concerns simply because they are unaware of options for addressing their concerns. This reality underscores the importance of adhering to legal and ethical obligations to ensure that parents receive information about their legal rights, including due process and mediation procedures. And, considering the concern that many parent information materials may not be comprehensible to a large number of parents because of high readability rates of those materials, special education professionals must be willing to commit the extra time necessary to ensure parental understanding of their legal rights (Roit & Pfohl, 1984).

Commitment of Time and Energy

Participation in formal conflict situations requires a considerable commitment of time and energy by both school personnel and parents. Any two parties have a greater chance of experiencing conflict as their opportunities for personal interactions increase (Deutsch, 1973). As an example, studies confirm that parents participating in due process hearing conflict were actively involved in visiting their child's school frequently to observe the classroom, discuss the educational program with the teacher, coordinate home/school activities, and discuss the child's progress (Fiedler, 1993):

> In parent-school interactions, therefore, greater parent involvement means more opportunities for actively involved parents to confirm or disconfirm that their expectations for their child are being met at school. Undoubtedly, some parents lack sufficient time and energy to be actively involved in their children's education. Therefore, compared to more actively involved parents, they do not have as many opportunities to realize differences of opinion or conflict with school personnel. (Fiedler, 1993, pp. 259–260)

The Prior Family/Professional Relationship

Conflict between families and professionals develops over time and is highly dependent on the quality of interpersonal interactions and the resulting relationship between the two parties (Simpson, 1996). A relationship built on mutual trust, respect, and effective communication is no guarantee that disagreement and even conflict will not develop between families and professionals. However, a positive preconflict relationship between the parties is likely to set the conditions for constructive conflict resolution. Special education professionals must recognize the importance of initial interactions between themselves and families (Losen & Diament, 1978). Simply stated, there is no second chance to make a favorable first impression. A positive or negative initial interaction may determine whether families view professionals as allies or adversaries.

The IEP conference represents a significant interaction opportunity for professionals and families to establish a mutually cooperative relationship. Unfortunately, many parents have reported that their interactions with professionals at IEP conferences left them feeling discouraged and devalued as educational planning partners (Fiedler, 1993). Professionals must view every interaction with family members as an opportunity to lay a solid foundation for constructive problem solving when the occasion calls for it.

The Nature of the Conflict and Its Perceived Importance

The nature of the conflict and its perceived importance to professionals and families is a major determinant in the evolution and ultimate resolution of a dispute (Simpson, 1996). In assessing the nature of conflict, important factors to consider are (1) the scope of the issues in dispute, (2) the rigidity of the parties, and (3) the perceived importance of the issue to the parties involved (Deutsch, 1973).

If the scope of the dispute concerns a large issue of principle (e.g, inclusion versus pull-out special education services), the parties will have more difficulty resolving their differences cooperatively than if the dispute is over a specific issue related to the application of a principle (e.g., using cooperative learning techniques to enhance the inclusion of a student with disabilities versus using peer tutoring).

Rigidity of the parties refers to their perceptions of the availability of mutually satisfactory solutions to resolve their dispute. If the parties in dispute perceive that there are no mutually satisfactory alternatives, they are likely to become entrenched in their positions and be reluctant to problem solve or compromise. The final factor, perceived importance of the issue to the parties in dispute, refers to the significance attached to the issue by both parties. If the issue is deemed highly significant, the parties will tend to act in a more steadfast and recalcitrant manner than would be the case with issues considered to be less significant.

The Social Environment within Which the Conflict Occurs

The school district's social environment involves the institutional rules and procedures established to handle parent/school conflict. School district rules and procedures may set the climate and expectations for a cooperative conflict resolution approach or, conversely, a competitive, win-lose conflict resolution approach. For instance, school district rules and procedures can endorse parent/school conflict as legitimate and healthy, thus fostering confidence that good-faith efforts will lead to mutually satisfactory outcomes (Himes, 1980).

Alternatively, school district rules and procedures may promote a competitive, zero sum perspective of parent/school conflict. In this perspective, achieving one's own goals means defeating the other party (McGuire, 1984). I conducted a study of special education due process hearings in a large, urban school district several years ago. In interviewing parents of children with disabilities who had been involved in due process disputes with the school district, it became evident that a principal reason for an inordinate number of hearings in this district was the parents' beliefs that the school district administration was not sincerely interested in their concerns about their children's education. The school district's rules and procedures emphasized its power vis-à-vis parents. The parents perceived the school district administrators as competitive in conflict situations and they responded in kind (Fiedler, 1985).

Interested Audiences to the Conflict

When a conflict extends beyond the immediate parties and becomes more public, both parties feel compelled not to back down. Deutsch (1973) referred to this as the need to "maintain face." Under these conditions, escalation of the dispute can be expected, as well as increasingly competitive conflict resolution approaches and a greater willingness to use adversarial procedures such as due process hearings. Further, when a parent/school conflict encompasses a larger interested audience, the school district becomes more concerned about the potential precedential impact of resolving a parent's concerns. For example, in the *Board of Education* v. *Rowley* (1982) case, as the conflict between the parents and the school became more public, the school district "grew increasingly concerned about the potential financial drain on its fiscal resources if they lost and parents of other hearing impaired children began to request full-time sign language interpreters for their children" (Fiedler, 1993, p. 263). As parent/school conflict becomes more public, with a larger audience interested in the outcome, the tendency is for both parties to become more entrenched in their positions, thus reducing the likelihood of reaching a mutually satisfactory resolution.

Willingness of Participants to Compromise or Concede

Parent/school conflict characterized as defensive, distrustful, and vindictive connotes a win-lose philosophy where the parties perceive their inability to win as a failure. This mindset is likely to foster positional bargaining, polarization of the conflict, excessive demands, and an unwillingness to compromise or concede to the demands of the other party. This situation will escalate the conflict.

Other Precipitating Factors in the Development of Interpersonal Conflict

Interpersonal conflicts experienced by professionals may also be categorized by the interaction of the goals of the individuals who are involved (Maurer, 1991). Using this classification scheme, Friend and Cook (1996) categorized the types of conflict into (1) conflict between individuals with different goals, (2) conflict between individuals with the same goals, and (3) conflict within individuals.

The advocacy scenarios presented in Chapter 1 contain examples of conflict between individuals with different goals. For instance, in Mary Kinney's advocacy dilemma, she was pursuing a goal of obtaining appropriate speech and language services for all eligible students; whereas, arguably, the school district administration's goal was to maintain the present school budget by not hiring additional staff.

The second type of goal conflict, conflict between individuals with the same goals, is reflected in the Steve Kern advocacy scenario. The school administration had employed punitive disciplinary sanctions, such as school suspension, in furthering its goal of maintaining a school atmosphere conducive to learning by removing unduly disruptive students from school. Many of Steve's students with emotional/behavioral disorders had been repeatedly suspended from school. Steve's goal for his students was to provide them with appropriate educational services to foster their learning and successful transition to community life. Essentially, the school administration's goal for all students and Steve's goal for his students were the same (i.e., to maintain a school environment conducive to learning). However, a conflict arose when the school administration achieved its goal at the expense of Steve's goal attainment.

The final goal conflict discussed by Friend and Cook (1996) involves conflict within individuals. This intrapersonal dilemma is demonstrated in Mary Kinney's advocacy scenario. Undoubtedly, as a conscientious and dedicated speech and language clinician, Mary was experiencing an internal conflict in wrestling with her ethical obligation to provide appropriate services for students on her current caseload versus her sense of duty to ensure appropriate educational services for all of the newly referred students.

Resistance

In addition to having to respond to interpersonal conflict, professionals engaged in advocacy activities can expect to encounter resistance from others. Resistance frequently occurs when people are asked to change (Dettmer, Dyck, & Thurston, 1996; Friend & Cook, 1996). As discussed in Chapter 7, advocacy usually involves some type of change, either at intrapersonal, interpersonal, or systems levels.

Ury (1991) identified four situations where individuals are more inclined to resist another person's proposal or idea for change. First, if the proposal/idea is not their own, individuals are likely to resist. Change is easier to contemplate when it is sparked by our own ideas; but when change is stimulated by another individual's ideas, the tendency is to resist. This type of resistance offers a partial explanation why both parties in a due process hearing dispute often fail to abide by the decision imposed on them by the hearing officer (see Chapter 6). Because the decision was imposed on the parents and school by someone else (i.e., the hearing officer), the changes required by the hearing decision are more difficult to accept than if the parties had mutually resolved their dispute.

Second, resistance from the other individual in a dispute is likely when the proposed resolution has overlooked a basic interest of that person. For example, when the director of pupil services proposed that any newly eligible students would simply be added to Mary Kinney's speech and language caseload, Mary's resistance to such a solution was highly predictable. The director's proposed solution failed to consider Mary's strong interest in ethically and competently providing appropriate educational services to the students already on her caseload, which would have been impossible, given more students to serve.

Third, individuals engaged in conflict resist proposed solutions because they are afraid of losing face. This situation was discussed earlier in this section as a factor causing conflict—interested audiences to the conflict. The more public the conflict becomes, the more the parties resist compromise because they fear looking weak or as if they are "backing down."

Fourth, sometimes resistance is the result of negotiations that are moving too fast for one party's comfort level. Under such circumstances, when feeling overwhelmed by the whirlwind of proposals, counterproposals, and decisions that must be made, it is often easier to resist—to say no. A parent advocacy group, for example, had quickly circulated a petition in a door-to-door campaign, demanding that the school board take immediate action to bring several students with severe disabilities back to their home school district instead of busing those students to a cooperative educational program in another school district. Although the parent advocacy group had very valid reasons supporting their demand, the school board was caught off guard by the petition drive and reacted with resistance. The parent advocacy group would have been more successful if they had systematically addressed their concerns with the school administration first and asked the administration to make a proposal to the school board. In the rush to rectify a perceived injustice, advocates must be careful not to act too hastily, as to do so may invite resistance. Specific problem-solving strategies for dealing with resistant individuals are presented later in this chapter.

DESTRUCTIVE AND CONSTRUCTIVE CONFLICT

Conflict is destructive if the involved parties are dissatisfied with the outcomes and feel they have lost as a result of the conflict (Deutsch, 1973). Conversely, constructive conflict leaves the involved parties satisfied with the outcomes and with a sense that they have benefitted as a result of the conflict. Whether conflict is destructive or constructive depends primarily on the skills, strategies, and tactics employed by the participants.

When participants in a conflict situation perceive each other as hostile or uncaring, a destructive chain reaction follows. Typically, one or both parties becomes defensive, and, quite often, withdrawal from interaction occurs. Without a sufficient opportunity to interact and communicate with each other, the conflicting parties fail to understand each other's goals and interests, which increases mutual mistrust, confirming the initial perceptions of hostility and uncaring, thereby creating a vicious cycle of increased negativity and competitiveness (Friedman, 1980). Without an adequate opportunity for the participants to express disagreements and differences of opinion, conflict is likely to be expressed as anger, hostility, or fear (Simpson, 1996). Anger or hostility typically engender coercive power or the use of threats as the primary conflict resolution tactics.

Deutsch (1973) noted that certain tactics are likely to elicit resistance or alienation of conflicting parties. These tactics include (1) illegitimate techniques that involve violations of values and norms governing interpersonal interactions (e.g., ridiculing or mocking the other party); (2) negative sanctions such as punishment or threats (e.g., threatening a parent with the withdrawal of all special education services if the parent continues to pursue a due process hearing); (3) sanctions that are inappropriate in kind (e.g., initiating a job retaliatory action against a school employee who challenges school policies or actions); and (4) influence that is excessive in magnitude (e.g., an administrator exerting undue pressure on a staff member or parent to concede to the demands of the administrator).

One destructive effect of employing threats in conflict situations is the tendency to use threat to force another person to yield; the more irreconcilable the conflict is perceived to be, the stronger this tendency. Also, if threat is used to intimidate, the threatened person will feel hostility toward the person engaged in threatening and will tend to respond with a counterthreat, leading to a competitive struggle between the parties and conflict escalation.

Conflict is likely to be resolved constructively in situations where the parties involved perceive that they have less at stake in the conflict than in continuing the relationship between them (Deutsch, 1973). Constructive conflict resolution is advanced by effective communication skills such as empathic listening, physical attending, assertiveness, positive reinforcement, and group decision-making techniques, such as agenda setting, reaching closure, and planning (Turnbull, 1983). In addition, the following characteristics promote constructive conflict resolution: (1) minimize differences in goals and emphasize cooperative strategies, (2) emphasize the desirability of mutually satisfactory outcomes, (3) refrain from harmful actions or statements, (4) emphasize mutual dependencies, (5) ensure equal status in negotiations, (6) attempt to understand others' motives and explanations, and (7) maintain openness about intentions and rationale (Walton, 1969).

Depending on a professional's skills in resolving conflict constructively, there are numerous potential benefits and results from conflict (Dettmer, Dyck, & Thurston, 1996; Fisher & Ellis, 1990; Friend & Cook, 1996):

- Conflict can help clarify issues, increase communicative interaction and individual participation in group decision making, and promote personal and professional growth.
- Conflict can strengthen relationships and school organizations when the problems are successfully resolved.
- Conflict can increase group cohesiveness by providing an appropriate and healthy outlet for hostility.
- Conflict requires a group to spend more time in its decision making, searching for alternatives, and preventing premature decisions from being made out of expediency. As diverse perspectives emerge during conflict, critical thinking is stimulated and this process yields higher-quality decisions.
- Conflict builds consensus in group decision making, as all perspectives and ideas have an opportunity to be aired.
- Conflict increases a sense of ownership by all of the participants for the resulting decisions, and thus the participants develop a stronger commitment to implement those decisions.
- Conflict that is successfully resolved enhances open communication and a more trusting relationship in future interpersonal interactions.
- Skills that are utilized in successfully resolving conflict increase the likelihood of successfully managing future conflict situations.

CONFLICT RESOLUTION APPROACHES

Special education professionals may approach conflict from several conflict management styles. This section discusses five common conflict resolution approaches: competition, accommodation, avoidance, compromise, and collaboration. Each approach will be analyzed along two dimensions: cooperativeness (e.g., the extent to which the parties involved in conflict value maintaining a cooperative relationship) and assertiveness (e.g., the extent to which the parties involved in conflict value achieving their individual goals). Individuals have preferred conflict management styles, although one's approach to conflict can change over time with new knowledge and skills. No single conflict resolution approach is always the desired mode of operation; specific situations will dictate selection of a particular approach.

Competition

A competitive conflict resolution approach reflects a win-lose strategy, indicating a high value for achieving individual goals and a corresponding low concern for maintaining a cooperative relationship with the other party to a conflict. A competitive approach engages in positional bargaining, trying to persuade another person to accept alternatives that favor one's own interests (Fisher & Ury, 1991). Typically, efforts are made to dominate the other party by the use of such pressure tactics as (1) demands that exceed what is acceptable, (2) commitments to unalterable positions, (3) persuasive arguments aimed at convincing the other person that concessions are in his or her own best interests, (4) threats, (5) impositions of time pressure to make a decision, and (6) attempts to conceal information to deceive the other person (Pruitt, 1983).

Filley (1975) identified several characteristics of a competitive approach to conflict resolution. First, competition involves a clear we-they distinction between the parties, rather than a we-versus-the problem orientation. Second, individual energies are directed toward the other person in an atmosphere of total victory or defeat. Third, each party sees the issue only from his or her own point of view, rather than defining the problem in terms of mutual needs. Fourth, emphasis is on attainment of a solution, rather than definition of goals, values, or motives to be attained. Fifth, conflicts are personalized rather than depersonalized through an objective focus on facts and issues. Sixth, no sequence of activities is planned for bringing about conflict resolution. Finally, the involved parties are conflict oriented (emphasizing their immediate disagreement) rather than relationship oriented (emphasizing the long-term effect of their differences and the way in which they are resolved).

However, even considering the negative tactics associated with a competitive conflict resolution approach, professionals might appropriately employ this style when ethical issues are at stake or when certain about the correctness of their position in promoting the best interests of a student with disabilities (Friend & Cook, 1996). For example, a special education teacher of students with emotional/behavioral disorders became embroiled in a conflict with her principal over the use of a seclusionary timeout procedure with a severely acting out and disruptive student. The principal insisted that the teacher institute the timeout procedure and had a corner of the classroom partitioned off to serve as the timeout area. The teacher felt this disciplinary procedure was excessively aversive and punitive. Further, the teacher had experienced some success with the student by using a more positive behavioral management strategy—differential reinforcement of other behavior.

In the context of this conflict, the teacher was highly competitive in her conflict resolution tactics with the principal because she was guided by the Council for Exceptional Children's Code of Ethics (see Chapter 3) and its prohibition against disciplinary methods that undermine the dignity and basic human rights of individuals with disabilities. Therefore, the teacher did not believe, given the success of the differential reinforcement technique, that the timeout procedure was in the student's best educational interest.

Accommodation

Accommodation is a yield-lose style of conflict resolution in that the accommodating person places a high value on maintaining a positive and cooperative relationship with the other person and sacrifices his or her own goals to maintain the relationship. There are several limitations with this approach to conflict resolution (Friend & Cook, 1996; Simpson, 1996). The accommodation approach will instill frustration and anger, and leave the person accommodating with a feeling that he or she is being taken advantage of in the negotiation process. Second, it is inappropriate to accommodate in situations where the other person is making demands or seeking concessions that are inappropriate or unachievable.

Accommodation can, however, be beneficial when the disputed issue or problem is relatively unimportant or when a situation cannot be altered under any set of circumstances. A parent of a learning disabled high school student accommodated the school's demand that she sign a homework sheet each night indicating that her son had completed his homework. (The parent truly felt her son was not learning about individual responsibility and consequences of personal actions if she was forced to police his homework completion every evening.) However, in terms of the overall educational experience her son was receiving, signing a homework sheet was a relatively insignificant issue to the mother. For the sake of maintaining a collaborative and positive relationship with school personnel, the mother was willing to accommodate.

Avoidance

When conflict is avoided or suppressed, the consequences are usually harmful or stagnating (Folberg & Taylor, 1984). Avoidance as a conflict resolution approach is typified by a lose-leave style of interpersonal interaction; participants consciously turn away from conflict. With this approach, there is a low value placed on obtaining individual goals and a similar low regard for the relationship with the other parties involved in the dispute. The basic weakness of this approach was captured by Friend and Cook (1996): "Avoidance is a seductive strategy because it gives the appearance that all is well; its hidden danger is that a situation may become more conflicted by inaction" (p. 204). A person who avoids conflict sees it as a hopeless, useless, and punishing experience. If somehow a resolution is reached or imposed on the parties, there will be very little commitment to carrying out that decision.

Avoidance of a conflict can be a reasonable temporary tactic, however, if it is designed to let the parties cool down or gather more information, if there is inadequate time to constructively address a conflict, or if the problem is tangential or symptomatic of other more basic issues (Thomas & Kilmann, 1974). During a very emotional and conflict-ridden IEP meeting, the parents of a daughter with moderate mental retardation decided to avoid the issue of including their child in general education classes because it was obvious that the school staff felt the child was not ready for such an experience. Although the parents felt strongly that their daughter could benefit from general education classroom experiences, they realized that they needed time to regain their emotional balance so they could rationally argue their opinion. Further, the parents wanted to gather some additional information from the local protection and advocacy agency on the law of educating students with disabilities in the least restrictive environment. The parents knew they could request another IEP meeting later to revisit this issue. However, as a long-term approach, avoidance of conflict will generally exacerbate the problem and will rarely solve the situation to everyone's mutual satisfaction.

Compromise

A compromising style of conflict resolution demonstrates a moderate concern for achieving personal goals paralleled by a moderate concern for maintaining a cooperative relationship. According to Filley (1975), compromising is a lose-lose approach because neither party accomplishes what it wants completely. This conceptualization may be somewhat harsh. By compromising, a person gives up more than through competing, but less

than by accommodating. A compromising style addresses an issue more directly than avoiding, but does not explore it in as much depth as collaboration (Thomas & Kilmann, 1974).

A compromising approach displays several characteristics: (1) the participants assume limited resources and conflict of interests, (2) there is relatively equal balance of power between the parties, (3) continued disagreement is viewed as more costly than compromise, (4) negotiation emphasizes the strategic use of information rather than full disclosure, (5) the parties' energies are directed toward each other rather than toward reaching a solution to a common problem, and (6) the parties are concerned with sacrificing and avoiding an unfavorable outcome rather than with achieving a solution beneficial to both sides (Filley, 1975).

Compromisers typically seek expedient solutions because they have limited time to resolve a problem. Compromising is also an appropriate approach when the problem to be resolved is not particularly significant and when two highly competitive individuals are involved in conflict and neither is likely to "back down" (Friend & Cook, 1996). As an example of compromise, consider the Steve Kern advocacy scenario from Chapter 1. During negotiations with the school administration on the issue of repeated use of out-of-school suspensions levied against many of his students, Steve and the administration agreed on an intermediary solution. Both parties compromised and initiated a new in-school suspension program for disruptive students. This compromise represented neither party's ideal solution, but both parties gained some of their objectives through this solution.

Collaboration

Collaboration or problem solving is the most highly recommended approach for effective conflict resolution (Deutsch, 1973; Fisher & Ury, 1991; Simpson, 1996; Ury, 1991). Collaboration is a win-win approach with the distinct advantage of "providing a means for meeting parents', families', and educators' needs while serving the best interests of the child" (Simpson, 1996, p. 333). Collaboration is characterized by a high concern for achieving personal goals as well as a high concern for maintaining a cooperative relationship.

Collaboration leads to constructive conflict resolution (Araki, 1983; Deutsch, 1973). Compared to competitive methods, cooperative problem-solving techniques are characterized by more effective communication processes; more friendly, helpful, and less obtrusive interpersonal interactions; better coordination of effort and task orientation; and a greater confidence in one's ideas for reaching a mutually satisfactory resolution (Deutsch, 1973). Problem solving is particularly beneficial when the parties respond creatively.

The following beliefs, according to Filley (1975), are conducive to collaborative problem solving: (1) belief in the availability of mutually acceptable solutions, (2) belief in the desirability of a mutually acceptable solution, (3) belief in cooperation rather than competition, (4) belief that everyone is of equal value and status during problem-solving negotiations, (5) belief in others' views as legitimate statements of their position, (6) belief in the trustworthiness of the other party, and (7) belief that the other party can compete but chooses to cooperate.

Although collaborative problem solving represents a positive approach to conflict resolution, it is a process that requires a substantial time commitment, a trust in one another, and a commitment to reaching a mutually beneficial solution (Friend & Cook, 1996). The specific steps in the implementation of collaborative problem solving are discussed in the next section.

CONSTRUCTIVE CONFLICT RESOLUTION STRATEGIES AND SKILLS

Principled Negotiation

The five basic strategies associated with principled negotiation are (1) separate the people from the problem; (2) focus on interests, not positions; (3) invent options for mutual gain; (4) insist on using objective criteria; and (5) prepare your BATNA—the best alternative to a negotiated agreement (Fisher & Ury, 1991).

Separate the People from the Problem

In every negotiation situation each party has interests in two areas: (1) in the substance of the problem or conflict and (2) in the relationship with the other party. In many conflicts, the parties' relationship becomes entangled with the problem. This creates an unnecessarily antagonistic and adversarial situation.

For instance, if Karen Snyder (advocacy scenario in Chapter 1) had said to the general education teachers in her building, " By your failure to implement the accommodations listed on the IEPs of students with disabilities included in your classes, you are acting irresponsibly and not in the best interests of your students," such a statement would have made the conflict an adversarial situation between the people involved. Instead, Karen should focus on the problem, stating, for example, "We must ensure that all of the accommodations listed on each student's IEP are implemented in general education classes." This second statement attacks the problem, not the people involved. Fisher and Ury (1991) offered several strategies for separating the person from the problem:

- Put yourself in your opponent's shoes.
- Do not presume to know your opponent's intentions based solely on what you fear might be his or her intentions.
- Do not blame your opponent for your problem.
- Discuss each other's perceptions.
- Look for opportunities to act inconsistently with your opponent's perceptions. For example, if your opponent perceives you as the enemy, look for any opportunity to act as an ally. (Karen Snyder could act as an ally of the general education teachers by expressing her intention to increase their collaborative planning time with the special education teachers in the building.)

- Give your opponent a stake in the outcome by ensuring that she participate in the problem-solving process.
- Make proposals that are consistent with your opponent's values.

Focus on Interests, Not Positions

This conflict resolution strategy involves identifying whether the parties in conflict have any underlying mutual interests or interests that can be reconciled with each other, instead of engaging in positional bargaining and, ultimately, a commitment to unalterable positions. A lucid example of this approach was provided by Fisher and Ury (1991):

> Consider the story of two men quarreling in a library. One wants the window open and the other wants it closed. They bicker back and forth about how much to leave it open: a crack, halfway, three quarters of the way. No solution satisfies them both. Enter the librarian. She asks one why he wants the window open: "To get some fresh air." She asks the other why he wants it closed: "To avoid the draft." After thinking a minute, she opens wide a window in the next room, bringing in fresh air without a draft. (p. 41)

Several strategies for identifying interests include (Fisher & Ury, 1991):

- Ask "Why?" or "Why not?" when examining your opponent's stated position. Why has your opponent taken a particular position? What interests of your opponent stand in the way of an agreement?
- Realize that each party has multiple interests.
- Recognize that the most powerful interests are basic human needs: security, economic well-being, a sense of belonging, recognition, and control over one's life.
- Make your interests come alive by providing concrete and graphic details.
- Acknowledge your opponent's interests as part of the problem.
- Put the problem before the solution. This means stating interests and reasoning first and conclusions or proposals later. This will increase the

other party's listening and understanding of the problem.
- Be concrete but flexible.
- Be hard on the problem but soft on the people.

Invent Options for Mutual Gain

The likelihood of reaching a mutually satisfactory conflict resolution greatly increases if the participants can invent a large number and variety of options for reaching agreement. Fisher and Ury (1991) classified four major obstacles that inhibit inventing options for mutual gain: (1) judging prematurely, (2) searching for the single answer, (3) assuming there is a fixed pie, and (4) thinking that solving your opponent's problem is not your problem. To overcome these obstacles and invent options for mutual gain, effective negotiators broaden their options through brainstorming. Brainstorming is designed to stimulate creative problem solving by producing as many ideas as possible to solve a problem. See Box 10.1 for a list of brainstorming guidelines.

Insist on Using Objective Criteria

Many special education disputes revolve around differences of opinion concerning a student's educational progress. These differences tend to escalate in the absence of mutually agreed upon objective criteria for evaluating a student's progress. The use of objective evaluation criteria allows the parties to evaluate solutions based on independent sources of information, not personal bias or subjectivity. How do participants in conflict over the educational services provided to a student with disabilities develop objective criteria? To produce an outcome independent of personal bias or subjectivity, parties in conflict must use either *fair standards* for the substantive issue or *fair procedures* for resolving the conflicting interests.

As an example of developing objective criteria, consider the Miguel Hernandez advocacy scenario (in Chapter 1), involving the seventh-grade student with learning disabilities, Susie Ortiz. Susie's mother was angry with the school because she felt Susie had not made sufficient academic progress during the past two years. Specifically, Mrs. Ortiz

Box 10.1 _____

Advocacy Actions: Brainstorming Guidelines

BEFORE BRAINSTORMING

1. Define your purpose.
2. Choose a few participants—an ideal number of participants is 5–8.
3. Change the environment—keep brainstorming sessions as distinct as possible from regular meetings by scheduling those sessions at a different time and place.
4. Provide an informal, relaxed atmosphere.
5. Choose a facilitator to enforce ground rules and to keep the discussion on track by asking questions.

DURING BRAINSTORMING

1. Seat the participants side by side (in a semi-circle) facing the problem (the facilitator will record ideas on a board or chart paper).

2. The facilitator clarifies the ground rules, including the key ground rule of no criticism and suspension of all judgment and evaluation of ideas.
3. Engage in brainstorming—approach the problem from every possible angle.
4. The facilitator records the ideas in full view of all participants—this reduces repetition and serves to stimulate ideas through piggybacking of one idea with another.

AFTER BRAINSTORMING

1. Star the most promising ideas.
2. Invent improvements for promising ideas—focus on one idea at a time and discuss how that idea can be better and more realistic and how that idea could be implemented.
3. Establish a time to evaluate and decide.

Source: Abridged from *Getting to Yes,* 2nd ed. by Roger Fisher, William Ury, and Bruce Patton. Copyright © 1981, 1991 by Roger Fisher and William Ury. Reprinted by Permission of Houghton Mifflin Co. All rights reserved.

was concerned about her daughter's poor reading skills. In this conflict situation, school professionals and Mrs. Ortiz needed to develop objective criteria to measure Susie's reading performance over the course of the year.

In establishing objective criteria, consider these possible "fair standards" to measure Susie's reading performance: (1) grades in language arts class; (2) self-reported perceptions of whether Susie likes to read; (3) teacher anecdotal reports of Susie's reading performance; or (4) Susie's reading rate and fluency, as determined by the number of words orally read correctly per minute and the number of comprehension questions answered correctly after each timed reading trial. Although all of these "fair standards" provide some information on Susie's reading performance, clearly the most objective criteria is the timed reading samples. The use of these data provides both school personnel and Mrs. Ortiz with a precise measure of Susie's reading performance.

In developing fair procedures for resolving conflicting interests of the parties, the scenario

with Susie Ortiz is again instructive. Another source of conflict between Susie's mother and the school revolved around Mrs. Ortiz's frustration with feeling that school personnel regularly dismissed her input in IEP decision making. Mrs. Ortiz has an interest in feeling empowered as a co-equal decision maker at her daughter's IEP meeting. The school professionals' interest is in having their opinions respected and trusted.

To resolve these potentially conflicting interests, the parties could agree to incorporate one of Mrs. Ortiz's suggestions (e.g., use of partner reading activities to increase Susie's motivation to read) into Susie's educational program on a trial basis. Prior to this trial procedure, the school and Mrs. Ortiz must establish objective criteria on how long this trial peer partner reading program will be implemented and what measures of reading performance will be used to determine whether Susie's reading performance is improving to a satisfactory level. This procedure attends to the mother's interest in having input in her daughter's educational program while acknowledging the professionals' opinion and skepticism that this partner reading program will not substantially improve Susie's reading skills. If the trial procedure does not produce mutually satisfactory objective evaluation data on Susie's reading performance, the professionals' opinion will be corroborated.

Prepare Your BATNA—The Best Alternative to a Negotiated Agreement

This final strategy in principled negotiation establishes in advance the worst possible outcome a negotiator will accept—a bottom line. By articulating their BATNA, effective negotiators have the security of knowing that they will not sacrifice important principles for expediency. The BATNA becomes the negotiator's fallback position if he or she has to walk away from the negotiations. Fisher and Ury (1991) recommended the following steps in developing possible BATNAs: (1) develop a list of possible actions to take in case an agreement is not reached, (2) embellish some of the best possible actions and develop specific action steps, and (3) select the one option that seems best. More information on developing BATNAs will be presented later in this section.

Although principled negotiation represents a positive and constructive approach to conflict resolution, the preceding strategies are not a panacea for every advocacy conflict situation. Goldberg and Huefner (1995) recognized several limitations in the use of principled negotiation: "Principled negotiation may fail when the hostility levels are too high, when the disputants have ego or power needs that require a win-lose outcome, when one party is irrational and unwilling to brainstorm or adopt objective criteria, or when one party really has no motivation to negotiate and is coerced into pretending to negotiate" (pp. 540–541).

Collaborative Problem Solving

The collaborative problem-solving process is composed of the following steps (Berry & Hardman, 1998; Fiedler, 1991; Simpson, 1996):

- *Define the problem.* In this step, it is critical that the problem definition encompasses both parties' perspective. For example, in the Karen Snyder advocacy scenario, the problem cannot solely be defined by Karen as "several general education teachers are failing to implement IEP accommodations for students with disabilities in their classes." This problem definition does not incorporate the general education teachers' concerns of having sufficient collaborative planning time to develop appropriate accommodations, being provided with sufficient support from special education teachers, and having legitimate input into IEP decision making regarding appropriate and feasible general education classroom accommodations.

- *Generate possible solutions.* This step involves brainstorming, which was discussed in the section on principled negotiation.

- *Choose a solution.* At this stage of the process, both parties must weigh the possible risks, gains, likelihood of success, and costs of each possible solution identified in the brainstorming session. It is at this point in problem solving that the parties evaluate real-world constraints —such as time, money, energy, and support— in determining which possible solutions are feasible.

- *Implement the chosen solution.* After the cost-benefit analysis is conducted (in the previous step), both parties mutually select one of the solutions to implement.

- *Evaluate the solution.* In this final step of the process, it is critical that both parties mutually agree on objective evaluation criteria to determine whether the implemented solution is or is not successful. In addition to developing objective evaluation criteria, the parties must agree on the length of time that the solution will be implemented prior to a formal evaluation of whether to continue the current course or select a different solution.

Managing Resistance and Conflict Effectively

This section discusses strategies for overcoming resistance from others in a professional's advocacy efforts. Shields (1987) identified several types of resistance or impasse that advocates are likely to encounter. He defined an *impasse* as "the inability to find or agree upon a course of action" (p. 94).

One common impasse is *the only reality*. This resistance is based on an individual's perspectives and assumptions about a problem situation. If an individual maintains that the only way to view a problem is his or her way, an impasse and debate over whose perspective of reality is correct is likely to ensue. Shields offers these strategies for responding to this impasse: (1) keep a problem solving focus on the child's best interests, (2) emphasize what's right rather than who's right, (3) begin with areas of agreement among the participants and proceed from there, and (4) accept all views of "reality" as equally valid and attempt to understand why there are different perspectives.

A second type of impasse is *preconceived limits*. This impasse is caused by excessive negativity where proposed alternatives are defined in terms of what is not possible. The tendency is to assume a solution is not possible without attempting to find out. A strategy to break this impasse is to shift the problem-solving discussion from negative assumptions to an identification of the desired goal and then, from there, work back to consider possible solutions to reach that goal.

For example, in the Mary Kinney advocacy dilemma, the director of pupil services set a preconceived limit by assuming that the school board would not support the hiring of a second speech and language clinician. At this point, Mary was at an impasse in her professional advocacy. Mary needed to refocus the discussion from budgetary limits to the desired goal—that of ensuring that all students' speech and language needs are appropriately addressed. With the focus on the desired goal, a more positive problem-solving discussion can occur where possible solutions may emerge, such as hiring a less expensive speech language assistant to work with Mary, applying for state or federal grant monies, or restructuring the local school budget by, for example, postponing the purchase of new band uniforms for one year.

A third typical type of impasse identified by Shields (1987) is the *never-ending past*. In this situation, the participants in conflict have some negative " baggage" in their past interactions and each new problem reverts to reliving past grievances and arguing about what happened in the past.

In the advocacy scenario involving the school counselor, Miguel Hernandez, an impasse occurred between Mrs. Ortiz and school personnel because for two years Mrs. Ortiz had been frustrated and dissatisfied in her educational decision making role vis-à-vis her daughter's teachers. These negative feelings based on past experiences always surfaced during present problem-solving interactions. In his advocacy role as a mediator, Miguel must refocus the discussions between Mrs. Ortiz and the teachers from their past difficulties to the present and future by asking questions such as: What will be the method of keeping Mrs. Ortiz regularly informed of Susie's progress on her IEP goals and objectives? How can we demonstrate to Mrs. Ortiz that her concerns and suggestions are incorporated into Susie's IEP and implemented by school staff? In other words, the strategy utilized to address the "never-ending past" impasse is to minimize past difficulties by focusing on present problem-solving circumstances.

A fourth type of impasse involves the *hidden dissuader*. This resistance is caused by underlying issues or concerns that are not out in the open during problem-solving discussions. As a result of this hidden agenda, the child's best interests are not directly addressed. This impasse is demonstrated in the experience of parents of a young son with autism at an IEP meeting. At the meeting, the parents requested that their son participate in an after-school student enrichment activity known as Odyssey of the Mind. The parents felt this creative problem-solving experience would provide much needed peer social interactions for their son and stimulate his expressive language skills. However, the principal and special education teacher were very resistant to the parents' request, expressing their belief that Odyssey of the Mind was not an appropriate experience for their son. The parents were surprised by this opposition because the principal and special education teacher had always been supportive advocates of inclusion and social interaction opportunities for their son.

When faced with an impasse resulting from unknown obstacles, as was the case here, the most effective strategy is to uncover those hidden issues/concerns in private conversations with the individuals involved. When the parents of the young boy with autism confronted the principal and special education teacher after the IEP meeting, the real issue about their son participating in Odyssey of the Mind surfaced. Both the principal and the special education teacher expressed concern that the coach of the school's Odyssey of the Mind team (a parent volunteer) would not be supportive of their son's special needs in this learning experience. Since the coach was the wife of the school psychologist who was at the IEP meeting, the principal and special education teacher were uncomfortable in identifying their true concerns about the Odyssey of the Mind experience for the young boy with autism at the meeting.

Once this hidden issue was revealed, the parents indicated that their desire was primarily for an after-school social interaction experience for their son—whether that opportunity came through participation in the Odyssey of the Mind team was not their primary objective. With this information, the principal, special education teacher, and parents were able to identify a more appropriate and supportive after-school activity that allowed the student with autism to interact with nondisabled peers in the school peer mediation project.

A final common type of impasse discussed by Shields (1987) is *intransigence*. Intransigent individuals refuse to reconsider their position or seek a mutually satisfactory resolution. In such situations, one strategy is to turn the tables on the intransigent individual by asking, What would you do in my situation? If this approach does not cause the person to reconsider and become more flexible, Shields suggests (1) changing to a different service provider or agency, (2) appealing to an administrator higher in the organizational chain of command, (3) lobbying other professionals to influence or overrule the intransigent individual, or (4) going outside the system for support.

Ury (1991) proposed a five-step process for conducting problem-solving negotiations with difficult, resistant individuals. Ury referred to this process as the *Break Through Strategy* of negotiation. It is a counterintuitive strategy because it requires negotiators to do the opposite of what feels natural to them. The five steps in this negotiation process are listed here, followed by a discussion of how you, the reader, might employ the strategies:

1. Do Not React

This first step in problem-solving negotiations with resistant individuals is critical because conflict often escalates when individuals respond to another person's anger and hostility with similar negative emotions. Responding with negative emotions is the natural response when individuals feel under attack. Three common reactions during difficult negotiations are striking back, giving in, and breaking off the relationship. However, as noted by Ury (1991), these three reactions lead to destructive conflict. As an alternative response, Ury suggests that negotiators "go to the balcony," which means adopting a mental attitude of objective detachment from the present conflict. This step permits one to regain mental and emotional balance and stay focused on the goal.

During this step, it is important to reflect on underlying interests in the conflict and to identify the best alternative to a negotiated agreement (BATNA). The BATNA becomes the walk-away alternative for a negotiator. That is, the BATNA assists the negotiator in evaluating any proposed solution. Any proposal that is worse than the BATNA should not be accepted. For example, in the Mary Kinney advocacy scenario, Mary's BATNA may be to provide consultation services to teachers in an effort to address some of the speech and language needs of the new students while, at the same time, informing and encouraging parents of those students to press the district to hire a second speech and language clinician. Knowing her BATNA allows Mary to negotiate with more confidence and assurance that the present situation will not, at least, deteriorate as a result of her negotiations with the school administration. The better one's BATNA, the more negotiating power that person possesses.

There are several "going to the balcony" tactics that help a negotiator restore his or her mental balance during difficult negotiations. First, it is helpful to recognize the other person's tactic and then neutralize that tactic. For example, in the Karen Snyder advocacy dilemma, if the general education teachers during their conflict with Karen attempted to make her feel guilty by stating, "How can you expect already overworked teachers to make all of these accommodations for students with disabilities in our classes?" Karen could respond, "It is not what I expect of you, it is what the law mandates from all teachers. Further, you are not solely responsible for making the accommodations; the special education teachers are part of the team in this process." In this example, Karen was able to identify the negotiating tactic of the general education teachers and defuse that tactic by not assuming guilt for the additional work imposed upon the teachers.

Second, a negotiator can buy time to think by simply pausing and saying nothing. This tactic prevents the natural impulse to strike back with negative emotions during difficult negotiations. A third tactic is to "rewind the tape" by reviewing the discussion. This buys time for a negotiator to regain mental balance and to plan a more thoughtful response. Finally, a negotiator may gain more time to collect his or her thoughts by finding a natural excuse to take a break (e.g., to check in with the office) or by requesting a caucus with colleagues.

2. Disarm Your Opponent

The second step in the Break Through Strategy of negotiation is to disarm your opponent by creating a favorable climate for problem solving. This climate can be created by doing the opposite of what most negotiation opponents expect. That is, in difficult negotiations, most participants expect that their threats will be met with counterthreats, that their hard line positions will generate similar pos-

turing, and that their animus will engender similar ill will. Instead, disarm your opponent by "stepping to his or her side." Most of the skills required for this technique were discussed in Chapter 8. Specifically, effective negotiators must be empathic listeners and employ verbal communication skills such as paraphrasing, reflecting affect, using clarifying statements, and questioning. In this step of the negotiation process, the goal is to create a climate for agreement by accepting as valid the other person's perspective and by acknowledging the other person's feelings.

As a problem-solving strategy, it is helpful to agree with your opponent whenever possible. Look for every opportunity to say yes without making any concessions. This approach attempts to change the mindset of parties involved in conflict from "either-or" thinking to a "both-and" perspective.

For example, instead of responding to an opponent's point by stating "But . . . ," which is a clear sign of disagreement and argument, respond with "Yes, and . . . ," which signals some agreement. Instead of presenting your views as a direct contradiction to the other person's views, present your perspective as an addition to your opponent's point of view. As an example, in advocating for his students with emotional/behavioral disorders, Steve Kern could respond to his principal's argument that out-of-school suspensions are necessary to maintain school wide discipline and to ensure an atmosphere conducive to learning with the following: "Yes, and I understand your position on wanting to ensure student discipline and an effective learning environment. I support those goals as well. In addition, I support effective and positive educational programming for my students. This is difficult to accomplish when they are suspended from school for several days. Under these circumstances I am unable to adequately monitor their behaviors. What if we could agree on a system where I am able to monitor my students' behavior and learning by having them attend school while preserving your goals of maintaining discipline and an orderly learning environment?" By stepping to the principal's side and emphasizing some common points of agreement, one establishes a negotiating climate that is more conducive to reaching a mutually satisfactory solution.

3. Change the Game

Typically, during the heat of battle in a difficult negotiation, the participants only want to discuss their own positions in an effort to persuade the opponent to see the problem and the solution "their way." This type of negotiating usually results in conflict escalation. As an alternative, a skillful negotiator can "change the game" by not rejecting the opponent's position but, instead, reframing the situation into a problem that serves the mutual interests of both parties. By putting a problem-solving frame around your opponent's position, it is possible to actively draw your opponent into the problem-solving process. An effective negotiator reframes by asking questions instead of making assertions or arguing his position. The following questions can serve as effective reframing tools: Why? Why not? What if? What's your advice? and What makes that fair? Problem-solving questions must be open ended questions that cannot be simply answered by a no. Successful negotiators ask lots of questions. By using reframing, and thus changing the game, a negotiator can change the dynamics of conflict from positional bargaining to problem solving.

As an example of reframing, consider the Miguel Hernandez advocacy scenario. As an advocate for Susie Ortiz and her mother, Miguel wanted to intervene with several of his colleagues to express Mrs. Ortiz's frustration at having school professionals discount and devalue her concerns about Susie's educational program. If Miguel engages in positional bargaining by reminding his colleagues of the legal requirements to involve parents in IEP decision making, the likely response from his colleagues would be defensive posturing that they have involved Mrs. Ortiz in IEP decision making and that her concerns have been seriously considered by the IEP team. The dynamics of such an interaction are unlikely to produce a mutually satisfactory resolution of the conflict.

Alternatively, Miguel could change the game through reframing in this manner: "I know the IEP committee members are interested in working productively with Mrs. Ortiz and in resolving her concerns within the committee so that Mrs. Ortiz does not take her concerns to the school administration. I share those same interests. What is your advice on how we can make Mrs. Ortiz feel more like a valued and respected decision maker in future IEP meetings?"

4. Make It Easy to Say "Yes"

Ury (1991) advocated "building a golden bridge" for your opponent as a metaphor to describe the strategies and process for avoiding resistance and positional bargaining. By building a golden bridge, an effective negotiator establishes a structure that allows the other party to cross over negative negotiating tactics to a mutual problem-solving process. There are four important considerations in making it easier for an opponent to say yes.

Involve your opponent in reaching a solution. In effective negotiation, the process is as important as the product. To overcome your opponent's resistance, bring him or her into the problem-solving process. This can be done by simply asking your opponent for ideas on how the current problem could be resolved to everyone's satisfaction. Another tactic is to propose a solution and ask the other person for feedback. In breaking an impasse during negotiations, another effective strategy is to offer a list of proposed solutions and ask the other party to choose an option from that list. When an opponent selects an idea or solution from a list of options, Ury maintained, it becomes your opponent's solution, and his or her psychological resistance is lessened.

For example, Mary Kinney, in an effort to adequately address the speech and language needs of the newly referred students, could propose a variety of options to the director of pupil services. Possible options include (1) hiring a second speech and language clinician (however, this does not appear to be a very viable short-term solution, given the budget situation); (2) employing a speech language assistant to work under Mary's supervision; (3) providing more speech and language services in a transdisciplinary model where Mary functions more as a consultant who trains teachers and classroom aides in some of the intervention techniques; or (4) using communication disorders majors from a local university as practicum students to increase the school district's capability to provide speech and language services.

These options, at least, provide the director of pupil services with some flexibility and serve to expand thinking from a rigid "either-or" perspective (e.g., "No, we cannot afford to hire a second speech and language clinician. You will have to do the best you can.") to a more creative problem solving approach. By providing more options to an opponent, you increase the possibility of that person saying "yes."

Satisfy your opponent's unmet interests.   If your opponent has an unmet need or interest at the end of the negotiating session, she is unlikely to agree to any proposed solution. For example, in Karen Snyder's conflict with several general education teachers in her building over the issue of implementing IEP accommodations for students with disabilities attending general education classes, the teachers had an interest in feeling like they have professional autonomy in making decisions affecting their own classrooms.

If Karen merely issued a directive that the "teachers better adhere to the IEP listed accommodations or else," the teachers would probably resist in many ways which could undermine the true intent and spirit of the least restrictive environment legal principle. However, if Karen recognized the teachers' strong interests in autonomy and decision making input and influence, she would reframe this problem as one of ensuring that general education teachers have ample opportunity to attend (the 1997 IDEA amendments require that a general education teacher must be present at an IEP meeting if the student spends any time in a general education setting) and actively participate in IEP decision making. This result may require increasing the planning time for general education teachers by providing them with substitute teacher coverage from time to time.

Help your opponent save face.   In many difficult negotiation situations, one or both parties will have to "sell" the proposed solution to their constituent group. The constituents may be the local school board, a parent group, school colleagues, other school administrators, students, or other agency personnel. Effective negotiators assist their opponents in explaining the agreement reached during the negotiation as a victory for all parties. A negotiator will resist any solution that portrays her as being weak, giving in, or losing the negotiation.

In the Mary Kinney advocacy dilemma, the director of pupil services may resist taking a request to the school board to authorize hiring a second speech and language clinician because of his fear that the school board would perceive him as a weak administrator who is unable to keep school costs down and as someone who bows to pressure from his staff. Mary can facilitate an agreement with the director by recognizing his need to save face in front of the school board. Therefore, Mary could propose that the request to the school board for funds to hire a second speech and language clinician be made by a parent spokesperson for a group of concerned parents who are dissatisfied with speech and language services in the district. In this scenario, Mary would simply ask the director not to oppose the parent request to the school board and to acknowledge the need for a second speech and language clinician if the school board so inquires.

Sum up the understanding when an agreement is reached.   In any negotiation, when the parties think they have reached a mutually satisfactory solution to the problem, their understanding of the agreement should be orally summarized; then, if the summary is accurate, it should be committed to writing. This is a helpful tactic even in informal discussions. The cardinal principle is to immediately follow up an oral agreement or understanding with written confirmation.

5. *Make It Hard to Say "No"*

In this final step of the Break Through Strategy of negotiation, the effective negotiator attempts to convince her opponent that the "golden bridge" she constructed is a better solution than her opponent's BATNA. During this step of the process, the negotiator asks reality testing questions to assist his or her opponent in understanding the consequences of not reaching a mutual resolution of the problem. Examples of these reality testing questions are:

- What will happen if we do not reach an agreement?
- What do you think I will do?
- What will you do?
- What will be the costs to both of us?

Effective negotiators use direct statements as to what will happen if the parties fail to reach a mutually satisfactory agreement. At this point, your opponent should be informed of your BATNA. One's BATNA is presented not as a threat (e.g., reflecting an intention to inflict pain or discomfort) but as a warning (e.g., what will happen if an agreement is not reached). In some difficult negotiations, a negotiator must be prepared to walk away and be willing to implement his or her BATNA. However, the door should always be left open for negotiations to resume.

SUMMARY

The ultimate success of a professional's advocacy efforts is largely dependent on the effectiveness of the advocate's conflict resolution skills. Special education professionals must not fear or be intimidated by conflict; in fact, as discussed in this chapter, conflict that is resolved constructively offers a number of potential benefits to the participants, to schools as organizations, and to children with disabilities. To engage in constructive conflict resolution, professionals must understand the causes of conflict between schools and families and among professionals themselves. Although a variety of conflict resolution approaches exist, the most salient approach in fostering constructive conflict resolution is collaborative problem solving. This process encourages mutual problem solving and demonstrates a win-win perspective to conflict. Collaborative problem solving seeks to meet individual goals of the parties in conflict while, at the same time, maintaining a trusting, respectful, and positive relationship between all of the participants. Finally, this chapter addressed a number of specific skills and strategies for managing difficult conflict negotiations.

CHAPTER 11

ADVOCACY SKILLS AND STRATEGIES

The reasonable man adapts himself to the world; the unreasonable man persists in trying to adapt the world to himself. Therefore, all progress depends on the unreasonable man.—George Bernard Shaw

When special education professionals consider the time and energy demands as well as the potential risks associated with fulfilling an advocate's role and responsibilities on behalf of children with disabilities, it would seem that the reasonable course of action is to ignore or avoid serving as an advocate. However, as recognized by George Bernard Shaw, progress is often the result of the efforts of unreasonable individuals who take risks and challenge the status quo.

Certainly, in terms of opportunities for students with disabilities, educational progress has occurred because families and professionals asked the difficult questions, fought for legal rights and protections, demanded better services, and refused to accept the status quo when those situations were not beneficial to students with disabilities. Mlawer (1993) argued that advocacy must be a part of any special education professional's job (see Box 11.1).

As noted by Turnbull and Turnbull (1997), advocacy by special education professionals can occur in a variety of places and situations: at IEP meetings, during interpersonal interactions with colleagues or administrators, while serving on school advisory committees, while testifying at due process hearings or before legislative bodies, during presentations at local school board meetings, during informal interactions with family members, or in any place or situation where a professional's judgment concludes that some action

must be taken to change the status quo on behalf of a student with a disability.

As noted in Chapter 1, special education professionals can function as either external advocates, working for change from outside of an organization, or as internal advocates, committed to changing organizations from within (Herbert & Mould, 1992; Hines, 1987; Schloss & Jayne, 1994). Both forms of advocacy have advantages and disadvantages. For instance, external advocates enjoy more independence and freedom in their advocacy efforts than internal advocates. However, external advocates usually lack complete access to information and an understanding of organizational norms and procedures.

In Chapter 2, essential advocacy dispositions for special education professionals were discussed; following is a review of those advocacy dispositions:

- Sense of autonomy
- Persistence
- Empathy
- Sense of self-efficacy
- Risk taker
- Humility
- Patience
- Self-reflective
- Self-confidence
- Passion in one's work
- Stimulated by challenges
- Intrinsically motivated
- Hopeful
- Realistic

Further, most of the essential knowledge bases (e.g., knowledge of special education law, dispute

Box 11.1 _____

Advocacy Anecdote: Advocacy Responsibilities
of Special Education Professionals

Mlawer (1993) wrote:

The answer, therefore, to the question "Who should fight?" is: professionals. Those of us who enter the special education and disability "fields" by choice rather than necessity, those of us who ask for the duties and responsibility of working on behalf of students with disabilities, are those with the obligations of advocacy. No matter what our job, advocacy must be part of it.

It is impossible to avoid one implication of this point of view: by engaging in advocacy, special education and disability professionals risk making their employers angry and may even risk their jobs. While the risks are usually overestimated, it cannot be denied that they exist. Nevertheless, it is time to accept that working on behalf of students with disabilities entails risks; and as with many other professionals, one should not enter this profession without accepting its values and all the risks that living in accordance with those values entails. And, in fact, some special education and disability professionals—particularly some classroom teachers—take these risks and have for some time. Parents will be spared the burdens of advocacy when others, especially more of those in administrative positions, join these courageous professionals.

Moreover, in order to truly empower parents, programs must be developed that are capable of engaging in advocacy along with and on behalf of parents; programs that are available regardless of income; programs that are well publicized and easy to access; and programs that have available a corps of independent, uncompromised special educators to serve as experts on behalf of students. Only by creating a true balance of power between parents and school systems, not just between some middle- and upper-class parents and school systems, will all parents be given the opportunity of empowerment. "Empowerment" without real power is an empty concept, a cruel sham that results in disempowerment for many. . . .

We can best assist children and youth with disabilities if we stop pushing their parents to become advocates and simply allow them to be parents. But this will only happen if we expand the ranks of, and access to, qualified advocates, and start doing our jobs as professionals; this can begin once we accept the responsibilities our roles entail, and once funding priorities are set based upon the real needs of parents and families, rather than upon what we wish those needs were. (pp. 112–114)

Source: From "Who Should Fight? Parents and the Advocacy Expectation" by M. A. Mlawer, 1993, *Journal of Disability Policy Studies, 4* (1), pp. 105–115.

resolution mechanisms, and systems change) and essential skills (e.g., interpersonal communication skills, collaboration skills, and conflict resolution skills) for effective advocacy were discussed in prior chapters. This chapter focuses on advocacy strategies along with the necessary skills to implement those actions. Prior to describing advocacy skills and strategies, however, this chapter will initially examine six types of advocacy that can occur on behalf of individuals with disabilities and their families: direct services advocacy, community advocacy, legislative advocacy, legal advocacy, systems advocacy, and self-advocacy.

TYPES OF ADVOCACY

Direct Services Advocacy

This type of advocacy involves direct intervention by the special education professional on behalf of an individual student with a disability and/or that student's family (Hines, 1987; Schloss, 1994; Schloss & Jayne, 1994). The goal of direct services advocacy is to "focus on the specific needs of an individual and specific steps that can be taken to meet these needs" (Schloss, 1994, p. 25). In most situations, this advocacy involves changing the attitudes, behaviors, or decisions of individuals providing services to a student with a disability. In addition, direct services advocacy may assist others (e.g., parents and students) in understanding their legal rights and ensuring that schools and other service providers are accountable for providing appropriate services (Schloss & Jayne, 1994).

Direct services advocacy often involves informal interactions between an advocate and a service provider; however, this type of advocacy may also include formal interactions, such as IEP meetings. In essence, special education professionals who serve as advocates constantly engage in "public relations" efforts on behalf of children with disabilities.

One of the most dedicated and competent special education teachers I ever knew made a conscious effort of spending time in the teachers' workroom on a daily basis. This teacher was not a naturally gregarious individual but she recognized the importance of positive public declarations about her students with disabilities. She would share with colleagues in the teachers' workroom positive examples of her students' abilities, their unique strengths and attributes, and the personal satisfaction she received in teaching students with disabilities. Whenever a general education teacher colleague was working successfully with a student with disabilities, the special education teacher publicly praised that teacher. In addition, this special education teacher was always open to engaging in problem solving when one of her colleagues had a concern about a student with a disability. This special education professional was functioning as an advocate for her students with disabilities each and every day.

Other brief examples of direct services advocacy activities include:

- A physical therapist who intervened on behalf of a student in need of physical therapy services by contacting the child's pediatrician and convincing the doctor to write a prescription so that the child could receive services at school
- A general education teacher and a special education teacher who collaboratively initiated a peer partners program for children without disabilities and children with severe disabilities

- A school psychologist who changed her school administration's thinking by arguing that the parents of a student with significant behavioral problems needed and were entitled to receive behavior management training from the school district as a related service to enable their child to benefit from special education
- A principal who intervened with the school district's transportation director to reroute one of the school buses so that a student with cerebral palsy was not arriving at school all tired out as a result of a one-hour bus ride
- A pupil services director who convinced the school board of the necessity of contracting with the local vocational and technical adult education institution to provide an alternative vocational training experience for a student with emotional and cognitive disabilities

Although direct services advocacy should always be attempted prior to resorting to more formal and adversarial advocacy options, Schloss (1994) noted, "While more adversarial approaches should be viewed as methods of last resort, not all providers operate in good faith. In these cases, the 'power' of interpersonal interactions may be insufficient to motivate a school district, rehabilitation agency, or other provider to extend services or rights to an individual student" (p. 25). In addition to the issue of whether the service provider is operating in good faith, Crosson (1977) acknowledged that sometimes legitimate differences of opinion exist between advocates and service providers in assessing the appropriateness of specific services. In those situations, direct services advocacy is unlikely to produce the requisite "meeting of the minds," which is the goal of collaborative problem solving.

Community Advocacy

The goal of community advocacy is to bring about change and improve services and conditions for individuals with disabilities in general (Schloss & Jayne, 1994). This type of advocacy attempts to educate the community on a particular issue or concern affecting individuals with disabilities. In an effort to foster change, community advocacy efforts define, document, educate, and organize the community on problems that have an adverse impact on individuals with disabilities. Community advocacy encompasses a wide range of activities designed to enhance the responsiveness of the public to the needs of individuals with disabilities. Some examples of community advocacy activities include:

- A parent advocacy group putting pressure on the state department of education and other professional educational organizations to improve monitoring of IEPs to ensure that schools appropriately implement and provide the services listed in an IEP
- A social worker organization seeking publicity on the issue of lack of adequate family foster care placements and services for children with disabilities
- Parents and professionals uniting together to educate the public on the need for more funding for special education
- A university professor conducting research to document the detrimental effects of social security disability cutbacks on families of children with disabilities
- Special education professionals documenting and informing the public and policy makers about the excessive use of punitive disciplinary sanctions, such as suspension and expulsions in public schools across the state

One effective strategy to enhance community advocacy efforts is to build a coalition. The important function of a coalition is noted by Bootel (1995): "A coalition is a union of people or organizations seeking similar ends. It presents a visible source of information and power and a unified voice to prevent the fragmentation of forces that share common goals. It also prevents governmental bodies from pitting one person/group against another" (p. 22). There are three major reasons for building a coalition: (1) to mobilize the maximum number of people on a given issue, (2) to represent more than one aspect of an issue, and (3) to avoid a situation in which similar agencies take contradictory approaches (Ross, 1985). As Fiedler (1991)

noted, "Coalitions can have significant system-wide advocacy impact because they can help public policy makers learn the needs of and services required by people with mental retardation [disabilities]" (p. 29).

Legislative Advocacy

There is a rich tradition in special education of effective legislative advocacy on behalf of students with disabilities (Turnbull & Turnbull, 1997). Legislative advocacy efforts seek to influence the political process and change public policies by passing laws that promote the rights of individuals with disabilities and provide effective educational and social services. Legislative advocacy efforts have been led by parent organizations representing all disability areas, and by numerous professional organizations such as the Council for Exceptional Children.

Examples of legislative advocacy actions have included (1) contacting state and federal legislators to press for new legislation; (2) inviting legislators to visit educational and social service programs for individuals with disabilities to see, firsthand, the issues and concerns raised by the advocates; (3) testifying at legislative hearings on disability issues; (4) using the media to publicize advocacy issues and solicit public support; and (5) cultivating the support of committed legislative insiders (e.g., legislators and key members of their legislative staff) to introduce new legislation.

Effective legislative advocacy by parents and professionals was directly responsible for the passage of the Education for All Handicapped Children Act (P.L. 94-142) in 1975 and each of the subsequent amendments to federal special education law, now known as the Individuals with Disabilities Education Act (P.L. 105-17). Effective legislative advocacy by parents and professionals developed a grassroots movement to secure family support laws (e.g., laws that initiated services that empowered families of individuals with disabilities to have more control over their lives) in more than half the states (Turnbull & Turnbull, 1997).

A final example of effective legislative advocacy by parents and professionals was the successful effort to thwart then President Reagan's administration's attempt to deemphasize the federal role in special education. Senator Lowell Weicker (1985), a legislative supporter of special education laws, noted the importance and impact of legislative advocacy in maintaining a strong federal presence in promoting special education rights for children with disabilities:

> The administration did not get its way. Why? Because the disabled people in this country and their advocates repudiated a long-held cliche that they were not a political constituency, or at least not a coherent one. It was assumed that in the rough and tumble world of politics they would not hold their own as a voting block or as advocates for their cause. But that assumption was blown to smithereens in the budget and policy deliberations of 1981, 1982, and again in 1983. (p. 284)

A good reference on legislative advocacy considerations and strategies is the *Council for Exceptional Children's Special Education Advocacy Handbook* (1995) developed by Jaclyn Bootel. This book contains (1) information on "what makes politicians tick," a useful set of advocacy considerations when contacting individual legislators; (2) a step-by-step description of how a federal bill becomes a law; (3) tips for testifying before a legislative body; (4) tips on writing letters to legislators and other public officials, including sample letters; and (5) information to aid in understanding the federal regulatory process, which results in the promulgation of administrative regulations to implement laws passed by Congress.

Legal Advocacy

Legal advocacy invokes the due process protections of federal and state special education laws in an effort to secure appropriate educational services for students with disabilities. Legal advocacy may proceed as an individual case, seeking to protect the rights and procure services for an individual student, or as a class action lawsuit, seeking to obtain judicial protection of educational rights and services for a group of students with disabilities who are in a similar situation (e.g., all students

with mental retardation being deprived of a right to a free and appropriate public education). Legal advocacy efforts are initiated with a request for a due process hearing. (Basic due process protections and hearing rights were reviewed in Chapter 5, and the procedural aspects of due process hearings and the negative consequences and limitations of conflict resolution via legal proceedings were discussed in Chapter 6.)

Legal advocacy should be viewed as a method of last resort employed only after direct services advocacy efforts have failed. An advocate's motivation to resolve disputes at the lowest, most informal level of mutual problem solving should be enhanced by being cognizant of the disadvantages of due process hearings versus advantages of mediation and other alternative dispute resolution mechanisms discussed in Chapter 6. Nevertheless, legal advocacy and litigation has been an important and sometimes necessary tactic in promoting and enforcing the rights of students with disabilities to appropriate educational services. Some of the following significant judicial decisions demonstrate the potential of legal advocacy on behalf of students with disabilities:

- *Mills* v. *District of Columbia Board of Education* (1972) and *PARC* v. *Commonwealth of Pennsylvania* (1971) served as a precursor to the passage of P.L. 94-142, the Education for All Handicapped Children's Act, in 1975 by establishing the constitutional right of children with disabilities to attend public schools.
- *Board of Education* v. *Rowley* (1982) required that local education agencies must develop and implement IEPs that provide some educational benefit for students with disabilities.
- *Irving Independent School District* v. *Tatro* (1984) clarified a school's obligation to provide related services (in this case, clean intermittent catheterization) when such services are necessary to assist a student in benefitting from special education services.
- *Daniel R.R.* v. *State Board of Education* (1989), *Oberti* v. *Board of Education* (1992), and *Board of Education* v. *Holland* (1994) expand-

ed the rights of students with disabilities to be educated, according to the least restrictive environment legal principle, in general education classrooms.

Although special education professionals will not represent families in formal legal advocacy proceedings, professionals do have a legal and ethical obligation to inform families as to the availability of free or low cost legal services. There are three organizations that provide information resources and/or legal representation to families embroiled in special education disputes: (1) Parent Training and Information Centers, (2) Protection and Advocacy Systems, and (3) the Legal Services Corporation. Special education professionals fulfill an important responsibility by ensuring that families are informed about each of these potential legal advocacy resources.

Parent Training and Information Centers

There are 71 Parent Training and Information Centers (PTIs) funded by the U.S. Department of Education, Office of Special Education and Rehabilitative Services (Turnbull & Turnbull, 1997). The Turnbulls' book, *Families, Professionals, and Exceptionality: A Special Partnership,* contains an appendix that lists the addresses for all of the PTIs. Each state has at least one PTI governed by a board of directors composed primarily of parents of individuals with disabilities. In fact, many PTIs employ parents as directors or staff members.

As described by Turnbull and Turnbull (1997), PTIs are legally mandated to provide these support services to families: (1) information to understand the nature and needs of their children's disabilities; (2) follow-up support to ensure appropriate educational programs; (3) training on effective interpersonal communication skills to improve interactions with school professionals; (4) training on how to participate in IEP and educational decision making; (5) information on programs, services, and resources available on the national, state, and local levels for children with disabilities; and (6) information about the IDEA provisions for educating infants, toddlers, and children with disabilities.

The national PTI network has created four regional PTI centers that provide technical assistance to other PTIs in their region:

- *West Regional Center* PAVE (Washington Parents Are Vital in Education), Tacoma, WA
- *Midwest Regional Center* PACER (Parent Advocacy Coalition for Educational Rights), Minneapolis, MN
- *South Regional Center* ECAC (Exceptional Children's Assistance Center), Davidson, NC
- *Northeast Regional Center* PIC (Parent Information Center), Concord, NH

Finally, professionals must be aware of PTIs that focus on specific topics or projects. The PEAK Parent Center in Colorado Springs, Colorado, provides technical assistance and information on inclusive education. In Billings, Montana, the Parents Let's Unite for Kids (PLUK) Program addresses issues related to assistive technology. Early childhood services are the focus of the Pilot Parent Partnerships in Phoenix, Arizona. In 1990, Congress established several Experimental Parent Training and Information Centers, which provide information and training for minority families. Finally, the Supported Employment, Parents, Transition, and Technical Assistance Project, based at the PACER Center in Minneapolis, Minnesota, offers technical assistance, information, and training on transition of students with disabilities from high school to the adult world.

Protection and Advocacy Systems

A second important legal advocacy resource for families and professionals are the Protection and Advocacy (P&A) systems that exist in all 50 states. Protection and Advocacy systems are federally funded and administered by the states. They were established to provide legal assistance and advocacy on behalf of individuals with disabilities and their families. P&A staff usually consists of attorneys and advocates with experience in disability issues who provide a variety of services, including information and referral, training and education, negotiations, legal assistance, investigation of complaints, and monitoring service providers.

In terms of litigation, P&A systems initiate lawsuits on behalf of individual clients and class action lawsuits involving large-scale rights violations or abuses. P&A staff handle a large number of special education cases, including representing incarcerated juveniles with disabilities. The National Association of Protection and Advocacy Systems (NAPAS) provides technical assistance, information, and training support to each of the Protection and Advocacy systems around the country. Advocates can find out how to contact the P & A system in their state by contacting NAPAS, 900 Second Street NE, Suite 211, Washington, DC 20002; Phone: 202-408-9514; website address: www.protectionandadvocacy.com/index.htm

The Protection and Advocacy Systems serve individuals with disabilities through these five programs:

Client Assistance Program (CAP). This program was authorized by the federal Rehabilitation Act Amendments of 1992 to assist individuals in obtaining services from programs funded by the Rehabilitation Act (a state's Department of Vocational Rehabilitation and Independent Living Programs). The CAP informs individuals with disabilities of all available benefits under the Rehabilitation Act, investigates complaints regarding services, helps individuals appeal adverse decisions by program personnel, and represents individuals in legal proceedings to ensure the protection of rights to rehabilitative services under the Rehabilitation Act.

Protection and Advocacy for Assistive Technology (PAAT). This program is designed to provide advocacy and legal assistance to individuals with disabilities who have been denied assistive technology devices and services as guaranteed by the Technology Related Assistance for Individuals with Disabilities Act of 1988, 29 U.S.C. Sec. 2201 et seq. This program not only advocates to secure assistive technology devices for individuals but it also ensures that individuals with disabilities receive appropriate training and maintenance for those devices.

Protection and Advocacy for Individuals with Developmental Disabilities (PADD). This program is mandated under the Developmental Disabilities Assistance and Bill of Rights Act of 1975 (the most recent amendment is P.L. 104-183, 42 U.S.C. Sec. 6000 et seq.). PADD provides advocacy and legal services to ensure the human, civil, and legal rights of individuals with developmental disabilities. The federal law requires that the state P&A agency must be independent of public and private service providers to avoid any conflict of interest. A person is eligible for PADD services if the disability is a result of a mental or physical impairment before the age of 22 and the disability is likely to continue throughout the person's lifetime, limiting the person's ability to function in three or more of the following areas: self-care, mobility, independent living, economic self-sufficiency, and receptive and expressive language.

Protection and Advocacy for Individuals with Mental Illness (PAIMI). This program was established by the Protection and Advocacy for Mentally Ill Individuals Act of 1986 (P.L. 99-319, 42 U.S.C. Sec. 10801 et seq.) to ensure the enforcement of the Constitution as well as federal and state statutes, and to investigate abuse and neglect of individuals with mental illness. This program, administered by the state P&A agency, serves only institutionalized or formerly institutionalized (within 90 days of discharge) individuals with mental illness. Students with mental illness detained in juvenile or correctional facilities could qualify for services under this program. Some of the services provided by this program include investigating reports of abuse and neglect, acting to eliminate or prevent imminent serious harm to individuals with mental illness, training on legal rights, obtaining services that individuals are entitled to receive, providing information and technical assistance, and promoting self-advocacy.

Protection and Advocacy for Individual Rights (PAIR). The purpose of the PAIR program is to provide advocacy to individuals with disabilities not covered by the PADD and PAIMI programs.

Essentially, any individual with a disability who has one or more major life activities substantially impaired qualifies for this program. Among the disabling conditions of individuals who qualify for PAIR program services are autism, cerebral palsy, epilepsy, hearing impairment, hemophilia, HIV, lupus, multiple sclerosis, muscular dystrophy, orthopedic impairment, spina bifida, spinal cord injury, traumatic brain injury, tourette syndrome, and visual impairment. This program provides a wide range of services such as information and referral, advocacy and legal representation to secure rights and prevent employment discrimination, self-advocacy training, and leadership training.

Legal Services Corporation

The Legal Services Corporation (LSC) is a private, nonprofit corporation established by Congress in 1974 to promote equal access to the judicial system and improve opportunities for low-income individuals throughout the United States by providing civil legal assistance to those who otherwise would be unable to afford legal counsel. The LSC is governed by an 11-member bipartisan Board of Directors appointed by the President and confirmed by the Senate. The LSC's 1998 budget from Congress was $283 million.

The LSC makes grants directly to 262 independent local legal services programs, serving every county in the nation. Each local legal services program is governed by a board of directors, which sets priorities and decides the types of cases that will be accepted. The local board members are appointed by local bar associations and client groups. In addition to federal funds, many local legal services programs receive state and local funding as well as pro bono (free) legal services provided by private attorneys.

In 1997, LSC-funded legal services programs resolved 1.5 million civil cases, benefitting over 4 million individuals, primarily women and children. The most common types of cases handled by legal services programs are family, housing, income maintenance, and consumer. In addition, legal services attorneys represent low-income clients in child custody and support, child abuse or neglect, access to health care, disability and unemployment claims, special education, and juvenile cases. To find the nearest legal services program, an LSC Program Directory is provided at this Internet address: www.ain.lsc.gov/pguide/pdir.htm The Legal Services Corporation's address is 750 First Street NE, 10th Floor, Washington, DC 20002-4250; Phone: 202-336-8800.

Systems Advocacy

Systems advocacy is defined as the process of influencing policies, rules, laws, or practices of social and political institutions to bring about change for persons in a certain group or class (Eklund, 1978; Hines, 1987; Schloss & Jayne, 1994). Systems advocacy works to change the situations of a whole group of persons who share a similar problem or to change a service system. Systems advocacy efforts may take various forms. For example, informal or formal interactions with agencies/organizations where a problem is identified and a change in policy or practice is requested may constitute systems advocacy. Further, systems advocacy may involve efforts to change federal or state laws adversely affecting individuals with disabilities. Specific examples of systems advocacy have included the following:

- Advocates concerned about employment discrimination against individuals with disabilities organized, filed lawsuits, and initiated a political discussion about the need for a federal law to protect persons with disabilities from discriminatory treatment. This systems advocacy eventually led to the passage of the Americans with Disabilities Act of 1990.
- Families and professionals concerned about the problem of protecting the rights of persons with developmental disabilities engaged in systems advocacy, which culminated in 1975 when Congress passed the Developmental Disabilities Assistance and Bill of Rights Act, which established the Protection and Advocacy Systems discussed earlier.

- Families and advocates for individuals with autism and traumatic brain injury employed systems advocacy tactics to change the Individuals with Disabilities Education Act to include autism and traumatic brain injury as new categories of eligibility for special education services in its 1990 reauthorization.

- Systems advocacy resulted in a state department of education improving its policies and practices on monitoring the IEPs of students with disabilities attending state institutions or child-care institutions.

- Families and professionals combined their systems advocacy efforts in changing a school district's practice of clustering students with mental retardation at only one of the elementary school buildings.

As noted by Hines (1987),

Because systems advocacy works to cause change in organizations, service systems or laws, it requires a long-term, sustained effort by a number of people. It is harder to change how an organization or system treats a whole group of persons than it is to change a decision made by one person about the situation of another. Although it is more work, a systems advocacy effort is needed when policies or laws cause the same problem for many people and the problems are expected to keep recurring. (pp. 117–118)

See Chapter 7 for a discussion of systems change issues and strategies.

A broad range of effective systems advocacy activities exists, including staging demonstrations, making demands, writing letters, holding fact-finding forums, using communication media and symbolic acts, negotiating, educating the public on the issue, initiating boycotts, lobbying, and creating model programs (Biklen, 1976). Hines (1987) identified these steps to effective systems advocacy:

1. Find others that are experiencing the same problem. This does not need to be a large group of individuals, but the group members must agree on the nature of the problem and be committed to a long-term effort to change the situation.

2. Keep members of the advocacy group involved by ensuring that everyone feels a sense of purpose. A sense of purpose is established by developing clear and specific goals that are achievable in a reasonable amount of time. The goals must make a real difference in the lives of individuals with disabilities. If the systems advocacy group has several goals, the goals should be prioritized and addressed one at a time.

3. Gather information. The pertinent information at this stage of systems advocacy is reflected in the questions posed in Box 11.2.

Box 11.2 _____

Advocacy Actions: Questions to Promote Systems Change

1. What is the problem? Identify your issues carefully. Prioritize them. Document the problem thoroughly. Double check your information.

2. Who is affected by the problem? How is each person you listed affected by the problem? Who benefits from continuation of the problem? Is someone's prestige or professional welfare being enhanced by the continuation of the problem?

3. When did the problem start? Has it been a continuous problem? Is it worse at certain times? What started the problem, made it worse, or caused you to notice the problem?

4. What kinds of changes would solve the problem? How will you know when the problem is solved?

5. By what date should the problem begin to be resolved? How long should this process take?

6. What has been done to address the problem so far? What happened as a result of this? Should this be confirmed or does something else need to be tried?

7. Are there laws and regulations which relate to the problem at hand? Know and be able to refer to the ethical standards of your professional association.

Source: From "Models and Methods of Advocacy" by C. N. Schloss and D. Jayne in *Families of Students with Disabilities: Consultaton and Advocacy* (pp. 229–250) by S. K. Alper, P. J. Schloss, and C. N. Schloss, 1994, Boston: Allyn and Bacon. Copyright © 1994 by Allyn and Bacon. Reprinted by permission.

4. Identify ways the organization could benefit from making the requested change. Often, organizations react to systems advocacy initiatives by doing nothing, waiting for the advocates to lose their motivation and quit. Change is fostered by creating positive incentives for the organization to change. To create positive organizational incentives to change, the advocacy group must know the organization well. For example, in the systems advocacy situation that is described in Box 11.5 (pages 206–207), the parent advocacy group knew that the requested change to bring their children with severe disabilities back to be educated in the home school district could save the district money in terms of escalating tuition costs and reduced transportation expenses. These positive incentives were a major factor in the success of this systems advocacy effort.

5. Create a visible and credible image for the systems advocacy group. Again, reference is made to Box 11.5 for an example of how the parent advocacy group created a visible and credible image of itself. First, visibility of the group was created by the threat to circulate a petition in the local community soliciting signatures from other residents in support of the effort to bring the children with severe disabilities back to their home school district. The parent advocacy group indicated it was prepared to present this petition to the school board. Credibility of the parent advocacy group was established by its membership. There were a couple of parents, myself included, who had established a reputation in the district for being very knowledgeable of special education law and procedures and of being assertive in pursuing their children's rights. Additional pressure for change can be created if the systems advocacy group has other groups with high credibility who are supportive of their proposed changes.

Self-Advocacy

Self-advocacy reflects our democratic form of government by directly involving students with disabilities in educational decision making. Rude and Aiken (1982) stated, "Self-advocacy is a street survival skill for all people, it is necessary for independence. Ideally, people with developmental disabilities are their own advocates, identifying needs and taking the steps to meet them. They usually know their own best interests better than someone acting on their behalf" (pp. 9–10). Special education professionals can promote self-advocacy in two basic ways: (1) helping to form a self-advocacy group, serving as the group's initial facilitator, and functioning as a resource support person to the group (Rhoades, Browning, & Thorin, 1986); and (2) teaching students with disabilities the skills necessary to actively participate in their own IEP meetings.

The self-advocacy movement has grown tremendously in the past decade. "It consists of community-based groups that provide a forum for their members to learn the rights and responsibilities of citizenship and to speak on their own behalf" (Fiedler, 1991, p. 27). The most popular self-advocacy group across the nation is called People First. The choice of this name denotes that individuals with disabilities want to be viewed as whole persons who happen to have a disability. As Fiedler (1991) noted, "Their disability does not totally define them nor is it their most important characteristic—they are more like than different from nondisabled people" (p. 28).

The issue of teaching students with disabilities self-advocacy skills was initially discussed in Chapter 3. The importance of teaching students self-advocacy skills to enhance their participation in IEP meetings is underscored by several research findings. One study reported that school personnel rarely acknowledge and consider student-initiated choice or preferences in classroom learning activities (Houghton, Bronicki, & Guess, 1987). A more recent national survey of adults with mental retardation revealed they had very little self-determination, choice, or control over key life decisions (Wehmeyer & Metzler, 1995).

To foster decision making and self-determination skills, students with disabilities must be constantly encouraged to develop those attributes in a variety of educational and life situations (Sands & Wehmeyer, 1996). In another study assessing student preparedness for IEP meetings, 26 parents of students with learning disabilities ranging in age from 5 to 16, were asked about their child's knowledge of the IEP process. Approximately one-fifth (19 percent) of the parent respondents indicated that their children did not even know they were coming to the IEP meeting, and 38 percent of the parents related that their children did not think they had a learning problem or knew anything about the common characteristics of a learning disability (Vaughn, Bos, Harrell, & Lasky, 1988).

Finally, the importance of teaching self-advocacy skills is stressed in a study by Fifield (1978), which concluded that the attitudes of mothers and special education teachers toward IEP meetings were more positive when the students participated in their own IEP decisions. Similar research has revealed that the majority of secondary students with disabilities want to be involved in their own IEP meetings (Gillespie & Turnbull, 1983). More professionals are calling for the inclusion of students with disabilities in IEP decision making, and special education regulations require the participation of students at transition IEPs (at age 14 and beyond) and allow for student involvement in other IEP situations, when deemed appropriate (Strickland & Turnbull, 1990).

Unfortunately, the majority of students with disabilities are still not actively participating in decision making at their own IEP meetings (Van Reusen & Bos, 1994). Van Reusen and colleagues have developed an instructional procedure called I-PLAN to enhance student participation at IEP meetings (Van Reusen, Bos, Schumaker, & Deshler, 1987). The I-PLAN instructional procedure involves the following five steps:

1. *Inventory.* In this first step, the student lists his or her perceived strengths, areas of improvement, educational goals, and learning choices. The student completes this inventory prior to the IEP meeting.
2. *Provide Your Inventory Information.* In this instructional step, students are taught how and when to provide their inventory information at the IEP meeting.
3. *Listen and Respond.* In this step of the instructional procedure, students learn effective listening skills and how and when to respond to statements and questions made by others at the IEP meeting.
4. *Ask Questions.* During this stage of instruction, students learn how and when to ask questions during the IEP meeting.
5. *Name Your Goals.* Finally, students are required to name the IEP goals that were discussed and agreed upon before the end of the IEP meeting.

The research on the efficacy of this self-advocacy instructional procedure is promising. One study found that students who received the I-PLAN instruction contributed more ideas and generated more IEP goals than students without this training (Van Reusen, Deshler, & Schumaker, 1989). Another study concluded that IEP meetings with students who had received I-PLAN instruction contained more positive communication by focusing more on student strengths (Van Reusen & Bos, 1994).

The multiple and diverse needs and situations of children with disabilities and their families require different types of advocacy actions. For example, in reviewing the advocacy scenarios from Chapter 1, several types of potential advocacy activities are indicated. Mary Kinney will likely be engaged in *direct services* advocacy efforts in working with families and school officials to secure appropriate speech and language services for newly eligible children. In addition, Mary may need to lobby the local school board (*systems* advocacy) for funds to hire a second speech and language clinician. Steve Kern's advocacy efforts on behalf of his students with emotional/behavioral disorders require *community, legislative,* and *systems* advocacy actions. In Karen Snyder's advocacy dilemma, she must focus on *direct services* advocacy in her efforts to ensure that IEP accommodations are implemented for students with disabilities in general education classes. Finally,

Miguel Hernandez, in his advocacy on behalf of Susie Ortiz and her mother, will be involved in *direct services* advocacy and perhaps *legal* advocacy.

ADVOCACY PRINCIPLES, PROCEDURES, SKILLS, AND STRATEGIES

This section discusses specific advocacy skills and strategies. First, several principles for effective advocacy are articulated. Second, a five-step process for engaging in effective advocacy is outlined. And, third, specific advocacy skills and strategies—including documentation, advocacy support for families, media strategies, and the use of persuasion—are presented.

Principles for Effective Advocacy

Although special education professionals who function as advocates for students with disabilities rely heavily on their instincts, intuition, and common sense, there are some distinct skills and strategies necessary for effective advocacy work. Bootel (1995) identified the following set of core principles for effective advocacy:

Ask for what you want.   Advocates must possess enough confidence and assertiveness to directly request the services or changes that their advocacy is seeking. When an advocate appears hesitant or unsure of what he or she wants, it is likely that others will not take the advocate seriously or will stall, assuming that the advocate lacks the commitment and resilience to pursue the matter any further.

Be specific in your request.   At an IEP meeting, parents of a 10-year-old son with significant behavioral and attention challenges expressed their dissatisfaction with the current school program and requested "more educational support" for their son. After an hour of nonproductive problem solving in which school personnel offered several kinds of support—such as after-school

tutorial assistance, a peer tutor during independent seatwork time in class, and modified grading—the parents finally got specific in their request. They requested a full-time aide for their son. At this point, then, the school was aware of the parents' specific concern and request and mutual problem solving could begin in earnest.

Organize, coordinate, orchestrate.   Some advocacy efforts may involve informing and organizing individuals into a coalition or group to seek changes in school district policies/practices, state or federal administrative policies/practices, or state or federal laws or regulations. A coalition quickly loses its political clout if it does not present a truly unified front to the legislative or policy-making body. Therefore, it is critical that a coalition spend the necessary initial time and energy in reaching a group consensus on advocacy goals and priorities.

As an example of this principle, I recall a loosely connected coalition of advocates for persons with developmental disabilities who took their concerns about adequate community housing options to the county board of supervisors. This board allocated state and local funds for social services, including housing assistance. At the board of supervisors meeting where the "coalition" presented its concerns, the group quickly lost its focus and momentum when several representatives of the coalition spoke on behalf of different, and sometimes contradictory, housing initiatives.

Although the members of the housing advocacy group had galvanized around a common dissatisfaction with current community housing options for persons with developmental disabilities, they had not come to agreement on solutions. Some members urged the county board of supervisors to provide more funding for group homes, others argued for more supported apartment living programs, one person spoke on behalf of establishing a fund to provide low-interest mortgage loans so that individuals with disabilities could purchase their own homes, and still other group members advocated for more adult foster care options.

Because this advocacy coalition had failed to coordinate and orchestrate its advocacy goals and priorities, the county board of supervisors heard mixed messages. In this situation, it is easier for a policy-making body to not accede to the political pressure because the group trying to apply the pressure does not present itself as truly unified.

Touch all the bases.   Another basic principle of effective coalition building is to solicit support from as many groups as possible that may have similar advocacy interests. Consider all the groups or constituents that might have a vested interest in the advocacy issue that the coalition is forming around. It is even helpful to discuss an advocacy issue with groups or individuals that may appear as likely opponents. This allows an advocacy group to gauge what kind of opposition they may encounter and to learn about their opponents' objections.

An example of touching all bases is demonstrated in the experiences of a group of parents of children with attention deficit disorder who organized around the issue of the local school district's failure to develop and implement specific behavioral intervention plans (for students qualifying for services under either the IDEA or Section 504 of the Rehabilitation Act of 1973) as a component of their children's IEP. The parents solicited support not just from families of children with attention deficit disorder but from families who might have children with behavioral challenges regardless of the disability label attached to their children.

In addition, the parent advocacy group contacted some professional groups (e.g., the state association of school psychologists) to ascertain whether those groups would be supportive of the parents' advocacy issue. As it turned out, several professional groups, including the state association of school psychologists, were interested in the issue and were eager to join the advocacy coalition because the professional associations saw this as an opportunity to inform their members on the legal requirement to develop behavioral intervention plans for children with disabilities who frequently misbehave, and to educate professional colleagues on the skills necessary to conduct functional behavioral assessments and develop positive behavioral support interventions. In this case, the parent advocacy group found allies that it had not anticipated would be supportive of its cause.

Stay flexible, be opportunistic.   Although effective advocates need to establish clear goals and a plan of action, they must remain flexible in their advocacy efforts to seize unexpected opportunities. In my own parent advocacy experience, I recall one IEP meeting where my wife and I expressed our concern over some of the IEP goals and objectives for our daughter. We went to that meeting with the advocacy mindset that we would try to have those objectionable IEP goals changed. After a lengthy discussion of our concerns, the pupil services director offered to have an outside consultant of our choosing conduct an independent evaluation of our daughter and her educational program. Although we had not anticipated and were somewhat surprised by this offer, we seized this opportunity as an excellent chance to enhance the educational programming for our daughter.

Keep it simple.   I remember a legislative forum session where an advocate for supported employment went on for 20 minutes about the current employment problems faced by individuals with disabilities and how sheltered workshops were not preparing their employees for independent jobs in integrated work settings. Although this advocate was well intentioned and had spoken on behalf of an important issue, the legislators in attendance tuned him out after 5 minutes. In fact, the advocate's lack of brevity hindered his message about the changes needed in vocational services for individuals with disabilities. Bootel (1995) stated this principle of advocacy:

> *You should be prepared to state your best case for the issues at hand in 30 seconds. You will have opportunities to discuss the issues in greater depth, but you should always strive to capture your audience's attention within the first few sentences. Always plan your presentations as if your audience will only remember one line from everything that you say. Decide ahead of time what that one line*

should be (think of it as the headline), and design your message around it. (p. 18)

Assume the perspective of others.   When advocating on behalf of students with disabilities to individuals or groups (i.e., school boards, legislative councils, policy-making bodies), remember that many individuals who are not special education professionals will lack knowledge about and personal insight into the issues, needs, and life circumstances faced by individuals with disabilities and their families. Therefore, an effective advocate carefully listens to the questions and comments of others to gain insight into their perspective. An effective advocate illuminates disability issues by relating through anecdotes how a problem has direct impact on a child with a disability. An effective advocate attempts to "bring to life" an advocacy issue by associating a real name and face to the problem at issue.

Build and preserve your credibility.   Effective advocates recognize that their personal reputation for integrity, honesty, and credibility are important advocacy tools. To build and enhance these tools, advocates must (1) not mislead anyone in their advocacy actions, (2) not spring any unfair surprises on others, and (3) not promise more than they can deliver.

Never burn your bridges.   Although advocacy often engenders strong emotions, it is important to avoid negative personal attacks on someone as a result of one's frustration, anger, or hurt. That is, effective advocates attempt to avoid making enemies in their advocacy actions. Advocacy alliances and oppositions shift, depending on the issues. A special education professional may find herself embroiled in a conflict with a colleague or an administrator on one issue while on another unrelated issue, that same colleague or administrator may be an ally.

For example, a school psychologist found himself in opposition with a special education teacher over the issue of whether a student with attention deficit disorder qualified for special education ser-

vices. Two months later, at a teacher assistance team meeting, this same school psychologist and teacher were allies over the question of whether to provide another student with a prereferral behavioral management intervention program in the general education classroom. As stated by Bootel (1995), "Remember, in advocacy, there are no permanent friends and no permanent enemies" (p. 20).

Follow up.   During advocacy interactions, effective advocates ensure that they complete their agreed upon tasks within the prescribed time frame. An advocate must be counted on, by allies and adversaries alike, to do what he says he will do. If not, advocates risk their credibility and, ultimately, their negotiating and problem-solving ability. Further, if an advocate is serving as a spokesperson for a coalition, the advocate must keep his or her allies regularly informed of the progress or problems encountered during the course of the advocacy efforts.

Steps in the Advocacy Process

Although the situations, issues, and problems encountered by advocates are unique, Hines (1987) has maintained that the process of engaging in effective advocacy consists of these five steps:

1. Problem Definition

Problem definition is the first step in the advocacy process. At the conclusion of this step, the advocate should have a clear perspective of what specifically is the problem, who is affected by the problem, what started the problem, what changes are needed to resolve the problem, and what has already been done in an attempt to address the problem. This step assists advocates in prioritizing problems. The goal during this step is to develop a specific problem definition that includes behavior, events and circumstances that led to the conclusion that something is wrong, along with a specific statement describing what is needed or desired to resolve the problem. The advocate should be mindful that it is important to separate the objective facts of a problem situation from an individual's feelings about the problem. An example of a poor problem definition and a better, specific problem definition follows:

Poor Problem Definition: Jeremy's special education program is not beneficial to him.

Specific Problem Definition: Jeremy is currently being served for 80 percent of his school day in a special education program for students with emotional/behavioral disorders where he receives instruction primarily in the general education core academic subjects. At 16 years old, Jeremy needs (1) instruction in "learning how to learn" skills to increase his efficiency and retention of the content in the core academic subjects; (2) social skills instruction to improve his abilities to engage in productive interpersonal interactions with peers and adults and to control his anger; (3) a vocational training program in different community settings; and (4) more general education classroom experiences to be removed from the negative behavioral contagion of his special education classroom and to learn collaborative behaviors in a larger group setting.

The questions identified in Box 11.2 are useful in the identification of a specific problem situation. These questions were applied in the example of Jeremy's problem situation above by his new special education teacher who is functioning as his advocate in an effort to improve this problem situation for Jeremy. This questioning process is illustrated here as an example:

- *How do you know there is a problem?*   Jeremy is falling further behind academically each year. His attitude toward school has deteriorated in the past year. He has no positive peer relationships at school. He is disobeying his parents on a regular basis, staying out late at night, and hanging around with adolescents who are gang "wannabes."
- *Who is affected by the problem and how?*   Obviously, Jeremy is affected by this problem

situation. He is becoming increasingly apathetic toward school, disrespectful to teachers and his parents, and engaging in dangerous behaviors. Jeremy's parents are worried about his negative school attitude and behaviors, his destructive peer influences, and his future in general. The school staff is affected by this problem as they struggle to turn this situation around for Jeremy.

- *When did the problem start?*   Jeremy had been a solid student until he entered the high school two years ago. At that time, he lost interest in sports and his studies, and he began hanging around with a different group of peers. *What started the problem, made it worse, or caused you to notice it?*   The special education teacher can identify no single cause of Jeremy's problem. This problem has slowly evolved over the past two years. When Jeremy's best friend moved out of town last year, Jeremy seemed even less interested in school. The teacher also knows that Jeremy is experiencing stress over his younger sister's battle with leukemia, which was diagnosed a little over one year ago.
- *What kinds of changes would solve the problem?*   In addition to the educational changes noted earlier in the specific problem definition, the special education teacher believes Jeremy could benefit from counseling to talk about his concerns regarding his sister's health problems. In addition, the teacher is trying to match Jeremy as a peer tutor for a younger student in a computer technology class. (Jeremy likes computers and he is quite skilled in computer applications.)
- *How will you know when the problem is solved?*   A number of behaviors could signal improvement in Jeremy's problem situation: a renewed interest in sports; a willingness to express his worries and feelings; improved grades; an interest in and regular attendance at his job placement; less opposition to his parents or teachers; better control over his anger; and involvement with more positive peers.
- *By what date should the problem begin to be resolved?*   Although Jeremy has two more

years of school before he could graduate (if he improved his grades and earned the required number of graduation credits), he has agreed to try the new IEP changes for six months before deciding whether he will continue in school.

- *What has been done to address the problem so far?* Jeremy's parents have agreed to try family counseling. The special education teacher has scheduled a new IEP meeting to address proposed educational changes and to write a new transitional IEP.
- *Are there any ethical or legal guidelines that relate to the problem?* It is questionable whether Jeremy is receiving an appropriate education as required by law. An appropriate education must provide some beneficial results for the student.

2. Information Gathering

Obviously, different problems require different kinds of information. However, Hines (1987) identified the informational gathering areas in Box 11.3, presented in a checklist, as critical in almost any advocacy situation.

3. Action Planning

Following the information gathering process, an action plan should be developed. This action plan includes step-by-step activities the advocate will take to resolve the problem. The action plan describes the current problem situation, articulates the advocacy goal, and outlines the actions necessary to reach the goal. Elements of the action plan include (1) a short statement of the problem (see the problem definition step described earlier); (2) a description of the ideal resolution of the problem; (3) a list of acceptable compromise solutions (e.g., the BATNA; see Chapter 10); (4) a list of all the information needed to reach the desired advocacy goal with information divided into two sections: information already collected (see the information gathering step described earlier) and information needed; (5) a description of how the requested changes or advocacy goal could benefit others, including those in direct opposition to the advocacy efforts; (6) a description of the other party's needs, priorities, or anticipated arguments and possible responses to each argument; (7) a step-by-step description of the proposed advocacy strategy and approach to the other party; (8) a time line for the completion of each step of the action plan; and (9) a discussion of what actions will be taken if the advocacy effort is not successful.

4. Assertive Action

In this step of the advocacy process, the advocate implements his or her action plan. Important elements in determining advocacy success are effective assertive communication skills (see Chapter 8) and negotiation and conflict resolution skills (see Chapter 10). Assertive actions are at the heart of effective advocacy. When a person is assertive, he or she stands up for his or her rights, while, at the same time, respecting the rights of others. The assertive person is a good listener, is able to control his or her emotions and work for mutually beneficial solutions, and is able to promote communication and problem solving. Some assertive verbal techniques include the following:

- *Simple assertion.* This is a straightforward statement in which the advocate expresses an opinion, belief, or request. The advocate, in making a simple assertion, does not attempt to explain or justify. (*Examples:* "I would like a copy of the student's file." "I would like to speak without being interrupted." "I believe this IEP does not comply with the law." "You did not answer my question.")
- *Acknowledgment and assertion.* This technique allows the advocate to demonstrate that he or she understands the other person's perspective while asserting his or her own point of view or needs. This technique is beneficial when interacting with someone who feels that the advocate does not understand his position. (*Example:* "I understand that you are concerned about the cost of a residential placement for Brian. However, the courts have consistently ruled that if a residential placement is necessary to provide a student with a disability an appropriate education, then the local school

Box 11.3 _____

Advocacy Actions:
An Informational Gathering Checklist

RESPONSIBLE AGENCIES

Who is the responsible agency to provide the requested services? In most special education advocacy situations, the responsible agency to provide the requested services is the local school district. (See Chapter 5 for a discussion of the services school districts are legally responsible to provide.) In some cases, there may be questions about whether a community agency (e.g., vocational services provider) is responsible for certain services or whether medical assistance will cover a therapy service or an assistive technology device.

RIGHTS AND RIGHTS PROCEDURE

An advocate must know the applicable legal rights (see Chapter 5) and complaint and appeals procedures (see Chapter 6) for formal advocacy activities. In terms of legal rights and protections, an advocate may discover that:

- A legal provision (e.g., statute, administrative regulation, case law) specifically requires the kind of service or change requested, or
- A legal provision permits the agency to provide the kind of service or change requested, or
- There is no directly applicable legal provision controlling the particular situation

In the case of the last two possibilities, an effective advocate must demonstrate that a service or change is necessary for the student with disabilities or the advocate must be able to make a logical argument that the agency should provide the service or change requested. Some possible reasons to support a request for change are:

- The current situation is inhumane or abusive.
- The current situation violates constitutional or statutory rights.

- The current situation is discriminatory.
- The current situation results in unnecessary segregation or isolation of a student with a disability.
- The current situation may endanger safety or health, in the short or long term.
- The current situation will result in no educational benefit or cause the student to regress.
- The current situation violates standards of good practice or professional ethics.

AGENCY CHAIN OF COMMAND

An advocate must know the agency administrative hierarchy and chain of command in case the problem cannot be resolved at the initial level and the complaint must be taken to subsequent administrative levels. Knowing the agency chain of command demonstrates that an advocate is serious about resolving the problem and is willing to take further action.

STUDENT RECORDS

Adhering to educational records access and confidentiality provisions (see Chapter 5), the advocate must carefully review the student's school file. Particular attention should be paid to the student's evaluation reports, IEP, and progress reports.

POLICY DOCUMENTS

School districts have a variety of policy documents, such as school board policies, school policies and procedures, and individual teacher policies and procedures. Especially in situations where there is no clearly controlling legal provision, an advocate must investigate various policy documents for relevant information to advance the advocacy efforts.

Source: Adapted from _Don't Get Mad: Get Powerful! A Manual for Building Advocacy Skills_ by M. L. Hines, 1987, Lansing, MI: Michigan Protection and Advocacy Service. (ERIC Document Reproduction Service No. ED 354 683).

district is responsible for the costs of the residential placement.")

— *Repeated assertion.* A repeated assertion is a useful technique when an advocate does not get a response to a request or when the other party attempts to shift the topic of conversation to avoid addressing the advocate's request or statement. (*Example:* "*Mrs. Adams:* I want to review my son's educational records. *Principal:* Those records are very complicated. I don't think you would understand them. *Mrs. Adams:* I am very interested in reviewing my son's educational records. *Principal:* I am sure I can answer any questions you have about your son's education. *Mrs. Adams:* I have a right to see my son's educational records and I would like to do so" (Hines, 1987, p. 98)).

— *Agreement and assertion.* In this assertive technique, an advocate agrees with those statements made by another person that are true while continuing to assert his or her point of view. This technique demonstrates an advocate's desire to listen and work with the other party. (*Example: Advocate:* I believe that Michael requires occupational therapy services on a daily basis. *Pupil Services Director:* We have a shortage of occupational therapists in the district right now. *Advocate:* I know there is a shortage of occupational therapists. However, the IEP committee maintains that occupational therapy needs to be provided daily and the courts have held that lack of available services is not an adequate excuse for failure to provide an appropriate education.)

5. Follow-Up

In this final step, the advocate monitors other individuals involved in the advocacy activities to ensure the implementation of agreed-upon services and changes. If the agreed-upon actions are implemented, the advocate should send a thank you letter to those individuals. If other individuals fail to fulfill their promises, the advocate should contact them in writing with a reminder of the earlier agreement and request that the individual implement the agreement within a prescribed time period. A copy of the letter should be sent to the next level in the agency chain of command to indicate that the advocate is willing to pursue this advocacy action to subsequent administrative levels if necessary.

Specific Advocacy Skills and Strategies

Documentation

An effective advocate must be able to organize the array of information that is typically gathered during the course of advocacy activities and must be able to document advocacy interactions and the manner in which they occur (e.g., at meetings or in phone conversations.) This section describes strategies for organizing relevant information and for documenting the content of advocacy interactions.

Organizing school records. Anderson, Chitwood, and Hayden (1997) developed a Four-Step Record Decoder process to assist advocates in organizing and reviewing the voluminous amount of school documents that comprise the school record of a student with disabilities. The four steps are organize, read, analyze, and evaluate. Important considerations for each step are as follows:

Organize

— Organize school documents into two general categories: documents describing the student (i.e., evaluation reports, IEPs, progress reports) and correspondence or administrative documents (i.e., meeting notices, consent forms, placement forms).

— Arrange documents in chronological order from oldest to most recent.

— Keep a chronological list of the documents, including the name of the document, the date, and the reporting individual.

Read

— Read through the student's entire school records to gather general impressions and the school's perspective on the student.

- Keep a list of questions or concerns related to specific documents. This list will highlight information in reports that the advocate does not understand or wishes to challenge.

Analyze

- Keep a list of the student's strengths (identify the document) and a list of the student's needs or weaknesses (identify the document).
- Keep a list of recommendations made by school personnel.
- Look for trends in the information. For example, is a strength, need, or recommendation mentioned by more than one school professional? Are similar observations and/or conclusions repeated over more than one school year?

Evaluate

- Are the conclusions and recommendations in the school reports in agreement with the perceptions, observations, and opinions of the advocate, the student's family, and the student?
- Are all of the required documents contained in the school records? Do all the reports (i.e., evaluation reports or IEPs) contain all the required legal components?
- Are school reports subjective (e.g., expressing personal biases or judgments) or objective (e.g., expressing behavioral descriptive information)? Do the evaluation reports take into account the student's disability and its likely effect on performance in a standardized test instrument? Is there any evidence of cultural or racial bias in any of the school reports?
- How current is the report information on the student's academic performance, social/behavioral performance, health status, and family background?
- Is there any inconsistency between the student descriptions of various school professionals?

Documenting the content of advocacy interactions. Prior to any advocacy-oriented meeting regarding educational services or changes for a student with disabilities, the advocate should request that minutes of the meeting be taken to capture and summarize the main points of the discussion (Shields, 1989). This request is especially important in case there are any agreements or promises made by any of the meeting participants. If there is no written record of a meeting, the advocate should summarize his or her understanding of the relevant points in a letter and ask for confirmation of their accuracy from the chair of the meeting or other participants. Effective advocates seek closure at the end of every meeting by (1) summarizing the substance/purpose of the discussion; (2) summarizing any agreements reached or promises made at the meeting; (3) articulating questions or information that remain to be answered or gathered; (4) describing the next tasks, identifying the responsible individuals, and stating the deadline for completion of those tasks; and (5) setting a subsequent meeting date, location, and time for any further meetings if necessary.

Many advocacy interactions occur via telephone conversations. An effective advocate documents those interactions by maintaining a written record of (1) the name, position, phone number, and address of the person spoken to; (2) the date of the phone conversation; (3) the reason(s) for the conversation; (4) a summary of the main points of the conversation; (5) a summary of any agreements or conclusions reached during the conversation; (6) deadlines for completion of specific tasks; and (7) a note of whether there is any need for a follow-up phone call, indicating by whom the call will be made, when the call will occur, and the purpose of the follow up contact (Anderson et al., 1997; Cutler, 1993; Hines, 1987; Learning Disabilities Association of America, 1992; Shields, 1989).

When advocates are at the stage of requesting an educational change on behalf of a student with a disability, a final important documentation strategy is sending a letter to the administrator or decision-making body who has the authority to grant the request. This request letter should normally be short, succinct, and specific. There are three main components to a good request letter (Hines,

1987). First, the opening paragraph should state the purpose for writing the letter (e.g., "I am writing to request that Kim Chang's IEP be revised to incorporate specific social skills goals and objectives.") Second, the body of the letter should provide specific details to support the request in the opening paragraph (e.g., "Over the past two months, Kim has become increasingly isolated from her peers. She rarely, if ever, freely chooses to interact with other children during recess, lunch or other free periods during the school day. Other children are beginning to tease and ridicule her. Kim's academic performance is starting to slide as well.")

Finally, the last paragraph of the letter should summarize the request and ask for a response to the request within a specific time period (e.g., "Therefore, for the above stated reasons, I request that the IEP committee reconvene as soon as possible for the purpose of developing some goals and objectives to address Kim's social skill deficits and her need for more peer interactions and friendships. Please respond to this request within 7 days of the date of this letter. I thank you for your prompt attention to this matter.")

Advocacy Support for Families

Cutler (1993) identified five types of support that advocates could provide to families of children with disabilities. First, an advocate can simply serve as a good *listener* for parents as they discuss their concerns and fears and their child's strengths and weaknesses, needs, and future goals. In practicing good listening skills, an advocate can empower families by helping them engage in active educational planning and in acknowledging the parents' expertise in terms of providing relevant and useful information about their children.

Second, advocates can assist families in *sorting out* their priorities and determining if more information is needed to secure appropriate educational services for their children. My daughter's high school special education teacher served this important advocacy function for my family as she helped us, as parents, determine what we could do to facilitate beneficial general education classroom experiences for our daughter. As a result of this advocacy support from the teacher, my wife and I prepared a letter that we sent to all of our daughter's general education teachers. The purpose of the letter was to provide information to teachers on our daughter's needs, our rationale for wanting her to participate in some general education classes, our goals for her general education classroom participation, and suggestions on how teachers could help her with functional skill development. All of the teachers reacted positively to this letter, which opened a clear line of communication between the school and home. See Box 11.4 for a copy of the letter my wife and I sent to Jennifer's general education teachers.

A third advocacy support function for families involves the advocate serving as a *spokesperson* and as a *source of information*. As an example of a special education professional fulfilling this advocacy support role, consider the Miguel Hernandez scenario from Chapter 1. Miguel has assumed the responsibility of being a spokesperson for Susie Ortiz and her mother by serving as a mediator between Mrs. Ortiz and IEP committee members. Miguel is assisting Mrs. Ortiz in communicating her frustration in not being treated as an equal educational decision maker at IEP meetings. Further, Miguel is providing the Ortiz family with information to address their family needs by informing Mrs. Ortiz about the availability of community services such as respite care, financial budgeting, a food pantry, and a parent advocacy center.

Special education professionals can fulfill a fourth advocacy support role by serving as *coplanners* to assist families in developing a plan of action. A specific strategy in facilitating family action planning is reframing. *Reframing* is defined as "the family's ability to redefine a demanding situation in a more rational and acceptable way in order to make the situation more manageable" (Olson, McCubbin, Barnes, Larsen, Muxen, & Wilson, 1983, p. 143). This strategy can be employed by families and professionals. In essence, this strategy involves two steps: (1) distinguishing situations that can be changed from those that are beyond

Box 11.4 _____

Advocacy Actions

Dear Educator:

We are parents of Jennifer Fiedler, a student in your general education classroom with exceptional educational needs, and we feel a need to write this letter and provide you with some information. We have tried to anticipate some of your questions/concerns and will address them in a question and answer format. However, please do not hesitate to contact us at any time if you have other questions or concerns. We are eager to work with you in an effort to best meet Jennifer's educational needs and the needs of the other students in your classes.

What are Jennifer's major disabling conditions and how do her disabilities impact on her functioning and learning?

Jennifer has severe and multiple disabilities. She was disabled at birth but the specific cause is unknown. Jennifer's major disability is a profound cognitive disability. She has no oral language skills, she is nonambulatory, and she is not toilet trained. She also has a seizure disorder that is under good control through medication (she receives tegretol and neurontin in the morning and evening at home). Jennifer also has moderate hearing and vision impairments. She has functional vision (it is best to hand her something from the side) and marginal hearing. We have tried FM receivers in the past and you might want to explore that with her special education teacher. Due to her disabilities, Jennifer learns at a very slow rate and only through constant drill and repetition of learning activities. We realize that Jennifer will always need considerable assistance from others in order to live as independently as possible.

What is Jennifer's most recent educational history?

This is Jennifer's first year at the high school. For the last three years, Jennifer attended the middle school. During those three years, Jennifer was in various general education classes for at least 3 periods a day. She also spent an hour or two almost every day in various community work settings.

Why do we want Jennifer to participate in general education classes?

We know our daughter is severely disabled; we are not denying that reality. The reality that has been the most painful for us as parents, however, has been the fact that Jennifer had no friends in her life. This sad reality began changing three years ago as we finally found a group of educators who were willing to work with Jennifer in general education classes. Since that time, Jennifer has developed some relationships with nondisabled peers. She has been invited to parties, school dances, and social outings in the community. It has not been easy but we feel it has been well worth all of the effort on the part of us, the teachers, and some special non-disabled students who have taken the time to get to know Jennifer. If Jennifer is really going to be an integral member of her community, she will need to rely on her friends who want to be involved with her because they are her friends.

What do we hope to accomplish by having Jennifer in general education classes?

First, we certainly realize that Jennifer is not going to function at grade level in any academic subject. That is not the reason for having her in general education classes. The most recent court decisions on a disabled student's rights to be educated in the "least restrictive environment" have recognized that there are legitimate educational reasons for general education placements aside from the issue of whether the disabled student can perform academically at grade level. In particular, the courts have recognized that having students with disabilities in general education classes can provide them with more appropriate language and social/ behavioral role models. Jennifer is clearly stimulated by human interaction which cannot be as rich in a segregated special education classroom where all or most of the other students are similarly language and behaviorally disabled. Second, as we have witnessed in the past three years, the only way for nondisabled peers to get to know Jennifer is to interact with her on a daily basis. It is only through Jennifer's general class participation that some relationships with nondisabled students have been formed.

What expectations do we have for general education teachers working with Jennifer?

Box 11.4   Continued

Obviously, we do not expect you to teach her the general education class curriculum. Instead, please be conscious of various adaptations that can enhance Jennifer's involvement and interaction in the class and that can facilitate her working on functional skills. For example, in terms of curricular/instructional adaptations to enhance Jennifer's class involvement, please consider the following strategies:

1. Change the lesson to include cooperative learning groups, small group instruction, partner learning or peer tutors.
2. Change the lesson format to allow for more active student participation instead of a strict lecture format.
3. Change lesson goals. For example, in a Foods class Jennifer could have a goal of using a touch plate to turn on a blender.
4. Change general classroom expectations to facilitate more active involvement. For example, are there any classroom chores that Jennifer could help with while the other students are engaged in seat work or listening to a lecture? For instance, perhaps Jennifer could pass out some materials to the other students or she could clean up a back table.
5. Change the curricular materials. For example, Jennifer could use a signature stamp to identify her belongings. Or she could listen to stories/music on headphones as a legitimate leisure/recreational activity.
6. Allow for some personal assistance to enhance Jennifer's class participation. As you know or will quickly discover, Jennifer needs lots of hand over hand assistance. Please invite her class peers to interact with Jennifer to provide some of that assistance. We feel it is important for nondisabled students to learn about individuals with disabilities and that can only occur in direct face-to-face interaction.
7. We recognize that there are some situations where it is inappropriate for Jennifer to work on learning activities in the general education classroom. She spends a good portion of her school day at various work sites to get exposure to different work environments. During times of end of the semester testing,

Jennifer should probably be educated outside of the general education classroom.

Another consideration we would like you to keep in mind is that Jennifer can work on a number of functional skills in general class settings that have nothing to do with a particular subject matter. For instance, here are some goals for Jennifer in your class that are not subject matter related: listening attentively without hand flapping; making eye contact when spoken to; staying alert; decreasing behaviors such as mouthing her clothing or sucking her thumb; passing materials to someone seated next to her; cleaning up her work space; weight-bearing as she stands at a table or sink; working on communication skills by either using her signature stamp or activating her speak easy tape player; performing any classroom chore where Jennifer could, with assistance, shred or cut paper, sort or distribute materials, or take a break to drink from a glass. Jennifer can also work on mobility skills by trying to move her wheelchair for short distances. These are just some examples of "functional oriented skills" that Jennifer should address in general education environments; because once she leaves school, we want her to live in the community and participate in as many community activities as possible.

There is no way that we can suggest all of the modifications that might add to Jennifer's involvement in your general education classrooms. Please do not hesitate to contact Jennifer's special education teacher for suggestions on class modifications. Also, trust your own ideas. You can facilitate nondisabled peer interaction with Jennifer by serving as a positive role model for your students. Please do not be afraid to interact with Jennifer. As we said earlier, she enjoys human interaction.

We greatly appreciate your willingness to work with Jennifer in your classroom. You are helping us realize a future vision for our daughter that includes maximum integration into her home community with the richness of interactions and personal relationships. Thank you.

Sincerely,

Craig and Sharon Fiedler

one's control and (2) taking action on alternative situations that can be changed.

Invoking the strategy of reframing involves use of the skills of problem solving and redefining stressful situations. Professionals can help families acquire problem-solving skills (discussed in Chapter 10) by teaching the distinct steps involved in the problem-solving process. Professionals can aid families in redefining stressful situations (i.e., reframing) by using positive comparisons, employing selective attention and selective ignoring, and redefining a situation that is beyond one's control to make the situation more manageable (Turnbull & Turnbull, 1990).

In the reframing strategy of positive comparisons, families consider others' problems and stresses, reaching a conclusion that their problems, by comparison, are not so great after all. The reframing strategy of selective attention and selective ignoring involves encouraging families to dwell more on the positive aspects of their children with disabilities rather than the negative factors (Pearlin & Schooler, 1978). Finally, learning how to redefine a situation that is beyond one's control in an effort to alleviate stress and make a demanding situation more manageable is exemplified in Box 11.5.

A final advocacy support engages professionals as a *source of personal support* for families as they go through the special education process in securing an appropriate educational program for their children. The components of this type of ad-

---

Box 11.5 _____

Advocacy Actions: Reframing as a
Coping and Advocacy Strategy

My family and some other families of children with severe disabilities successfully employed the strategy of reframing in our advocacy efforts on behalf of our children several years ago. For the first five years that we lived in our home school district, our daughter Jennifer was transported to a neighboring school district and attended a special education program for children with severe and multiple disabilities. This school district was larger than our home district and operated a regional program for students with severe and multiple disabilities. Our home school district claimed that it had too few children with similar needs as our daughter, thus necessitating the out of district placement. Jennifer spent approximately 45 minutes each way on the bus every day. Although Jennifer received some excellent educational services from a number of dedicated and competent professionals, we wanted our daughter to attend school in her home district. Our desire to have Jennifer attend school in her home district was primarily fueled by the lack of social interaction opportunities with nondisabled peers. Those peers at school who demonstrated an interest in getting to know Jennifer lived in other communities 15 to 20 miles away from our home.

During each of those five years, my wife and I expressed our dissatisfaction with this out of district special education placement to our home school district administration. We encountered the same obstacle each year: "There are not enough students with needs similar to your daughter's in our district to justify operating our own special education program." With my law background, I approached this "problem" as a matter of legal rights, specifically the right of my daughter to be educated in the least restrictive environment. Unfortunately, all of my legal research concluded that we would probably not prevail if we challenged this out of district placement in a due process hearing. Although special education administrative regulations require that children with disabilities be educated as close to home as possible and (unless the IEP requires a different educational placement) in the school they would attend if they were not disabled, there have been no court decisions obligating school districts to educate every student with a disability in his or her neighborhood school. In fact, the court decisions have ruled that school districts may exercise proper administrative discretion in using its resources in an efficient manner, which may include addressing some students' needs with out of district educational placements.

We were stuck, unable to change an unacceptable situation, until we reframed the problem. Instead of viewing our daughter's educational placement situation as a "legal problem," which offered us no viable solu-

Box 11.5 Continued

tion, we reframed the situation as a "political problem." My wife and I asked these questions: "Are there any other families in our community who have children with severe disabilities and are their children receiving special education services via out of district placements?" "If so, are those families similarly dissatisfied with their children's out of district special education placements?" With this simple reframing of the problem, we were able to develop an alternative advocacy strategy.

First, we were able to locate two other families in our community whose severely disabled children were also being educated out of district. Both of those families preferred to have their children attend school in their home district. We had several meetings with these two families and developed the following strategy. We gave our group (consisting of three families) a name—Taxpayers and Parents for Educational Fairness—and we sent a letter to the local school administration. In our letter, we expressed our dissatisfaction with the current out of district placements of our children and requested that the school district bring our children back to school in their home district. We requested a meeting with school district officials to discuss our concerns. We also enclosed a copy of a petition that we were prepared to circulate around the community to get signatures from other residents in support of our efforts to have our children educated in their home school district. We indicated in the letter that we intended to circulate this petition and present it at a school board meeting if the administration refused to meet with us and take our concerns seriously. The letter also mentioned that we knew the education reporter for the local newspaper and we felt this was a newsworthy event and would contact that reporter if the school administration ignored us.

Our strategy clearly reflected a reframed view of this problem as a political one, calling for pressure to be put on the school administration to address our concerns. Within a couple of days after sending our letter, the school administration contacted us and stated they would be happy to meet with our group. We had several productive meetings with school administrators in the middle of the school year, resulting in the district's commitment to bring all students with severe disabilities back to their home district by the start of the next school year. For the past seven years, our daughter has been attending school at her neighborhood middle school and now our local high school. The strategy of reframing caused this successful outcome.

---

vocacy are multifaceted, including such support functions as explaining special education procedures and legal rights, preparing families in advance of evaluation and IEP meetings (e.g., encouraging parents to review educational records, make a list of questions they have for the meeting, and make a list of information that they want to share at the meeting), and acknowledging the emotional aspects of parenting a child with a disability by maintaining a family support and empowerment disposition (see Chapter 4) during interactions with parents.

Media Strategies

Bootel (1995) defined *media advocacy* as "the strategic use of mass media as a resource for advancing social or public policy change" (p. 53).

In certain situations, advocates may need to consider using media strategies to accomplish their goals. Media strategies are especially relevant when an advocate is involved in community, legislative, or systems advocacy work. In such advocacy situations, the issues are usually broader and affect a larger number of individuals with disabilities. The media can help draw public attention to a perceived problem or inadequacy in the educational or social services systems. The first element of any media strategy is to determine whether an advocacy issue is "newsworthy" enough for the media to be interested in the issue. The following factors (Bootel, 1995) largely determine whether a story has sufficient news value:

- *Timeliness.* Topics that raise new issues are more likely to generate media interest than topics that have already been reported.

■ *Proximity.* The news story must directly involve members of the local community where the story is being reported.

■ *Consequence.* The news story must affect the viewer or reader in some manner.

■ *Human interest.* An appeal to fundamental emotions or a story that illustrates a universal moral truth are more likely newsworthy items.

■ *Conflict.* Stories about disputes between opposing parties tend to garner media interest.

■ *Prominence.* Stories that feature a prominent celebrity who is associated with a particular issue are more newsworthy.

■ *Unusualness.* More unique or unusual stories attract more media attention.

■ *Brevity.* A story must be able to be packaged in short "news bites."

Once an advocate or advocacy organization has determined the newsworthy angle that will be employed to sell the story to the media, the second step in media advocacy is to skillfully "frame the issue." One strategy in framing an issue is to relate the issue to the audience's existing knowledge framework or informational background. This tactic helps place an issue into a context that the audience can better understand or relate to. Bootel (1995) cites an effective example of framing the issue: "If you're advocating for increased special education funding for your state, you might want to relay some 'success' stories of students who benefitted from a special education program in your legislator's district. When done well, framing makes bare facts come alive. It personalizes abstract ideas and illuminates their relevance and importance" (p. 27).

A second strategy in framing the issue is to relate your advocacy concern or change request to a fundamental public value, such as freedom, security, fairness, opportunity, independence, or caring. Stories that evoke these values enhance the audience's receptiveness to the underlying message and allow for a closer identification to individuals affected by the advocacy issue. A third framing strategy is to translate the central message in a particular advocacy issue into a simple concept that can evoke strong emotions in the audience. For example, the issue of adequate training and support for school personnel to be able to provide fairly sophisticated support services to medically fragile children such as suctioning of a tracheostomy, ventilator setting checks, ambubag administrations, and blood pressure monitoring can get quite technical with lots of jargon. An advocate seeking media coverage of this issue would want to promote the story as dealing with potential "life and death issues" if school personnel are inadequately trained and supervised. This framing distills the issue to a basic concept that highlights the significance of the issue.

A final framing strategy is to emphasize the positive, constructive elements of an advocacy issue as opposed to conveying a message that is nothing but a complaint. Most people react more favorably to constructive messages than to complaints.

The next step in this media advocacy process is to access the media through any of these strategies: (1) issuing a press release; (2) sending a pitch letter to a specific journalist who may be interested in the story (e.g., the education reporter for the local newspaper); (3) scheduling a news conference (this is best if held in conjunction with a professional conference or as part of the celebration of National Disability Awareness Month or some similar event); (4) scheduling a well-known speaker who is likely to attract press coverage; or (5) distributing a press kit that contains background information on a particular advocacy issue and includes brief one-page fact sheets for easy reference and a list of contact persons for a follow-up interview (Bootel, 1995).

Persuasion as a Strategy

Advocates seek change on behalf of students with disabilities and their families in an attempt to improve the status quo in terms of educational services. As should be anticipated, advocates will often encounter resistance to their change efforts. Therefore, an effective advocate must be able to employ persuasion as an advocacy strategy. *Per-*

suasion is one's ability to convince another person to agree to one's perception, plan, or idea for change (Perloff, 1993).

Kenton (1989) identified several personal qualities that enhance an individual's persuasive credibility with others. First, the persuader must possess the quality of *goodwill and fairness*. This quality requires the persuader to attend appropriately to the other party during an interpersonal interaction, to express concern about the other person's perspective, and to be generous and magnanimous toward the other person. Second, a persuader must have the requisite *expertise* related to the issue that he or she is seeking to discuss with another individual. A third personal quality contributing to credibility is *prestige*. Some individuals acquire prestige through their position, status, or rank. Others gain prestige because they are perceived as being very competent in their professional role. The final quality is *self-presentation,* which refers to the persuader's verbal communication skills, dynamism, energy, and confidence.

Friend and Cook (1996) discuss four strategies or approaches for persuading others: behavioral, consistency, perceptual, and functional approaches. Each approach will be briefly examined.

Behavioral Approach

The behavioral approach seeks to persuade others by associating positive characteristics with the persuader's change request. Specific behavioral strategies include (1) providing incentives, (2) imposing negative consequences, (3) relating the proposed change to a positive image, and (4) providing opportunities for others to become familiar with the change through observation. Examples of each strategy are considered in the context of the Karen Snyder advocacy scenario from Chapter 1.

Karen could provide the recalcitrant general education teachers who are refusing to implement IEP accommodations for students with disabilities with a positive incentive of more collaborative planning time during the week. An example of a negative consequence Karen could impose would be to file a grievance against the teachers, claiming that they are insubordinate. Obviously, negative

sanctions like this should only be contemplated as an absolute last resort. An example of how Karen could relate the change of having more students with disabilities in general education classes to a positive image is to focus the change request on enhanced professional development that is promoted through teacher collaboration. Finally, as an example of the fourth strategy, Karen could have the teachers visit another elementary school where inclusion of students with disabilities is working well and the general education teachers are excited and positive about their new roles and responsibilities.

Consistency Approach

This approach to persuasion assumes that individuals seek cognitive consistency. When faced with inconsistent information or dissonance in their thinking, individuals attempt to resolve the inconsistency and, at that point, they are more open to change (Festinger, 1957). Consistency theory advances three major persuasion strategies (Friend & Cook, 1996).

One strategy involves the persuader systematically pointing out the discrepancies in another person's thinking that may create cognitive dissonance. For instance, in the Steve Kern advocacy dilemma, the thinking of the school administration presented an obstacle in the path of Steve's advocacy on behalf of more positive and supportive disciplinary interventions for his students with emotional/behavioral disorders. In this advocacy example, the school administration believed that Steve's students were disruptive and detracted from an efficient learning environment. Steve was able to gather data from the past two school years that refuted this administrative perception by demonstrating there was a greater percentage of students without disabilities involved in serious behavioral incidents at school than his students.

A second strategy involves the persuader creating a discrepancy that can be brought to the attention of a resistant individual. Steve might employ this strategy by having other teachers who work with his students share their positive experiences with the principal.

A third persuasion strategy associated with the consistency approach involves the persuader linking the proposed change with the resolution of the discrepancy. As an example of this strategy, Steve could provide the school administration with professional literature indicating that developing positive alternatives to punitive disciplinary techniques (out-of-school suspension and expulsion) represents "best practices," and outlining for the administration how his disciplinary proposal reflects those best practices.

Perceptual Approach

The perceptual approach maintains that each person has a unique frame of reference based on his or her experiences and attitudes. An individual's frame of reference impacts his or her willingness to tolerate and adjust to change. Change requests that fall within a person's frame of reference and toleration levels are more likely to be accepted. Specific strategies associated with the perceptual approach include (1) relating the change request to others' knowledge and experience, (2) proposing changes within the value system of others, and (3) gaining a public commitment.

Using the Mary Kinney advocacy dilemma from Chapter 1, Mary could employ the first strategy—that is, relating the change request to others' knowledge and experience—during her presentation to the school board to request funds to hire a second speech and language clinician. In doing her research, Mary learned that several board members were business people who either owned their own small business or were employed by larger businesses. Mary used the background knowledge and experiences of the school board members to her advocacy advantage by asking the board to consider what would happen to their own businesses if they did not have enough employees to provide the services and products requested by their customers. The outcome would, obviously, be detrimental to any business. She could explain that the school district faced a similar problem by not having a second speech and language clinician to provide the necessary and required services to

eligible students. The detrimental impact to the school district as an organization and to its "customers" might be more easily recognized by the school board if Mary were to put the problem into a frame of reference that most of the board members could readily relate to.

Employing the second perceptual approach strategy, appealing to the value system of others, Mary must be able to demonstrate how critically important and fundamental speech and language services are for some students (appealing to administration and school board values of providing all students with, at least, basic educational services). She might also demonstrate how long-term educational costs could increase if students do not receive adequate early intervention services when needed (appealing to administration and school board values of efficiency and cost containment).

A third strategy associated with the perceptual approach is to gain a public commitment from resistant individuals. A public commitment significantly increases the likelihood that a change request will be implemented. This is an important tactic to remember when advocating for a particular change at a public forum or meeting.

Functional Approach

This approach to persuasion attempts to identify and address others' needs. To the extent that this can be accomplished, the persuader is likely to be successful. For example, as discussed previously in Chapter 10, Karen Snyder could increase her persuasiveness by identifying and addressing the general education teachers' strong needs for autonomy and decision making input into the IEP listed accommodations for students with disabilities in their classrooms. Karen can address the teachers' needs by involving them early in the IEP process, increasing their sense of ownership for the IEP decisions that are made, and obtaining and using the teachers' feedback on their satisfaction with IEP meetings and their level of decision making participation.

SUMMARY

There are many dimensions to special education advocacy work. Effective advocates must be able to recognize the type of advocacy that is required to address a specific situation and need. Direct services advocacy is required to initiate changes on behalf of an individual student with a disability. If an issue is adversely affecting a number of individuals with disabilities, initial steps may involve community advocacy efforts to publicize a particular concern and to educate the public on the need for change. When issues emerge due to inadequate legal protections for individuals with disabilities, advocates may need to organize and lobby for legislative changes. Legal advocacy, invoking the due process protections and procedures of federal and state laws, may be necessary when collaborative problem solving efforts fail. Systems advocacy may be required to respond to a broad problem involving organizational policies, rules, or practices that are detrimental to the best interests of individuals with disabilities. Finally, self-advocacy efforts instill a greater sense of independence and autonomy in students with disabilities by providing them with the skills and opportunities to participate in their own educational decision making.

This chapter also discussed some principles, decision-making processes, skills, and strategies necessary to engage in effective advocacy. Core principles for effective advocacy as well as the steps involved in the advocacy process were articulated. Finally, specific skills and strategies such as documentation, advocacy support for families, media tactics, and the effective use of persuasion techniques were reviewed. Indeed, an effective advocate must possess a diverse repertoire of skills and strategies to successfully navigate in the various advocacy venues.

CHAPTER 12

ETHICAL ANALYSIS SKILLS

*When an apparently good policy, perhaps even a law, tells us
to do something that our knowledge of the individual case
tells us is wrong, what is the right thing to do?*
—*James Kauffman (1992)*

Previous chapters have discussed requisite dispositions, knowledge bases, and skills to enable a special education professional to serve as an effective advocate for students with disabilities and their families. The implicit assumption related to these essential advocacy dispositions, knowledge bases, and skills is that special education professionals will always be able to identify clearly the "right course of action" to take on behalf of a student with a disability. However, as recognized by Kauffman in the above quote, determining the right course of action is often difficult and beset by legal and ethical ambiguities. Ethical reasoning and decision making involves thinking about the duties and obligations school professionals have to each other and to students and their families, determining what constitutes just or fair treatment of another individual, and articulating the rights of another person.

The objective of this chapter is to enhance the ethical competencies of school professionals. A list of relevant ethical competencies for school professionals is presented in Box 12.1. This list includes some competencies originally addressed in Chapter 3 (e.g., the relationship between law and ethics, professional ethical codes, a personal ethical framework, specific characteristics of ethical professionals). A competent school professional must be able to (1) articulate relevant principles on which to base ethical decision making and (2) employ a reasoned decision-making

process in rendering decisions when confronted with difficult moral choices. This chapter concentrates on these two topics of professional development as the foundation for ethical reasoning and decision making.

EXAMPLES INDICATING A NEED FOR ETHICAL REASONING AND DECISION MAKING

The need for ethical reasoning and decision making in special education arises when a professional encounters an ethical dilemma. An *ethical dilemma* is defined as "conflict(s) between two or more core values. They involve hard choices that force us to give up something important" (Kipnis, 1987, p. 28). Specific examples of special education ethical dilemmas are provided by Howe and Miramontes (1992) in several hypothetical case scenarios summarized here:

At a special education initial evaluation and eligibility determination meeting, a professional difference of opinion emerged as to whether a fifth-grade student qualified for special education services based on a learning disability. The general education teacher and the special education teacher both agreed that the student did not have a learning disability. The school psychologist, however, maintained that his findings indicated a learning disability and recommended that the student be placed in special

Box 12.1 _____

Advocacy Actions: Ethical Competencies for School Professionals

1. Competent school professionals are sensitive to the ethical aspects of their work and are aware that their actions have real consequences that can harm or help others.
2. Competent school professionals have a working knowledge of the content of professional ethical codes, professional standards, and legal principles relevant to providing educational services.
3. Competent school professionals are committed to proactive ethical thinking and conduct in an effort to anticipate and prevent problems from developing.
4. Competent school professionals are able to analyze the ethical issues in a situation and to systematically reason and problem solve.
5. Competent school professionals are aware of their feelings and values and the role their feelings and values play in ethical decision making.
6. Competent school professionals acknowledge the complexity of ethical decisions and accept some ambiguity and uncertainty. Further, they acknowledge and accept that there may be more than one appropriate course of action.
7. Competent school professionals possess the personal strength to make and implement tough decisions and accept responsibility for their actions.

Source: From *Ethics and Law for School Psychologists* by S. Jacob and T. Hartshorne, 1991, Brandon, VT: Clinical Psychology Publishing. Copyright 1991 by John Wiley & Sons. Reprinted by permission of John Wiley & Sons, Inc.

---

education. As the chair of the evaluation committee, the school psychologist was very forceful in pressing for his recommendation. In fact, the student's mother was being "pressured" by the school psychologist to consent to the special education placement. The school psychologist faced an ethical dilemma of arguing for what he believed was the best interests of the student versus maintaining integrity and parity in edu-

cational decision-making relations with parents and his colleagues.

In the interests of providing a student with emotional/behavioral disorders more positive peer social interactions and role models, a special education teacher placed the student into a general education classroom for a major portion of his school day. The student was extremely disruptive in the general education classroom, negatively affecting the learning experiences of the other students. The general and special education teachers had an ethical dilemma that involved evaluating legitimate, but competing interests: the best interests of the one student with emotional/behavioral disorders versus the best interests of the rest of the students in the general education classroom.

A ninth-grade student enrolled in a gifted and talented program began to engage in negative behaviors in and out of school. These behaviors included using drugs, rebelling against his parents, skipping school, and failing his classes. The district resources to support the gifted and talented program were limited, resulting in some very qualified students not receiving those services and support. The school staff were divided on how to handle this situation with the recalcitrant ninth-grade student. Some staff believed the gifted and talented program would eventually stimulate and sufficiently challenge the student so that the negative behaviors would dissipate. Other staff maintained that the student had forfeited his right to receive these limited services and a more deserving student should be entitled to enroll instead. The ethical dilemma concerned the value of giving a person a second chance versus the just and beneficial distribution of limited educational resources.

A veteran special education teacher agreed to transfer to a new teaching position the next school year. The new position involved developing a program for students with severe disabilities. The director of special education promised the teacher a budget to provide the new classroom with sufficient materials and supplies. At the start of the new school year, the teacher found her new program inadequately stocked with materials and supplies. After several failed attempts to solicit the necessary resources from the director of special education, the teacher sought the support of parents. Parents began contacting the school district administration demanding more resources for the new special education program. The special education teacher was reprimanded by the administration for "unprofessional" behavior in terms of involving parents in an issue that should have been handled internally. The special education teacher faced an ethical dilemma of "playing by the rules" and maintaining loyalty to her employer versus acting in her students' best interests.

A special education teacher, committed to advancing inclusion in her building, finally convinced a reluctant general education teacher to accept some of her students with disabilities into his classroom. The problem was that the general education teacher's perspective on inclusion permitted students with disabilities to be in the same classroom with general education students but the special education students were still, essentially, segregated as a group for social and academic activities. The special education teacher was hopeful that, with her support and encouragement, the general education teacher's attitudes and practices would change. In the meantime, the special education teacher must grapple with the dilemma of promoting her professional agenda and following the least restrictive environment mandate versus acting in the best interests of her students.

A fifth-grade student who was failing in general education classes was referred for a special education evaluation. After a comprehensive evaluation, the school team concluded that the student's academic problems were not attributable to any disability; thus, the student did not qualify for either special education services or Section 504 accommodations. However, all the school staff acknowledged that the student still required intensive and individualized support that could not be provided to him in the general education classroom. The school professionals had an ethical dilemma of potentially undermining the integrity of the special education eligibility determination process by labeling a student as disabled when there is no supporting evidence for that label versus engaging in preventive efforts to address the needs of a student now in the hope of forestalling an academic decline.

A special education teacher believed that one of her kindergarten students could benefit socially and academically from participation in the general education kindergarten classroom. When the teacher proposed this placement to the child's mother, the mother flatly refused the placement offer. The mother wanted her daughter to remain in the early childhood special education classroom on a full-time basis. The ethical tension in this case revolved around the teacher's sense of responsibility to act in the child's best interests and to abide by the least restrictive environment legal mandate versus the teacher's sense of responsibility to adhere to legal requirements that empower parents of children with disabilities to function as equal educational decision makers.

These hypothetical case scenarios provide a glimpse into the varied and complex situations and issues that embroil special education professionals in ethical dilemmas. The need for ethical reasoning and decision making in special education has been further conceptualized as involving four specific conditions (Paul, Gallagher, Kendrick, Thomas, & Young, 1992).

First, special education professionals encounter many decisions that involve shared values presumed to be held by all in determining options. Examples of broad ethical values or principles include (1) beneficence or responsible caring, (2) integrity in professional relationships, (3) responsibility to community and society, (4) the principle of benefit maximization, and (5) the principle of equal respect (Howe & Miramontes, 1992; Jacob & Hartshorne, 1991; Strike, Haller, & Soltis, 1998). Each of these ethical principles will be discussed in detail later in this chapter. In a situation involving a presumed ethical value or principle, ethical reasoning enhances decision making by identifying the relevant values involved and evaluating the merits of those values in relation to different options.

Special education professionals must be careful, however, because some educational decisions are mistakenly cast as ethical dilemmas. For example, issues of educational placement of students with disabilities are often approached as contingent on whether the school professionals or parents *value* inclusion or pull-out special education services. As noted by Howe and Miramontes, however, the ethical question about delivery of educational services depends more on a *factual* rather than a *value* issue. This "ethical dilemma" can and should be decided by empirical evidence on which educational delivery model (inclusion or pull-out services) is more beneficial for the student involved. Sometimes ethical dilemmas are mistakenly cast as value differences when the issue really is dependent on relevant facts.

A second condition requiring ethical reasoning involves situations when a professional must render a decision that is more than merely a reflection of his or her own personal beliefs. As observed by Howe and Miramontes (1992), "Special education has a particularly strong ethical mission, and decisions made through the special education process have lifelong ramifications for individuals" (p. 1). Because special education decisions have a profound effect on others' lives, the decision-making process must be more rigorous and bound by the use of sound ethical principles as guideposts over and above what would be required for personal decisions. That is, decisions that profoundly affect others ought to be based on reasoning and ethical decision making that is free from *personal* values, prejudice, benefit, and factual error.

The third condition necessitating ethical reasoning and decision making has evolved from the difficulty of making moral choices when confronted with so many diverse cultural and religious beliefs and values that conflict. For example, some families, for religious beliefs, refuse invasive medical procedures for their children. Other families, as a result of cultural values, place more or less emphasis on competition or collaboration in their children's educational programs.

Now, more than at any other time in our country's educational history, school professionals are likely to encounter conflict with families revolving around different religious or cultural values. As a society, we celebrate diversity from a cultural enrichment perspective, but diversity in cultural and religious beliefs and values makes it difficult, at times, to achieve a consensus on moral questions. The value of ethical reasoning and decision making in this condition is not in guaranteeing consensus decision making. The value of ethical reasoning lies in acknowledging and explicitly articulating principles on which difficult decisions are made and consciously considering diverse perspectives prior to reaching any decision.

The final condition compelling a reasoned approach to ethical decision making encompasses situations where an opportunity exists to improve circumstances for individuals with disabilities by basing decisions on what *ought* to be as opposed to what *is*. Each of the school professionals in the advocacy scenarios from Chapter 1 faced this condition and is trying to change what *is* to what *ought* to be for students with disabilities. Sound ethical reasoning can illuminate the underlying principles on which to base arguments for changing the status quo.

RELEVANT PRINCIPLES FOR ETHICAL DECISION MAKING IN SPECIAL EDUCATION

As briefly discussed in Chapter 3, the law provides some standards to govern professional ethical decision making. However, legal principles are not always solely sufficient in resolving ethical dilemmas. In some instances, professionals must be able to turn to relevant ethical principles for moral guidance. This section articulates several principle-based theories (referred to as a *rational approach* to moral decision making in Chapter 3). These theories identify some relevant guiding principle and apply it to determine the ethically right decision in a particular situation. Principle-based ethical theories are in contrast to virtue-based theories, which "identify the characteristics of the ethically virtuous person and then determine the morally right choice in a given situation by asking how the ethically virtuous person would deliberate in that situation" (Howe & Miramontes, 1992, p. 12).

As noted in Chapter 3 one presumed advantage of a virtue-based approach to ethical decision making is that it is less abstract and more specific to a given situation than principle-based ethical theories, which apply universal principles to similar cases. Noddings's (1984, 1993) advocacy of a caring approach to ethical decision making exemplifies this virtue-based approach. Further guidance for employing a virtue-based approach to ethical decision making was provided in Chapter 3 along with a discussion of characteristics of ethical educational professionals (e.g., discretion, candor, competence, fairness, avoidance of dual relationships, protection, allowing autonomy, diligence, and respectfulness).

This chapter provides special education professionals with an alternative to the virtue-based approach to ethical decision making outlined in Chapter 3, without arguing for the supremacy of either approach. In fact, as will be discussed later in this chapter, the choice of either approach should be primarily dependent on the ethical circumstances at issue and the closeness of the relationship between the decision maker and individuals affected by the decision. Principle-based ethical theories identify relevant ethical principles and evaluate ethical choices in terms of how well specific decisions comport with those principles. The following ethical principles will be briefly discussed: (1) beneficence or responsible caring, (2) integrity in professional relationships, (3) respon-

sibility to community and society, (4) the principle of benefit maximization, and (5) the principle of equal respect (Howe & Miramontes, 1992; Jacob & Hartshorne, 1991; Strike et al., 1998).

Beneficence or Responsible Caring

This ethical principle obligates special education professionals to engage in actions that are beneficial to others, or, at the very least, that do no harm (Jacob & Hartshorne, 1991). This principle fosters professional decision making based on the "best interests of the child" as the ethical standard (Bowe, 1995). Jacob and Hartshorne have maintained that actions are likely to benefit others or be in the child's best interests when professionals practice within the boundaries of their competence and accept responsibility for their actions.

The notions of benefit to others or best interests of the child is reflected in the Council for Exceptional Children's (CEC) Code of Ethics (CEC, 1983, p. 205) (e.g., "I. Special education professionals are committed to developing the highest educational and quality of life potential of exceptional individuals"; and "III. Special educational professionals engage in professional activities which benefit exceptional individuals, their families, other colleagues, students, or research subjects"). Similarly, the responsibility of professionals to engage in competent practices is promoted by the CEC Code of Ethics (e.g., "II. Special education professionals promote and maintain a high level of competence and integrity in practicing their profession"; and "V. Special education professionals strive to advance their knowledge and skills regarding the education of exceptional individuals"). Competence was also one of the characteristics of ethical school professionals discussed in chapter 3.

Of what decision-making value is this ethical principle of beneficence or responsible caring for a special education professional faced with an ethical dilemma? Consider the Mary Kinney advocacy scenario from Chapter 1. As the only speech and language clinician employed by a small but rapidly growing rural school district, Mary is faced with some choices in responding to her dilemma of how to manage all of the newly referred students who qualify for speech and language services when she already has a full caseload. Clearly, one choice Mary could make would be to deny services to all the newly referred students. This decision, however, would certainly not benefit the students who are denied a service that they need and for which they qualify.

Another possible decision would have Mary assume the extra responsibility of trying to serve all of the newly referred students while, at the same time, maintaining her current caseload. The ethical limitation of this course of action is that it is unlikely that Mary would be able to provide her speech and language expertise in a competent and beneficial manner to all students when she is overloaded with too many students to serve. The ethical decision that comports with this principle is for Mary to advocate for additional speech and language services to benefit both the current students and the newly referred students who qualify for those services. In her advocacy efforts, Mary should be able to articulate relevant legal and ethical principles that advance her cause.

Integrity in Professional Relationships

There are several important components of this principle of maintaining integrity in professional relationships with both colleagues, families, and students. First, as discussed in Chapter 3, candor or honesty is essential in forming trusting and collaborative relationships with professional colleagues and parents. Second, Chapter 3 also highlighted the importance of professional discretion in safeguarding confidential information. Third, ethical professionals preserve the integrity of their professional relationships by disclosing potential conflicts of interests.

As an example, if Mary Kinney, in the advocacy scenario about insufficient speech and language services for increasing numbers of students, decides to inform the parents of those students of their legal rights, Mary must also disclose to the parents that she faces a potential conflict of interest (see Chapter 2). Mary may still decide to challenge the school district in not meeting its legal obligation to provide appropriate educational services to all eligible students with disabilities, but she must acknowledge that, at some point during her advocacy, she may face a conflict of interest in adhering to the dictates of her employer versus fulfilling her advocacy role and responsibility. In this case, parents must be informed of this dual role conflict of interest so that they are in an informed position to evaluate all of Mary's advocacy actions on their behalf. Finally, this principle of integrity in professional relationships also suggests that special education professionals must be honest about their competencies. When a professional does not possess the requisite expertise to provide a particular educational service, that professional is ethically bound to inform any individual impacted by such services.

The CEC Standards for Professional Practice provide further ethical guidance for this principle of integrity in professional relationships with parents. The following standards apply to parent relationships:

- *1.4.1 Professionals seek to develop relationships with parents based on mutual respect for their roles in achieving benefits for the exceptional person. Special education professionals:*
  - *1.4.1.1 Develop effective communication with parents, avoiding technical terminology, using the primary language of the home, and other modes of communication when appropriate.*
  - *1.4.1.2 Seek and use parents' knowledge and expertise in planning, conducting, and evaluating special education and related services for exceptional persons.*
  - *1.4.1.3 Maintain communications between parents and professionals with appropriate respect for privacy and confidentiality.*

- *1.4.1.4 Extend opportunities for parent education, utilizing accurate information and professional methods.*
- *1.4.1.5 Inform parents of the educational rights of their children and of any proposed or actual practices which violate those rights.*
- *1.4.1.6 Recognize and respect cultural diversities which exist in some families with exceptional persons.*
- *1.4.1.7 Recognize that the relationships of home and community environmental conditions affects the behavior and outlook of the exceptional person. (CEC, 1983, p. 207)*

Integrity in professional relationships is crucial in several of the advocacy scenarios from Chapter 1. For instance, Steve Kern has several ethical obligations to other professionals: (1) to develop more positive attitudes among his school administration toward students with emotional/behavioral disorders, (2) to cooperate with other community agencies to improve transitional and vocational services for students, and (3) to provide consultation support to other school staff on more positive behavior management techniques and procedures.

In the Karen Snyder advocacy situation, as building principal, Karen must candidly inform the general and special education teachers of their joint obligations to implement all IEP accommodations for students with disabilities attending general education classes. Further, Karen must assist the school staff in acknowledging their need for assistance in competently performing their professional duties. For example, the general education teachers will most likely require assistance from the special education teachers on how to make appropriate behavioral, instructional, and evaluative accommodations for students with disabilities. In turn, the special education teachers may require support and assistance from the general education teachers in understanding the scope and sequence of the curricula in certain subject areas.

Finally, in the Miguel Hernandez scenario, Miguel must exercise these ethical obligations to Mrs. Ortiz and his school colleagues: (1) assist his colleagues in developing more effective commu-

nication and decision-making functions with Mrs. Ortiz, (2) assist his colleagues in more effectively utilizing Mrs. Ortiz's knowledge and expertise in IEP decision making, (3) inform Mrs. Ortiz of her legal rights to equally participate in educational decision making, (4) expand training opportunities for Mrs. Ortiz to enhance her skills in participating as an equal educational decision maker at IEP meetings, and (5) assist his colleagues in recognizing and respecting the cultural values of the Ortiz family.

Responsibility to Community and Society

The ethical principle of responsibility to community and society extends beyond specific moral obligations to individual students to encompass broader duties of enhancing services and rights for all individuals with disabilities. In this regard, the ethical principle of responsibility to community and society is compatible with community, legislative, and systems advocacy efforts (see Chapter 11). There are several relevant facets of this ethical principle. First, special education professionals have an ethical obligation to promote the general welfare of all students with disabilities. This moral responsibility is reflected in the CEC Code of Ethics: "VII. Special education professionals seek to uphold and improve where necessary the laws, regulations, and policies governing the delivery of special education and related services and the practice of their profession" (CEC, 1983, p. 205). Further, all of the CEC Standards for Professional Practice pertaining to advocacy seek to advance the general welfare of students with disabilities.

Second, professionals demonstrate responsibility to community and society by enhancing the public's trust and confidence in the profession of special education. The CEC Standards for Professional Practice acknowledges this ethical principle in these particular standards:

- *3.1.1 Special education professionals assume responsibility for participating in professional organizations and adherence to the standards and codes of ethics of those organizations.*

- *3.1.3 Special education professionals refrain from using professional relationships with students and parents for personal advantage.*
- *3.1.4 Special education professionals take an active position in the regulation of the profession through use of appropriate procedures for bringing about changes. (CEC, 1983, p. 208)*

A third important facet of a special education professional's ethical responsibility to community and society is to monitor and intervene when other professionals engage in illegal or unethical conduct toward individuals with disabilities and their families. This ethical responsibility is revealed in the CEC Code of Ethics: "VIII. Special education professionals do not condone or participate in unethical or illegal acts, nor violate professional standards adopted by the Delegate Assembly of CEC" (CEC, 1983, p. 205). A specific CEC Standard addresses this ethical duty: "1.2.1.4 Take adequate measures to discourage, prevent, and intervene when a colleague's behavior is perceived as being detrimental to exceptional persons" (CEC, 1983, p. 206).

A final aspect of this ethical principle requires professionals to contribute to the knowledge base of special education in order to improve educational services for students with disabilities. Evidence of this ethical responsibility is displayed in CEC Standard: "3.1.5 Special education professionals initiate support and/or participate in research related to the education of exceptional persons with the aim of improving the quality of educational services, increasing the accountability of programs, and generally benefitting exceptional persons" (CEC, 1983, pp. 208–209).

In the advocacy scenarios from Chapter 1, each of the professionals facing an ethical dilemma could resort to the principle of responsibility to community and society for justification for his or her advocacy efforts. For example, Mary Kinney, Steve Kern, and Karen Snyder are seeking to improve educational services and practices for all students with disabilities. Miguel Hernandez, in his attempts to enhance Mrs. Ortiz's level of input and participation in IEP decisions, is enhancing public trust and confidence in special education procedures. Both Miguel Hernandez and Mary Kinney are intervening in situations where other school professionals have engaged in legally and/or ethically questionable conduct. Finally, Steve Kern's and Karen Snyder's advocacy is intended to improve educational services for students with disabilities by enhancing other professionals' knowledge and skills in employing positive behavior management techniques and developing and implementing accommodations for students with disabilities attending general education classes respectively.

Principle of Benefit Maximization

The principle of benefit maximization, also referred to as *utilitarianism* or *consequentialism,* is primarily associated with the moral philosophy of John Stuart Mill (Howe & Miramontes, 1992; Strike et al., 1998). This principle argues that the consequences of a decision or action are the sole basis for determining morally correct behavior (Greenspan & Negron, 1994). The morally correct or just decision or action is the one that results in the greatest good or benefit for the greatest number of people (Strike et al., 1998). As noted by Howe and Miramontes, "The intuitive idea behind utilitarianism is by no means strange. It fits perfectly well with a large majority of common ethical beliefs. Rules in schools against cheating, stealing, disturbing others, destroying books, and so on, can easily be justified in terms of the belief that such prohibitions maximize the good" (p. 13).

There have been, however, several prominent criticisms levied against the principle of benefit maximization. One criticism surrounds the difficulty of determining what counts as a benefit or good (Strike et al., 1998). Most philosophers have cited happiness or human welfare as typical examples of benefits or goods to be maximized. However, these are vague standards on which to base educational policy and decision making. Another criticism relates to the difficulty in calculating what constitutes the greatest good for the greatest number of people. As Howe and Miramontes (1992) argued, it would be difficult to calculate whether an educational policy which provided for more resources for the education of students with disabilities or a policy which committed more resources to gifted and talented students produced the greatest good.

A third criticism of consequentialism is that the basic rights of a minority could be sacrificed if the majority experienced a greater overall increase in their "good." The vulnerability of those individuals in the minority, such as students with disabilities, was recognized by Scruggs (1993): "Since schools tend to operate on utilitarian lines, the role of the special educator is often one of advocating for justice in the individual case in an environment that is not predisposed to reason along these lines" (p. 444).

Finally, the principle of benefit maximization has been criticized because it sometimes justifies results that seem intuitively unfair (Strike et al., 1998). For example, the principle of benefit maximization could be used to justify greater educational expenditures for gifted and talented students as opposed to students with disabilities on the theory that gifted and talented students are more likely to contribute to overall societal welfare and progress than students with disabilities. Therefore, gifted and talented programs demand a greater share of limited educational resources. Although the principle of benefit maximization could justify such a conclusion, the moral sensibilities of many people would be offended by this outcome.

As an example of ethical decision making employing the principle of benefit maximization, consider one of the hypothetical cases cited at the beginning of this chapter. This ethical dilemma involved the placement of a highly disruptive student with an emotional/behavioral disorder into a general education classroom. The disruptive student was having a detrimental impact on the educational experiences of the other students while consuming an inordinate amount of the classroom teacher's time and energy. In the analysis of this case, Howe and Miramontes (1992) concluded that the interests of the one disruptive student would yield to the interests of the majority of students in the general education class. That is, a greater good

would accrue to the majority of students by having the disruptive student placed in a self-contained special education program. "Under these conditions, where resource limitations entail that *someone's* interests have to be sacrificed, it appears there is no escape from endorsing a utilitarian brand of reasoning" (Howe & Miramontes, 1992, p. 44).

Principle of Equal Respect

The principle of equal respect, also known as *nonconsequentialism,* maintains that ethically correct actions or decisions must respect the equal worth of individuals (Howe & Miramontes, 1992; Strike et al., 1998). This principle is embodied in the Golden Rule: Treat others as you would want them to treat you. Strike and colleagues (1998) have identified three key features of the principle of equal respect: (1) People should be treated as ends rather than means. This notion requires that other people should not be viewed as simply a means to advance another person's goals; ethical decision making must consider and respect the goals of other individuals. (2) People are regarded as free and rational, which requires that they be accorded freedom of choice. (3) All people, regardless of differences, have equal value and enjoy the same basic rights. It is important to note that this idea does not mean that relevant differences between individuals (e.g., a disabling condition) should be ignored in deciding how to treat them.

Significant differences exist between the principle of equal respect and the principle of benefit maximization. First and foremost, with the principle of equal respect, the consequences of an action or decision are not always decisive in terms of determining the ethically correct course of action. The decisive factor, according to nonconsequentialism, is that the action or decision must respect the dignity and worth of the individuals involved. In contrast to consequentialism, according to the principle of equal respect, ethical decisions do not always lead to the most efficient use of resources by achieving the greatest good for the greatest number of people.

Second, the principle of equal respect bestows more concern about the welfare of the most disadvantaged individuals than utilitarian decision making typically produces. Third, the principle of equal respect avoids some of the problematic features of the principle of benefit maximization by not requiring that ethical decision makers define what constitutes a measure of the greatest "good" nor that consequences of decisions be known before a decision can be rendered. For these reasons, most educational ethicists argue that the principle of benefit maximization should be subordinate to the principle of equal respect as moral guidance in ethical dilemmas (Greenspan & Negron, 1994; Howe & Miramontes, 1992; Strike et al., 1998).

As a contrast to utilitarian decision making, the principle of equal respect will be applied to the same ethical dilemma involving the placement of a highly disruptive student with an emotional/behavioral disorder into a general education classroom. As previously indicated, the principle of benefit maximization (i.e., utilitarianism) would likely produce a decision to place the disruptive student in a self-contained special education because a greater good (i.e., improved learning opportunities for the other students in the general education class) would be achieved by such a decision. Applying the principle of equal respect to this dilemma would probably produce the same outcome (i.e., removal of the disruptive student) but for different reasons. Instead of reliance on a calculation of what decision produces the greatest good for the greatest number of people, the principle of equal respect would address the following reasons in rendering a decision.

First, the disruptive student is currently probably not experiencing much educational benefit in the general education classroom. In fact, a placement in an educational setting that could better attend to his behavioral needs and teach him more appropriate social skills would be treating him with more dignity and respect.

Second, the disruptive student would have a better chance of an equal opportunity to an appropriate education if his special needs are fully recognized and remediated by providing intensive social skills instruction in a special education program.

Third, the decision to remove the disruptive student from the general education class must be made in a fair manner at an IEP meeting according to due process procedures. As noted by Strike and colleagues (1998), the concept of due process, with its concern for establishing fair procedures which promote rational decision making, is more closely aligned with the principle of equal respect than the principle of benefit maximization, which is more concerned with the actual decision rendered and its consequences.

In this case, a reasoned decision according to due process procedures would (1) allow for input from all affected parties in the decision on whether to remove the disruptive student; (2) apply a standard of what is in the best interests of the disruptive student and the other students in the general education class; (3) provide objective behavioral data that have been systematically collected over time to reveal the performance of the disruptive student and other students in the general education class; and (4) justify the correct decision on the best interests standard, which has a rational connection to the legitimate educational purpose of adequately addressing all students' needs. A fair consideration of all relevant interests of the people involved would acknowledge that the legitimate interests of the disruptive student and the other students in the general education class are best served by a removal decision.

The Coexistence of Principle-Based and Virtue-Based Approaches to Ethical Reasoning

Chapter 3 advanced a virtue-based perspective, an ethic of caring, as an appropriate framework for ethical reasoning and decision making. This chapter has offered another perspective, that of principle-based theories, as a guide for ethical reasoning and decision making. Is it possible and desirable that special education professionals encompass both principle-based and virtue-based perspectives in their ethical reasoning and decision making? Effective advocates possess multiple and diverse tools in their advocacy arsenal. The art of effective advocacy involves knowing what tool to employ in what situation. Both ethical reasoning perspectives, then, can be useful to the special education professional in determining morally correct actions.

Principle-based theories identify relevant ethical principles and evaluate ethical choices in terms of how well each option conforms with those principles (Howe & Miramontes, 1992). Principle-based theories are more abstract than a virtue-based approach because the guiding principles must be *universal,* applicable to all similar cases, and the decision maker must be *impartial* in applying "the principles indifferently so that in making ethical choices, personal histories and family and community relationships are pushed into the background or altogether ignored" (Howe & Miramontes, 1992, p. 18). Special education professionals will encounter situations where they must be able to apply broad ethical principles universally and impartially to all individuals similarly situated. For example, a special education professional would be deemed unethical if she promoted equality of educational opportunity for some students while denying this same right to other students.

A virtue-based approach to ethical reasoning identifies relevant characteristics of the ethically virtuous individual and evaluates ethical choices in terms of how each decision embodies the deliberations of the ethically virtuous individual (Howe & Miramontes, 1992). A virtue-based approach is a more particular and personal model of ethical reasoning. This perspective forsakes universal principles when the reasoned outcome utilizing principle-based perspectives to a particular dilemma seems intuitively unjust. Virtue-based theories maintain that the impartial application of universal principles often "distorts ethical deliberations, because individuals, when they are confronted with ethical choices, can (and should) neither forget who they are and where they come from, nor ignore the special attachments and obligations they have to family and community" (Howe & Miramontes, 1992, p. 18). In this sense, one would expect par-

ents to adhere to a virtue-based approach as guidance for ethical decision making. That is, abstract ethical principles should never circumvent the welfare of individuals with whom a caring relationship exists.

Howe and Miramontes (1992) argued that the appropriate ethical reasoning perspective to adopt in a given situation, principle-based or virtue-based theories, depends on (1) the nature of the ethical dilemma and (2) whether there exists a close and personal caring relationship between the decision maker and affected individuals. As recognized by Howe and Miramontes, special education professionals are often caught between these two ethical reasoning perspectives because they have commitments to both the general mission of special education, and thus must apply universal and impartial ethical principles in the treatment of all students, and also to individual students, where a personal caring relationship has developed, demanding a more virtue-based approach to ethical decision making.

The compromise between principle-based and virtue-based approaches to ethical reasoning and decision making is found in the role-related obligations of special education professionals (Howe & Miramontes, 1992). Ethical special education professionals must incorporate the characteristics of the virtuous professional in ethical deliberations while maintaining adherence to relevant ethical principles that can be consistently and impartially applied. In Box 12.2, the Steve Kern advocacy scenario from Chapter 1 is used as an example of a special education professional employing a principle-based approach to address one dilemma and a virtue-based ethical reasoning approach to use as a model in resolving a second situation.

A MODEL FOR ETHICAL REASONING AND DECISION MAKING

Advocates who encounter ethical dilemmas should be motivated to take the *right, fair,* and *just* action, not merely the most expedient or least trouble making action (Strike et al., 1998). In difficult ethical dilemmas, special education professionals

Box 12.2 _____

Advocacy Anecdote

As an ethical special education professional and advocate for his students, Steve Kern faces a dilemma in terms of how to handle the following inadequate educational services for his students with emotional/behavioral disorders:

- Vocational and career education services
- Nonparticipation of community agency personnel in transition planning
- Use of excessively punitive disciplinary interventions (e.g., out-of-school suspensions)

A further complication is that one of Steve's 16-year-old students has recently sustained a severe traumatic brain injury, which requires, in Steve's professional opinion, a highly structured residential program consisting of education in basic living skills, socialization, and behavior therapy.

As a relatively new employee to the district who has inherited these problems, Steve is rightfully concerned about "challenging his school administration and these practices" without a sound justification for his actions. A justification for his advocacy actions can be found in principle-based and virtue-based approaches to ethical reasoning and decision making.

First, employing a principle-based perspective to ethical reasoning, Steve identifies the following principles as relevant to his dilemma: (1) integrity in professional relationships, (2) responsibility to community and society, and (3) the principle of equal respect. In terms of the principle of integrity in professional relationships, Steve concludes that he is ethically obligated to foster better cooperation and relations with community agency personnel, to enhance the attitudes of school administrators toward his students with emotional/behavioral disorders, and to provide consultation support to school administrators and staff on positive behavior management procedures. In regard to the principle of responsibility to community and service, Steve recognizes his ethical duty to attempt to improve the quality of vocational and transition services for his students and to intervene when other professionals' behavior (i.e., re-

peatedly suspending his students from school) is detrimental to his students. Finally, Steve reasons that the principle of equal respect requires that his students not be treated as "second-class citizens" but be treated with the same dignity and respect that all students deserve.

Second, Steve enjoys a close relationship with the student who has sustained a traumatic brain injury. To meet this student's educational needs, Steve is best served by not searching for some universal principle that can be impartially applied to this situation. Instead, Steve and his student are best served by asking what a virtuous professional would do in this particular circumstance. The deliberation of an ethically virtuous professional would likely involve these considerations: (1) A virtuous professional would act with *candor* by recommending at an IEP meeting whatever educational service that was necessary, regardless of cost, to provide a student with an appropriate education. In this case, Steve would recommend a residential program. (2) A virtuous professional would display *competence* by acknowledging his own limitations and referring a student to appropriately trained professionals who can provide the necessary services. (Steve lacks the training, experience, and resources to adequately address this student's needs.) (3) A virtuous professional *protects* his students from harm. In this situation, Steve recognizes that the student with the traumatic brain injury is likely to regress without appropriate educational services. (4) A virtuous professional is *diligent* by going beyond the minimum requirements for his job. Steve displayed this virtue through his relentless investigation of appropriate residential programs for students with needs similar to his student with a traumatic brain injury.

Steve Kern has fulfilled his role-related obligations as an ethical professional by identifying relevant principles and impartially applying those principles to the educational circumstances of his students. Further, Steve has exemplified the behavior of an ethically virtuous professional through his reasoning process and advocacy actions on behalf of his student with a traumatic brain injury.

can expect that their decisions and actions will be questioned and challenged. Use of a systematic model or process for ethical reasoning and decision making will produce several beneficial results for school professionals, such as (1) more responsible moral decisions, (2) a better understanding of the relevant issues, and (3) an ability to describe how a decision was reached (Tymchuk, 1986). This systematic ethical reasoning process will not guarantee that others will automatically agree with the decision, but at least the decision maker will be afforded some protection when difficult decisions come under the scrutiny of others.

This section presents a model for ethical reasoning and decision making. This model is adapted from the work of several researchers (Howe &

Miramontes, 1992; Jacob & Hartshorne, 1991; Paul et al., 1992; Reynolds, 1996; Schloss & Henley, 1994) and is outlined in Box 12.3.

To illustrate the application of this model for ethical reasoning and decision making, reference will be made to one of the hypothetical cases from Howe and Miramontes (1992) which was briefly introduced at the beginning of the chapter. The illustrative case involves a special education teacher struggling with implementing inclusion in her building but concerned that one of the general education teachers who has agreed to accept students with disabilities into his classroom is not truly "including" the students with disabilities, and that those students might not be receiving an appropriate educational experience as a result. The purpose

---

Box 12.3 _____

Advocacy Actions: A Model for Ethical Reasoning and Decision Making (Howe & Miramontes, 1992; Jacob & Hartshorne, 1991; Paul et al., 1992; Reynolds, 1996; Schloss & Henley, 1994)

1. Describe the problem/dilemma with objective facts.
   - Are there any related problems?
   - Are there any specific professional concerns?
   - Is additional information needed?
2. Define the potential ethical and/or legal issues involved.
   - Are there any functional issues?
3. Identify potential value conflicts.
4. Consult ethical and legal guidelines for standards in resolving each issue.
   - What are the relevant legal guidelines?
   - Are there any relevant professional organization (e.g., code of ethics) standards?
   - What personal ethical principles apply?
5. Evaluate the rights, responsibilities, and welfare of all affected individuals.
6. Generate a list of alternative decisions for resolving the issues.
   - Brainstorm potential solutions.
   - Identify the necessary steps for implementing each decision.
   - Consider any potential problems in implementing each decision.

7. Identify the short- and long-term consequences of each alternative decision.
   - How will each decision affect other individuals?
   - Can the perspectives of others be accommodated while still acting ethically?
8. Conduct a risk-benefit analysis by considering any evidence that potential consequences or benefits from each alternative decision are likely to occur.
9. Make a decision by choosing one of the alternatives.
   - Delineate the reasons that support the chosen alternative over the rejected alternatives.
   - Check the chosen alternative with intuitive moral judgment.
10. Implement the chosen deliberative decision.
11. Evaluate the outcomes of the implemented decision.
    - Has the decision resulted in the desired functional outcome for the student(s)?
    - Has the decision resulted in the desired ethical outcome?
    - Are personal ethical standards/principles influenced by the outcome?

of this case analysis is not to suggest all possible issues, decisions, considerations, or outcomes. Instead, this case analysis merely illustrates a model that can produce more thoroughly reasoned ethical decisions. This case and analysis will be presented from the perspective of the special education teacher as the professional confronted with an ethical dilemma who wants to make a reasoned ethical decision.

1. Describe the problem/dilemma with objective facts.

The first step in systematic ethical reasoning is to articulate clearly all of the relevant and objective facts of the dilemma. It is imperative to distinguish objective facts from subjective feelings and opinions at this stage. The relevant objective facts in this case are as follows:

- Jane Rollins is a special education resource room teacher at a junior high school. She works with students with learning disabilities and emotional/behavioral disorders.
- Ms. Rollins is eager to promote the inclusion of five of her students into general education classrooms but no teachers have agreed to work with students with disabilities in their classrooms. The prevailing attitude among the school staff is that "problem students" belong in special education classes, not general education classrooms.
- The building principal, Mr. Jones, is not willing to interfere in student placement issues, believing that these decisions are prerogatives of the teachers and that a principal cannot effectively order or force inclusion on any teacher.
- Mr. Jones did discuss the issue of inclusion with one of the new social studies teachers, Mr. Young. Although Mr. Young was not enthusiastic about inclusion, he somewhat reluctantly told Mr. Jones that Ms. Rollins could work with her special education students in the back of his classroom.
- Ms. Rollins explained the concept of inclusion to Mr. Young but he was only willing to allow the special education students into his classroom if (1) Ms. Rollins assumed full responsibility for working with them, (2) Mr. Young would not have to change his grading standards, (3) Ms. Rollins would be responsible for grading the special education students in Mr. Young's class, and (4) Ms. Rollins would work with one of Mr. Young's more difficult students in the group of special education students.

Ms. Rollins has some related problems in this ethical dilemma. First, she has very little administrative support to advance new educational initiatives in her building. Second, there appears to be a serious misunderstanding or lack of knowledge about inclusionary practices and team teaching by some of the general education teachers—Mr. Young included. Third, Ms. Rollins has a concern about not alienating nor antagonizing her general education teacher colleagues by pushing inclusion too forcefully on them.

Additional information would be helpful to Ms. Rollins in deciding how to address this ethical dilemma. Are there any teachers in the building who are supportive of inclusion or who are at least willing to make a good-faith effort to try it? Is Mr. Young an extremely rigid teacher or is it possible that his attitudes and practices could change with some more encouragement by Ms. Rollins? How many parents of special and general education students are in favor of inclusion? Are there any administrators in the central district office who support more inclusion of students with disabilities into general education classrooms? These are some of the critical questions that Ms. Rollins should ponder as she gathers more information.

2. Define the potential ethical and/or legal issues involved.

This hypothetical case poses several ethical questions, including: (1) Will promoting inclusion and the least restrictive environment principle serve the "best interests" of the students with disabilities? (2) What constitutes an equal educational opportunity for the students with disabilities? (3) Is the responsibility to work on behalf of students with disabilities only an obligation owned by special education professionals or is it a total school obligation shared by all staff?

In addition to identifying relevant ethical and legal issues, it is important to address functional issues. As Schloss and Henley (1994) noted, "Functional aspects may be viewed as matters of expedience, convenience, or utility" (p. 300). For example, a functional issue in this case is whether Ms. Rollins has any support in her building, in the district, or from parents in advancing inclusion for students with disabilities. This functional issue should be factored into the decision-making equation. Without this kind of practical consideration, ethical decision making may, in some cases, become too abstract and divorced from reality constraints.

3. Identify potential value conflicts.

There appears to be a value conflict between Ms. Rollins, who supports equal respect for all students, and many of the other teachers who, apparently, place a high value on benefit maximization. There also is a value conflict over the presumed advantages of team teaching. Ms. Rollins values collaborative relationships with other teachers; Mr. Young and many other general education teachers in the building apparently prefer to teach in a traditional and isolated work environment. A third potential value conflict exists between Ms. Rollins and her principal, Mr. Jones. Ms. Rollins values strong administrative leadership; Mr. Jones values a laissez-faire leadership style. Finally, a potential conflict of values exists between Ms. Rollins, who values risk taking and changing the status quo, versus Mr. Young, Mr. Jones, and many other teachers in the building, who seem to value the status quo.

4. Consult ethical and legal guidelines for standards in resolving each issue.

Legal guidelines.   To expedite this analysis and discussion, the remaining steps in the model for ethical reasoning enunciated in Box 12.3 will be demonstrated in terms of the first ethical issue identified in step 2: *Will promoting inclusion and the least restrictive environment principle serve the "best interests" of the students with disabilities?* The least restrictive environment (LRE) principle requires that "to the maximum extent appropriate, children with disabilities . . . are educated with children who are not disabled, and that special classes, separate schooling, or other removal of children with disabilities from the regular educational environment occurs only when the nature or severity of the disability is such that education in regular classes with the use of supplementary aids and services cannot be achieved satisfactorily" (IDEA, 20 U.S.C. Sec. 1412). (See Chapter 5 for a discussion of the least restrictive environment legal principle.)

In addition to the LRE principle, one must consider the application of the appropriate education (FAPE) legal principle, as well. The FAPE principle takes priority over the LRE principle in situations where the student with disabilities cannot receive an appropriate education in the general education classroom. An appropriate education has been interpreted by the *Rowley* case and subsequent cases to mean that special education services must confer meaningful benefits to the student, not merely minimal or trivial benefits.

Professional organization ethical standards. The CEC Code of Ethics and Standards for Professional Practice provide some relevant guidelines for contemplating a course of action regarding this issue of LRE and the best interests of the students. For example, both the CEC Code and the Standards contain mandates that obligate special education professionals (1) to develop the highest educational potential in their students, (2) to create safe and effective learning environments, (3) to uphold the laws and policies governing the delivery of special education services, and (4) to encourage other professionals to improve special education services to students with disabilities.

Personal ethical principles.   The beneficence or responsible caring principle addresses the ethical obligation of acting in a student's best interests and the responsibility to provide competent professional services. Second, the integrity in professional relationships principle offers some guidance relevant to this dilemma by requiring candor and honesty in establishing collaborative professional relationships, by disclosing possible conflicts of interests (e.g., Does Ms. Rollins have a conflict of interest in her personal agenda to promote inclusion versus ensuring the best interests of her students?), and by honestly discussing one's professional competencies (e.g., Is Mr. Young being honest with Ms. Rollins, in respect to his reasons, for his reluctance to truly include the students with disabilities into his general education classroom?)

Third, the principle of responsibility to community and society requires Ms. Rollins to (1) promote the general welfare of her students, (2) monitor for inappropriate placements and services, and (3) intervene when a colleague's conduct is detrimental to students with disabilities. Fourth, the principle of benefit maximization would require Ms. Rollins to consider what action brings about the greatest good for the greatest number of people. Finally, in contemplating the application of the principle of equal respect in this case, Ms. Rollins would need to decide what action accords her students with disabilities equal worth and dignity. How would Ms. Rollins want to be treated if she were in the same situation as her students?

5. Evaluate the rights, responsibilities, and welfare of all affected individuals.

Some of the potential rights, responsibilities, and welfare of the individuals involved in this dilemma are briefly articulated in Box 12.4. These include (1) students with disabilities facing possible inclusion into Mr. Young's general education classroom, (2) students without disabilities in Mr. Young's classroom, (3) Ms Rollins, (4) Mr. Young, and (5) Mr. Jones. Arguably, this evaluation step could involve other individuals (e.g., parents of these students, other special education teachers, other general education teachers), but for reasons of brevity, discussion will focus on the previously mentioned individuals. This step in the ethical reasoning model helps the decision maker identify relevant interests and obligations of all affected parties before making a decision.

6. Generate a list of alternative decisions for resolving the issues.

Will promoting inclusion and the least restrictive environment principle serve the "best interests" of the students with disabilities? Some possible decisions to resolve this issue include (1) placing the students with disabilities into Mr. Young's general education classroom, (2) keeping the students in the special education resource room with Ms. Rollins, or (3) keeping the students in the resource room while Ms. Rollins continues to cultivate more support and awareness for inclusion in the building. For each possible decision, Ms. Rollins would identify requisite steps and possible problems in implementing a particular decision. For example, in considering the third possible decision just listed, Ms. Rollins identified these implementation steps:

- Work with the school administration and staff to establish a task force (with diverse composition, including parents) to study the issue of inclusion and to develop recommendations.
- Develop inservice workshops for school staff on inclusion-related topics, such as team teaching, curriculum and instructional modifications, cooperative learning, positive behavioral supports, and modified grading.
- Start small by developing a collaborative relationship with one general education teacher who expresses interest in team teaching.
- Build on any successes to gradually expand inclusion efforts in the building.

Some likely problems in implementing this decision include (1) lack of administrative support, (2) negative staff attitudes toward inclusion, and (3) ownership and professional turf issues that make team teaching difficult.

In considering the best interests of her students, Ms. Rollins could decide that the risk of exposing them to a nonsupportive environment may further stigmatize her students and not be in their best interests. On the other hand, Ms. Rollins may decide that the potential benefits of exposure to positive peer models and a challenging curriculum is worth taking this risk. The problems in implementing ei-

Box 12.4 _____

Advocacy Actions: Evaluation of the Rights, Responsibilities, and Welfare of Individuals Affected by Jane Rollins's Decision

Affected Individual(s)	Rights	Responsibilities	Welfare
Students with disabilities	■ To be educated in the LRE ■ To receive a FAPE ■ To receive general education classroom accommodations	■ To perform to capabilities ■ To not disrupt learning of other students	■ To achieve maximum potential
Students without disabilities	■ To receive an education that addresses their needs ■ To learn to appreciate and respect human differences	■ To treat all students with respect ■ To support other students	■ To achieve maximum potential
Ms. Rollins	■ To express her opinions and be treated with respect	■ To secure appropriate educational services in the LRE for students with disabilities ■ To provide support to other professionals working with students with disabilities ■ To not use her students as a means to advance her own agenda	■ To be provided a stimulating work environment in which to grow and develop
Mr. Young	■ To express his opinions and be treated with respect ■ To receive necessary support for new teaching responsibilities	■ To make good-faith efforts to provide appropriate education to all students ■ To treat students fairly ■ To seriously consider suggestions offered by his colleague, Ms. Rollins	■ To be provided a stimulating work environment in which to grow and develop
Mr. Jones	■ To determine his administrative style	■ To act in all of the students best interests ■ To provide leadership in his building	■ To be provided a stimulating work environment in which to grow and develop

ther decision include adequately addressing the students' needs in either setting, ensuring that the educational experiences of the students in the general education classroom do not suffer if inclusion is pursued, and developing a true team teaching relationship with Mr. Young.

7. Identify the short- and long-term consequences of making each alternative decision.

Contemplating the consequences of all possible decisions is highly speculative work. As discussed earlier in this chapter, one of the criticisms levied against the principle of benefit maximization relates to the need to identify consequences of decisions prior to implementing a decision. However, the process of thinking through the possible consequences of one's actions does prevent rash decisions and can provide the decision maker with some beneficial insight. Here are some possible consequences for the key individuals affected by Ms. Rollins's decision of whether to include students with disabilities into Mr. Young's general education classroom.

Students with disabilities. Given the facts as described in step 1, a general education classroom placement of the students with disabilities is likely to subject them to peer ridicule, embarrassment, and a negative educational situation as a whole. If Ms. Rollins decides to keep the students with disabilities in her special education resource room, she will have more control over their learning experiences, although the attitude that inclusion is not appropriate for students with disabilities will be reinforced in the minds of the general education teachers. If Ms. Rollins decides to take a middle position and keep the students in the resource room while working on establishing a more appropriate team teaching relationship, the students with disabilities will continue to receive special education services from Ms. Rollins while the possibility of being educated in the least restrictive environment remains open without having to sacrifice the students' rights to an appropriate educational experience.

Students without disabilities. If the students with disabilities are included in the general education classroom in the manner envisioned by Mr. Young, the students without disabilities may have some stereotypical views toward the special education students reinforced. Because the students with disabilities will still be essentially segregated within the general education classroom, the perception of the other students will be that the students with disabilities are less capable and must be educated in separate groups. This same consequence is the likely result if Ms. Rollins maintains the status quo and teaches the students with disabilities in the resource room. If a mutual team teaching relationship could be developed between Ms. Rollins and Mr. Young, the students without disabilities could experience positive interactions with students with disabilities in an atmosphere where mutual respect and tolerance are modeled.

Ms. Rollins. If the decision is to keep the students in the special education resource room, Ms. Rollins is effectively isolating herself and risking disillusionment and burnout. Alternatively, if Ms. Rollins goes ahead with inclusion, she is likely to be frustrated because the teaching arrangement with Mr. Young is not a true collaborative relationship. The decision to gradually try to build some collaborative relationships with other general education colleagues at least provides Ms. Rollins with a goal that offers her some opportunity for continued professional growth and development.

Mr. Young. If the students with disabilities are included in his classroom, Mr. Young is probably, because he appears to be somewhat resistant to inclusion in the first place, going to look for any excuse to conclude that his original thinking that inclusion is inappropriate was correct. If Mr. Young develops a level of satisfaction with the inclusion arrangement as he has dictated it to Ms. Rollins (i.e., with his contingencies), his distorted perspective of team teaching, collaboration, and inclusion will become more entrenched. If Ms. Rollins keeps the students with disabilities in the resource room, Mr. Young and other general education teachers will not be forced to examine their instructional assumptions and practices. This status quo may be comfortable for Mr. Young but it does not provide for a stimulating and enriching work environment.

8. Conduct a risk-benefit analysis by considering any evidence that potential consequences or benefits from each alternative are likely to occur.

This step of the ethical reasoning model requires the decision maker to consider any known facts that increase the likelihood that the consequences identified in the previous step will actually occur. An objective consideration of the existing facts as identified in step 1 leads to a reasoned opinion that the potential consequences are overwhelmingly negative for either of the first two alternative decisions considered (identified in step 6): (1) place the students with disabilities into Mr. Young's general education classroom or (2) keep the students with disabilities in Ms. Rollins special education resource room.

Further, there are very few identifiable benefits emanating from either decision. This risk-benefit analysis favors the third alternative decision (i.e., keep the students with disabilities in the resource room while Ms. Rollins continues to cultivate more support and awareness for inclusion in her building.) As discussed in step 7, there are more potential benefits to both students with disabilities and students without disabilities if this course of action is pursued. In addition, if Ms. Rollins is able to develop a collaborative relationship with Mr. Young, there will be benefits in terms of professional growth and development for both teachers.

9. Make a decision by choosing one of the alternatives.

Based on the foregoing analysis, Ms. Rollins chooses the third alternative decision. She decides to keep the students with disabilities in the resource room and to continue developing a collaborative relationship by informing Mr. Young, or any other general education teachers, about

inclusive educational practices. Ms. Rollins offers the following reasons as justification for her decision:

- If the students with disabilities were placed in Mr. Young's classroom under the current stipulated conditions, they would most likely be stigmatized even more than if educated in a separate setting, because the students without disabilities would still be educated in a different group and the presumed instructional and learning differences between the two groups of students would be accentuated.
- It is likely that inclusion under Mr. Young's constraints will fail, thus solidifying the opposition in the building to future inclusion efforts.
- On the other hand, if inclusion was deemed a success by Mr. Young's standards, he and other general education teachers would have a distorted and inaccurate perception of inclusion more firmly entrenched in their thinking.
- Basically, there is too much uncertainty and risk in trying to include the students with disabilities in Mr. Young's classroom under the present constraints. The apparent benefits from inclusion, at this point, seem negligible.
- The more prudent course of action is for Ms. Rollins to work on creating a more promising inclusion opportunity by laying the foundation with her general education colleagues. This foundation must be based on attitudinal changes that foster a sense of mutual ownership among all the teachers for the educational needs of all students, the development of collaborative relationships between special and general education teachers, and a commitment of necessary support for general education teachers who engage in team teaching in their classrooms.

This step in the ethical reasoning model also requires the decision maker to check the chosen alternative decision with her intuitive moral judgment. The importance of incorporating the decision maker's moral intuitions was addressed by Strike and colleagues (1998): "Moral decisions regarding choice and action require moral sensitivity, rationality, and the development of moral theory for which the initial evidence is our moral intuitions. Moral intuitions—that is, our intuitive sense of right and wrong—are important data for moral reasoning and the construction of moral theory" (p. 101). That is, an ethically reasoned decision must feel right according to the decision maker's intuitive sense of right and wrong. The decision maker's moral intuitions serve as a sort of a litmus test for judging the moral soundness and appropriateness of the chosen decision. In this respect, the decision maker's feelings or emotions function as an important gauge of morally correct actions.

First, feelings help the decision maker establish empathy for others and to put herself in the shoes of others that are affected by her decisions. This is the essence of what Noddings (1984, 1993) referred to as the personal ethic of caring. Second, feelings provide the ethical decision maker with the motivation to engage in right conduct (Strike et al., 1998). Ms. Rollins's chosen alternative decision "feels right" because she will be able to provide the students with disabilities an appropriate educational experience, she will not be promoting a distorted and misunderstood notion of inclusion, she will continue to work toward educating her students in the least restrictive environment, and she still can work on developing collaborative teaching relationships.

10. Implement the chosen deliberative decision.

The challenge for Ms. Rollins in implementing her decision involves stimulating interpersonal change in her relationships with the general education teachers. Chapter 7 discussed change issues and strategies. Ms. Rollins would be well served by reflecting on two approaches for promoting interpersonal change that were discussed in Chapter 7: The six thinking hats and the Concerns Based Adoption Model (CBAM). By employing the perspective of the six thinking hats, Ms. Rollins is less likely to become frustrated by the reality that the other teachers do not have the same perspective on inclusion that she maintains. In fact, the six thinking hats promotes diverse perspectives and person-

alities. In particular, Ms. Rollins must recognize that in this situation, the general education teachers are primarily wearing "black hats." They are currently pessimistic, arguing that inclusion will not work. In responding to this perspective, Ms. Rollins should be prepared to address difficult implementation issues head on, such as: How can we continue to meet the educational needs of students without disabilities while including students with disabilities in our classes? If I team teach, will I have to give up my instructional style and preferences? Given that as a general education teacher I am not trained to teach students with disabilities, how can I effectively meet this responsibility?

Also, Ms. Rollins can conceptualize the interpersonal change process as proceeding through stages of concern as identified in CBAM. At each stage, the general education teachers will have different concerns and support needs. Examples of relevant strategies for addressing concerns at each of the CBAM stages are provided in Box 7.2.

11. Evaluate the outcomes of the implemented decision.

This last step of the ethical reasoning model establishes accountability for professional decisions and actions. Schloss and Henley (1994) have recommended consideration of the following three questions in evaluating decision outcomes.

Has the decision resulted in the desired functional outcome? A *functional outcome* refers to the practical effect of the decision on students and their families. In this case, the functional outcome for the students with disabilities is that they will receive an appropriate education from Ms. Rollins with an opportunity in the future to spend more time in an appropriately structured and supportive general education setting. The students without disabilities will not have prejudicial stereotypes of students with disabilities reinforced by seeing them in a negative light, as would be the situation if inclusion would occur in Mr. Young's classroom.

Has the decision resulted in the desired ethical outcome? The decision can be judged *ethical* if it conforms to accepted legal and ethical principles. In this case, Ms. Rollins's decision affords the students with disabilities an appropriate education, albeit in a segregated setting, because, under the present circumstances, the students could not receive an appropriate education in Mr. Young's general education classroom. Ms. Rollins is attempting to adhere to the LRE principle by developing collaborative relationships with general education teachers, which will, hopefully, provide appropriately supportive educational opportunities in general education classrooms in the future.

In terms of the CEC Code of Ethics and Standards for Professional Practice, Ms. Rollins is adhering to mandates to create safe and effective learning environments and to encourage other professionals to improve special education services to students with disabilities. Ms. Rollins is acting in the students' best interests by not allowing her personal agenda to promote inclusion at the cost of sacrificing an appropriate educational experience for the students with disabilities. Further, Ms. Rollins is adhering to the principle of responsibility to community and society by monitoring for inappropriate educational placements and services and intervening when a colleague's actions are detrimental to students with disabilities. Finally, Ms. Rollins is acting according to the principle of equal respect by making a decision that treats the students with disabilities with respect and dignity.

Are personal ethical standards/principles influenced by the outcome? The decision reached by Ms. Rollins as a result of this ethical reasoning process reaffirms her commitment to relevant legal, professional organization ethical mandates as well as personal ethical principles. This realization should afford some comfort and satisfaction to the professional confronted with a difficult ethical dilemma.

A final issue in regard to ethical reasoning was raised by Howe and Miramontes (1992), who questioned the appropriateness and circumstances of engaging in moral compromise. By *moral compromise,* Howe and Miramontes were referring to a conscious decision of "splitting the difference"

between one's ethical perspective and opposing perspectives. Benjamin (1990) identified the following five circumstances as giving rise to the need for moral compromise:

- *Factual uncertainty.* This automatically reduces the decision maker's degree of confidence in any decision because the facts are not completely known or are in dispute. In many special education dilemmas, the facts will be uncertain, therefore an open mind, a willingness to compromise, and a commitment to empirical verification of the appropriateness of any decisions are important professional traits.
- *Moral complexity.* In Ms. Rollins's dilemma, how adherence to the least restrictive environment principle should be interpreted vis-à-vis the principles of responsible caring and equal respect was a source of moral complexity.
- *Need to maintain a continuing cooperative relationship.* In her decision making, Ms. Rollins must certainly consider the effects of any decision on her continuing relationships with school colleagues. This was an important factor in Ms. Rollins's compromise decision to keep the students in the resource room while continuing to foster collaborative relationships with general education teachers.
- *Need to make an immediate decision.* Many difficult decisions affecting students with disabilities require immediate decisions that eliminate the luxury of protracted personal reflection. In such circumstances, it is important for professionals to remember that decisions should be viewed as formative, not summative. That is, as experience yields new information, decisions may have to be revisited and revised.
- *Scarcity of resources.* When resources are scarce, moral compromise becomes a practical necessity. For example, in her decision making, Ms. Rollins must be realistic in considering the amount of time and energy she has available to foster collaborative relationships and support to her general education teacher colleagues.

Each of the preceding circumstances should cause professionals to exercise humility and caution in their ethical decision making because of various constraints such as time, uncertainty, lack of resources, or collegiality issues. Any reasoned decision-making process must leave room for compromise as a practical and feasible resolution.

SUMMARY

Special education professionals frequently encounter ethical dilemmas in their work. These dilemmas emerge for myriad reasons but ethical issues are often associated with the significant challenges presented by some students with disabilities, the highly personal nature of the services provided, and the lack of adequate resources to provide appropriate services. An advocate must be able to identify ethical issues and apply a reasoned decision-making process in resolving ethical dilemmas. This chapter offered some tools to enhance the ethical advocacy efforts of special education professionals. Specifically, several principle-based theories were discussed as decision-making frameworks. Further, a model for ethical reasoning and decision making was presented. An important measure of the effectiveness of advocacy work is whether the advocate's decisions and actions have adhered to acceptable ethical guidelines.

CHAPTER 13

SPECIAL EDUCATION ADVOCACY OUTCOMES

Even if you are on the right track, you will get run over if you just sit there.—Will Rogers

Special education professionals who advocate on behalf of students with disabilities and their families experience institutional constraints when their advocacy "exceeds what is sanctioned by the norms of action in schools" (Mawhinney & Smrekar, 1996, p. 1). That is, school structures and rules often limit an educator's advocacy to a "zone of acceptable action." Certainly, special education professionals who engage in advocacy efforts must be realistic in their assessment of institutional constraints. However, this book has challenged special education professionals in addressing advocacy constraints that are self-imposed.

Self-imposed constraints to advocacy occur when school professionals lose their sense of idealism with which they began their careers (Luckner, 1996). With this loss of idealism, school professionals experience disillusionment, feel powerless, and, ultimately, lack concern for their students. Self-imposed constraints to advocacy develop when school professionals no longer believe they can make a difference in the lives of their students (Littrell, Billingsley, & Cross, 1994). Self-imposed constraints to advocacy thrive when school professionals no longer feel compelled by a sense of justice or a "service ethic" to assert, defend, and extend the rights of students with disabilities (Mawhinney & Smrekar, 1996). And self-imposed constraints to advocacy abound when school professionals fail to recognize that advocacy can result from simple acts and that even

small efforts can make a difference. Special education professionals who ignore their advocacy role and responsibilities in an attempt to create a tensionless work environment fail to appreciate that it is only through the struggle for goals that expand and improve services for students with disabilities that true personal and professional fulfillment occurs (Benson & Stuart, 1992).

In considering the wisdom of Will Rogers's quote above, the right track for special education professionals is to assume the role and responsibilities of serving as an advocate for students with disabilities and their families. Further, to avoid "just sitting there and getting run over," special education professionals must develop and hone their advocacy competencies (dispositions, knowledge, and skills).

McLaughlin, Irby, and Langman (1994) have referred to professionals who, through their advocacy efforts, have overcome constraining conditions for students with disabilities and their families as "wizards." Perhaps more wizards will be necessary in the future to protect the rights of students with disabilities to receive appropriate educational services, because, as noted by Williams (1995), progress and entitlements for individuals with disabilities are secured on a fragile foundation: "As we approach the millennium, progress is measured by the number of steps taken in retreat. Perhaps we are moving back to the future."

This final chapter briefly reviews how special education professionals' advocacy efforts can foster desirable outcomes. This chapter also summarizes some of the essential advocacy competencies exhibited by the four special education professionals originally introduced in Chapter 1.

ADVOCACY OUTCOMES

A review of the advocacy scenarios from Chapter 1 reveals significant advocacy outcomes that can be attributed to the efforts of the four special education professionals. In each situation, a special education professional confronted and accepted an advocacy role and responsibilities on behalf of students with disabilities and their families. As a result of each professional's advocacy, the following outcomes were promoted: (1) enhanced professional growth and development, (2) family empowerment, (3) improved educational services, and (4) a more responsive and collaborative educational system.

Professional Growth and Development

Special education professionals are at considerable risk of job-related stress, burnout, and a higher attrition rate than general educators. Further, studies reveal the following factors are some of the significant causes of stress and burnout in the special education profession: isolated working conditions and lack of professional collaboration, role ambiguity and conflict, poor communication and relationships with other professionals and families of students with disabilities, and lack of administrative support and encouragement for autonomous decision making (Brownell & Smith, 1992; Cooley & Yovanoff, 1996; Frank & McKenzie, 1993; Pullis, 1992).

The dispositions, knowledge, and skills displayed by the four special education professionals in the Chapter 1 scenarios counteract the causes of stress and job-related burnout. By fostering professional collaboration as opposed to isolation, a special education professional is empowered and supported in taking risks. By clarifying one's ethical and legal obligations to promote the best interests of students with disabilities, a special education professional resolves a potential role conflict concerning the issue of whether one's primary loyalty should be to one's employer or to the students for whom services are provided. By improving interpersonal communication skills and fostering more productive partnerships with colleagues and families, a special education professional enhances problem solving and constructive conflict resolution processes. By exercising greater independence and autonomy in decision making, a special education professional experiences more control over how her work is performed.

There is an increasing recognition that special education professional development should focus more on serving as an advocate for children and families (Miller, 1992). Kagan (1992) asserted that one of the key growth areas for special education professionals is a shift in focus and attention from self to one's students and their best interests. Perceived lack of professional growth opportunities is a notable reason for special education professionals leaving the field (Brownell & Smith, 1992).

There is a long-standing debate over whether education qualifies as a "profession" (Heller & Ridenhour, 1982). In a review of the literature on criteria essential to professional status, Reynolds and Birch (1982) identified a number of relevant criteria. Some of the most relevant criteria to special education advocacy work include:

- The work done is acknowledged to be a vital public service.
- Learning to do the work calls for extended and specialized education based, in part, on undergirding disciplines.
- Performance of the activities requires major public trust and accountability.
- The application of the thinking process to the solution of problems is a predominant ingredient.
- Decisions and procedures are based on reliable knowledge that is constantly refreshed by new facts and ideas from other disciplines.

- The activity has a practical object, a definite and useful purpose in the eyes of both the practitioner and of society.
- Communicability is represented by an agreed upon criteria of knowledge and skills essential for carrying out the object of the profession, and organized in such a way that it is passed on to new entrants as an orderly discipline.
- Procedures exist to ensure that all members are qualified to perform a basic and common body of practice at a safe level.
- Members are motivated primarily by concern about other individuals' and society's objectives rather than their own rights and interests.

To the extent that professionals adhere, in their advocacy efforts, to these criteria, the field of special education solidifies its "professional status" and the attainment of the mission of special education for students with disabilities is accelerated.

Family Empowerment

In the past decade, a significant shift in philosophy and practice has occurred in the relationship between families of children with disabilities and school professionals who serve them (Winton, 1994; Turnbull & Turnbull, 1997). This shift is changing the perspective of schools "as places where parents go when there is a problem and, once there, feel uncomfortable or intimidated by school officials" (Mawhinney & Smrekar, 1996, p. 494) to places where professionals strive to understand the support needs and strengths of families in an effort to foster collaborative decision-making partnerships (Turnbull & Turnbull, 1997). Special education professionals now increasingly recognize that the goal of supporting and empowering families to improve their functioning and enhance their participation in educational decision making fosters positive educational results for students with disabilities (U.S. Department of Education, 1997).

For example, in one study, families receiving early intervention services for their children with disabilities reported more family-centered practices where the educational professionals showed concern for the entire family, not just the child with disabilities. Further, the professionals indicated their perspective and practices had shifted from child-focused to family-focused (McBride, Brotherson, Joanning, Whidden, & Demmitt, 1993). In another study, Bailey, Palsha, and Simeonsson (1991) reported that special education professionals considered their role of working with families as important, although they were concerned as to whether they possessed the necessary skills to engage successfully in such practices.

Special education professionals who assume an advocate's role on behalf of students with disabilities and their families embrace a family support and empowerment disposition (see Chapter 4). Further, advocates support and empower families through their knowledge of special education law and alternative dispute resolution mechanisms (see Chapters 5 and 6) and their skills in interpersonal communication (see Chapter 8), collaboration (see Chapter 9), constructive conflict resolution (see Chapter 10), and advocacy (see Chapter 11).

Although notable progress has been made in family/professional collaboration and empowerment, several challenges remain. First, parents of children in primary and secondary special education programs are still given less support and have less input into their children's education than parents of children in early childhood programs (Winton, 1994). Second, family input regarding transition planning must be incorporated into the IEP process in a more meaningful manner (Morningstar, Turnbull, & Turnbull, 1995). And third, Birenbaum (1996) has issued a warning that "family empowerment could mean 'fend-for-yourself' in an age of down-sizing" (p. 320).

The U.S. Department of Education (1995) has proposed a four-step plan to strengthen the working relationship between families and schools: (1) increase involvement of families in decision making, (2) improve information available to families, (3) link families to other resources and supports in the community, and (4) reduce adversarial dispute resolution by using mediation.

Improved Educational Services

The central impetus and motivation to engage in advocacy is the perception that there is a need to improve educational services for students with disabilities and their families. Through their advocacy efforts, the four special education professionals from the Chapter 1 scenarios improved educational services for students with disabilities. Specifically, Mary Kinney's advocacy reaffirmed the right of all students to receive a FAPE by convincing her school district to hire a second speech and language clinician to meet the expanded student needs for those services. Steve Kern's advocacy secured more appropriate and beneficial transitional, vocational, and behavioral intervention services for students with emotional/behavioral disorders. Karen Snyder's advocacy resulted in affirming the obligation of general education teachers to make appropriate IEP listed accommodations for students with disabilities attending general education classrooms. And finally, Miguel Hernandez's advocacy empowered a family of a student with disabilities by linking the family up with community resources to address functional needs and by fostering more active parent participation in IEP decision-making activities.

Despite substantial progress in improving educational services since the original passage of the Education for All Handicapped Children's Act in 1975, the educational achievement of students with disabilities remains less than satisfactory (U.S. Department of Education, 1997). The continuing need for special education professionals to fulfill an advocacy role is underscored by the following data from the U.S. Department of Education:

- The number of children requiring special education services continues to grow with increasing incidences of children born in poverty, children suffering from abuse and neglect, children from diverse ethnic backgrounds, children born to teenage mothers, infants and children with severe disorders who are saved by medical advances, babies infected with AIDS or HIV, and children born to drug-dependent mothers.

- There is still a disproportionate representation of minority students in special education programs. For example, in 1992, the national data revealed that although African American students accounted for 16 percent of the total student population, they represented 32 percent of the students in programs for students with mental retardation.

- The cost of educating a student with disabilities has risen at a higher rate than the cost of general education as a whole. Although the costs of special education are rising, there has not been a corresponding increase in federal educational funds to serve students with disabilities, thus creating more financial pressures on state and local educational agencies.

- General education reforms of the past decade (e.g., standards development, assessment, accountability, governance, teacher licensure, and school systems finance) will have an impact on special education services in some yet to be determined ways (Goertz & Friedman, 1996).

- Although great progress has been made in appropriately educating larger percentages of students with disabilities in general education classrooms, that progress is characterized as inconsistent across disability groups, age groups, and states.

- The most recent U.S. Department of Education, Office of Special Education Programs (OSEP) state compliance monitoring reports on 13 states revealed continuing compliance challenges with regard to student access to appropriate instruction and vocational preparation in the least restrictive environment, transition from school to employment and other postsecondary activities, procedural safeguards for students with disabilities and their parents, and overall state education agency monitoring responsibilities.

- As discussed in Chapter 1, students with disabilities are less likely to graduate from high school than their peers without disabilities. Students who do not complete high school are more likely to be unemployed, employed less than full time, and a disproportionate percentage of the prison population in this country.

More Responsive and Collaborative Educational System

Advocacy fosters a more responsive and collaborative educational system in the following two respects. First, advocates identify educational system deficiencies or issues that require reflection and attention. To the extent that the educational system is made aware of issues related to improving educational services for students with disabilities and to the extent that the educational system attempts to address those concerns, the educational system becomes more responsive and dynamic. Second, advocacy work typically involves collaborative interactions between professional colleagues and families. Each advocacy interaction represents an opportunity for the participants to enhance their knowledge of special education laws and procedures and their skills in interpersonal communication, collaboration, constructive conflict resolution, advocacy, and ethical decision making.

Collaboration among school professionals and with families requires subtle shifts in professionals' perceptions of their duties, work routines, and attitudes toward their clients (Knapp, 1995). As special education professionals engage in more collaborative advocacy work on behalf of students with disabilities and their families, they discover the personal and professional satisfaction that results from developing a network of support from colleagues who openly discuss problems and solutions to those problems (Cooley & Yovanoff, 1996: Gillet, 1987; Pullis, 1992). Luckner (1996) urged special education professionals to surround themselves with positive people, to maintain a positive mindset, and to continually retool their skills to enhance their effectiveness. Although advocacy is challenging work, it is, ultimately, a very positive act on behalf of another person.

SUMMARY OF THE ESSENTIAL ADVOCACY COMPETENCIES EXHIBITED BY THE FOUR SPECIAL EDUCATION PROFESSIONALS

This section will highlight some of the essential professional advocacy competencies exhibited by the four special education professionals introduced in Chapter 1 (Mary Kinney, Steve Kern, Karen Snyder, and Miguel Hernandez). Their advocacy considerations and actions have been interspersed in discussions throughout this book. This summary synthesizes the relevant and necessary advocacy competencies into composite portraits of four special education professionals who strive to make a difference for their students with disabilities.

Mary Kinney

In her advocacy efforts on behalf of children in need of speech and language services, Mary displayed an advocacy *disposition* by taking an empathic perspective toward the students and their families who were being denied appropriate speech and language services due to inadequate staffing. Mary's empathy for these students fueled her ethical responsibility to document and report to her school administration the need for a second speech and language clinician. In addition, Mary demonstrated a family support and empowerment disposition by informing parents of their children's legal rights to a free and appropriate public education.

Mary's advocacy was based on her *knowledge* of special education law, specifically the zero reject principle. According to the zero reject principle, all eligible children (speech or language impairment is 1 of 13 categorical disability criteria recognized by the IDEA), birth through age 21, are entitled to free and appropriate educational services. School districts may not use financial constraints as an excuse in denying eligible students appropriate services.

Mary's knowledge of alternative dispute resolution mechanisms in special education, such as the IDEA complaint process, was useful information to impart to parents as she informed them of their legal rights and options. A complaint may be filed with the state education agency (SEA) if anyone believes that a local education agency (LEA) has violated a procedural or substantive provision of state or federal special education laws. Under the IDEA complaint process, the SEA is legally obligated to investigate the complaint and, if the evidence reveals a violation, issue a corrective plan of action to ensure the LEA comes into legal compliance. In her advocacy efforts in front of the local school board, Mary was mindful of systems change issues and strategies as she attempted to have an impact on the budgeting and decision making at the local level.

To be successful in her advocacy, Mary possessed a variety of *skills*. First, good interpersonal communication skills allowed Mary to refrain from personalizing the problem in her interactions with the director of pupil services. Instead of criticizing the director and increasing his defensiveness, Mary concentrated on resolving the problem by objectively documenting the number of students in need of speech and language services and the time she spent on each student on her caseload. These data clearly revealed the need for a second speech and language clinician.

Second, Mary displayed collaboration skills by supporting the viewpoints of others. In this case, Mary assisted the parents of the newly referred children to articulate their concerns to the school administration.

Third, in addressing this problem, the director of pupil services set a preconceived limit by assuming that the school board would not authorize the hiring of a second speech and language clinician. Mary recognized that this tactic created an impasse. To circumvent this impasse, Mary refocused the discussion from budgetary constraints to the desired goal—ensuring the newly referred and eligible students a FAPE.

Fourth, Mary employed the perceptual approach to persuasion in her advocacy in front of the school board. She skillfully framed the issue of the need to hire a second speech and language clinician in terms that the school board members, many of whom were small business owners or employees of large companies, related to from their own experiences. Simply, Mary pointed out that any business was at risk if it could not satisfy its customers. The school district was faced with a similar problem and needed to satisfy its customers—namely, parents of children entitled to an educational service that the school district was not appropriately providing. Finally, Mary reflected on the ethical principle of beneficence or responsible caring as a justification for her advocacy efforts for additional speech and language services.

Steve Kern

Steve Kern brought passion and hope to his job as a teacher of students with emotional/behavioral disorders. This advocacy *disposition* motivated Steve to improve transitional and vocational services for his students as well as change the current disciplinary system and its emphasis on punitive interventions. Steve's commitment to his students fostered an ethical disposition to adhere to the CEC Standard for Professional Practice by working cooperatively and encouraging other professionals to improve the provision of special education and related services to students with disabilities. His advocacy and positive attitude about the future potential of his students empowered families by instilling hope in them.

In addressing the issue of repeated suspensions of some of his students, Steve possessed *knowledge* of special education law and the 1997 IDEA amendment that requires school districts to conduct functional behavioral assessments and to implement proactive and positive behavioral intervention plans for students with behavioral problems. If a student is suspended for inappropriate behavior and the student's IEP does not contain a behavioral intervention plan, the school must complete a functional behavioral assessment and develop a plan.

Steve's advocacy to improve educational services for his students was also partially fueled by his knowledge that the formal due process hearing system is accessible primarily to parents who are more highly educated and in the middle- and upper-income levels. Since the majority of his students come from families who are poorly educated and in the lower income levels, it was unlikely that those parents would challenge the current educational services by requesting a due process hearing. In the absence of the parents' advocacy, Steve recognized his responsibility to seek necessary changes. In addressing changes in transition planning and programming and positive behavior management techniques, the Concerns Based Adoption Model (CBAM) became a valuable tool for Steve by identifying strategies for overcoming resistance to change initiatives.

In pursuing more positive disciplinary interventions for his students, Steve needed to demonstrate flexibility in his interpersonal communication *skills* by compromising with the school administration and agreeing to employ in-school suspensions for his students. Steve's ability to work collaboratively with his school administration was put to the test as he advocated for more proactive and positive behavioral interventions. He introduced his ideas on behavior management in a nonthreatening, noncompetitive manner by initially agreeing with the school administration's concerns in regard to school violence and safety.

Steve created a favorable climate for problem solving by disarming his building principal's opposition. That is, Steve agreed with the principal that discipline was necessary to ensure an effective learning environment. With an acknowledged goal that was the same as his principal's, Steve effectively outlined his plan for implementing a more proactive and positive behavioral management system in the school. Steve engaged in both legislative and systems advocacy work as the state education agency implemented new regulations expanding vocational services, provided for closer monitoring of transitional programming, and developed statewide inservice training on functional behavioral assessments and positive behavioral interventions.

Finally, Steve's advocacy promoted the ethical principle of integrity in professional relationships by developing more positive attitudes among school administrators toward his students, by cooperating with other community agency personnel to improve transitional and vocational services, and by providing consultation support to school staff in implementing positive behavioral interventions.

Karen Snyder

Karen Snyder displayed an advocacy *disposition* through her autonomous actions to enforce IEP accommodations for students with disabilities attending general education classes. Her actions as principal further demonstrated the ethical characteristic of fairness by ensuring that students with disabilities received the services they were entitled to and that provided them with an equal educational opportunity to be successful in general education classrooms. Karen's leadership also supported families of the students with disabilities by monitoring classroom services to secure implementation of all IEP listed services.

Karen's *knowledge* of special education law gave her confidence when she confronted the general education teachers and their failure to implement accommodations listed in students' IEPs. She knew that schools are legally obligated to provide all special education and related services that are listed in an IEP. Further, school personnel must make a good-faith effort to achieve IEP goals and objectives. In other words, the mandate to provide supplementary aids and services to students with disabilities in general education settings requires more than a mere token gesture of implementation. In trying to resolve this situation, Karen knew that collaborative problem solving with her staff was more beneficial than taking an adversarial stance. This problem-solving approach fostered interpersonal change among the school staff (both general and special education teachers) by using the Concerns Based Adoption Model as a conceptual framework for identifying the different informational needs and supports for various staff dependent upon their individual levels of concern.

By employing constructive confrontation in her interpersonal communication *skills,* Karen was able to point out the discrepancy in the general education teachers' verbal behaviors when they agreed to the accommodations at the IEP meetings and their subsequent actions in failing to implement the IEP listed accommodations. Karen chose not to assert her authority and dictate to the teachers what they had to do in their classrooms (realizing that this approach would, at best, lead to half-hearted compliance by the teachers). Instead, she established a collaborative, problem-solving partnership with the teachers. This partnership was based on parity among all the participants in determining an appropriate resolution to the problem. As a component of this collaborative arrangement, Karen employed the principled negotiation tactic of separating people from the problem. That is, she did not threaten or criticize the general education teachers for failing to implement IEP accommodations.

Karen focused on the problem of ensuring that IEP accommodations are implemented and functioned as an ally with the teachers by creating more collaborative planning time each week. This increased collaborative planning time served as a powerful incentive to the teachers and was an effective persuasion tool for Karen in encouraging the teachers to implement the accommodations in their classrooms. By fostering more teacher collaboration, Karen was also able to associate inclusion with a more positive image of professional development for her staff. Karen's advocacy actions were justified from the ethical principle of equal respect. By receiving the necessary classroom accommodations, the students with disabilities were treated with dignity and equal worth in terms of having an equal opportunity to be successful as was afforded all students.

Miguel Hernandez

In assuming a role and responsibility to assist the Ortiz family beyond "school issues," Miguel Hernandez exhibited an advocacy *disposition* and an understanding of family systems by recognizing that Mrs. Ortiz's inability to adequately meet all of her family's functional needs (e.g., economic, daily care, socialization, education) created stress for the family. As a caring professional, Miguel provided information to assist Mrs. Ortiz in identifying community services to help her family address some of their functional needs.

Miguel's *knowledge* of special education law enhanced his resolve to ensure that Mrs. Ortiz had input into IEP decisions for her daughter Susie. In fact, Miguel knew that IEPs developed without a legitimate opportunity for parental input have been repealed and declared invalid. Miguel decided to function as a mediator between Mrs. Ortiz and other IEP committee members because he realized that Mrs. Ortiz's dissatisfaction with how school personnel had treated her was not an appropriate issue for resolution at a due process hearing. Miguel attempted to stimulate interpersonal change in IEP decision-making dynamics between Mrs. Ortiz and school personnel by linking Mrs. Ortiz up with a parent advocate.

Miguel's sensitivity to Mrs. Ortiz's frustration with school personnel was enhanced by his interpersonal communication *skill* in recognizing the importance of different assumptions and expectations concerning a student's present abilities and future educational needs as determinants of the quality of interpersonal interactions between families and school professionals. Further, Miguel displayed a collaborative disposition by demonstrating empathy to the needs and perspectives of the Ortiz family.

In resolving Mrs. Ortiz's concern over Susie's poor reading and lack of progress in her reading skills, Miguel used the principled negotiation strategy of insisting on objective criteria (e.g., measuring Susie's progress by taking weekly timed reading samples and calculating words read correctly per minute) to document whether Susie's reading was or was not improving. Miguel provided advocacy support by functioning as a mediator in interactions between Mrs. Ortiz and the other IEP committee members. Finally, Miguel demonstrated adherence to the ethical principle of responsibility to community and society as the justification for his mediator's role and attempt to improve Mrs. Ortiz's trust and confidence in special education decision-making procedures.

SUMMARY

Although most special education professionals would probably acknowledge a responsibility to serve as an advocate for students with disabilities and their families, the number of professionals who actually function in that capacity is less. For professionals reflecting on their advocacy role, a fundamental question must be addressed: Why did you choose a career in special education? For a special education professional who possesses the essential advocacy dispositions, knowledge, and skills presented in this book, the answer to that question is simple and direct: To make a difference.

REFERENCES

Adams, R. D., Hutchinson, S., & Martray, C. (1980). *A developmental study of teacher concerns across time*. Paper presented at the annual meeting of the American Educational Research Association, Boston.

Agostini v. Felton, 65 LW 4524 (Supreme Court, June 24, 1997).

Aguilar v. Felton, 473 U.S. 402 (1985).

Ahearn, E. M. (1994). *Mediation and due process procedures in special education: An analysis of state policies.* Alexandria, VA: Project Forum, National Association of State Directors of Special Education. (ERIC Document Reproduction Service No. ED 378 714)

Ahearn, E. M. (1997). *Due process hearings: An update.* Alexandria, VA: National Association of State Directors of Special Education. (ERIC Document Reproduction Service No. ED 403 717)

Alper, S. K., Schloss, P. J., & Schloss, C. N. (Eds.). (1994). *Families of students with disabilities: Consultation and advocacy.* Boston: Allyn and Bacon.

American Psychological Association. (1992). *Ethical principles of psychologists and code of conduct.* Washington, DC: Author.

Anderson, W., Chitwood, S., & Hayden, D. (1997). *Negotiating the special education maze: A guide for parents and teachers.* Bethesda, MD: Woodbine House.

Araki, C. T. (1983). A practical approach to conflict resolution. *Educational Perspectives, 22*(1), 11–16.

Arcia, E., Keyes, L., Gallagher, J. J., & Herrick, H. (1992). *Potential underutilization of Part H services: An empirical study of national demographic factors.* Chapel Hill, NC: Carolina Policy Studies Program.

Arends, R. I., & Arends, J. H. (1977). *Systems change strategies in educational settings.* New York: Human Sciences Press.

Arizona Department of Education. (1993). *Special education negotiation and mediation skills training manual* (rev. ed.). Phoenix, AZ: Author.

Ashton, P., & Webb, R. (1996). *Making a difference: Teacher's sense of efficacy.* New York: Longman.

Audette, B., & Algozzine, B. (1997). Re-inventing government? Let's re-invent special education. *Journal of Learning Disabilities, 30*(4), 378–383.

Audette, D. (1982). Private school placement: A local director's perspective. *Exceptional Children, 49*(3), 214–219.

Ayers, J. B. (1980). *A longitudinal study of teachers.* Paper presented at the annual meeting of the American Educational Research Association, Boston.

Bailey, D. B., McWilliams, P. J., Winton, P. J., & Simeonsson, R. J. (1992). *Implementing family-centered services in early intervention: A team-based model for change.* Cambridge, MA: Brookline.

Bailey, D. B., Palsha, S. A., & Simeonsson, R. J. (1991). Professional skills, concerns, and perceived importance of work with families in early intervention. *Exceptional Children, 58*(2), 156–165.

Bailey, D. B., & Wolery, M. (1992). *Teaching infants and preschoolers with disabilities* (2nd ed.). New York: Merrill.

Balcazar, F. E., Keys, C. B., Bertram, J. F., & Rizzo, T. (1996). Advocate development in the field of developmental disabilities: A data-based conceptual model. *Mental Retardation, 34*(6), 341–351.

Bateman, B. (1982). Legal and ethical dilemmas of special educators. *Exceptional Education Quarterly, 2*(4), 57–69.

Bateman, B. D., & Linden, M. A. (1998). *Better IEPs: How to develop legally correct and educationally useful programs* (3rd ed.). Longmont, CO: Sopris West.

Bayles, M. D. (1989). *Professional ethics.* Belmont, CA: Wadsworth.

Beekman, L. E. (1993). Making due process hearings more efficient and effective (aka How to run a hearing—and get away with it!). In *Proceedings of the 14th National Institute on Legal Issues of Educating Individuals with Disabilities.* Horsham, PA: LRP Publications.

Benjamin, A. (1969). *The helping interview.* Boston: Houghton Mifflin.

Benjamin, M. (1990). *Splitting the difference.* Lawrence: University Press of Kansas.

Benson, H., & Stuart, E. M. (1992). *The wellness book: The comprehensive guide to maintaining health and treating stress-related illness.* New York: Birch Lane Press.

Benson, H. A., & Turnbull, A. P. (1986). Approaching families from an individualized perspective. In R. H. Horner, L. H. Meyer, & H. D. Fredericks (Eds.), *Education of learners with severe handicaps: Exemplary service strategies* (pp. 127–157). Baltimore: Brookes.

Bernasconi v. Tempe Elementary School District No. 3, 548 F.2d 857 (9th Cir. 1977).

Berry, J. O., & Hardman, M. L. (1998). *Lifespan perspectives on the family and disability.* Boston: Allyn and Bacon.

Bettelheim, B. (1967). *The empty fortress: Infantile autism and the birth of the self.* London: Collier-Macmillan.

Beyer, L. E. (1997). The moral contours of teacher education. *Journal of Teacher Education, 48*(4), 245–254.

Biklen, D. P. (1976). Advocacy comes of age. *Exceptional Children, 42,* 308–313.

Birenbaum, A. (1996). Can family empowerment survive a smaller federal government? *Mental Retardation, 34*(5), 320–322.

Blackorby, J., Edgar, E., & Kortering, L. J. (1991). A third of our youth? A look at the problem of high school dropout among students with mild handicaps. *Journal of Special Education, 25*(1), 102–114.

Board of Education of Community Consolidated School District No. 21 v. Illinois State Board of Education, 938 F.2d 712 (7th Cir. 1991).

Board of Education of the Hendrick Hudson School District v. Rowley, 458 U.S. 176 (1982).

Board of Education of Northfield High School District 225 v. Roy H. and Lynn H., 21 IDELR N. D. Ill. (1995).

Board of Education of Sacramento Unified School District v. Holland, 14 F. 3d 1398 (9th Cir., 1994).

Bonney, L. G., & Moore, S. (1992). Advocacy: Noun, verb, adjective or profanity. *Impact, 5*(2), 7.

Bootel, J. A. (1995). *CEC special education advocacy handbook.* Reston, VA: Council for Exceptional Children.

Bowe, F. G. (1995). Ethics in early childhood special education. *Infants and Young Children, 7*(3), 28–37.

Brantlinger, E. (1991). Home-school partnerships that benefit children with special needs. *The Elementary School Journal, 91*(3), 249–259.

Brock, K. A., & Shanberg, R. (1990). Avoiding unnecessary due process hearings. *Journal of Reading, Writing, and Learning Disabilities, 6*(1), 33–39.

Brookhart v. Illinois State Board of Education, 697 F.2d 179 (7th Cir. 1983).

Brown v. Board of Education, 347 U.S. 483 (1954).

Brownell, M. T., & Smith, S. W. (1992). Attrition/retention of special education teachers: Critique of current research and recommendations for retention efforts. *Teacher Education and Special Education, 15*(4), 229–248.

Budoff, M. (1976). *Procedural due process: Its application to special education and its implications for teacher training.* Paper presented at the meeting of the American Educational Research Association, San Francisco.

Budoff, M., & Orenstein, A. (1981). Special education appeals hearings: Are they fair and are they helping? *Exceptional Education Quarterly, 2*(2), 37–48.

Budoff, M., & Orenstein, A. (1982). *Due process in special education: On going to a hearing.* Cambridge, MA: Ware Press.

Budoff, M., Orenstein, A., & Sachitano, J. (1987). *Informal resolution of special education disputes: A review of state practices.* Boston: Research Institute for Educational Problems.

Burgdorf, R. (Ed.). (1980). *Legal rights of handicapped persons: Cases, materials, and texts.* Baltimore: Brookes.

Burlington School Committee v. Department of Education, 471 U.S. 359 (1985).

Burton, Letter to, 17 EHLR 1182 (OSERS, 1991).

Cahill, B. F. (1986). Training volunteers as child advocates. *Child Welfare, 65*(6), 545–553.

Campbell, E. (1997). Connecting the ethics of teaching and moral education. *Journal of Teacher Education, 48*(4), 255–263.

Canady, R. L., & Seyfarth, J. T. (1979). *How parent-teacher conferences build partnerships.* Bloomington, IN: Phi Delta Kappa Educational Foundation.

Caplan, P. J., & Hall-McCorquodale, I. (1985). Mother-blaming in major clinical journals. *American Journal of Orthopsychiatry, 55*(3), 345–353.

Carlson, R. (1997). *Don't sweat the small stuff . . . And it's all small stuff.* New York: Hyperion.

Carr, D. (1993). Questions of competence. *British Journal of Educational Studies, 43*(3), 253–271.

Carter, M. (1996). Master teacher evaluation. *Child Care Information Exchange,* 60–61.

Chadsey-Rusch, J., Rusch, F. R., & O'Reilly, M. F. (1991). Transition from school to integrated communities. *Remedial and Special Education, 12*(6), 23–33.

Champagne, J. F. (1993). Decisions in sequence: How to make placements in the least restrictive environment. *EdLaw Briefing Paper, 9 & 10,* 1–16.

Cheney, D., & Osher, T. (1997). Collaborate with families. *Journal of Emotional and Behavioral Disorders, 5*(1), 36–45.

Christensen, C. A., & Dorn, S. (1997). Competing notions of social justice and contradictions in special education reform. *Journal of Special Education, 31*(2), 181–199.

Christensen, S. L., & Cleary, M. (1990). Consultation and the parent-education partnership: A perspective. *Journal of Educational and Psychological Consultation, 1,* 219–241.

Chynoweth, J. K. (1995, December). *Systems change strategies* (SARRC Reports: Emerging Issues and Trends in Education). Plantation, FL: South Atlantic Regional Resource Center.

Cobb, H. B., & Horn, C. J. (1989). *Implementation of professional standards in special education: A national study.* Paper presented at the Council for Exceptional Children, Teacher Education Division Annual Conference, Memphis, TN.

Cochran, M. (1992). Parent empowerment: Developing a conceptual framework. *Family Science Review, 51*(1 & 2), 3–21.

Cohen, M. L., Berring, R. C., & Olson, K. C. (1989). *How to find the law* (9th ed.). St. Paul, MN: West.

Cohen, M. L., & Olson, K. C. (1992). *Legal research in a nutshell.* St. Paul, MN: West.

Connick v. Myers, 461 U.S. 138 (1983).

Cook, L., & Friend, M. (1991). Collaboration in special education. *Preventing School Failure, 35*(2), 24–27.

Cooley, E., & Yovanoff, P. (1996). Supporting professionals-at-risk: Evaluating interventions to reduce burnout and improve retention of special educators. *Exceptional Children, 62*(4), 336–355.

Cooley, W. C. (1994). The ecology of support for caregiving families. *Developmental and Behavioral Pediatrics, 15,* 117–119.

Corey, G., Corey, M. S., & Callanan, P. (1993). *Issues and ethics in the helping professions* (4th ed.). Pacific Grove, CA: Brooks/Cole.

Council for Exceptional Children. (1983). Code of ethics and standards for professional practice. *Exceptional Children, 50*(3), 205–209.

Covey, S. R. (1989). *The 7 habits of highly effective people: Restoring the character ethic.* New York: Simon & Schuster.

Crawford v. Honig, 37 F.3d 485 (9th Cir. 1994).

Crosson, A. (1977). *Advocacy and the developmentally disabled.* Eugene: Rehabilitation Research and Training Center in Mental Retardation, University of Oregon.

Cuban, L. (1996). Myths about changing schools and the case of special education. *Remedial and Special Education, 17*(2), 75–82.

Cutler, B. C. (1993). *You, your child, and special education: A guide to making the system work.* Baltimore: Brookes.

Dagley, D. L., McGuire, M. D., & Evans, C. W. (1994). The relationship test in the discipline of disabled students. *Education Law Reporter, 88,* 13–31.

Damasio, A. (1994). *Descartes error.* New York: Grossert Putnam.

Daniel R.R. v. State Board of Education, 874 F.2d 1036 (5th Cir. 1989).

Darling-Hammond, L. (1988). Policy and professionalism. In A. Lieberman (Ed.), *Building a professional culture in schools.* New York: Teachers College Press.

De Bono, E. (1985). *Six thinking hats.* Boston: Little, Brown.

de Gues, A. (1997). *The living company.* Cambridge, MA: Harvard Business School Press.

DeMitchell, T. A., & Fossey, R. (1997). *The limits of law-based school reform: Vain hopes and false promises.* Lancaster, PA: Technomic Publishing.

Des Jardins, C. (1993). *How to get services by being assertive.* Chicago: Family Resource Center on Disabilities.

Destefano, L., & Wagner, M. (1993). Outcome assessment in special education: Implications for decision-making and long-term planning in vocational rehabilitation. *Career Development for Exceptional Individuals, 16*(2), 147–158.

Dettmer, P. A., Dyck, N. T., & Thurston, L. P. (1996). *Consultation, collaboration, and teamwork for students with special needs.* Boston: Allyn and Bacon.

Deutsch, M. (1973). *The resolution of conflict: Constructive and destructive process.* New Haven, CT: Yale University Press.

Developmental Disabilities Assistance and Bill of Rights Act of 1975, 42 U.S.C. Sec. 6000 et seq.

Diamond, S. (1981). Growing up with parents of a handicapped child: A handicapped person's perspective. In J. L. Paul (Ed.), *Understanding and working with parents of children with special needs* (pp. 23–50). New York: Holt, Rinehart and Winston.

Dobbs, R. F., Primm, E. B., & Primm, B. (1991). Mediation: A common sense approach for resolving conflicts in special education. *Focus on Exceptional Children, 24*, 1–11.

Doe v. Withers, 20 IDELR 442 (W.Va. Cir. Ct. 1993).

Dunst, C. J., Johanson, C., Trivette, C. M., & Hamby, D. (1991). Family-oriented early intervention policies and practices: Family centered or not? *Exceptional Children, 58*(2), 115–126.

Dunst, C. J., Trivette, C. M., & LaPoint, N. (1992). Toward clarification of the meaning and key elements of empowerment. *Family Studies Review, 5*(1 & 2), 111–130.

Edgar, E. (1991). Providing ongoing support and making appropriate placements. *Preventing School Failure, 35*(2), 36–39.

Edgar, E. (1995). *First decade after graduation: Final report.* Seattle: University of Washington. (ERIC Document Reproduction Service No. ED 397 573)

Edgar, E., & Levine, P. (1986). *Washington state follow-up studies of postsecondary special education students in transition.* Unpublished manuscript. Seattle: University of Washington, Child Development and Mental Retardation Center.

Edgar, E., & Polloway, E. (1994). Education for adolescents with disabilities: Curriculum and placement issues. *Journal of Special Education, 27*(4), 438–453.

Eklund, E. (1978). *Systems advocacy.* Lawrence: University of Kansas, Affiliated Facility.

Elias, S., & Levinkind, S. (1992). *How to find and understand the law* (3rd ed.). Berkeley, CA: Nolo Press.

Elmore, R. F. (1990). Introduction: On changing the structure of public schools. In R. F. Elmore and associates (Eds.), *Restructuring schools: The next generation of educational reform.* San Francisco: Jossey-Bass.

Engiles, A., Peter, M., Baxter Quash-Mah, S., & Todis, B. (1996). *Team-based conflict resolution in special education.* Eugene, OR: Lane Education Service District. (ERIC Document Reproduction Service No. ED 401 69)

Epstein, J. L. (1992). School and family partnerships: Leadership roles for school psychologists. In S. Christenson & J. Conoley (Eds.), *Homeschool collaboration: Enhancing children's academic and social competence* (pp. 499–515). Silver Spring, NY: National Association of School Psychologists.

Esperanza, K., & Powell, P. (1996). 10 ways to have more fun at your IEP. *Exceptional Parent, 26*(4), 34–35.

Etzioni, A. (1993). *The spirit of community.* New York: Croan Publishers.

Falvey, M. A., Forest, M., Pearpoint, J., & Rosenberg, R. (1994). Building connections. In J. S. Thousand, R. A. Villa, & A. I. Nevin (Eds.), *Creativity and collaborative learning: A practical guide to empowering students and teachers* (pp. 347–368). Baltimore: Brookes.

Feeney, S., & Kipnis, K. (1985). Professional ethics in early childhood education. *Young Children, 42*(3), 54–58.

Feeney, S., & Kipnis, K. (1992). *Code of ethical conduct and statement of commitment.* Washington, DC: National Association for the Education of Young Children.

Festinger, L. (1957). *A theory of cognitive dissonance.* Stanford, CA: Stanford University Press.

Fiedler, C. R. (1985). *Conflict prevention, containment, and resolution in special education due process disputes: Parents' and school personnel's perceptions of variables associated with the development and escalation of due process conflict.* Unpublished doctoral dissertation, University of Kansas, Lawrence.

Fiedler, C. R. (1986). Enhancing parent-school personnel partnerships. *Focus on Autistic Behavior, 1*(4), 1–8.

Fiedler, C. R. (1991). Preparing parents to participate: Advocacy and education. In M. J. Fine (Ed.), *Collaboration with parents of exceptional children* (pp. 313–333). New York: Clinical Psychology Publishing.

Fiedler, C. R. (1993). Parents and the law: Conflict development and legal safeguards. In J. L. Paul & R. J. Simeonsson (Eds.), *Children with special needs: Family, culture, and society* (pp. 256–278). Fort Worth, TX: Harcourt Brace Jovanovich.

Fiedler, C. R. (1994). Inclusion: Recognition of the giftedness of all children. *Network, 4*(2), 15–23.

Fiedler, C. R. (1997). *Interviews with professional educators who serve as advocates for children with disabilities and their families: Findings and insights.* Unpublished manuscript.

Fiedler, C. R., & Antonak, R. F. (1991). Advocacy. In J. L. Matson & J. A. Mulick (Eds.), *Handbook of mental retardation* (pp. 23–32) New York: Pergamon Press.

Fiedler, C. R., & Prasse, D. P. (1996). Legal and ethical issues in the educational assessment and programming for youth with emotional or behavioral disorders. In M. J. Breen & C. R. Fiedler (Eds.), *Behavioral approach to assessment of youth with emotional/behavioral disorders: A handbook for school-based practitioners* (pp. 23–79). Austin, TX: Pro-Ed.

Fifield, V. J. (1978). *Parent and school staff attitudes toward meetings to develop individualized education programs which include/exclude the child.* Unpublished manuscript, Utah State University, Department of Special Education.

Filley, A. C. (1975). *Interpersonal conflict resolution.* Glenview, IL: Scott, Foresman.

First, P. (1992). *Educational policy for school administrators.* Boston: Allyn and Bacon.

Fischer, L., Schimmel, D., & Kelly, C. (1999). *Teachers and the law* (5th ed.). New York: Longman.

Fishbaugh, M. S. E. (1997). *Models of collaboration.* Boston: Allyn and Bacon.

Fisher, B. A., & Ellis, D. G. (1990). *Small group decision making: Communication and the group process.* New York: McGraw-Hill.

Fisher, R., & Ury, W. (1991). *Getting to yes: Negotiating agreement without giving in* (2nd ed.). Boston: Houghton Mifflin.

Folberg, J., & Taylor, A. (1984). *Mediation: A comprehensive guide to resolving conflicts without litigation.* San Francisco: Jossey-Bass.

Frank, A. R., & McKenzie, R. (1993). The development of burnout among special educators. *Teacher Education and Special Education, 16*(2), 161–170.

Freeman, A. (1991). Being transformative in special educational needs. *Educational Change and Development, 11*(2), 15–19.

Friedman, P. G. (1980). *Communicating in conferences: Parent-teacher-student interaction.* Urbana, IL: ERIC Clearinghouse on Reading and Communication Skills.

Friend, M., & Cook, L. (1996). *Interactions: Collaboration skills for school professionals.* White Plains, NY: Longman.

Friesen, B., & Huff, B. (1990). Parents and professionals as advocacy partners. *Preventing School Failure, 34*(3), 31–37.

Frith, G. H. (1981). "Advocate" vs. "professional employee": A question of priorities for special educators. *Exceptional Children, 47*, 486–492.

Fullan, M. (1991). *The new meaning of educational change.* New York: Teachers College Press.

Fullan, M. (1993). *Change forces: Probing the depths of educational reform.* New York: Falmer Press.

Fullan, M., & Hargreaves, A. (1991). *What's worth fighting for in your school?* New York: Teachers College Press.

Fuller, F. (1969). Concerns of teachers: A developmental conceptualization. *American Educational Research Journal, 6*(2), 207–226.

Gallagher, J. J., & Gallagher, G. G. (1985). Family adaptation to a handicapped child and assorted professionals. In H. R. Turnbull & A. P. Turnbull (Eds.), *Parents speak out: Then and now* (2nd ed.) (pp. 233–244). Englewood Cliffs, NJ: Merrill/Prentice-Hall.

Gehrke, N. J. (1979). Renewing teacher enthusiasm: A professional dilemma. *Theory into Practice, 18*(3), 188–193.

Gersten, R., Vaughn, S., Deshler, D., & Schiller, E. (1997). What we know about using research findings: Implications for improving special education practices. *Journal of Learning Disabilities, 30*(5), 446–457.

Gillespie, E., & Turnbull, A. P. (1983). Involving special education students in planning the IEP. *Teaching Exceptional Children, 16*(1), 27–29.

Gillet, P. (1987). Preventing discipline-related teacher stress and burnout. *Teaching Exceptional Children, 19*(4), 62–65.

Gilligan, C. (1982). *In a different voice.* Cambridge, MA: Harvard University Press.

Gilligan, C. (1988). Remapping the moral domain: New images of self in relationship. In C. Gilligan, J. V. Ward, & J. M. Taylor (Eds.), *Mapping the moral domain: A contribution of women's thinking to psychological theory and education* (pp. 3–19). Cambridge, MA: Center for the Study of Gender, Education, and Human Development.

Givhan v. Western Line Consolidated School District, 439 U.S. 410 (1979).

Glaser, R., & Glaser, C. (1985). *Group facilitators intervention guidebook, a quick reference to team development interventions* (2nd ed.). Bryn Mawr, PA: Organization Design and Development.

Glickman, C. D. (1990). *Supervision of instruction: A developmental approach* (2nd ed.). Boston: Allyn and Bacon.

Glickman, C. D., Gordon, S. R., & Ross-Gordon, J. M. (1998). *Supervision of instruction: A developmental approach* (4th ed.). Boston: Allyn and Bacon.

Glickman, C., & Tamashiro, R. T. (1982). A comparison of first year, fifth year, and former teachers on efficacy, ego development and problem solving. *Psychology in the Schools, 19*(4), 558–562.

Goens, G. A. (1996, October). Shared decisions, empowerment, and ethics: A mission impossible for district leaders? *The School Administrator,* 12–14.

Goertz, M. E., & Friedman, D. H. (1996). *State education reform and students with disabilities: A preliminary analysis.* Alexandria, VA: Center for Policy Research on the Impact of General and Special Education Reform, National Association of State Boards of Education.

Goldberg, S. S. (1989). The failure of legalization in education: Alternative dispute resolution and The Education for All Handicapped Children Act of 1975. *Journal of Law and Education, 18*(3), 441–454.

Goldberg, S. S., & Huefner, D. S. (1995). Dispute resolution in special education: An introduction to litigative alternatives. *Education Law Reporter, 99,* 703–803.

Goldberg, S. S., & Kuriloff, P. J. (1991). Evaluating the fairness of special education hearings. *Exceptional Children, 57*(6), 546–555.

Goldstein, S., Strickland, B., Turnbull, A. P., & Curry, L. (1980). An observational analysis of the IEP conference. *Exceptional Children, 46*(4), 278–286.

Goleman, D. (1995). *Emotional intelligence.* New York: Bantam Books.

Gordon, T. (1977). *Leader effectiveness training. L.E.T.: The no-lose way to release the productive potential in people.* Toronto: Bantam.

Gorn, S. (1996). *What do I do when: The answer book on special education law.* Horsham, PA: LRP Publications.

Goss v. Lopez, 419 U.S. 565 (1975).

Gowen, J. W., Christy, D. S., & Sparling, J. (1993). Informational needs of parents of young children with special needs. *Journal of Early Intervention, 17*(2), 194–210.

Greenspan, S., & Negron, E. (1994). Ethical obligations of special services personnel. *Special Services in the Schools, 8*(2), 185–209.

Guernsey, T. F., & Klare, K. (1993). *Special education law.* Durham, NC: Carolina Academic Press.

Hall, G. E., & Hord, S. M. (1987). *Change in schools: Facilitating the process.* Albany: State University of New York.

Hall, G. E., Loucks, S. F., Rutherford, W. L., & Newlove, B. W. (1975). Levels of use of the innovation: A framework for analyzing innovation adoption. *Journal of Teacher Education, 26*(1), 52–56.

Halpern, A. S. (1985). Transition: A look at the foundations. *Exceptional Children, 51,* 479–486.

Hanline, M. F., & Halvorsen, A. (1989). Parent perceptions of the integration transition process: Overcoming artificial barriers. *Exceptional Children, 55*(6), 487–492.

Hargreaves, A. (1997). Introduction. In A. Hargreaves (Ed.), *1997 ASCD yearbook: Rethinking educational change with heart and mind* (pp. vii–xv). Alexandria, VA: Association of Supervision and Curriculum Development.

Hargreaves, A., & Fullan, M. (1998). *What's worth fighting for out there?* New York: Teachers College Press.

Harry, B., Allen, N., & McLaughlin, M. (1995). Communication versus compliance: African-American parents' involvement in special education. *Exceptional Children, 61*(4), 354–377.

Harste, J. (1990). Introduction to *Jevon doesn't sit at the back anymore* by C. White. New York: Scholastic.

Hartmann v. Loudoun County Board of Education (4th Cir. 1997).

Harvey, O. J. (1970). Beliefs and behavior: Some implications for education. *The Science Teacher, 37,* 10–14.

Hasazi, S. B., Gordon, L. R., & Roe, C. A. (1985). Factors associated with the employment status of handicapped youth exiting high school from 1979 to 1983. *Exceptional Children, 51,* 455–469.

Haslett, B., & Ogilvie, J. R. (1988). Feedback processes in task groups. In R. Cathcart & L. Samovar (Eds.), *Small group communication* (5th ed.) (pp. 385–401). Dubuque, IA: Brown.

Heller, H., & Ridenhour, N. (1982). Professional standards: Foundation for the future. *Exceptional Children, 49*(4), 294–298.

Hepworth, D. H., & Larsen, J. A. (1982). *Direct social work practice: Theory and skills.* Homewood, IL: Dorsey.

Herbert, M. D., & Mould, J. W. (1992). The advocacy role in public child welfare. *Child Welfare, 70*(2), 114–130.

Heron, T. E., Martz, S. A., & Margolis, H. (1996). Ethical and legal issues in consultation. *Remedial and Special Education, 17*(6), 377–385.

Herr, S. S. (1984). Advocacy and the future of communitization. In J. A. Mulick & B. L. Mallory (Eds.), *Transitions in mental retardation: Vol. 1: Advocacy, technology, and science* (pp. 3–15). Norwood, NJ: Ablex.

Himes, J. S. (1980). *Conflict and conflict management.* Athens: University of Georgia Press.

Hines, M. L. (1987). *Don't get mad: Get powerful! A manual for building advocacy skills.* Lansing: Michigan Protection and Advocacy Service. (ERIC Document Reproduction Service No. ED 354 683)

Hoover-Dempsey, K. V., Bassler, D. C., & Brissie, J. S. (1992). Explorations in parent-school relations. *Journal of Educational Research, 85*(5), 287–294.

Houghton, J., Bronicki, G. J., & Guess, D. (1987). Opportunities to express preferences and make choices among students with severe disabilities in classroom settings. *The Journal of the Association for Persons with Severe Handicaps, 12*(1), 18–27.

Howe, K. R., & Miramontes, O. B. (1992). *The ethics of special education.* New York: Teachers College Press.

Huberman, A. M., & Miles, M. B. (1984). *Innovation up close: How school improvement works.* New York: Plenum Press.

Huefner, D. S. (1994). The mainstreaming cases: Tensions and trends for school administrators. *Educational Administration Quarterly, 30,* 27–55.

Huszczo, G. E. (1990). Training for team building. *Training and Development Journal, 44*(2), 37–43.

Illinois Planning Council on Developmental Disabilities. (1991). *Policy statements of the Illinois Planning Council on Developmental Disabilities.* Springfield: Illinois Planning Council on Developmental Disabilities. (ERIC Document Reproduction Service No. ED 343 349)

Individuals with Disabilities Education Act of 1990, 20 U.S.C. Sec. 1400 et seq.

Ingraham v. Wright, 430 U.S. 651 (1977).

Irving Independent School District v. Tatro, 468 U.S. 883 (1984).

Jacob, S., & Hartshorne, T. (1991). *Ethics and law for school psychologists.* Brandon, VT: Clinical Psychology Publishing.

Jacobstein, J. M., & Mersky, R. M. (1990). *Fundamentals of legal research* (5th ed.). Mineola, CA: Foundation Press.

Johnson, D. W., & Johnson, F. P. (1997). *Joining together: Group therapy and group skills* (6th ed.). Boston: Allyn and Bacon.

Johnson, N. P., Berring, R. C., & Woxland, T. A. (1991). *Winning research skills.* St. Paul, MN: West.

Kagan, D. M. (1992). Professional growth among preservice and beginning teachers. *Review of Educational Research, 62*(1), 129–169.

Kagan, S. L. (1989). The new advocacy in early childhood education. *Teachers College Record, 90*(3), 465–473.

Karasoff, P. (1991, Winter). Systems change: Critical activities. *TASH Newsletter,* pp. 7, 10.

Kauffman, J. M. (1984). Saving children in the age of big brother: Moral and ethical issues in the identification of deviance. *Behavioral Disorders, 10*(1), 60–70.

Kauffman, J. M. (1993). How we might achieve the radical reform of special education. *Exceptional Children, 60*(1), 6–16.

Kauffman, J. M. (1997). *Characteristics of children's behavioral disorders.* Columbus, OH: Merrill.

Kaufman, T. U., & Adema, J. L. (1998). The learning support center: A systems approach to special needs. *Intervention in School and Clinic, 33*(2), 163–168, 183.

Kenton, S. B. (1989). Speaker credibility in persuasive business communication: A model which explains gender differences. *Journal of Business Communication, 26,* 143–157.

Kerns, G. M. (1992). Helping professionals understand families. *Teacher Education and Special Education, 15*(1), 49–55.

Kibodeaux v. Jefferson Parish School Board, 381 So.2d 1268 (La.App. 1980).

Kieffer, C. H. (1983). Citizen empowerment: A developmental perspective. *Prevention and Human Services, 3*(2/3), 19–30.

Kipnis, K. (1987). How to discuss professional ethics. *Young Children, 42*(4), 26–30.

Knapp, M. S. (1995). How shall we study comprehensive, collaborative services for children and families? *Educational Researcher, 24*(4), 5–16.

Kohlberg, L., & Armon, C. (1984). Three types of stage models used in the study of adult development. In M. Commons, F. A. Richards, & C. A. Armon (Eds.), *Beyond formal operations: Late adolescence and adult cognitive development.* New York: Praeger.

Krehbiel, R., & Kroth, R. L. (1991). Communicating with families of children with disabilities or chronic illness. In M. J. Fine (Ed.), *Collaboration with parents of exceptional children* (pp. 103–127). Brandon, VT: Clinical Psychology Publishing.

Kroth, R. L. (1985). *Communicating with parents of exceptional children.* Denver: Love.

Kuriloff, P. J. (1985). Is justice served by due process? Affecting the outcome of special education hearings in Pennsylvania. *Law and Contemporary Problems, 48,* 89–117.

Lambie, R., & Daniels-Mohring, D. (1993). *Family systems within educational contexts: Understanding students with special needs.* Denver: Love.

LaMorte, M. W. (1996). *School law: Cases and concepts.* Boston: Allyn and Bacon.

Lane County Direction Service. (1996). *Team conciliator's manual.* Eugene, OR: Lane Education Service District. (ERIC Document Reproduction Service No. ED 401 699)

Larry P. v. Riles, 495 F.Supp. 926 (N.D. Cal. 1979), aff'd in part, rev'd in part, 793 F.2d 969 (9th Cir. 1986).

Lear, R. (1995). The extent of public schools' responsibility to provide health-related services. In *Proceedings of the 16th Annual Institute on Legal Issues of Educating Students with Disabilities.* Alexandria, VA: LRP Conference Division.

Learning Disabilities Association of America. (1992). *Advocacy manual: A parent's how-to guide for special education services.* Pittsburgh, PA: Author. (ERIC Document Reproduction Service No. ED 363 051)

Lee, G. V., & Barnett, B. G. (1994). Using reflective questioning to promote collaborative dialogue. *Journal of Staff Development, 15*(1), 16–21.

Lemon v. Kurtzman, 403 U.S. 602 (1971).

Levine, P., & Edgar, E. (1994). An analysis by gender of long-term post school outcomes for youth with and without disabilities. *Exceptional Children, 61*(3), 282–300.

Levine, S. L. (1989). *Promoting adult growth in schools.* Boston: Allyn and Bacon.

Light v. Parkway School District, 21 IDELR 933 (8th Cir. 1994).

Littrell, P. C., Billingsley, B. S., & Cross, L. H. (1994). The effects of principal support on special and general educators' stress, job satisfaction, school commitment, health, and intent to stay in teaching. *Remedial and Special Education, 15*(5), 297–310.

Loevinger, J. (1976). *Ego development.* San Francisco: Jossey-Bass.

Lortie, D. (1975). *School teacher: A sociological study.* Chicago: University of Chicago Press.

Losen, S. M., & Diament, B. (1978). *Parent conferences in the schools: Procedures for developing effective partnership.* Boston: Allyn and Bacon.

Louis, K. S., & Miles, M. (1990). *Improving the urban high school: What works and why.* New York: Teachers College Press.

Lubet, S. (1994). Ethics and theory choice in advocacy education. *Journal of Legal Education, 44*(1), 81–88.

Luckner, J. L. (1996). Juggling roles and making changes: Suggestions for meeting the challenges of being a special educator. *Teaching Exceptional Children, 28*(2), 24–28.

Maloney, M. H. (1993). The seven deadly sins: Common mistakes which can lead to due process hearings. In *Proceedings of the 14th National Institute on Legal Issues of Educating Individuals with Disabilities.* Horsham, PA: LRP Publications.

Maurer, R. E. (1991). *Managing conflict: Tactics for school administrators.* Boston: Allyn and Bacon.

Marston, P. J., & Hecht, M. L. (1988). Group satisfaction. In R. Cathcart & L. Samovar (Eds.), *Small group communication* (pp. 236–246). Dubuque, IA: Brown.

Mawhinney, H. B., & Smrekar, C. (1996). Institutional constraints to advocacy in collaborative services. *Educational Policy, 10*(4), 480–502.

McBride, M. (1992). Self-determination and empowerment: The parent case management program. *Impact, 5*(2), 14.

McBride, S. L., Brotherson, M. J., Joanning, H., Whidden, D., & Demmitt, A. (1993). Implementation of family-centered services: Perceptions of families and professionals. *Journal of Early Intervention, 17*(4), 414–430.

McGuire, J. B. (1984). Strategies of school district conflict. *Sociology of Education, 57,* 31–42.

McLaughlin, M. W., Irby, M. A., & Langman, J. (1994). *Urban sanctuaries.* San Francisco: Jossey-Bass.

McLoughlin, J. A., Edge, D., Petrosko, J., & Strenecky, B. (1981). P.L. 94-142 and information dissemination: A step forward. *Journal of Special Education Technology, 4*(4), 50–56.

Mentink, Letter to, 18 IDELR 276 (OSERS, 1991).

Merriam-Webster's collegiate dictionary. (10th ed.). (1994). Springfield, MA: Merriam-Webster.

Mesibov, G. B., & LaGreca, A. M. (1981). Ethical issues in parent-professional service interaction. In J. L. Paul (Ed.), *Understanding and working with parents of children with special needs* (pp. 154–179). New York: Holt, Rinehart and Winston.

Miller, P. S. (1992). Segregated programs of teacher education in early childhood: Immoral and inefficient practice. *Topics in Early Childhood Special Education, 11*(4), 39–52.

Mills v. District of Columbia Board of Education, 348 F.Supp. 866 (D. D.C., 1972).

Misra, A. (1994). Partnership with multicultural families. In S. K. Alper, P. J. Schloss, & C. N. Schloss (Eds.), *Families of students with disabilities: Consultation and advocacy* (pp. 143–179). Boston: Allyn and Bacon.

Mithaug, D. E., Horiuchi, C. N., & Fanning, P. N. (1985). A report on the Colorado statewide follow-up survey of special education students. *Exceptional Children, 51,* 397–404.

Mlawer, M. A. (1993). Who should fight? Parents and the advocacy expectation. *Journal of Disability Policy Studies, 4*(1), 105–115.

Moore, R. (1992). *Stories of teacher identity: An analysis of conflict between social and personal identity in life stories of women teachers in Maryland, 1927–1967.* Unpublished doctoral dissertation, University of Maryland.

Morningstar, M. E., Turnbull, A. P., & Turnbull, H. R. (1995). What do students with disabilities tell us about the importance of involvement in the transition from school to adult life. *Exceptional Children, 62*(3), 249–260.

Mt. Healthy City School District Board of Education v. Doyle, 429 U.S. 274 (1977).

National Association of School Psychologists. (1992). *Principles for professional ethics.* Stratford, CT: Author.

National Association of State Directors of Special Education (NASDSE). (1993). *Leading and managing for performance: An examination of challenges confronting special education.* Alexandria, VA: Author. (ERIC Document Reproduction Services No. ED 389 116)

National Council on Disability. (1989). *The education of students with disabilities: Where do we stand?* Washington, DC: Author.

Nelson, J. R. (1996). Designing schools to meet the needs of students who exhibit disruptive behavior. *Journal of Emotional and Behavioral Disorders, 4*(3), 147–161.

Nelson, R. A. (1994). Issues, communication and advocacy: Contemporary ethical challenges. *Public Relations Review, 20*(3), 225–231.

Nevin, A., Thousand, J., Paolucci-Whitcomb, P., & Villa, R. (1990). Collaborative consultation: Empowering public school personnel to provide heterogeneous schooling for all—Or, who rang that bell? *Journal of Educational and Psychological Consultation, 1*(1), 41–67.

New York City School District Board of Education, 19 IDELR 169 (SEA N.Y., 1992).

Newman, J. (1993). Ethical issues in consultation. *Journal of Counseling and Development, 72,* 148–156.

Niebuhr, H. R. (1963). *The responsible self: An essay in christian moral philosophy.* New York: Harper and Row.

Noddings, N. (1984). *Caring: A feminine approach to ethics and moral education.* Berkeley: University of California Press.

Noddings, N. (1993). Caring: A feminist perspective. In K. A. Strike & P. L. Ternasky (Eds.), *Ethics for professionals in education: Perspectives for preparation and practice* (pp. 43–53). New York: Teachers College Press.

Oberti v. Board of Education, 789 F.Supp. 1322 (D. N.J., 1992).

Oja, S. N., & Pine, G. J. (1981). *Toward a theory of staff development.* Paper presented at the annual meeting of the American Educational Research Association, Los Angeles.

Oliver, J. M., Cole, N. H., & Hollingsworth, H. (1991). Learning disabilities as functions of familial learning problems and developmental problems. *Exceptional Children, 57*(5), 427–440.

Olson, D. H., McCubbin, H. I., Barnes, H., Larsen, A., Muxen, M., & Wilson, M. (1983). *Families: What makes them work.* Beverly Hills: Sage.

Osborne, A. G. (1995). Procedural due process rights for parents under the IDEA. *Preventing School Failure, 39,* 22–26.

Osborne, A. G. (1996). *Legal issues in special education.* Boston: Allyn and Bacon.

OSEP Memorandum 94-16, 21 IDELR 85 (OSEP 1994).

OSEP Policy Letter, 18 IDELR 627 (OSEP 1991a).

OSEP Policy Letter, 18 IDELR 969 (OSEP 1991b).

OSEP Policy Letter, 20 IDELR 1219 (OSEP 1993).

OSEP Policy Letter, 21 IDELR 998 (OSEP 1994).

OSEP Policy Letter, 22 IDELR 637 (OSEP 1995).

Oser, F., & Althof, W. (1993). Trust in advance: On the professional morality of teachers. *Journal of Moral Education, 22*(3), 253–275.

Paul, J. L., Gallagher, J. J., Kendrick, S. B., Thomas, D. D., & Young, J. F. (1992). *Handbook for ethical policy making.* Chapel Hill: North Carolina Institute for Policy Studies. (ERIC Document Reproduction Service No. ED 348 810)

Pardeck, J. T. (1996). Advocacy and parents of special needs children. *Early Child Development and Care, 120,* 45–53.

Parents in Action on Special Education (PASE) v. Hannon, 506 F.Supp. 831 (N.D. Ill. 1980).

Pazey, B. (1995). An essential link for the administration of special education: The ethic of care. *Journal for a Just and Caring Education, 1*(3), 296–310.

Pearlin, L. I., & Schooler, C. (1978). The structure of coping. *Journal of Health and Social Behavior, 19,* 2–21.

Pearson, J. (1992). A parent's quest for credibility. *Impact, 5*(2), 5.

Peck, C. A. (1995). Some further reflections on the difficulties and dilemmas of inclusion. *Journal of Early Intervention, 19*(3), 197–199.

Perloff, R. M. (1993). *The dynamics of persuasion.* Hillsdale, NJ: Erlbaum.

Pickering v. Board of Education, 391 U.S. 563 (1968).

Pennsylvania Association for Retarded Citizens v. Commonwealth of Pennsylvania, 343 F.Supp. 279 (E.D. Pa. 1972).

Postman, N., & Weingartner, C. (1969). *Teaching as a subversive activity.* New York: Delacorte.

Primm, E. B. (1988). *Mediation of school disputes in Georgia.* Atlanta, GA: Justice Center of Atlanta.

Protection and Advocacy for Mentally Ill Individuals Act of 1986, 42 U.S.C. Sec. 10801 et seq.

Pruitt, D. G. (1983). Strategic choice in negotiation. *American Behavioral Scientist, 27*(2), 167–194.

Pullis, M. (1992). An analysis of the occupational stress of teachers of the behaviorally disordered: Sources, effects, and strategies for coping. *Behavioral Disorders, 17*(3), 191–201.

Rainforth, B., York, J., & Macdonald, C. (1992). *Collaborative teams for students with severe disabilities: Integrating therapy and educational services.* Baltimore: Brookes.

Rapid City School District v. Vahle, 733 F.Supp. 1364 (D.S.D. 1990).

Rees, S. (1991). *Achieving power: Practice and policy in social welfare.* North Sydney, Australia: Allen and Unwin.

Reinert, H. R., & Huang, A. (1987). *Children in conflict: Educational strategies for the emotionally disturbed and behaviorally disordered.* Columbus, OH: Merrill.

Rest, J. (1983). Morality. In P. Mussen (Ed.), *Manual of child psychology: Vol. 3: Cognitive development* (pp. 556–629). J. Flavell & E. Markham (Eds.). New York: Wiley.

Rest, J. (1986). *Moral development: Advances in research and theory.* New York: Praeger.

Reynolds, C. H. (1996). Making responsible academic ethical decisions. *New Directions for Teaching and Learning, 66,* 65–74.

Reynolds, M. C., & Birch, J. W. (1982). Special education as a profession. *Exceptional Education Quarterly, 2*(4), 1–13.

Rhoades, C., Browning, P., & Thorin, E. (1986). Self-help advocacy movement: A promising peer support system for people with mental disabilities. *Rehabilitation Literature, 47*(1-2), 2–7.

Riley, D. (1976). The mystique of lawyers. In R. Nader & M. Green (Eds.), *Verdicts on lawyers* (pp. 80–93). New York: Crowell.

Riley, P. V. (1971). Family advocacy: Case to cause and back to case. *Child Welfare, 50*(7), 374–383.

Robinson, E. L., & Fine, M. V. (1994). Developing collaborative home-school relationships. *Preventing School Failure, 39*(1), 9–15.

Rock, S. L., Geiger, W. L., & Hood, G. (1992). CEC's standards for professional practice in advocacy: Members' attitudes and activities. *Exceptional Children, 58,* 541–547.

Roger, B., Gorevin, R., Fellows, M., & Kelly, D. (1992). *Schools are for all kids: School site implementation Level II training.* San Francisco: California Research Institute, San Francisco State University. (ED 365 052)

Rogers, C. R. (1951). *Client-centered therapy.* Boston: Houghton Mifflin.

Rogers, C. R. (1969). *Freedom to learn.* Columbus, OH: Merrill.

Roit, M. L., & Pfohl, W. (1984). The readability of P.L. 94-142 parent materials: Are parents truly informed? *Exceptional Children, 50*(6), 496–505.

Roncker v. Walter, 700 F.2d 1058 (6th Cir. 1983).

Ross, E. C. (1985). Coalition development in legislative advocacy. *Exceptional Children, 51,* 342–344.

Rothstein, L. F. (1995). *Special education law* (2nd ed.). New York: Longman.

Rude, C. D., & Aiken, P. A. (Eds.). (1982). *Advocacy in residential programs.* Lubbock: Texas Tech University Research and Training Center in Mental Retardation.

Rudestam, K. E. (1988). The experiential group. In R. S. Cathcart & L. A. Samovar (Eds.), *Small group communication* (pp. 102–116). Dubuque, IA: Brown.

Ryndak, D. L. (1994a). A systems change approach to advocacy. In S. K. Alper, P. J. Schloss, & C. N. Schloss (Eds.), *Families of students with disabilities: Consultation and advocacy* (pp. 251–267). Boston: Allyn and Bacon.

Ryndak, D. L. (1994b). Strategies for advocating through systems change. In S. K. Alper, P. J. Schloss, & C. N. Schloss (Eds.), *Families of students with disabilities: Consultation and advocacy* (pp. 269–285). Boston: Allyn and Bacon.

Sacramento City Unified School District Board of Education v. Rachel H., 14 F.3d 1398 (9th Cir. 1994).

Sailor, W., & Skrtic, T. M. (1996). School/community partnerships and educational reform. *Remedial and Special Education, 17*(5), 267–270.

Salend, S. J., & Zirkel, P. A. (1984). Special education hearings: Prevailing problems and practical proposals. *Education and Training of the Mentally Retarded, 19*(1), 29–34.

Sands, D., & Wehmeyer, M. (Eds.). (1996). *Self-determination across the life span: Theory and practice.* Baltimore: Brookes.

Sarason, S. (1990). *The predictable failure of educational reform.* San Francisco: Jossey-Bass.

Saye v. St. Vrain Valley School District, 785 F.2d 862 (10th Cir. 1986).

Scheerenberger, R. C. (1983). *A history of mental retardation.* Baltimore: Brookes.

Schlalock, R. L., Holl, C., Elliott, B., & Ross, I. (1992). A longitudinal follow-up of graduates from a rural special education program. *Learning Disability Quarterly, 15*(1), 29–38.

Schloss, C. N., & Jayne, D. (1994). Models and methods of advocacy. In S. K. Alper, P. J. Schloss, & C. N. Schloss (Eds.), *Families of students with disabilities: Consultation and advocacy* (pp. 229–250). Boston: Allyn and Bacon.

Schloss, P. J. (1994). Historical and legal foundations for parent advocacy. In S. K. Alper, P. J. Schloss, & C. N. Schloss (Eds.), *Families of students with disabilities: Consultation and advocacy* (pp. 17–49). Boston: Allyn and Bacon.

Schloss, P. J., & Henley, J. G. (1994). Ethical issues relating to families of persons with disabilities. In S. K. Alper, P. J. Schloss, & C. N. Schloss (Eds.), *Families of students with disabilities: Consultation and advocacy* (pp. 287–306). Boston: Allyn and Bacon.

Schorr, L. (1997). *Common purpose: Strengthening families and neighborhoods to rebuild America.* New York: Doubleday, Anchor Books.

Schrag, J. A. (1996a). *Mediation and other alternative dispute resolution procedures in special education.* Alexandria, VA: Project FORUM, National Association of State Directors of Special Education. (ERIC Document Reproduction Services No. ED 399 736)

Schrag, J. A. (1996b). *Mediation in special education: A resource manual for mediators*. Alexandria, VA: Project FORUM, National Association of State Directors of Special Education. (ERIC Document Reproduction Services No. ED 399 735)

Scruggs, T. E. (1993). Special education and the problems of schooling. *Educational Theory, 43*(4), 433–447.

Seligman, M., & Darling, R. B. (1989). *Ordinary families, special children: A systems approach to childhood disability*. New York: Guilford.

Seligman, M. E. P. (1990). *Learned optimism: How to change your mind and your life*. New York: PocketBooks.

Senge, P. M. (1990). *The fifth discipline: The art and practice of the learning organization*. New York: Doubleday.

Sergiovanni, T. J. (1996). *Leadership for the schoolhouse: How is it different? Why is it important?* San Francisco: Jossey-Bass.

Shea, T. M., & Bauer, A. M. (1991). *Parents and teachers of children with exceptionalities: A handbook for collaboration*. Boston: Allyn and Bacon.

Shields, C. V. (1987). *Strategies: A practical guide for dealing with professionals and human service systems*. Richmond Hill, Ontario: Human Services Press.

Shrybman, J. A. (1982). *Due process in special education*. Rockville, MD: Aspen.

Simons, R. (1987). *After the tears: Parents talk about raising a child with a disability*. San Diego: Harcourt Brace Jovanovich.

Simpson, R. L. (1996). *Working with parents and families of exceptional children and youth: Techniques for successful conferencing and collaboration*. Austin, TX: Pro-Ed.

Simpson, R. L., & Fiedler, C. R. (1989). Parent participation in individualized educational program (IEP) conferences: A case for individualization. In M. J. Fine (Ed.), *The second handbook on parent education* (pp. 145–171). San Diego: Academic Press.

Singer, E., & Nace, L. R. (1985). Mediation in special education: Two states' experiences. *Exceptional Education Quaterly, 3*, 41–49.

Singer, G. H. S., & Powers, L. E. (1993). Contributing to resilience in families. In G. H. S. Singer & L. E. Powers (Eds.), *Families, disability, and empowerment: Active coping skills and strategies for family interventions* (pp. 1–25). Baltimore: Brookes.

Skinner, M. E. (1991). Facilitating parental participation during individualized education program conferences. *Journal of Educational and Psychological Consultation, 2*, 285–289.

Skrtic, T. (1987). *An organizational analysis of special education reform*. Paper presented at the annual meeting of the American Educational Research Association, Washington, DC.

Skynner, R., & Cleese, J. (1993). *Life and how to survive it*. London: Methuen.

Smith, J. (1992). Making the system work: The multicultural family inclusion project. *Impact, 5*(2), 10.

Smith, B. J., & Rose, D. F. (1993). *Administrative policy handbook for preschool mainstreaming*. Cambridge, MA: Brookline.

Sonnenschein, P. (1984). Parents and professionals: An uneasy relationship. In M. L. Henniger & E. M. Nesselroad (Eds.), *Working with parents of handicapped children: A book of readings for school personnel* (pp. 129–139). Lanham, MD: University Press of America.

Sontag, J. C., & Schacht, R. (1994). An ethnic comparison of participation and information needs in early intervention. *Exceptional Children, 60*, 422–433.

South Dakota Statewide Systems Change Project. (1995). *Welcoming parents as partners*. Pierre: South Dakota State Department of Education and Cultural Affairs. (ERIC Document Reproduction Service No. ED 391 324)

Spiegel-McGill, P., Reed, D. J., Konig, C. S., & McGowan, P. (1990). Parent education: Easing the transition to preschool. *Topics in Early Childhood Special Education, 9*(4), 66–77.

Stainback, S., Stainback, W., & Forest, M. (1989). *Educating students in the mainstream of regular education*. Baltimore: Brookes.

Stephens, T. M., & Wolf, J. S. (1980). *Effective skills in parent/teacher conferencing*. Columbus, OH: NCEMMH.

Stoecklin, V. L. (1994). Advocating for young children with disabilities. *Quarterly Resource, 8*(3), 1–35.

Strickland, B. (1982). Parental participation, school accountability, and due process. *Exceptional Education Quarterly, 3*, 41–49.

Strickland, B. (1983). Legal issues that affect parents. In M. Seligman (Ed.), *The family with a handicapped child: Understanding and treatment*. New York: Grune & Stratton.

Strickland, B., & Turnbull, A. P. (1990). Developing and implementing individualized education programs (3rd ed.). Columbus, OH: Merrill.

Strike, K. A., Haller, E. J., & Soltis, J. F. (1998). *The ethics of school administration* (2nd ed.). New York: Teachers College Press.

Strike, K. A., & Soltis, J. F. (1992). *The ethics of teaching*. New York: Teachers College Press.

Suchey, N., & Huefner, D. S. (1998). The state complaint procedure under the Individuals with Disabilities Education Act. *Exceptional Children, 64*(4), 529–542.

Summers, J. A. (1992). Decision making in the 90's: A new paradigm for family, professional, and consumer roles. *Impact, 5*(2), 2–3, 20.

Symington, G. T. (1995). *Mediation as an option in special education*. Alexandria, VA: Project FORUM, National Association of State Directors of Special Education. (ERIC Document Reproduction Services No. ED 378 768)

Taylor, D., Coughlin, D., & Marasco, J. (Eds.). (1997). *Teaching and advocacy*. York, ME: Stenhouse Publishers.

Technology Related Assistance for Individuals with Disabilities Act of 1988, 29 U.S.C. Sec. 2201 et seq.

Thomas, K. W., & Kilmann, R. H. (1974). *Thomas-Kilmann conflict mode instrument*. Tuxedo, NY: Xicom.

Thurston, P., Clift, R., & Schacht, M. (1993). Preparing leaders for change-oriented schools. *Phi Delta Kappan, 75*, 259–265.

Tiegerman-Farber, E., & Radziewicz, C. (1998). *Collaborative decision making: The pathway to inclusion*. Upper Saddle River, NJ: Prentice-Hall.

Timothy W. v. Rochester, New Hampshire School District, 875 F.2d 954 (1st Cir. 1989).

Tinsley, Letter to, 16 EHLR (OSEP, 1990).

Toffler, A. (1990). *Power shift*. New York: Bantam Books.

Trainer, M. (1991). *Differences in common: Straight talk on mental retardation, Down syndrome, and life*. Rockville, MD: Woodbine.

Tucker, B. P., & Goldstein, B. A. (1992). *Legal rights of persons with disabilities: An analysis of public law*. Horsham, PA: LRP Publications.

Tuckman, B. W. (1965). Developmental sequence in small groups. *Psychological Bulletin, 63*, 384–399.

Turnbull, A. P. (1983). Parental participation in the IEP process. In J. A. Mulick & S. M. Pueschel (Eds.), *Parent-professional partnerships in developmental disability services* (pp. 107–122). Cambridge, MA: Ware Press.

Turnbull, A. P., & Strickland, B. (1981). Parents and the educational system. In J. L. Paul (Ed.), *Understanding and working with parents of children with special needs* (pp. 231–263). New York: Holt, Rinehart and Winston.

Turnbull, A. P., Summers, J. A., & Brotherson, M. J. (1984). *Working with families with disabled members: A family systems approach.* Lawrence: University of Kansas, Kansas Affiliated Facility.

Turnbull, A. P., & Turnbull, H. R. (1990). *Families, professionals, and exceptionality: A special partnership* (2nd ed.). Columbus, OH: Merrill.

Turnbull, A. P., & Turnbull, H. R. (1997). *Families, professionals, and exceptionality: A special partnership* (3rd ed.). Columbus, OH: Merrill.

Turnbull, A. P., Turnbull, H. R., Shank, M., & Leal, D. (1995). *Exceptional lives: Special education in today's schools.* Englewood Cliffs, NJ: Merrill/Prentice-Hall.

Turnbull, H. R. (1993). *Free appropriate public education: The law and children with disabilities* (4th ed.). Denver: Love.

Turnbull, H. R., & McGinley, K. H. (1987). *Evaluating the effectiveness of mediation as an alternative to the due process theory in special education.* Lawrence: University of Kansas. (ERIC Document Reproduction Services No. ED 345 422)

Tymchuk, A. J. (1986). Guidelines for ethical decision making. *Canadian Psychology, 27,* 36–43.

Underwood, J. K., & Mead, J. M. (1995). *Legal aspects of special education and pupil services.* Boston: Allyn and Bacon.

Ury, W. (1991). *Getting past no: Negotiating with difficult people.* New York: Bantam Books.

U.S. Department of Education. (1980). General Administrative Regulations, 34 C.F.R. Sections 76.780–782.

U.S. Department of Education. (1992). IDEA Part B Regulations, 34 C.F.R. Sections 300.660–662.

U.S. Department of Education. (1995). *Individuals with Disabilities Education Act Amendments of 1995.* Washington, DC: Author.

U.S. Department of Education. (1997). *Nineteenth annual report to Congress on the implementation of the Individuals with Disabilities Education Act.* Washington, DC: Author.

Vandercook, T., York, J., & Forest, M. (1989). The McGill Action Planning System (MAPS): A strategy for building the vision. *The Journal of the Association for Persons with Severe Handicaps, 14*(3), 205–215.

Van Reusen, A. K., & Bos, C. S. (1990). I-PLAN: Helping students communicate in planning conferences. *Teaching Exceptional Children, 22*(4), 30–32.

Van Reusen, A. K., & Bos, C. S. (1994). Facilitating student participation in Individualized Education Programs through motivation strategy instruction. *Exceptional Children, 60*(5), 466–475.

Van Reusen, A. K., Bos, C. S., Schumaker, J. B., & Deshler, D. D. (1987). *The education planning strategy.* Lawrence, KS: Edge Enterprises.

Van Reusen, A. K., Deshler, D. D., & Schumaker, J. B. (1989). Effects of a student participation strategy in facilitating the involvement of adolescents with learning disabilities in the Individualized Educational Program planning process. *Learning Disabilities, 1*(2), 23–34.

Vaughn, S., Bos, C., Harrell, J., & Lasky, B. (1988). Parent participation in the initial placement/IEP conference ten years after mandated involvement. *Journal of Learning Disabilities, 21*(2), 82–89.

Villa, R. A., & Thousand, J. S. (1992). Restructuring public school systems: Strategies for organizational change and progress. In R. A. Villa & J. S. Thousand (Eds.), *Restructuring for caring and effective education: An administrative guide to creating heterogeneous schools* (pp. 109–137). Baltimore: Brookes.

Vincent, C. (1996). *Parents and teachers.* London: Falmer Press.

Vitello, S. J. (1990). *The efficacy of mediation in the resolution of parent-school special education disputes.* New Brunswick, NJ: Rutgers University. (ED 367 074)

Voltz, D. L. (1994). Developing collaborative parent-teacher relationships with culturally diverse parents. *Intervention in School and Clinic, 29*(5), 288–291.

Wagner, M. (1989). *The transition experiences of youth with disabilities: A report from the national longitudinal transition study.* Paper presented to the Division of Research, Council for Exceptional Children, San Francisco, CA.

Walker, B., & Singer, G. H. S. (1993). Improving collaborative communication between professionals and parents. In G. H. S. Singer & L. E. Powers (Eds.), *Families, disability, and empowerment: Active coping skills and strategies for family interventions* (pp. 285–316). Baltimore: Brookes.

Walton, R. E. (1969). *Interpersonal peacemaking: Confrontation and third party consultation.* Reading, MA: Addison-Wesley.

Wehmeyer, M. L., & Metzler, C. A. (1995). How self-determined are people with mental retardation? The national consumer survey. *Mental Retardation, 33*(2), 111–119.

Weicker, L. (1985). Sonny and public policy. In H. R. Turnbull & A. P. Turnbull (Eds.), *Parents speak out: Then and now* (2nd ed.) (pp. 281–287). Englewood Cliffs, NJ: Merrill/Prentice-Hall.

Weisenstein, G. R., & Pelz, R. (1986). *Administrative desk reference on special education.* Rockville, MD: Aspen.

Whelan, R. J. (1996). *Mediation in special education.* Lawrence, KS: Author.

Wilkins, R. A. (1980). If the moral reasoning of teachers is deficient, what hope is there for pupils. *Kappan, 61*(8), 548–549.

Williams, R. (1995, November 15). Videotaped welcoming remarks at the United States–Israel Bi-National Conference on Coordination and Integration of Children's Health, Education, Rehabilitation, and Social Service: Policies and Practice in a Time of Health Care Reform, Tel Aviv.

Williams, Letter to, 18 IDELR 534 (OSEP, 1991).

Williams-Murphy, T., DeChillo, N., Koren, P. E., & Hunter, R. (1994). *Family/professional collaboration: The perspectives of those who have tried.* Portland, OR: Portland State University, Research and Training Center on Family Support and Children's Mental Health. (ERIC Document Reproduction Service No. ED 385 103)

Wilson, S. (1993). Letter to a friend. In J. A. Spiegle & R. A. van den Pol (Eds.), *Making changes: Family voices on living with disabilities* (pp. 25–30). Cambridge, MA: Brookline.

Winton, P. J. (1994). Families of children with disabilities. In N. G. Haring, L. McCormick, & T. G. Haring (Eds.), *Exceptional children and youth* (6th ed.) (pp. 502–525). New York: Merrill.

Winton, P. J., & Bailey, D. B. (1993). Communicating with parents: Examining practices and facilitating change. In J. L. Paul & R. J. Simeonsson (Eds.), *Children with special needs: Family, culture, and society* (pp. 210–230). Forth Worth, TX: Harcourt Brace Jovanovich.

Wisniewski, L. (1994). Interpersonal effectiveness in consultation and advocacy. In S. K. Alper, P. J. Schloss, & C. N. Schloss (Eds.), *Families of students with disabilities: Consultation and advocacy* (pp. 205–228). Boston: Allyn and Bacon.

Witt, J. C., Miller, C. D., McIntyre, R. M., & Smith, D. (1984). Effects of variables on parental perceptions of staffings. *Exceptional Children, 51*(1), 27–32.

Wolfe, B. L., Petty, V. G., & McNellis, K. (1990). *Special training for special needs*. Boston: Allyn and Bacon.

Yell, M. L. (1998). *The law and special education*. Upper Saddle River, NJ: Merrill/Prentice-Hall.

Yoshida, R. K., Fenton, K., Kaufman, M. J., & Maxwell, J. P. (1978). Parental involvement in the special education pupil planning process: The school's perspective. *Exceptional Children, 44,* 531–534.

Ysseldyke, J. E., Algozzine, B., & Mitchell, J. (1982). Special education team decision making: An analysis of current practice. *Personnel and Guidance Journal, 60*(5), 308–313.

Ysseldyke, J. E., Thurlow, M. L., McGrew, K., & Vanderwood, M. (1994). *Making decisions about the inclusion of students with disabilities in large-scale assessments* (Synthesis Report 13). Minneapolis: University of Minnesota and National Center on Education Outcomes.

Zirkel, P. A. (1993). *Section 504 and the schools*. Horsham, PA: LRP Publications.

Zirkel, P. A. (1994). Over-due process revisions for the Individuals with Disabilities Education Act. *Montana Law Review, 55,* 403–414.

Zirkel, P. A. (1996). The substandard for FAPE: Does Section 504 require less than the IDEA? *Education Law Reporter, 106,* 471–477.

Zirkel, P. A., & Suppa, R. J. (1986). Legal-ethical conflicts for educator-advocates of handicapped students. *West's Education Law Reporter, 35,* 9–15.

Zobrest v. Catalina Foothills School District, 113 S.Ct. 2462 (1993).